Exam Ref MD-100 Windows 10

Second Edition

Andrew Bettany
Andrew Warren

Exam Ref MD-100 Windows 10, Second Edition

Published with the authorization of Microsoft Corporation by:
Pearson Education, Inc.

ISBN-13: 978-013-747219-2
ISBN-10: 0-137-47219-6

33614082807107

Library of Congress Control Number: 2021942771

1 2021

TRADEMARKS

WARNING AND DISCLAIMER

SPECIAL SALES

For information about buying this title in bulk quantities, or for special sales opportunities (which may include electronic versions; custom cover designs; and content particular to your business, training goals, marketing focus, or branding interests), please contact our corporate sales department at corpsales@pearsoned.com or (800) 382-3419.

For government sales inquiries, please contact governmentsales@pearsoned.com.

For questions about sales outside the U.S., please contact intlcs@pearson.com.

CREDITS

EDITOR-IN-CHIEF
Brett Bartow

EXECUTIVE EDITOR
Loretta Yates

SPONSORING EDITOR
Charvi Arora

DEVELOPMENT EDITOR
Songlin Qiu

MANAGING EDITOR
Sandra Schroeder

SENIOR PROJECT EDITOR
Tracey Croom

COPY EDITOR
Liz Welch

INDEXER
Timothy Wright

PROOFREADER
Abigail Bass

TECHNICAL EDITOR
Tommy B. Kobberøe

EDITORIAL ASSISTANT
Cindy Teeters

COVER DESIGNER
Twist Creative, Seattle

Contents at a glance

Contents

Acknowledgments

I want to thank the production team who help make the book production process painless. I would like to dedicate this Windows 10 2nd Edition book to Annette and Tommy for being supportive and encouraging. This book is also for the reader. Having taught thousands of IT professionals over my career, I hope this book helps you become proficient with Windows 10. The world of IT is ever changing, and we should all strive to stay up-to-date and use the most appropriate tools. I hope this book helps you achieve success!

—ANDREW BETTANY

The publication of the second edition of this book coincides with the 25th anniversary of my certification as a Microsoft Certified Trainer. Over the last quarter century, I've enjoyed the challenge of helping students gain the necessary skills to become better at their jobs. This book gives me the opportunity to continue doing so.

—ANDREW WARREN

About the authors

ANDREW BETTANY was awarded the Microsoft Most Valuable Professional (Windows and Devices for IT) for 8 years before joining Microsoft. He is a loving dad, IT geek, training mentor and consultant, entrepreneur, and author.

Andrew is recognized for his Windows expertise, and he is the author of many publications, including several Windows exam certification prep guides and Microsoft official training materials. He is the author of video training materials for LinkedIn Learning and Pluralsight. As a Microsoft Certified Trainer for 16 years, Andrew delivers learning and consultancy to businesses in many technical areas, including Microsoft 365, Azure, and Windows 10.

He has co-founded the "IT Masterclasses" series of short, intensive technical courses (see *www.itmasterclasses.com*), and he is passionate about helping others learn technology. He is a frequent speaker at Microsoft Ignite and other technical conferences worldwide.

Andrew is active on social media and can be found on LinkedIn, Facebook, and Twitter. He lives in a village just outside the beautiful city of York in Yorkshire, England.

ANDREW WARREN, MCT, has been writing for Microsoft for many years, helping to develop their official curriculum of instructor-led training material. He has served as a subject matter expert on many of the current Windows Server courses, was technical lead on several of the Windows 10 titles, and was involved in Microsoft 365, Azure, and Intune course development. When not writing about Microsoft technologies, he can be found in the classroom, teaching other IT professionals what they need to know to manage their organization's IT infrastructure.

Introduction

With the Microsoft 365 Certified: Modern Desktop Administrator Associate certification, Microsoft has changed the way that IT pro certifications work. Rather than being based on a technology area, they are focused on a specific job role. The Microsoft MD-100: Windows 10 exam provides the foundation of this Modern Desktop Administrator Associate certification.

This book covers every major topic area found on the exam, but it does not cover every exam question. Only the Microsoft exam team has access to the exam questions, and Microsoft regularly adds new questions to the exam, making it impossible to cover specific questions. You should consider this book a supplement to your relevant real-world experience and other study materials. If you encounter a topic in this book that you do not feel completely comfortable with, use the "Need more review?" links you'll find in the text to find more information and take the time to research and study the topic. Great information is available on the Microsoft website at *docs.microsoft.com*.

Organization of this book

This book is organized by the "Skills measured" list published for the exam. The "Skills measured" list is available for each exam on the Microsoft Learn website: *https://aka.ms/examlist*. Each chapter in this book corresponds to a major topic area in the list, and the technical tasks in each topic area determine a chapter's organization. If an exam covers six major topic areas, for example, the book will contain six chapters.

Preparing for the exam

Microsoft certification exams are a great way to build your résumé and let the world know about your level of expertise. Certification exams validate your on-the-job experience and product knowledge. Although there is no substitute for on-the-job experience, preparation through study and hands-on practice can help you prepare for the exam. This book is *not* designed to teach you new skills.

We recommend that you augment your exam preparation plan by using a combination of available study materials and courses. For example, you might use the Exam Ref and another study guide for your "at home" preparation and take a Microsoft Official Curriculum course for the classroom experience. Choose the combination that you think works best for you. Learn more about available classroom training and find free online courses and live events at *http://microsoft.com/learn*. Microsoft Official Practice Tests are available for many exams at *http://aka.ms/practicetests*.

Note that this Exam Ref is based on publicly available information about the exam and the authors' experience. To safeguard the integrity of the exam, authors do not have access to the live exam.

Microsoft certifications

Microsoft certifications distinguish you by proving your command of a broad set of skills and experience with current Microsoft products and technologies. The exams and corresponding certifications are developed to validate your mastery of critical competencies as you design and develop, or implement and support, solutions with Microsoft products and technologies both on-premises and in the cloud. Certification brings a variety of benefits to the individual and to employers and organizations.

> **MORE INFO ALL MICROSOFT CERTIFICATIONS**
>
> For information about Microsoft certifications, including a full list of available certifications, go to *http://www.microsoft.com/learn.*

Check back often to see what is new!

Errata, updates, & book support

We've made every effort to ensure the accuracy of this book and its companion content. You can access updates to this book—in the form of a list of submitted errata and their related corrections—at:

MicrosoftPressStore.com/ExamRefMD1002e/errata

If you discover an error that is not already listed, please submit it to us at the same page.

For additional book support and information, please visit:

MicrosoftPressStore.com/Support

Please note that product support for Microsoft software and hardware is not offered through the previous addresses. For help with Microsoft software or hardware, go to *http://support.microsoft.com.*

Stay in touch

Let's keep the conversation going! We're on Twitter: *http://twitter.com/MicrosoftPress.*

Deploy Windows

The MD-100 Windows 10 exam focuses on how to install Windows 10 efficiently and with the least amount of administrative effort. You need to understand how to plan and prepare the Windows 10 installation, along with the installation process itself, activation, and any potential issues along the way. You'll be expected to know how to perform an in-place upgrade from another version of Windows and how to migrate user data, configure hardware devices, manage device drivers, and perform post-installation configuration. For users who operate Windows 10 using a different language, you will also be expected to know how to configure additional languages and regional settings.

Skills covered in this chapter:

- Skill 1.1: Deploy Windows 10
- Skill 1.2: Perform post-installation configuration

Skill 1.1: Deploy Windows 10

Devices will be shipped with a ready-to-use version of Windows 10. For a number of reasons, you may want to replace it with a newer or different version of Windows. In a corporate environment, you may need to install Windows 10 on many devices, which requires careful consideration, planning, and preparation. This skill explores the requirements and preparations necessary for the deployment of Windows 10.

It is important to select the appropriate edition of Windows 10 for your organization. Windows 10 is available across many device types, including tablets, laptops, and desktop computers. Also, also it is available in multiple editions and in both 32-bit and 64-bit architecture versions. You need to choose the appropriate edition and version that provides the capabilities your users require.

After determining which edition you want to install, consider how best to deploy Windows 10. You can choose between simple interactive installations using local Windows 10 media, or you can deploy Windows 10 to your organization's devices by using one of several deployment technologies.

Select the appropriate Windows edition

Windows 10 is available in several different editions, and you should choose the most appropriate version for your personal or business needs. The specific editions of Windows 10, listed in Table 1-1, are designed to address the varying needs of this diverse user base.

TABLE 1-1 Windows 10 editions

Edition	Features
Windows 10 Home	Designed primarily for home users with features such as: ■ Microsoft Edge, the new web browser ■ Continuum Tablet mode for touch-capable devices ■ Cortana, the new personal digital assistant ■ Windows Hello biometric sign-in ■ Virtual Desktops ■ Projecting To This PC ■ Activity History ■ Windows Ink ■ A number of built-in universal Windows apps, such as Photos, Maps, Mail, Calendar, Music, and Video ■ Supports maximum 128 GB of RAM Note that in Windows 10 Home, you cannot control Windows feature and quality updates as was possible on earlier Windows versions; these updates are received and installed automatically.
Windows 10 Pro	Includes the same features as in Windows 10 Home but also provides: ■ Domain Join ■ Group Policy Management ■ Ability to join Azure Active Directory ■ BitLocker ■ Enterprise Mode Internet Explorer ■ Client Hyper-V ■ Remote Server Administration Tools For Windows 10 ■ Assigned Access ■ Remote Desktop ■ Windows Update for Business ■ Enterprise Data Protection ■ Microsoft Store For Business ■ Support for 2 CPUs and maximum 2 TB of RAM

Edition	Features
Windows 10 Pro for Workstations	Includes the same features as in Windows 10 Pro but also provides: ■ SMB Direct using RDMA (Remote Direct Memory Access) ■ ReFS (Resilient File System) ■ Licensed for installation on PCs using server-grade Intel Xeon and AMD Opteron processors, and up to 4 CPUs and maximum 6 TB of RAM ■ Persistent Memory using NVDIMM-N memory modules ■ Ultimate Performance power plan for desktop devices
Windows 10 Enterprise	Windows 10 Enterprise builds on the features of Windows 10 Pro and is available to Volume Licensing customers only. Windows 10 Enterprise provides additional features of relevance to larger organizations, including: ■ Always On VPN (introduced in the Windows 10 Anniversary Update) ■ DirectAccess ■ Windows To Go Creator (prior to the May 2020 update) ■ AppLocker ■ Support for BranchCache ■ Start Screen Control with Group Policy ■ Managed User Experience ■ Windows Defender Credential Guard ■ Windows Defender Application Control ■ Windows Defender Application Guard ■ Microsoft Application Virtualization (App-V) ■ Microsoft User Experience Virtualization (UE-V) In addition to the ability to manage updates to Windows with Windows Update for Business, Enterprise customers can access the Long-Term Servicing Channel (LTSC) deployment version of Windows 10 Enterprise.
Windows 10 Enterprise LTSC	Long-Term Servicing Channel is a specialized edition of Windows 10 Enterprise that receives security and other important updates in the normal way but does not receive feature updates. This enables organizations to know that their environment will not change over time. Windows 10 Enterprise LTSC does not include built-in apps that are subject to change, including: ■ Chromium-based Microsoft Edge browser ■ Microsoft Store client ■ Cortana ■ Many built-in universal Windows apps
Windows 10 Education	Provides the same features as Windows 10 Pro and Windows 10 Enterprise but does not offer support for LTSC. Windows 10 Education is only available through academic Volume Licensing.

The Windows 10 in S mode is a mode of Windows 10 and not an edition. It is designed to be the safest and most stable version of Windows ever. Windows 10 in S mode is a limited, locked-down version of Windows 10. To reduce the total cost of ownership (TCO), you can only install applications from the Microsoft Store and browse the internet using the Microsoft Edge browser. Windows 10 in S mode allows the following usage:

■ Microsoft Edge only

■ Bing search engine

■ Microsoft Store apps only

- Not able join Active Directory Domain Services (AD DS) domain
- Azure AD Domain Join, which is available in Windows 10 Pro in S mode and Windows 10 Enterprise in S mode

PCs ship with one of three versions of Windows 10 in S mode:

- Windows 10 Home in S mode
- Windows 10 Professional in S mode
- Windows 10 Enterprise in S mode

Users can freely opt to leave S mode—for example, to switch to Windows 10 Pro—by installing the Switch out of S mode app from the Microsoft Store. This action is a one-time decision—once you've taken the PC out of S mode, it cannot be put it back into S mode.

> **NOTE   WINDOWS 10 BUSINESS**
>
> Microsoft also provides a special business-focused license that can be applied to the Windows 10 Pro edition. This is called Windows 10 Business, and the upgrade license is included as part of Microsoft 365 Business Premium. You can upgrade Windows 7, 8, and 8.1 Professional to Windows 10 Pro and then apply the Windows 10 Business license. You cannot purchase the standalone version of Windows 10 Business edition; therefore, it is not listed in Table 1-1. To review further details about Microsoft 365 Business Premium, visit the Microsoft website at *https://docs.microsoft.com/en-us/microsoft-365/business/support/microsoft-365-business-faqs?view=o365-worldwide*.

Also, Microsoft has released Windows 10 Internet of Things (IoT) editions—Windows IoT Core and Windows IoT Enterprise. These can be used to operate small industrial devices, such as control devices and specialist industrial computing systems.

For businesses that require a long period of support for their IoT installations, Microsoft has released Windows 10 IoT Core Long-Term Servicing Channel (LTSC) together with Windows 10 IoT Core Services, which provides a subscription with access to 10 years of support for the IoT releases.

> **NEED MORE REVIEW?   LEARN MORE ABOUT THE WINDOWS 10 EDITIONS**
>
> To find out more about these Windows 10 editions, visit the Microsoft website at *https://www.microsoft.com/en-us/windowsforbusiness/compare*.

Choose 32-bit or 64-bit versions

If you are installing Windows 10, you can choose between 32-bit and 64-bit versions of all desktop editions of Windows 10. Nowadays, you should choose 64-bit versions unless there is a compelling reason to use 32-bit versions, such as your hardware does not support the 64-bit architecture. As of this writing, nearly all devices are supplied with 64-bit versions of Windows 10 on 64-bit architecture.

The various edition features described in Table 1-1 are applicable for both 32-bit and 64-bit versions. However, the 32-bit version of Windows 10 is no longer offered to original equipment manufacturers (OEMs) since Windows 10 version 2004. The majority of devices will ship with the 64-bit versions of Windows 10 as they provide a number of advantages, including the following:

- **Memory**   The 64-bit versions of Windows 10 can address more physical memory than 32-bit versions. Specifically, 32-bit versions are physically limited to just under 4 GB of RAM, whereas 64-bit versions of Windows are limited by the edition of Windows 10 installed.

- **Security**   Features such as Kernel Patch Protection, mandatory kernel-mode driver signing, and Data Execution Prevention (DEP) are available only in 64-bit versions of Windows 10.

- **Client Hyper-V**   This feature is only available on 64-bit versions of Windows 10. Your hardware must also support second-level address translation (SLAT).

- **Performance**   The 64-bit processors can handle more data during each CPU clock cycle. This benefit is only realized when running a 64-bit operating system.

EXAM TIP

You cannot perform a direct in-place upgrade from a 32-bit version of Windows 10 directly to the 64-bit version. Therefore, ensure that you know that in this scenario, you must perform a wipe-and-load installation.

Determine Windows 10 Edition requirements for particular features

A number of general and security features available in some editions of Windows 10 require specialist hardware or software configuration that you should know. This section covers how to:

- Identify hardware and configuration requirements for general Windows 10 features
- Identify hardware and configuration requirements for Windows 10 security features

EXAM TIP

It is important to know that some features of Windows 10 are available only on computers and devices that support specific hardware components.

GENERAL FEATURES

These features provide general usability and functional improvements and include the following:

- **Client Hyper-V**   Enables you to create, manage, and run virtual machines that you can install with different guest operating systems to support, perhaps, earlier line-of-business (LOB) apps that will not run natively on Windows 10. Requirements of the Client Hyper-V feature are as follows:

  - A 64-bit version of either the Windows 10 Pro or Windows 10 Enterprise and Education edition.

  - A computer that supports SLAT.

  - Additional physical memory to support running the virtual machines. A minimum of 4 GB of memory is recommended.

EXAM TIP

To use Client Hyper-V to run virtual machines, you also need additional physical memory in your computer. It is recommended that the device have at least 4 GB of RAM to support this feature.

- **Cortana**   You can use Cortana as a digital assistant to control Windows 10 and perform tasks such as writing email, setting reminders, and performing web searches. Because Cortana is voice-activated and -controlled, your Windows 10 device requires a microphone.

- **Continuum**   Windows 10 is available on a variety of devices types and form factors. With Continuum, Microsoft endeavors to optimize the user experience across device types by detecting the hardware on your device and changing to that hardware. For example, Windows 10 determines when you are using a non-touch desktop computer and enables traditional interaction with the operating system by use of a mouse. For users of hybrid devices, such as the Microsoft Surface Pro, when you disconnect a keyboard cover, Windows 10 switches to Tablet mode.

- **Miracast**   Windows 10 uses Miracast to connect your Windows device wirelessly to an external monitor or projector. You will need a Miracast-compatible external monitor or projector to use this functionality. If your display device doesn't support Miracast, you use a Miracast display adapter that supports Windows Display Driver Model (WDDM), such as a Microsoft Wireless Display adapter, and a Wi-Fi adapter that supports Wi-Fi Direct.

- **InstantGo**   Included with computers designed for connected standby, InstantGo allows network connectivity in standby mode. This way, the device can receive updates, mail, and Skype calls even with the screen turned off.

- **Touch**   Windows 10 is a touch-centric operating system. Although you do not need touch to use Windows 10, some features are made more usable through the use of touch. To use touch, your tablet or display monitor must support touch.

- **OneDrive** Users of OneDrive are entitled to 5 GB of free online storage. OneDrive provides this storage. OneDrive functionality is built into the Windows 10 operating system, and it is easy to use. You must have a Microsoft account to use OneDrive.

- **Sync your settings** When you use more than one Windows 10 device, it is convenient for your user settings to move with you to the new device. You can use the Sync Your Settings feature of Windows 10 to ensure that settings such as theme, Internet Explorer and Edge settings (including favorites), passwords, language, and ease of access are synchronized between your devices. You must have a Microsoft account to use this feature.

> **NOTE ACTIVE STYLUS SUPPORT**
>
> Some touch devices have screens that support active stylus input. Active styluses provide for pressure-sensitive input and enable you to use your device for accurate note taking and drawing. Passive styluses are supported on all touch devices but do not support these more advanced features.

SECURITY FEATURES

Windows 10 also has a number of features that can help make your device more secure, including:

- **BitLocker Drive Encryption** A Trusted Platform Module (TPM) version 1.2 or higher works with BitLocker to store encryption keys. This helps protect against data theft and offline tampering by providing for whole-drive encryption. Requirements for BitLocker are:

  - A device with either Windows 10 Pro or Windows 10 Enterprise installed.

  - Optionally, you should use a TPM. Using a TPM with BitLocker enables Windows to verify startup component integrity. You do not require a TPM in your computer to use BitLocker, but using a TPM does increase the security of the encryption keys.

- **Windows Device Health Attestation** With the increase in use of users' own devices, it is important to ensure that Windows 10 devices connecting to your organization meet the security and compliance requirements of your organization. Device health attestation uses measured boot data to help perform this verification. To implement device health attestation, your Windows 10 devices must have TPM version 2.0 or higher.

- **Secure Boot** Secure Boot protects the platform until the Windows kernel is loaded. When Secure Boot is enabled, you can only start the operating system by using an operating system loader that is signed using a digital certificate stored in the UEFI Secure Boot signature database. This helps prevent malicious code from loading during the Windows 10 start process. Requirements for Secure Boot include:

  - Computer firmware that supports Unified Extensible Firmware Interface (UEFI) v2.3.1 Errata B, and for which the Microsoft Windows Certification Authority is in the UEFI signature database

- **Multifactor authentication (MFA)** This is a process that provides user authentication based on at least two factors: something the user knows, such as a password, and something the user has, such as a biometric feature (fingerprint or facial features), or a device, such as a cell phone. Requirements for two-factor authentication are:
  - Biometric devices that support the Windows Biometric Framework, such as a fingerprint reader, a smartphone, or an illuminated infrared camera using Windows Hello
  - A biometric attribute, such as facial recognition, iris detection, or a fingerprint

> *NOTE* **WINDOWS HELLO**
>
> Windows Hello for Business provides enterprises with the tools and policies to implement and manage multifactor authentication within their organization's infrastructure.

- **Virtual Secure Mode** This feature moves some sensitive elements of the operating system to *trustlets* that run in a Hyper-V container that the Windows 10 operating system cannot access. This helps make the operating system more secure. Currently, this feature is only available in the Windows 10 Enterprise edition.
- **Virtual Smart Card** This feature offers comparable security benefits in two-factor authentication to that provided by physical smart cards. Virtual smart cards require a compatible TPM (version 1.2 or later).

EXAM TIP

If your organization requires the use of Windows Hello and your existing devices do not have the necessary hardware, then you can use an aftermarket add-on. You can purchase USB-connected infrared cameras, which provide secure facial recognition and USB-connected external fingerprint readers to the specifications required to support Windows Hello.

Perform a clean installation

Although most computers are purchased preinstalled with Windows 10, many organizations prefer to reinstall the operating system to avoid the additional software that OEMs often include with their computers. This software is often referred to as *bloatware* and can include utilities and tools or trial versions of software such as Microsoft 365 or antispyware software that are unwanted.

As shown in Table 1-2, there are several methods of installing Windows 10 on a device, and you should familiarize yourself with each prior to taking the exam.

TABLE 1-2 Windows installation methods

Installation Method	Description
Install from DVD	Windows 10 is no longer shipped on DVDs. You can use the downloadable media obtained from the Windows 10 website, Microsoft Volume Licensing Service Center (VLSC), or Visual Studio Subscriptions and burn it to DVD media.
Install from USB	Use this method to install the operating system on one computer at a time. Installation from a USB device is quicker than using a DVD. You must modify BIOS or UEFI settings to enable booting from USB.
Install from Windows Deployment Services	Requires Windows Deployment Services (WDS), which is a role installed on Windows Server 2019. WDS also requires Dynamic Host Configuration Protocol (DHCP) on the network. The target computer network card must support Preboot Execution Environment (PXE). Using WDS allows automated installation of system images and deployment of Windows to multiple computers simultaneously by using multicast.
Install an image from Windows Preinstallation Environment (Windows PE)	Boot the device by using Windows PE, and then use one of the following deployment options. ■ Use Deployment Image Servicing and Management (DISM) to apply the Windows image. ■ Use the Microsoft Deployment Toolkit (MDT) deployment solution. ■ Use the System Center Configuration Manager (Current Branch) deployment solution (Configuration Manager). Both MDT and Configuration Manager are enterprise-level solutions that enable you to deploy Windows to hundreds or thousands of devices at once and configure lite-touch installation (LTI) or zero-touch installation (ZTI) for either minimal user interaction or no user interaction, respectively, during the deployment.
Install over the network	Start the computer by using Windows PE and connect to a copy of the installation files stored on a shared network folder. You would use this method when you are unable to use a USB device, WDS, MDT, or Configuration Manager.

> **NOTE** **CREATE WINDOWS 10 INSTALLATION MEDIA**
>
> To obtain the latest version of Windows 10 that you can use to upgrade a device or download to create installation media on a DVD or USB, visit *https://www.microsoft.com/software-download/windows10*.

If you intend to start your PC from your installation media, such as a USB drive, you may need to configure your BIOS or UEFI to allow this. You can do so by modifying the BIOS or UEFI setting or choosing a custom boot order during the startup process.

During a clean installation on a new hard drive, perform the following steps to install Windows 10:

1. Insert your installation media and start your computer.

2. At the **Windows Setup** screen, choose the appropriate language and regional settings and then select **Next**.

3. In the **Windows Setup** window, select **Install Now**.

4. In the **Activate Windows** dialog box, enter your product key or select **I Don't Have a Product Key**, and then select **Next**.

5. On the **Applicable notices and license terms** page, accept the **License Terms** and select **Next**.

6. On the **Which type of installation do you want?** page, choose **Custom: Install Windows only (Advanced)**.

7. On the **Where do you want to install Windows?** page, select **Drive 0 Unallocated Space** and select **Next**.

> **NOTE EXISTING OPERATING SYSTEM DRIVE**
>
> For a clean installation of Windows 10 on a device on which an operating system is already installed, erase this partition by either formatting or deleting any partitions present during the setup process.

The installation begins. To install Windows 10 for personal use, perform the following steps:

1. On the **Let's start with region. Is this right?** page, select the regional settings.

2. On the **Is this the right keyboard layout?** page, select the keyboard layout settings.

3. On the **Want to add a second keyboard layout?** page, add a layout or select **Skip**.

4. On the **Let's connect you to a network** page, select a network connection.

5. On the **How would you like to set up?** page, choose **Set up for personal use** and select **Next**.

6. On the **Let's add your account** page, create a local offline account by selecting **Offline account**. Or you can enter your Microsoft account and password or select **Create account**.

7. On the **Create a PIN** page, select **Create PIN** and enter a PIN.

8. On the **Choose privacy settings for your device** page, choose your settings and then select **Accept**.

9. On the **Use your phone from your PC** page, select **Skip for now** or **Remind me later**.

10. On the **Back up your files with OneDrive** page, select **Next**. Or select **Only save files to this PC** to skip this step.

11. On the **Make the most of your 365 with a free Microsoft 365 trial** page, select **I have a product key**, select **No thanks**, or select **Try for free**.

12. On the **Let Cortana help you get things done** page, choose whether to enable Cortana. The remainder of the setup process will continue. You are now signed in.

Depending on your hardware performance, Windows should complete the clean installation process within 10–15 minutes, and the machine will restart several times. Nowadays most devices are fitted with a solid-state drive (SSD), which will outperform slower traditional hard drives. During the final stages of installation, Windows installs device drivers specific to the hardware.

Identify an installation strategy

You can choose among a number of methods when considering how best to install Windows 10. Generally, the size of your organization and the number of devices that you must install will determine the strategy that you select. The available strategies have different prerequisites, and some might require additional software components and configuration before you can begin installing Windows 10. Table 1-3 describes the strategies available.

TABLE 1-3 Windows 10 installation strategies

Deployment option	Description
High-touch retail media deployment	Suitable for small organizations with few devices to install with Windows 10. Requires no specialist IT skills or additional services or components. All that is required is one or more copies of the Windows 10 installation media, which can be provided on a DVD or on a USB storage device, or even from a shared folder on a network file server.
Low-touch deployment	Suitable for larger organizations that intend to install a few hundred devices, using limited installer intervention. Because the strategy relies on the use of image deployment and additional services, such as Windows Deployment Services (WDS) and, optionally, Microsoft Deployment Toolkit (MDT), some specialist IT skills are also required.
Zero-touch deployment	For very large organizations with thousands of devices. Requires a considerable investment in IT skills to facilitate this strategy. Also requires the use of MDT and System Center Configuration Manager (Current Branch) to deploy Windows 10 using no installer intervention.

Determine the appropriate installation media

Windows 10 uses an image-based installation and deployment model, with the Windows operating system installation files packaged inside an image file that is used as an installation source during the installation process.

A default installation image, Install.wim, is provided on the installation media in the \ Sources folder. Although you can choose to use this default image, you can also configure it to create custom installation images that better suit the needs of your organization. Customizations might include:

- Selecting a particular edition of Windows 10
- Choosing which Windows features are enabled
- Including Wi-Fi profiles and virtual private network (VPN) profiles
- Adding universal apps or desktop applications

The Windows Assessment and Deployment Kit (Windows ADK) contains a number of tools that you can use to create and manage Windows 10 images to support your installation needs:

- **DISM** The Deployment Image Servicing and Management (DISM) command-line tool enables you to capture, deploy, and manage Windows images. You can use the tool to install, uninstall, configure, and update Windows features, packages, drivers, and international settings in a WIM file or VHD, which can be either online or offline.

- **Windows Configuration Designer** This tool, as shown in Figure 1-1, enables you to provision Windows 10 features and runtime settings by using provisioning packages (with the extension .ppkg) to quickly configure a Windows 10 device without having to install a new image.

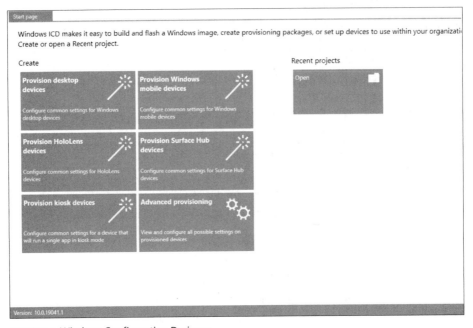

FIGURE 1-1 Windows Configuration Designer

You can then deploy these custom images and packages to target computers within your organization that require Windows 10. You can perform this deployment in a number of ways and by using a variety of deployment technologies and tools, depending on the installation strategy you previously selected. Options include:

- **DVD installation** You can create installation DVD media, or you can use a customized image that you created. The device you are installing to requires an optical drive.

- **USB installation** You can use the default or custom Windows images. This method is quicker than using a DVD, and although it does not require an optical drive, you might need to reconfigure your computer's BIOS or UEFI firmware settings to support startup from USB.

You can perform an unattended installation using these methods, provided an unattended answer file is present on the media. Answer files are discussed in the following section.

- **WDS deployment** To use this method, Dynamic Host Configuration Protocol (DHCP) must be available to network clients on your network, and your target computers running Windows 10 must support Preboot Execution Environment (PXE). Combined with unattended answer files and custom images, you can use this method to deploy multiple images to multiple computers at the same time by using multicast.

- **Image-based installation** By starting your computer into Windows Preinstallation Environment (Windows PE), you can use DISM to apply an image locally to the target computer. Alternatively, you can use MDT and System Center Configuration Manager (Current Branch) to deploy the image and desktop apps to the target devices.

- **Shared network folder installation** You can use Windows PE to start your computer and map a network drive to installation files and images on a network file shared folder. This method is comparatively inefficient and has been replaced by the other methods previously described.

FIGURE 1-2 Windows System Image Manager

- **Windows SIM** The Windows System Image Manager (Windows SIM) shown in Figure 1-2 enables you to create installation answer files for use in automated deployments. These answer files contain the configuration options used to install Windows 10. You can then associate these answer files with a local copy of the installation media, perhaps on a USB memory stick to provision Windows 10 using a semi-automated interactive installation.

> **NOTE   NAMING THE ANSWER FILE**
>
> If you copy the answer file you create by using Windows SIM to the location of the installation media, name the file **autounattend.xml.** Windows setup knows to search for this named file in the root of the installation media.

- **Windows PE**   Windows PE (WinPE) is used to start a computer that is being deployed with Windows 10. It enables access to Windows file systems and is, in essence, a small Windows operating system. You can use the generic Windows PE provided on the product DVD, or you can create your own using tools found in the Windows ADK to address your specific deployment needs. You can then launch Windows PE from a DVD or a USB memory stick or across the network using PXE.

> **NOTE   DOWNLOAD AND INSTALL THE WINDOWS ADK**
>
> A Windows ADK for Windows 10, version 20H2 is not available and will not be released. You should use the Windows ADK for Windows 10, version 2004 to deploy Windows 10, version 20H2. To obtain the latest version of the Windows Assessment and Deployment Kit, you should visit *https://docs.microsoft.com/en-us/windows-hardware/get-started/adk-install.*

Perform an in-place upgrade

The most efficient method of installing Windows 10 on existing computers is to perform an in-place upgrade. This method is fully supported and recommended by Microsoft.

It is important to understand the terminology used when describing the process of upgrading to Windows 10. *Upgrade* is often used generically to explain the licensing process of upgrading from an earlier version of Windows to a later version. You can also upgrade the edition of Windows that replaces an existing operating system, such as Windows 8.1 to Windows 10. On a semi-annual basis, Windows 10 will automatically perform an in-place upgrade of Windows 10 to the latest version of Windows 10.

When manually upgrading to Windows 10, you update the existing operating system and perform what is called an *in-place upgrade* on existing.hardware. All user data and settings are retained. For most users, this is now the recommended procedure.

Supported upgrade paths

Performing an *in-place upgrade* can be the simplest option, especially when you have only a few computers to upgrade. However, you cannot perform an in-place upgrade on computers running a Windows version that does not share the same feature set as the edition of Windows 10 that you want to install.

Table 1-4 lists the supported upgrade paths based on the Windows edition.

TABLE 1-4 Supported upgrade paths to Windows 10

Earlier Windows Edition	Windows 10 Home	Windows 10 Pro	Windows 10 Enterprise
Windows 8/8.1	X		
Windows 8/8.1 Pro		X	
Windows 8/8.1 Enterprise			X
Windows 7 Starter	X		
Windows 7 Home Basic	X		
Windows 7 Home Premium	X		
Windows 7 Professional		X	
Windows 7 Ultimate		X	
Windows 7 Enterprise			X

You will notice from Table 1-4 that direct upgrades between different editions are not supported. That is, you cannot upgrade directly from Windows 7 Home to Windows 10 Enterprise.

> **NOTE** **UPGRADING FROM WINDOWS 7 HOME**
>
> If you want to upgrade from Windows 7 Home to Windows 10 Enterprise, you can achieve that in a two-stage process. First, upgrade to Windows 10 Home and then upgrade to Windows 10 Enterprise.

After you have determined whether your upgrade path is supported, choose how to perform the process of upgrading to Windows 10.

CONSIDERATIONS FOR PERFORMING AN IN-PLACE UPGRADE

When determining whether to use the in-place upgrade method to upgrade to Windows 10, consider the following factors:

- It is a simple process and is ideal for small groups of computers.
- It provides for rollback to the earlier version of Windows.
- User and application settings and user data files are retained automatically.

- Installed applications are retained; however, retained applications might not work correctly after upgrading from an earlier Windows version.

- You do not need to provide for external storage space for data and settings migration.

- It does not allow for edition changes and is available only on supported operating systems (see Table 1-4).

- It does not provide the opportunity to start with a clean, standardized configuration.

Perform an in-place upgrade to Windows 10

As you have seen, there are three ways to upgrade to Windows 10. The recommended method by Microsoft is to use an in-place upgrade. This is the method that will be used for all future upgrades of Windows 10 using Windows Update. Using an in-place upgrade enables you to retain all the users' applications, data files, and user and application settings. During the in-place upgrade, the Windows 10 setup program automatically retains these settings.

> **IMPORTANT   BACK UP DATA FILES**
>
> It is important to perform a backup of user data files that may be stored locally prior to launching an in-place upgrade to guard against possible data loss.

You perform an in-place upgrade to Windows 10 when your users will continue to use their existing computers. To perform an in-place upgrade, complete the following procedure:

1. Evaluate the user's computer to determine that it meets minimum hardware requirements for Windows 10 and that Windows 10 supports all hardware.

2. Verify that all applications work on Windows 10.

3. Optionally, back up the user's data files.

4. Run the Setup.exe program from the root of the Windows 10 installation media.

5. Choose **Upgrade** when prompted and complete the setup wizard.

> **NOTE   UPGRADING DEVICES WITHIN A CORPORATE ENVIRONMENT**
>
> If your existing operating system is unstable or runs slowly, you may not want to perform an in-place upgrade to Windows 10. If the device is in a corporate environment and you previously deployed the earlier version of Windows using an automated deployment method, you can re-deploy the operating system again. Once complete, allow the corporate apps and settings to be applied and then perform an in-place upgrade to Windows 10. This two-stage process will take longer to perform, but it can provide an alternative method of deploying Windows 10 until you evaluate your deployment strategy.

The in-place upgrade process works well and is now the recommended deployment method Microsoft suggests for upgrading devices that run Windows 7 or Windows 8.1 to Windows 10.

Upgrade Windows 10 using enterprise tools

An enterprise that needs to upgrade existing devices will typically use tools that allow the process to be automated, with multiple devices being upgraded simultaneously.

Two of the most common tools for an enterprise to use are Windows Deployment Services (WDS) and Microsoft Deployment Toolkit.

WINDOWS DEPLOYMENT SERVICES

Windows Deployment Services is a Windows Server 2019 role that allows you to deploy Windows 10 within an on-premises environment. WDS can set up new clients with a network-based installation remotely, without needing to install directly from CD or DVD media. The Windows 10 image to be deployed can be customized and added to a server running WDS, which then transmits the image to clients using multicast functionality across the network.

WDS is installed on a Windows 2019 server and requires several prerequisites to be in place, including AD DS, DHCP, and DNS. When you deploy images using WDS you can also manage device drivers that will be needed by the client, though you are more likely to perform driver management through either MDT or Configuration Manager because these deployment tools offer more flexibility but with an increased level of complexity.

MICROSOFT DEPLOYMENT TOOLKIT (MDT)

MDT is a free, fully supported deployment toolkit from Microsoft. In addition to the tools required to deploy Windows 10, MDT provides end-to-end guidance and best practices guidelines that you can use to plan, build, and deploy Windows operating systems. MDT builds on top of the core deployment tools in the Windows ADK and can be fully integrated with Configuration Manager to customize, capture, and deploy images, applications, and device drivers to devices.

At the core of MDT are Task Sequences that allow you to automate each stage of an image capture and subsequent deployment. Because each item within the Task Sequence, as shown in Figure 1-3, can be independently configured you have a huge amount of flexibility and control over each stage of the processes.

MDT allows you to deploy images using either a Lite Touch or Zero Touch method. Lite Touch and Zero Touch are names of the two solutions, and both can be fully automated and used with the standalone MDT solution (Lite Touch) or integrated with Configuration Manager (Lite Touch and Zero Touch).

FIGURE 1-3 MDT Task Sequence

A Lite Touch installation requires someone on the remote computer to boot from a boot image. After the boot image is started, the entire installation process for the operating system and apps can be automated. With Zero Touch you utilize the tools within Configuration Manager current branch to deploy to a device. Devices with a BIOS and network card that support Wake-on-LAN can be sent a "Magic Packet" across the network that allows it to be powered on or awakened from standby. The device then receives the image and completes the installation completely unattended.

> **NOTE GET STARTED WITH MDT**
>
> The detailed capabilities of the MDT and the Windows Assessment and Deployment Kit (Windows ADK) are beyond the scope of this book. If you need to deploy hundreds or even thousands of devices within an on-premises environment, consider using MDT. You can review an overview of the features, components, and capabilities of the Microsoft Deployment Toolkit by visiting *https://docs.microsoft.com/windows/deployment/deploy-windows-mdt/get-started-with-the-microsoft-deployment-toolkit.*

Upgrade using installation media

An enterprise will normally obtain Windows 10 media through the volume licensing channel and can download it from the Volume Licensing Service Center (VLSC) at *https://www.microsoft.com/licensing/servicecenter/default.aspx*. VLSC media can use either a Multiple Activation Key (MAK) or Key Management Service (KMS), which is used during the installation process and is tied to the enterprise license agreement with Microsoft.

Alternatively, purchased retail media can be used, which is supplied on a USB thumb drive or by a direct download from the online Microsoft Store.

Another option is to use the Media Creation Tool (MCT), which generates a ready-to-use, bootable USB flash drive. You can also download an ISO file that can be used for the installation, which would need to be burned to a writable DVD. Media created with the MCT cannot be used for upgrading a Windows Enterprise edition client. When you run the MCT, when prompted on the What Do You Want To Do? page, select Create Installation Media and then select Next.

> **NOTE MEDIA CREATION TOOL (MCT)**
>
> You can download the MCT at *https://www.microsoft.com/software-download/windows10*.

If you are trying to use the wrong media or if you are trying to upgrade from an unsupported operating system, there should be an entry such as the following:

```
Info [windeploy.exe] OEM license detected, will not run SetupComplete.cmd
```

With all upgrades, you must ensure that you understand the requirements for a successful upgrade, such as having at least 2 GB of RAM and enough disk space. On the exam, you might face scenarios in which you are asked to upgrade from one architecture to another architecture that is not supported. You may be presented with the current system drive having insufficient disk space. To resolve disk space issues, you could attempt one of the following resolutions to complete the upgrade:

- Run the Disk CleanUp Wizard, remove any unwanted files, and empty the Recycle Bin.
- Uninstall apps, files, and language packs that you do not need.
- If possible, expand the volume by using the Disk Management tool.
- Move personal files off the system drive and onto another drive or external drive.

If the system fails during the upgrade due to a compatibility issue, you can troubleshoot the cause by reviewing the setupact.log and setuperr.log files found at C:\$Windows.~BT\Sources\panther\. You will need to grant yourself read permissions to the log file to open it. Some of the most common codes are shown in Table 1-5.

TABLE 1-5 Setuperr.log errors relating to upgrading

Error Code	Description
`CsetupHost::Execute result = 0xC1900200`	PC not meeting the system requirements for Windows 10.
`CsetupHost::Execute result = 0xC190020E`	Insufficient free hard drive space.
`CsetupHost::Execute result = 0xC1900204`	Migration choice (auto upgrade) not available—wrong Windows 10 SKU or architecture.
`CsetupHost::Execute result = 0xC1900208`	Compatibility issues found (hard block).
`CsetupHost::Execute result = 0xC1900210`	No issues found.

If you want to check the system for compatibility only, you can run Setup.exe with a command-line switch, which will check for compatibility but not perform the actual upgrade. The following command is an example:

```
Setup.exe /Auto Upgrade /Quiet /NoReboot /DynamicUpdate Disable /Compat ScanOnly
```

Windows 8.1 and later editions of Windows support mounting an ISO disk image directly in File Explorer. You can download the Windows 10 ISO and upgrade Windows 8.1 without first having to create installation media such as a DVD or bootable USB. For Windows 7, you must use bootable media, extract the files contained in the ISO, or use a third-party tool to mount the ISO.

A major advantage of upgrading rather than performing a clean installation (sometimes referred to as a *wipe-and-load* scenario) is that all the applications, settings, and data on the PC are retained during an upgrade. This often results in a much quicker process, and the device can be returned to the user in the shortest possible time.

> **NEED MORE REVIEW? WINDOWS 10 ENTERPRISE: FAQ FOR IT PROFESSIONALS**
>
> This Microsoft resource is useful to obtain answers to common questions about installation for Windows 10 Enterprise. Visit *https://docs.microsoft.com/windows/deployment/planning/ windows-10-enterprise-faq-itpro#administration*.

As part of the pre-upgrade checks, Windows 10 will validate the following:

- Whether UEFI is used (UEFI v2.3.1 or later is required for Secure Boot).
- System Host is not configured to boot from VHD.
- The system is not installed as a Portable Workspace (for example, using Windows To Go).

Details of the setup compatibility checks can be reviewed in the log file found at C:\$WINDOWS.~BT\Sources\Panther\setupact.log. The installation process proceeds in the same way as the in-place upgrade using Windows Update.

Migrate user data

With the rapid adoption of Microsoft 365, more data than ever before is now stored in cloud-based storage such as OneDrive for Business and SharePoint Online. Despite this trend, file server–based shared storage and local storage is still the most common data storage location for businesses.

Both cloud-based and server-based storage data backup and migration are outside of the scope of this exam, but you need to know how enterprises can migrate both user data and Windows settings from an earlier version of Windows to Windows 10. The procedure for migrating user data has not changed over the years, but you will be expected to understand the process.

Migrate from previous versions of Windows

The amount of user affinity with their devices is often overlooked by support professionals. If allowed, users can invest significant time and effort to customize and personalize their working environment, and this can include the Windows operating system and applications. When upgrading from an older operating system, it is very common for the user to be presented with a new device running the new version of Windows after the old device is removed. This can sometimes cause significant loss of productivity while the user becomes familiar with the updated operating system and reconfigures settings to their preferences.

The level of user personalization of the device can include the following:

- Desktop appearance, sounds, themes, and backgrounds
- Start menu customization
- Icons and file associations
- Files and folders stored locally
- Device and power settings
- Application settings, such as autotype and template locations

Migration strategies

You perform a migration to Windows 10 when your users have new computers on which to install Windows 10 and you want to preserve settings and data from their old computers. During the process, you perform the following high-level procedures:

1. Verify that all existing required applications work on Windows 10.
2. Ensure that the appropriate edition of Windows 10 is installed on the user's new computer.
3. On the new computer, install the required applications.
4. Back up the user's data files and settings from the old computer using User State Migration Tool (USMT).
5. Restore the user's data files and settings on the new computer using USMT.

You can use either a side-by-side migration or a wipe-and-load migration strategy to perform a migration. These migration scenarios are summarized as follows:

- **A side-by-side migration** In this scenario, the source and destination computers for the upgrade are different machines. You install a new computer with Windows 10 and then migrate the data and most user settings from the earlier operating system to the new computer.

- **A wipe-and-load migration** In this scenario, the source and destination computer are the same. You back up the user data and settings to an external location and then install Windows 10 on the user's existing computer. Afterward, you restore user data and settings.

PERFORM A SIDE-BY-SIDE MIGRATION

When you opt to use the *side-by-side* migration strategy, illustrated in Figure 1-4, use the following procedure to complete the task:

1. Either obtain a computer with Windows 10 preinstalled or install Windows 10 on a new computer. When Setup.exe prompts you, choose **Custom (Advanced). This is the destination computer**.

2. Install the same applications on the destination computer as are presently on the source computer.

3. Create an external intermediate storage location, such as a file server–shared folder or an external hard drive, for the storage of user data and settings. This storage must be accessible from both the source and destination computers.

4. Use USMT to collect the user's data and settings from the source computer and store them to the external intermediate store.

5. Use USMT to collect the user's data and settings from the external intermediate store and install them in the destination computer.

FIGURE 1-4 Side-by-side migration to Windows 10

PERFORM A WIPE-AND-LOAD MIGRATION

When you opt to use the *wipe-and-load* migration strategy, illustrated in Figure 1-5, use the following procedure to complete the task:

1. Create an external storage location, such as a file server–shared folder or an external hard drive, for the storage of user data and settings.

2. Use USMT to collect the user's data and settings and store them in the external location.

3. Install Windows 10 on the existing computer. When Setup.exe prompts you, choose **Custom (Advanced)**.

4. Reinstall the applications on the computer.

5. Use USMT to restore the user's data and settings from the external location.

FIGURE 1-5 Wipe-and-load migration to Windows 10

CONSIDERATIONS FOR PERFORMING A MIGRATION

When determining whether to use one of the two migration methods outlined to upgrade to Windows 10, consider the following factors:

- You have an opportunity to create a clean installation, free from remnant files and settings.
- You can reconfigure the existing disk partitions.
- You can upgrade to any Windows 10 edition, regardless of the earlier Windows edition.
- Migration is a more complex process, and you must use migration tools such as USMT to migrate user data and settings.
- You need to provide storage space for user settings and files to be migrated.
- Applications are not retained, and you must manually reinstall these.

Perform a user state migration

When computers are being replaced or refreshed on a large scale, the loss of user productivity can be significant. In this scenario, you can use USMT version 10, which is available as part of the Windows ADK.

EXAM TIP

You should always use the version of the Windows ADK for your version of Windows 10. For example, ensure you download Windows ADK, version 2004, if that's the version of Windows 10 you are deploying. As of this writing, Windows 10 2004 is the current feature release that can be used to deploy Windows 10, version 20H2.

The Windows ADK is available from the following Microsoft website at *https://docs.microsoft.com/windows-hardware/get-started/adk-install.*

User state migration is performed in two phases as follows:

1. Settings and data are captured (collected) from the source computer and stored in a secure migration store using the ScanState.exe tool.

2. Captured settings and data are restored on the destination computer, using the LoadState.exe tool.

USMT is a collection of the following three command-line tools that can be scripted to capture and migrate data efficiently and securely; it is intended for performing large-scale automated deployments:

- ScanState.exe
- LoadState.exe
- UsmtUtils.exe

You choose which data is captured, and these settings are stored in migration XML files as follows:

- MigApp.xml
- MigDocs.xml
- MigUser.xml
- Custom XML files that you can create

The XML files provide the migration rules that USMT needs to process.

You can also create a Config.xml file that is used to specify files or settings, which will be excluded from the migration.

> **IMPORTANT   INSTALL APPLICATIONS**
>
> USMT does not migrate applications; only the supported applications' settings are migrated. Therefore, any required applications must be already installed on the destination computer so that the captured app settings can be reinstated.

As part of both migration strategies, you must migrate user data and settings to the destination computer. Consequently, it is important to determine where these data and settings reside. The types of data that USMT can capture and migrate are shown in Table 1-6.

TABLE 1-6 Data types accessible by USMT

Data Type	Example	Description
User data	Documents, video, music, pictures, desktop files, Start menu, Quick Launch settings, and Favorites	Folders from each user profile.

Data Type	Example	Description
	Shared Documents, Shared Video, Shared Music, Shared Desktop files, Shared Pictures, Shared Start menu, and Shared Favorites	Folders from the Public profiles.
	File	USMT searches fixed drives, collecting files that have any of the file name extensions that are defined in the configuration XML file.
	Access control lists (ACLs)	USMT can migrate the ACL for specified files and folders.
Operating system components	Mapped network drives, network printers, folder options, users' personal certificates, and Internet Explorer settings	USMT migrates most standard operating system settings.
Supported applications settings	Microsoft Office, Skype, Google Chrome, Adobe Acrobat Reader, Apple iTunes, and more	USMT migrates settings for many applications, which can be specified in the MigApp.xml file. The version of each application must match on the source and destination computers. With Microsoft Office, USMT allows migration of the settings from an earlier version of an Office application.

> **NEED MORE REVIEW?** **USMT 10.0 OVERVIEW**
>
> This Microsoft resource provides an in-depth review of USMT, usage considerations, and in-depth references. Visit *https://docs.microsoft.com/en-us/windows/deployment/usmt/usmt-overview#*.

The following settings are not migrated when you use USMT:

- Local printers, hardware-related settings
- Device drivers
- Passwords
- Customized icons for shortcuts
- Shared folder permissions
- Files and settings, if the operating systems have different languages installed

After you have installed the USMT included in the Windows ADK, you have the components described in Table 1-7.

TABLE 1-7 USMT components

Component	Description
ScanState	Scans a source computer and collects files and settings, writing them to a migration store. (The store file can be password protected and can be compressed and encrypted if required, although you cannot use the /nocompress option with the /encrypt option.) You can turn off the default compression with the /nocompress option.
LoadState	Migrates the files and settings from the migration store to the destination computer.
USMTUtils	Compresses, encrypts, and validates the migration store files.
Migration XML files	MigApp.xml, MigUser.xml, or MigDocs.xml files, and custom XML files USMT uses to configure the process.
Config.xml	Used with /genconfig to exclude data from a migration.
Component manifests	Controls which operating system settings are to be migrated. These are specific to the operating system and are not modifiable.

> **NEED MORE REVIEW?** **USER STATE MIGRATION TOOL COMMAND-LINE SYNTAX**
>
> To review further details about using USMT or the syntax of the ScanState and LoadState commands, refer to the Microsoft website at *https://docs.microsoft.com/windows/deployment/usmt/usmt-command-line-syntax.*

To initiate the collection of the files and settings from the source computer, use the following steps:

1. Ensure that you have a backup of the source computer.

2. Close all applications.

3. Open an elevated command prompt, and run ScanState using this command:

   ```
   ScanState \\remotelocation\migration\mystore /config:config.xml / i:migdocs.xml
   /i:migapp.xml /v:13 /l:scan.log
   ```

4. Run UsmtUtils with the /verify switch to ensure that the migration store is not corrupted, using UsmtUtils /verify C:\mystore\storename.img.

5. On the destination computer, install the operating system, install any applications that were on the source computer, and then close any open applications.

6. Run the LoadState command, specifying the same XML files that you used when you ran ScanState using this command:

   ```
   LoadState \\remotelocation\migration\mystore /config:config.xml / i:migdocs.xml
   /i:migapp.xml /v:13 /l:load.log
   ```

7. Restart the device and verify whether some of the settings have changed.

You can also use ScanState to migrate user settings from an offline Windows system, including the Windows.old folder. A Windows.old folder is created when you perform an in-place upgrade of a modern version of Windows to Windows 10. The ability to access user settings contained within the offline Windows.old folder can be advantageous in the following scenarios:

- Improved performance if the Windows.old folder is local
- Simplified end-to-end deployment process by migrating data from Windows.old by enabling the migration process to occur after the new operating system is installed
- Improved success of migration, because files will not be locked for editing while offline
- The ability to recover and migrate data from an unbootable computer
- The flexibility to perform the migration at any time

Configure Windows for additional regional and language support

When Windows 10 was released, it offered support for 111 languages, spanning 190 countries and regions. You can download any of the additional languages for Windows 10, which allows users to view menus, dialog boxes, and other user interface items in their preferred languages.

To add an input language to your device, perform the following steps:

1. Open **Settings > Time & Language > Language**.
2. Under **Language**, select **Add A Language**.
3. Select the language you want to use from the list or enter the language name in the search bar.
4. Select **Next**.
5. Choose the optional language features you want for the selected language, as shown in Figure 1-6, and select **Install.** The language pack is downloaded and installed.
6. Log out of the device and then sign in to display the new default display language.

FIGURE 1-6 Choose a language to install

When adding a language to Windows 10, you can see which language features are available. These include:

- Display language
- Text-to-speech
- Speech recognition
- Handwriting support

You also have the option to set the language as your primary Windows display language after the language pack has been installed. Additional language options are available for common languages. Select the installed language and then select the Options button to configure features such as region-specific fonts (e.g., accents), regional formats, handwriting, pen settings, keyboards, and spell-checking options.

Installing Local Experience Packs

You can also modify the default language used by Windows 10 by adding a Local Experience Pack from the Microsoft Store. These packs perform the same configuration changes as the Language options in the Settings app, allowing you to enhance Windows with your chosen language, including navigation, menus, settings, and help topics.

To add a local language using the Microsoft Store, search for the required language and download it or use the link to add a Local Experience Pack on the Language page in the Settings app. If you need to add a Local Experience Pack to an offline image, you can add the Language Interface Packs (LIPs) APPX files and their associated license files, which can be found in the LocalExperiencePack folder on the Language Pack ISO. OEMs and system builders with Microsoft Software License Terms can download the Language Pack ISO and Feature on Demand ISO from the Microsoft OEM site or the Device Partner Center. IT professionals can find ISOs containing all available language resources on the Microsoft Next Generation Volume Licensing site at *https://licensing.microsoft.com.*

EXAM TIP

LIPs are delivered as Local Experience Packs (LXPs) APPX files, such as LanguageExperience-Pack.am-et.neutral.appx.

After the language is installed, you can set it to be the default language for your device or remove the language. On the Language page in the Settings app, you can also configure the Administrative Language Settings to copy your international settings to the Windows welcome screen, system accounts, and new user accounts, as shown in Figure 1-7. Systemwide changes require administrative privileges.

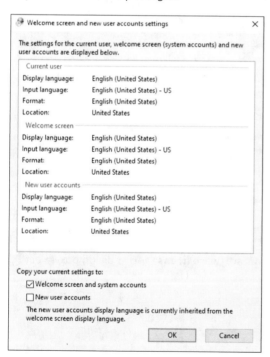

FIGURE 1-7 Modifying administrative language settings

Using the DISM command-line tool

You can also use the DISM command prompt to perform deployment of language components. As an example, if you want to modify an offline Windows image to add a language pack, first mount the Windows image, mount the Language Pack ISO and the Features on Demand ISO with File Explorer, and then use the following command:

```
Dism /Image:"C:\mount\windows" /Add-Package /PackagePath="D:\x64\langpacks\
Microsoft-Windows-Client-Language-Pack_x64_fr-fr.cab"
```

To add the Luxembourgish language, which requires the fr-FR base language and is delivered as an LXP (learning experience platform) file, use the following command:

```
DISM /Image:"C:\mount\windows" /Add-ProvisionedAppxPackage /PackagePath=
"D:\LocalExperiencePack\lb-lu\LanguageExperiencePack.lb-LU.Neutral.appx"
/LicensePath: "D:\LocalExperiencePack\lb-lu\License.xml"
```

To remove the same LIP, which was added through LXP, you would use this command:

```
Dism /remove-provisionedappxpackage /packagename:Microsoft.LanguageExperiencePack.
lb-LU._neutral__8wekyb3d8bbwe
```

Once you have completed the configuration, you need to capture the changes by committing the changes to the Windows image using the following command:

```
Dism /Commit-Image /MountDir:"C:\mount\windows"
```

Using the Lpksetup command-line tool

You can also use the Lpksetup tool to perform language pack operations on language pack CAB files.

To launch the Lpksetup Wizard, use the following steps:

1. Download and then mount the **Language Pack ISO**.

2. Select the **Windows key+R** to open the **Run** dialog box.

3. Enter **lpksetup.exe** and then select **OK**.

4. Step through the wizard and browse to the Language Pack location on the mounted ISO.

5. Locate the language pack as shown in Figure 1-8 and select **Next**.

6. In the **Review and accept the Microsoft software license terms** dialog box, select **I accept the license terms** and select **Next**.

7. The language pack installation completes.

8. Select **Close**.

FIGURE 1-8 Perform language pack operations using Lpksetup

If you want to automate the process or bypass the user interface (UI) and perform unattended or silent-mode language pack installations, you can also use the Lpksetup.exe command-line tool. You need to run the Lpksetup command using an elevated command prompt. The syntax is

```
lpksetup.exe /i * /p <path>
```

This example installs all language packs that are located on installation media specified in the *<path>* location. The command-line options available for Lpksetup are shown in Table 1-8.

TABLE 1-8 Lpksetup command-line options

Option	Description
/i	Installs the specified language packs. If you do not include * or language after /i, you are asked to continue the installation through the UI.
*	Wildcard character that represents all language packs found in the language_pack_path or the directory where lpksetup.exe is located.
Language-region	Specifies the language pack or packs to be installed or uninstalled.
/u	Uninstalls the specified language packs. If you do not include * or a language after /u, you are asked to continue the uninstall through the UI.
/r	Suppresses the need to restart after an operation is complete.
/p language_pack_path	Indicates the path of the language packs to install.
/s	Performs a silent and unattended operation that requires no user input.
/f	If the computer is required to restart, forces a restart even if other users are logged on to the computer.

Skill 1.2: Perform post-installation configuration

After you have provisioned Windows 10, you must ensure that the user is productive as soon as possible. Enabling a consistent Windows environment that looks and behaves the same regardless of the device used can be helpful. Users should be able to browse the internet safely and in accordance with corporate policies. Devices that are used by mobile users can be configured dynamically to provide them with optimal power settings and preconfigured connectivity to resources such as secure VPNs and Wi-Fi networks.

This skill covers how to:

- Customize the Windows desktop
- Configure Microsoft Edge
- Configure Internet Explorer
- Implement activation
- Configure mobility settings
- Configure printers and external devices
- Configure Windows 10 by using provisioning packages
- Configure Microsoft Store settings
- Configure application settings
- Configure and manage services

Customize the Windows desktop

After Windows 10 has been activated, you can customize the user interface and personalize Windows. Devices enrolled in Microsoft Intune or joined to Azure Active Directory will be activated automatically if a digital license has been assigned. The Windows 10 user interface may be familiar to users of Windows 7 because it has a Start menu, a desktop, and a taskbar.

It is important for you to understand how to customize the Windows 10 user interface, including Start and taskbar layout, desktop, and notification settings. That way, you can ensure that the operating system interface meets the needs of the users in your organization.

Customize Windows 10 Start

For users of earlier versions of Windows, the appearance of Start may be significantly different to what they have been used to. Start is dynamic, and its appearance depends on your device type. For example, on a device with a small screen such as a tablet, Start appears full screen, by default, which is easier to navigate when using a touch device.

If you are using a non-touch device, then, by default, Windows 10 displays Start as a menu that combines aspects that may be similar to the Start menu found in Windows 7 and Windows 8.1 (see Figure 1-9). This display is more easily navigated by using a mouse rather than touch.

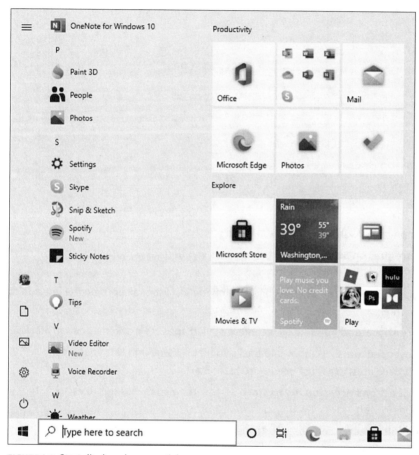

FIGURE 1-9 Start displayed as a partial screen

You can configure the Start menu behavior from the Settings app. Open the Settings app, select Personalization, and then select the Start tab. You can then select the option Use Start Full Screen, as shown in Figure 1-10.

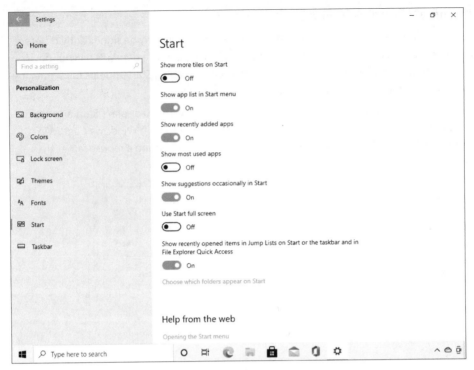

FIGURE 1-10 Start menu settings

The Start customizations shown in Figure 1-10 are:

- **Show more tiles on Start**   This setting enables you to display more tiles when Start is configured for partial-screen mode.

- **Show app list in Start menu**   Displays an alphabetical list of all apps on the left side of the Start screen.

- **Show recently added apps**   Any recently installed apps are marked as new in Start.

- **Show most used apps**   Windows 10 tracks your app usage and lists your most frequently used apps in a Most Used Apps list in Start.

- **Show suggestions occasionally in Start**   This setting enables or disables app suggestions in Start.

- **Use Start full screen**   Enables Start to display full screen. This is more useful on a tablet device than on a device with a mouse.

- **Show recently opened items in Jump Lists on Start or the taskbar and in File Explorer Quick Access**   This setting enables Windows 10 to remember recently opened files and list those in the context menu of apps appearing in Start or on the taskbar.

- **Choose which folders appear on Start**   This setting enables you to set shortcuts for the following folders on Start: File Explorer, Settings, Documents, Downloads, Music, Pictures, Videos, Network, and Personal Folders.

CONVERTIBLE DEVICES

Convertible devices, including the Microsoft Surface Pro, can switch in and out of Tablet mode with the removal and reattachment of the keyboard, or by reorienting the device. When a device switches like this, you can choose whether Windows should switch to full-screen Start (Tablet mode) automatically, as shown in Figure 1-11.

FIGURE 1-11 The Tablet mode prompt on a convertible laptop

You can configure the default behavior through the Settings app. Select System and then open the Tablet Mode tab. As shown in Figure 1-12, you can then configure the following options:

- When I Sign In:
  - Use Tablet Mode
  - Use Desktop Mode
  - Use The Appropriate Mode For My Hardware
- When This Device Automatically Switches Tablet Mode On Or Off:
  - Don't Ask Me And Don't Switch
  - Always Ask Me Before Switching
  - Don't Ask Me And Always Switch
- Hide App Icons On The Taskbar In Tablet Mode
- Automatically Hide The Taskbar In Tablet Mode

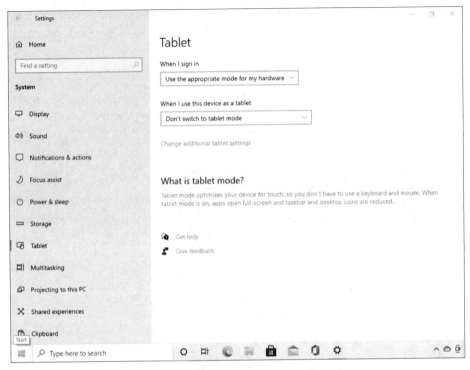

FIGURE 1-12 Tablet mode options

> **NOTE** **TABLET MODE**
>
> Tablet mode also changes applications so that they run full screen.

CONFIGURING START TILES

In addition to enabling or disabling Start full-screen behavior, you can customize the application tiles that appear on Start and how those tiles look and behave. From Start, right-select the appropriate app, as shown in Figure 1-13. Select Unpin From Start.

When a tile is pinned to Start, you can configure it. Right-select the tile, and from the context menu, you can choose:

- Unpin From Start
- Resize
    - Choose from Small, Medium, Large, and Wide, depending on the app.

- More
  - If the app is a Microsoft Store app, choose from Turn Live Tile Off, Pin To Taskbar, App Settings, Rate And Review, and Share.
  - If the app is a desktop app, choose from Pin To Taskbar, Run As Administrator, and Open File Location.
- Uninstall

> **NOTE** **UNINSTALLING DESKTOP APPS FROM START**
>
> If the app you select to uninstall is a desktop app, Programs And Features opens in Control Panel enabling you to manually remove the desktop app.

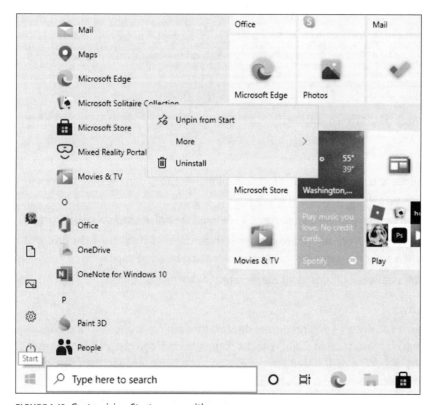

FIGURE 1-13 Customizing Start screen with a mouse

If your device is touch-enabled, the procedure is slightly different from using a mouse to configure tiles. Rather than right-selecting a tile from Start, you must touch and hold a tile. Then you can unpin the tile by using the Unpin icon. Use the ellipse button (three dots) to access the context menu, as shown in Figure 1-14.

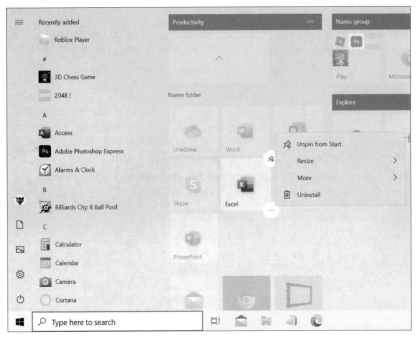

FIGURE 1-14 Customizing Start screen with touch

GROUPING START TILES

After you have added the required tiles to Start, you might want to group the tiles. You can perform the following actions on groups:

- To create a new group of tiles, simply drag a tile to an area of unused space on Start.
- To name a group, hover your mouse or tap the screen immediately above the group of tiles and then enter the name for your group in the text box that appears.
- To move tiles between groups, drag the required tile to the new group.

EXPORT START LAYOUT

Although you can manually drag and resize tiles on Start for each computer in your organization, this approach is not practical at scale. Within a corporate environment, you can control the Start layout by creating a customized Start screen on a test computer and then export the layout to other devices.

Not all editions of Windows 10 support customizing Windows 10 Start and taskbar with Group Policy. These are shown in Table 1-9.

TABLE 1-9 Windows 10 Start and taskbar support

Windows Version	Supported Edition
Windows 10, version 1607	Windows 10 Enterprise and Windows 10 Education
Windows 10, version 1703	Windows 10 Pro, Windows 10 Enterprise, and Windows 10 Education

You can choose to export a layout that applies a full or partial Start layout:

- **Full Start layout** Users cannot pin, unpin, or uninstall apps from Start. Users cannot pin any apps to Start.
- **Partial Start layout** The contents of the specified tile groups cannot be changed. Users can move groups and can create and customize their own groups.

The Start layout is exported as an XML file, which can then be deployed to devices using one of the following:

- Group Policy
- Windows Configuration Designer provisioning package
- Mobile device management (MDM)

On your test computer, you can customize the Start layout prior to exporting the layout. Customization can include:

- Pin apps to Start.
- Unpin the apps that you don't want to display.
- Drag the tiles on Start to reorder or group apps.
- Resize tiles.
- Create your own app groups.
- Name groups.

Once you have configured the desired Start layout, you use the `Export-StartLayout` Windows PowerShell cmdlet to export the Start layout to an XML file using the following procedure:

1. Open **Windows PowerShell**.
2. Run the `Export-StartLayout –path <path><file name>.xml` cmdlet.
3. You can optionally edit the XML file to add a taskbar configuration.
4. Copy the exported file to a shared folder.
5. Deploy the XML file using any of the deployment methods.

If you use Group Policy, you must specify the XML file in the GPO: User Configuration\Policies\Administrative Templates\Start Menu and Taskbar\Start Layout. To do this, complete the following procedure:

1. Open **Group Policy Management Console (GPMC)** to configure a domain-based GPO.
2. Navigate to the appropriate AD DS container, such as your domain.

3. Open an existing GPO for editing or create a new GPO, link it to your chosen container, and open it for editing.

4. Navigate to the **User Configuration\Policies\Administrative Templates\Start Menu And Taskbar** folder and open the **Start Layout** GPO.

5. Enable the GPO and, in the Start Layout File text box, type the full UNC path name to your XML file; for example, **\\LON-SVR1\Marketing\Marketing.XML** as shown in Figure 1-15.

6. Select **OK** and close **Group Policy Management**.

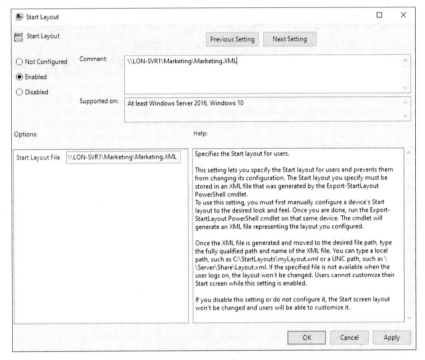

FIGURE 1-15 Deploy custom Start using Group Policy

For the policy to be effective, users must sign out and sign back in. Alternatively, you can issue a Gpupdate.exe /force command from an elevated command prompt to force GPO propagation.

To configure a partial Start screen layout, you should export the Start layout and then open the layout XML file. You should then add LayoutCustomizationRestrictionType="Only SpecifiedGroups" to the <DefaultLayoutOverride> element as follows:

```
<DefaultLayoutOverride LayoutCustomizationRestrictionType="OnlySpecifiedGroups">
```

Then save the file and deploy the settings.

If you like, you can update an existing Start layout by replacing the XML file that is specified in the Start Layout policy settings with an XML file that has a newer time stamp.

In addition to the Start layout, you can control other aspects of Start with Group Policy. Table 1-10 shows the elements that you can control with GPOs and the respective values to use within GPOs. Unless otherwise noted, the path for these GPO settings is User Configuration\ Policies\Administrative Templates\Start Menu And Taskbar.

TABLE 1-10   USING GROUP POLICY TO CONFIGURE START

Start Element	Policy
User Tile	Remove Logoff On The Start Menu
Most Used	Remove Frequent Programs List From The Start Menu
Suggestions	Computer Configuration\Policies\Administrative Templates\Windows Components \Cloud Content\Turn Off Microsoft Consumer Experiences
Power	Remove And Prevent Access To The Shut Down, Restart, Sleep, And Hibernate Commands
All Apps	Remove All Programs List From The Start Menu
Jump Lists	Do Not Keep History Of Recently Opened Documents
Start Size	Force Start To Be Either Full Screen Size Or Menu Size
All Settings	Prevent Changes To Taskbar And Start Menu Settings

CUSTOMIZE THE DESKTOP

In addition to customizing Start to your requirements, you can configure the desktop and related settings. To configure the desktop, select Start > Settings > Personalization.

From the Personalization Settings app, you can configure the following settings:

- **Background**   You can select and configure a desktop background color or picture image, or you can select a slideshow of images.
- **Colors**   On the Color tab, you can choose a color scheme and optionally configure the following options:
    - Enable transparency effects.

- Show accent color on the following surfaces: Start, taskbar, Action Center, title bars, and window borders.
- Choose the default app mode: Light or Dark.
- Access the High Contrast Settings.

- **Lock Screen**   From the Lock Screen tab, as shown in Figure 1-16, you can select and configure a background image to display when your Windows 10 device is locked. A feature called Windows Spotlight allows you to display different background images on the lock screen each day and will occasionally suggest Windows 10 features that the user hasn't tried yet, such as Snap Assist. In addition, you can:
  - Choose a Lock Screen background image.
  - Choose an app to show Detailed Status (for example, Calendar).
  - Choose apps to Show Quick Status (for example, Facebook, Mail, Calendar, or Alarms & Clock).
  - Configure Cortana Lock Screen Settings.
  - Show Lock Screen background picture on the Sign-In Screen.
  - Configure Screen Timeout Settings and Screen Saver Settings.

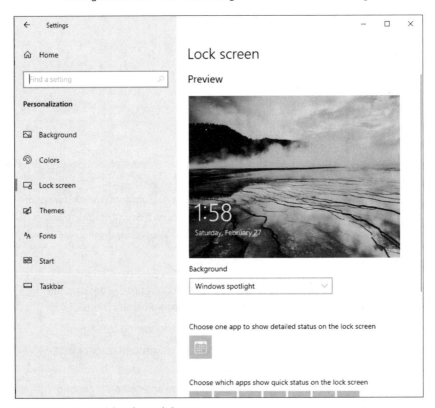

FIGURE 1-16 Customizing the Lock Screen

- **Themes**   This setting enables you to configure and apply theme settings. Themes enable you to define combinations of background, color, sound, and mouse cursor settings. You can also configure desktop icon settings, such as whether to display the Recycle Bin on the desktop. Underneath the Change Theme section is a link to Get More Themes in Microsoft Store. In the Microsoft Store, you can download of additional themes that are available free, as shown in Figure 1-17.

- **Start**   You can also configure Start settings, as previously discussed.

- **Taskbar**   From this tab, among other settings, you can:

  - Lock the taskbar.

  - Automatically hide the taskbar when in Desktop or Tablet mode.

  - Use small taskbar buttons.

  - Configure the way running tasks and apps combine on the taskbar.

  - Configure whether the Command Prompt will appear instead of Windows Power-Shell on Start; you can also configure whether the Command Prompt appears in the menu when the Windows key+X is pressed.

  - Change the taskbar location.

  - Customize the notifications area.

  - Turn system icons on or off.

  - Customize the taskbar appearance when using multiple displays.

  - Customize the People settings.

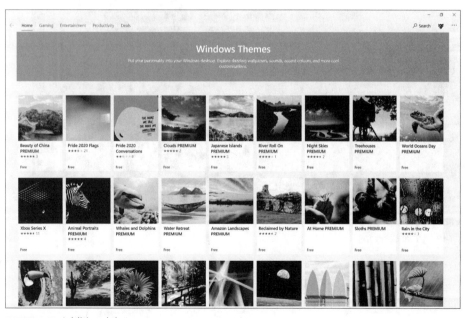

FIGURE 1-17 Additional themes

Multiple desktops

Windows 10 provides support for multiple desktops. This provides a simplistic multitasking view. Rather than running apps in multiple windows on the same desktop, you can create additional desktops for groups of apps or for individual apps. Multiple desktops can be useful for keeping unrelated windows or projects organized; multiple desktops are also useful for quickly switching to a clean desktop before a meeting.

To add a new desktop, select the Task View button on the taskbar and then select New Desktop in the upper-left of the display. You can also add a new desktop by pressing Windows key+Tab on your keyboard, or you can swipe with one finger from the left of your screen if you have touch.

To switch between desktops, select the Task View button, press Windows key+Tab, or swipe with one finger from the left of your touchscreen. You can then select the appropriate desktop, as shown in Figure 1-18.

To remove a desktop, select the Task View button on the taskbar and then hover over the desktop that you want to delete and then select the X on the desktop.

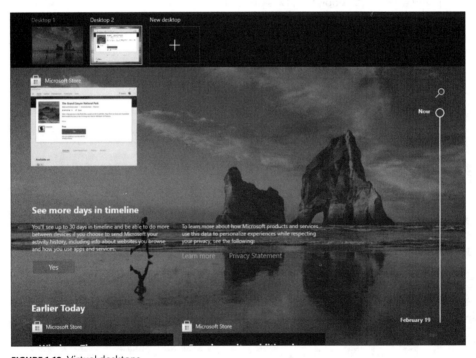

FIGURE 1-18 Virtual desktops

Configure Action Center and taskbar

In Windows 10, Microsoft introduces an improved Action Center, as shown in Figure 1-19. The Action Center is accessible by swiping from the right or by selecting the Notifications icon in the system tray.

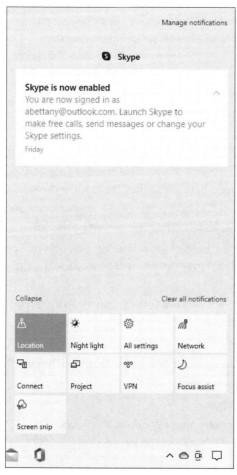

FIGURE 1-19 The Action Center

Action Center includes the following elements:

- **Quick Action tiles** As shown at the bottom of Figure 1-19, the displayed tiles are configurable and dependent on your device.

- **Notifications area** You can configure how Windows notifies you of events.

CONFIGURE QUICK ACTION TILES

The Quick Action tiles are shortcuts to commonly used features of the Windows 10 operating system. The expanded view allows a larger number of tiles to become visible, as shown in

Figure 1-20. The specific tiles that appear in the expanded view will depend on your device type and orientation. For example, if your computer is not a tablet and is not capable of converting into a tablet, the Tablet Mode tile is not available. By default, in the expanded view, the following tiles are available:

- **Tablet mode**   Enables you to switch between Tablet and Desktop modes.
- **Rotation Lock**   Enables or disables the rotation lock. Normally, the display orients itself based on the orientation of your Windows 10 device, switching between landscape and portrait modes. Use this option to lock the orientation regardless of physical orientation.
- **Airplane Mode**   Disables all internal radios in the device, including Wi-Fi and Bluetooth, for use when you travel on an aircraft. This mode is also convenient when you want to conserve battery power.
- **All Settings**   Provides a convenient shortcut to the Settings app.
- **Connect**   Enables you to find and connect to media servers. This includes Xbox and other devices running Windows that are sharing their media files. It can also include devices, such as TV set-top boxes.
- **Project**   Enables you to link your device to an external monitor or wireless display.
- **Battery Saver**   Only available when your device is running on battery alone; helps reduce power consumption. You can configure Power Options and Battery Saver in the Settings app.
- **VPN**   Switches to the VPN tab in the Network & Internet Settings app. From there, you can set up, configure, or connect to a VPN.
- **Bluetooth**   Enable or disable the Bluetooth radio.
- **Brightness**   Enables you to control display brightness. Select this tile to step through brightness levels in 25 percent increments.
- **Wi-Fi**   Enables or disables the Wi-Fi connection.
- **Focus Assist**   (Called Quiet Hours in earlier versions of Windows 10) Allows you to avoid distracting notifications when you need to stay focused by reducing the notifications you receive.
- **Night Light**   Toggles your display to remove white light. You can configure Night Light in the Settings app.
- **Location**   Enables or disables location services. Many services use location to customize services, such as mapping apps, for your device.

You can modify which Quick Action tiles are displayed by selecting the Edit Your Quick Actions link and then rearranging the location of the tiles by dragging and dropping them within the Settings app, as shown in Figure 1-20.

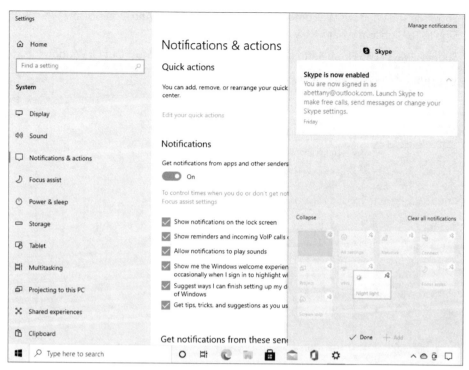

FIGURE 1-20 Windows 10 Quick Actions settings

CONFIGURE NOTIFICATIONS

When Windows 10 wants to inform you about something, it raises a notification. You can see and act on the notifications in a list shown in Action Center. To respond to a notification, select it. You can remove notifications by selecting Clear All at the top of the page.

Windows notifies you about a variety of operating system events and situations, including the need to obtain updates or perform an antivirus scan, and Windows also prompts you about which actions you want to take when a new device, such as a USB memory stick, has been detected.

As shown in Figure 1-21, you can configure which notifications you receive by opening Settings. Select System > Notifications & Actions. Under Notifications, you can configure the following options:

- Show Notifications On The Lock Screen
- Show Reminders And Incoming VoIP Calls On The Lock Screen
- Allow Notifications To Play Sounds

- Show Me The Windows Welcome Experience After Updates And Occasionally When I Sign In To Highlight What's New And Suggested

- Suggest Ways I Can Finish Setting Up My Device To Get The Most Out Of Windows

- Get Tips, Tricks, And Suggestions As You Use Windows

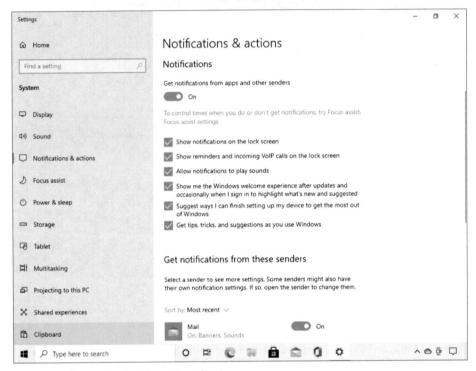

FIGURE 1-21 Configuring Windows 10 notifications

You can also configure notifications from individual apps. As shown in Figure 1-22 under the Get Notifications From These Senders heading, you can enable or disable notifications for each listed sender. If you select a sender from the list, such as for Skype, as shown in Figure 1-22, you can fine-tune the notifications for the application, including turning them on or off:

- Notifications

- Show Notification Banners

- Show Notifications In Action Center

- Hide Content When A Notification Arrives

- Number Of Notifications Visible In Action Center

- Priority Of Notifications In Action Center

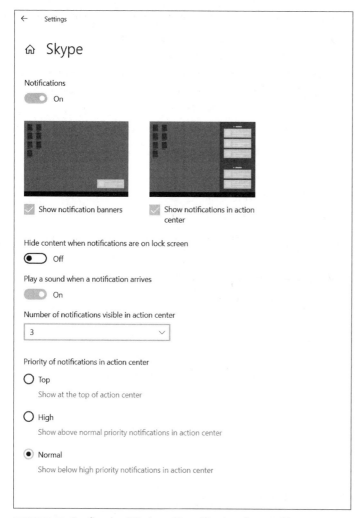

FIGURE 1-22 Configuring Windows 10 notifications for specific apps

EXAM TIP

You can remove the Notification & Action Center from the notifications area on the taskbar using Group Policy. Notifications will pop up, but users won't be able to review any notifications they miss. Use the User Configuration\Policies\Administrative Templates\Start Menu And Taskbar node and enable the Remove Notifications And Action Center GPO.

CONFIGURE THE TASKBAR

You have seen how to configure the taskbar using the Settings app. The same functionality is available if you right-select the taskbar. Administrators can also pin additional apps to the taskbar and remove default pinned apps from the taskbar.

This is achieved by adding a `<TaskbarLayout>` section to a layout modification XML file used to configure the Start screen.

You can specify which apps are added to the taskbar using the Application User Model ID (AUMID) or Desktop Application Link Path (the local path to the application). The easiest method to obtain the AUMID or Desktop Application Link Path is to extract the information from the `Export-StartLayout` cmdlet we saw earlier by following these steps:

1. Pin the required application to the Start menu on a reference or testing PC.

2. Open **Windows PowerShell** and run the `Export-StartLayout` cmdlet.

3. Open the generated XML file.

4. Identify the entry corresponding to the app you pinned.

5. Look for a property labeled `AppUserModelID` or `DesktopApplicationLinkPath`.

Once you have obtained the app information, you can configure the taskbar using these steps:

1. Create the XML file and include the `<CustomTaskbarLayoutCollection>` section.

2. Use the **AUMID** or **Desktop Application Link Path** to identify the apps to pin to the taskbar.

3. Add `xmlns:taskbar="http://schemas.microsoft.com/Start/2014/TaskbarLayout"` to the first line of the file, before the closing **>**.

4. Use `<taskbar:UWA>` and **AUMID** to pin Universal Windows Platform apps.

5. Use `<taskbar:DesktopApp>` and the **Desktop Application Link Path** to pin desktop applications.

The layout modification XML file can be applied to devices using Group Policy or a provisioning package created in Windows Configuration Designer.

> ***NEED MORE REVIEW?*** **CONFIGURE WINDOWS 10 TASKBAR**
>
> This Microsoft resource contains sample taskbar configuration XML files that can help you configure the taskbar, and it discusses how to remove default apps. Visit *https://docs. microsoft.com/windows/configuration/configure-windows-10-taskbar#sample-taskbar- configuration-added-to-start-layout-xml-file.*

CONFIGURE THE NOTIFICATIONS AREA

As shown in Figure 1-23, you can also configure taskbar options from the Personalization area of the Settings app. Open the Personalization area and then select the Taskbar tab. There are several headings on the Taskbar page with options for each:

- Taskbar

Options include:

- Lock The Taskbar
- Automatically Hide The Taskbar In Desktop Mode

- Automatically Hide The Taskbar In Tablet Mode
- Use Small Taskbar Buttons
- Use Peek To Preview The Desktop When You Move Your Mouse To The Show Desktop Button At The End Of The Taskbar
- Replace Command Prompt With Windows PowerShell In The Menu When I Right-Click The Start Button Or Press Windows Key + X
- Show Badges On Taskbar Buttons
- Taskbar Location On Screen
- Combine Taskbar Buttons
- How Do I Customize Taskbars?

- Notifications Area

Options include:

- Select Which Icons Appear On The Taskbar
- Turn System Icons On Or Off

Options include:

- Clock
- Volume
- Network
- Power
- Input Indicator
- Location
- Action Center
- Touch Keyboard
- Windows Ink Workspace
- Touchpad
- Microphone
- Meet Now

- Multiple Displays

Options include:

- Show Taskbar On All Displays
- Show Taskbar Buttons On
- Combine Buttons On Other Taskbars

- People

Options include:

- Show Contacts On The Taskbar
- Choose How Many Contacts To Show

- Show My People Notifications
- Play A Sound When A My People Notification Arrives
- Show My People App Suggestions
- Help From The Web

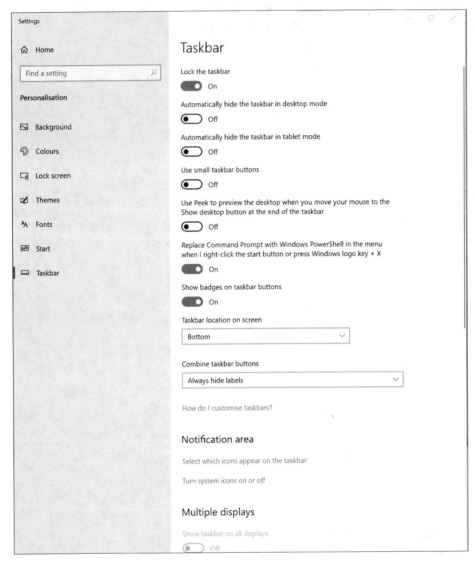

FIGURE 1-23 Configuring the notifications area

Configure Microsoft Edge

Microsoft Edge, shown in Figure 1-24, is a web browser that provides a consistent interface across device types, such as Windows 10–based tablets, laptops, and smartphones. The interface is simple and touch-centric, making it the ideal browser for devices running Windows 10. Microsoft Edge is also available on Android and iOS devices.

For readers not familiar with Microsoft Edge, it is the default browser for all Windows 10 devices. Windows 10 shipped originally with an HTML-based browser, but this was replaced in January 2020 with a new version of Edge, which uses the open source Chromium browser engine. All versions of Windows 10, version 1803 and newer will support the updated version of Microsoft Edge. In addition to Microsoft Edge, Windows 10 provides Internet Explorer 11 (IE11). Microsoft Edge is used for modern websites, and IE11 is included for compatibility with enterprise web apps that use older web technologies like ActiveX.

Because Microsoft Edge supports only the latest web standards, it offers users a fast and safe browsing experience. Microsoft Edge is like Windows 10 in that it is regularly updated. Because it was first introduced with Windows 10, many new features and functionality have been added, including the ability to manage tabs, read e-books, write on webpages, and more.

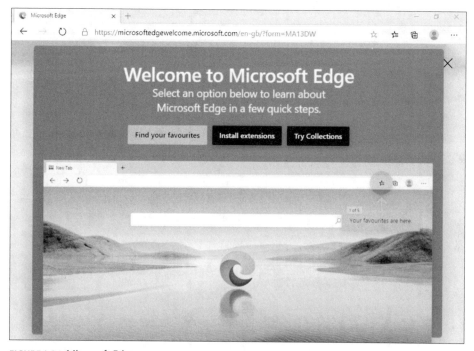

FIGURE 1-24 Microsoft Edge

Microsoft Edge includes a number of features not available in Internet Explorer 11. These include:

- Kiosk mode, which allows only Microsoft Edge to display a specific site in full-screen mode as used in digital/interactive signage or for public browsing
- Collections, which allow you organize webpages; similar to favorites

- Extensions, which allow you add additional functionality from the Microsoft Store or Chrome Web Store to enhance and customize your browser

You can install extensions in Microsoft Edge by performing the following steps:

1. Launch **Microsoft Edge**.

2. On the **Settings and More** menu (the three ellipsis in the top-right corner), select **Extensions**.

3. On the Extensions page, select **Get extensions for Microsoft Edge**, as shown in Figure 1-25.

4. In the **Edge Add-ons** site, select the extension that you want to install.

5. Select **Get** and then select **Add Extension**.

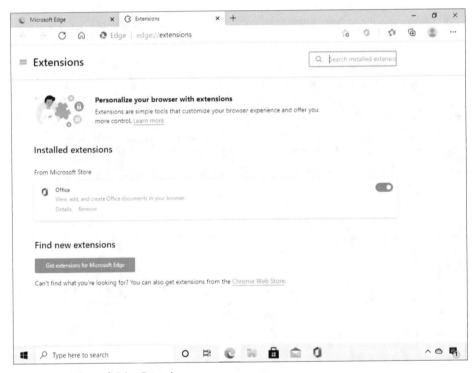

FIGURE 1-25 Microsoft Edge Extensions

It is important to know how to configure Microsoft Edge, including how to migrate web favorites to this new browser, to support your organization's users. Microsoft Edge has streamlined settings that you can easily configure from the to Settings link in the browser, as shown in Figure 1-26.

FIGURE 1-26 Configuring settings in Microsoft Edge

From this window, you can access the following options:

- **New Tab**   Enables you to open a new browser tab
- **New Window**   Enables you to open a new browser window
- **New InPrivate Window**   Provides the same privacy options enabled by InPrivate browsing in Internet Explorer
- **Zoom**   Enables you to zoom in or out on a webpage
- **Favorites**   Opens your webpage favorites
- **History**   Opens your webpage history
- **Downloads**   Opens your download history
- **Apps**   Enables you to install browser web apps

- **Extensions**   Opens your browser add-ins and offers a list of suggested extensions
- **Collections**   Enables you customize your collections of webpages
- **Print**   Enables you to print the webpage
- **Web Capture**   Enables you create a snip of part of whole of a webpage and optionally add notes
- **Share**   Enables you to quickly share a webpage or web URL to OneNote, your phone, and email
- **Find On Page**   Searches for content on the current webpage
- **Read Aloud**   Narrates the content on the current webpage
- **More Tools**   Provides additional tools:
  - **Save Page As**   Allows you to save a webpage
  - **Cast Media To Device**   Enables you to send content, such as a video, to wireless media devices
  - **Pin To Taskbar**   Enables you to pin frequently accessed webpages directly to the taskbar
  - **Pin To Start**   Enables you to pin frequently accessed webpages directly to your Start page
  - **Launch Taskbar Pinning Wizard**   Helps you find the websites that you use most, and then pin them to the taskbar
  - **Browser Task Manager**   Opens the version of Task Manager that enables you to end specific browser tasks that are misbehaving, as shown in Figure 1-27
  - **Developer Tools**   Opens a new developer console

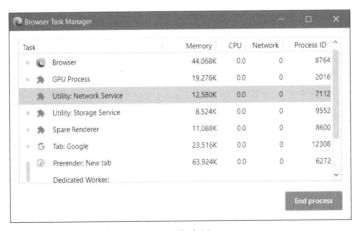

FIGURE 1-27   Microsoft Edge Browser Task Manager

From the Settings cog at the bottom of the window, you can access additional submenus that enable you to add and configure your browser profiles, view browser-stored passwords, review store payment information, review stored addresses, import browser data, and configure your profile preferences.

In the previous version of Microsoft Edge, the sync was limited to the Windows sync ecosystem based on OneDrive. With the new Microsoft Edge Chromium, Edge will sync across all the platforms, such as Windows 7, Windows 8.1, iOS, Android, and macOS.

If you create a browser profile and allow the profile to sync your browsing data across devices, you can then access additional settings within the Settings area, including:

- Favorites
- Passwords
- Addresses and more (form-fill)
- Collections
- Settings

Customize Microsoft Edge

One of the benefits of the integration between Windows 10 and Microsoft Edge is the extensive ability to customize Microsoft Edge for your organization. These settings cover every aspect of the modern browser, including configuring default tabs, security settings, allowed extensions, browser experience preferences, and more.

There are over 160 configuration options relating to Microsoft Edge, version 77 and later that can be applied to devices using either Group Policy management or Microsoft Intune.

To view the available policies for Microsoft Edge within Intune, follow these steps:

1. Sign in to the **Microsoft Endpoint Manager** portal.
2. Select **Devices** in the left-hand navigation pane.
3. Select **Configuration Profiles** (under the Policy heading).
4. On the top command bar, select **Create Profile**.
5. In the drop-down list below **Platform**, select **Windows 10 and later**.

6. In the drop-down list below **Profile Type**, select **Templates**.

7. In the drop-down list below **Template Name**, select **Administrative Templates**.

8. Select the **Create** button.

9. On the **Create Profile** page, enter a profile name and then select **Next**.

10. On the **Configuration Settings** page, select the folder category containing the templates, or select the individual policy from the policies listed below the folders, as shown in Figure 1-28. The policies are sorted alphabetically.

11. Select a policy to open a dialog box on the right side where you can configure the policy.

FIGURE 1-28 Microsoft Edge configuration policies

NEED MORE REVIEW? **CONFIGURE MICROSOFT EDGE POLICY SETTINGS WITH MICROSOFT INTUNE**

For more information about configuring Microsoft Edge policy settings using Microsoft Intune, visit the Microsoft website at *https://docs.microsoft.com/deployedge/configure-edge-with-intune*.

If your organization uses Group Policy, you can locate 55 Microsoft Edge Group Policy settings in the following location:

Computer Configuration\Administrative Templates\Windows Components\Microsoft Edge

Microsoft Edge kiosk mode

If you are running Windows 10, version 1809 (Professional, Enterprise, and Education editions only), you can use Microsoft Edge in a kiosk environment using assigned access. The assigned access feature allows you to lock down a Windows 10 device to run a single app or multiple apps only; the device can then be used in a public space such as a kiosk.

Microsoft Edge in kiosk mode allows you to operate a digital signage for presentation in a public area or to deploy devices for members of the public to use for web browsing in InPrivate mode. You can modify the behavior of Microsoft Edge when it's running in kiosk mode by configuring the appropriate policy, as shown in Table 1-11.

TABLE 1-11 Microsoft Edge kiosk mode policy

Management Tool	Policy
Group Policy	Configure Kiosk Mode
Microsoft Intune	ConfigureKioskMode

Microsoft Edge in kiosk mode supports four configuration types, as shown in Table 1-12. The Group Policy settings are shown in Figure 1-29.

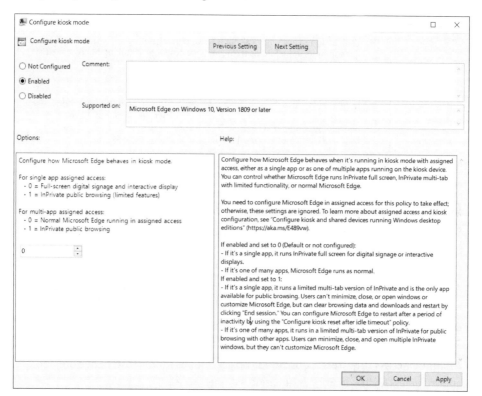

FIGURE 1-29 Microsoft Edge kiosk mode GPO

Microsoft Edge kiosk mode can be set up in various configurations depending on your requirements, as listed in Table 1-12.

TABLE 1-12 Microsoft Edge kiosk mode configuration types

configuration Type	Description

Single-app – Digital/interactive signage	■ Runs Microsoft Edge InPrivate displaying a single website running in full-screen mode for the following scenarios:
	  ■ **Digital signage** Rotating advertisement or menu requiring no user interaction.
	  ■ **Interactive signage** Allows user interaction, which is restricted to within the page, such as a building business directory or restaurant order/pay station.
	■ Prevents any other uses, such as browsing the internet.
	■ Policy setting = Not configured (0 default).

Single-app – InPrivate Public browsing	■ Runs a limited, multi-tab version of Microsoft Edge. ■ Microsoft Edge is the only app users can use on the device—they can browse publicly or close Microsoft Edge using the End Session button. ■ The session will reset after 5 minutes of user inactivity, which will restart Microsoft Edge with a new session. ■ Public browsing is useful within a public library or hotel concierge desk. ■ Policy setting = Enabled (1).
Multi-app – Normal browsing	■ Runs Microsoft Edge with all browsing features and preserves the user data and state between sessions. ■ With assigned access, apps that have dependents may not work as expected. For example, if the Microsoft Store is not available, installing Microsoft Edge extensions will not work. ■ Policy setting = Not configured (0 default).
Multi-app – InPrivate Public browsing	■ Runs a multi-tab version of Microsoft Edge InPrivate in full-screen mode. Users can open and close Microsoft Edge and launch other apps that have been allowed by assigned access. No "End session button" is shown and users close Microsoft Edge normally, which clears their browsing session. ■ Policy setting = Enabled (1).

When you use Microsoft Edge in kiosk mode, the default experience includes:

- **Safer browsing** Microsoft Edge in kiosk mode for public browsing runs Microsoft Edge InPrivate mode. This protects user data and deletes the browsing history, temporary internet files, and cookies once the session has ended or is reset.

- **Automatic browser session reset** Microsoft Edge kiosk mode has a built-in timer, which resets the browser session to the default URL after 5 minutes of idle time.

- **Default URLs** You must configure the URL to load when the kiosk session launches. The URL sets the Home button, Start page, and New Tab page.

- **Assigned access required** Kiosk mode policy settings for Microsoft Edge are not applied unless Microsoft Edge is run using assigned access.

CONFIGURE KIOSK MODE

To set up a single-app device using Microsoft Edge kiosk mode on a device running Professional, Enterprise, or Education edition, follow these steps:

1. On the kiosk device, select **Start**, search for **kiosk,** and then select **Set up a kiosk (assigned access)**.
2. On the **Set up a kiosk** page, select **Get started**.
3. Enter a name to create a new kiosk local account and select **Next**.
4. On the **Choose a kiosk app** page, select **Microsoft Edge** and then select **Next**.
5. Select how Microsoft Edge displays when running in kiosk mode:
   a. As a digital sign or interactive display
   b. As a public browser
6. Select **Next**.
7. Enter the URL to load when the kiosk launches.
8. Configure the idle time before Microsoft Edge resets (options include **never**, **five minutes** to **24 hours**), and select **Next**.
9. On the **You're done!** page, select **Close**.
10. Review the settings on the **Set up a kiosk** page. Under **Advanced settings**, you will see that if the device crashes, no error message will be displayed, and the device will automatically restart.
11. Restart the device for Microsoft Edge kiosk mode to run.

> **NOTE** **MICROSOFT EDGE KIOSK MODE FIRST RUN**
> The Welcome To The Best Windows Ever page will appear the first time you run Microsoft Edge kiosk mode. You should end this session by selecting the End Session button and then selecting Yes, which will restart Microsoft Edge and display the configured home page.

To end Microsoft Edge kiosk mode, you need to select Ctrl+Alt+Delete and then sign in to the device using another account. Once kiosk mode is enabled, the device will always automatically sign in and launch the configured app as a kiosk using assigned access.

To disable using Microsoft Edge as a kiosk using assigned access, follow these steps:

1. On the kiosk device, select Ctrl+Alt+Delete.
2. On the sign-in screen, sign in using another account.
3. Select Start, search for **kiosk**, and then select **Set up a kiosk (assigned access)**. (If Search is not available, you can access **Set up a kiosk** in **Settings app > Accounts > Other users**.)
4. On the **Set up a kiosk** page, **under kiosk Info**, select the kiosk username.
5. Select **Remove kiosk**.
6. On the **Remove kiosk** page, select **Remove**.

IE MODE ON MICROSOFT EDGE

You have seen how Microsoft Edge offers safer browsing for modern websites and apps, but the majority of the web—including company intranet sites—is still using older versions of HTML, ActiveX controls, and unsupported third-party add-ins. Internet Explorer 11 (IE11) is included with Windows 10 to allow users to continue to access these websites in a supported, safe, and secure way.

IE mode on Microsoft Edge is a business-focused feature that allows you to operate a dual-browser experience, using Microsoft Edge as your default browser but automatically switching to use the Trident MSHTML engine from IE11 for legacy sites that cannot be viewed in Microsoft Edge.

It is unrealistic to expect enterprises to permit viewing of websites and apps that can only be viewed by Microsoft Edge. We can expect that newer development projects will be written using modern web standards, which will be supported by Microsoft Edge.

For widespread compatibility problems with your popular, or required, websites and apps opening in Microsoft Edge, you can populate the Enterprise Mode Site List with these sites so that they seamlessly open in IE mode. Once the user finishes browsing the site, they can continue to browse using Microsoft Edge.

Using IE mode allows you to continue to use Microsoft Edge as your default browser, while also ensuring that websites and apps needed by your users continue working.

IE mode includes the following features:

- **Web app and website compatibility**   Allows many legacy web apps to run unmodified within Microsoft Edge.
- **Enterprise Mode Site List Manager**   Provides a management tool for website lists.
- **Centralized Control**   Specify the websites or web apps that IE Mode will use and store this XML file on a website or network, or you can store it locally.
- **Integrated Browsing**   Once set up, users can browse the web normally, letting the browser change modes automatically.
- **Data Gathering**   IE mode can be used to collect website compatibility issues from your users' browsing activity, which you can use to add URLs to your central site list.

CONFIGURE IE MODE

To enable and configure IE mode for Microsoft Edge, first download and install the latest Microsoft Edge Policy Template from *https://www.microsoft.com/en-us/edge/business/download*. Then use the following steps:

1. Open **Group Policy Editor**.

2. Select **Computer Configuration > Administrative Templates > Microsoft Edge**.

3. Select **Configure Internet Explorer integration**.

4. Select **Enabled**.

5. Under **Options**, as shown in Figure 1-30, set the drop-down value to:

   a. **Internet Explorer mode**, if you want sites to open in IE mode on Microsoft Edge

   b. **Internet Explorer 11**, if you want sites to open in a standalone Internet Explorer 11 window

   c. **None**, if you want to stop users from configuring Internet Explorer mode via edge://flags or through the command line

6. Select **OK** or **Apply** to save this policy setting.

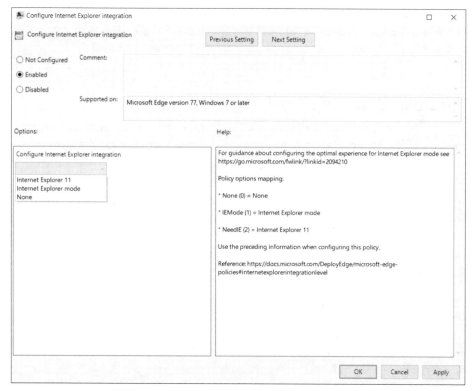

FIGURE 1-30 IE Mode Site List GPO

Once you have enabled Internet Explorer mode, you can configure the IE Mode.

In the Site List XML file, all sites that have the element `<open-in>IE11</open-in>` will open in IE mode. To create or reuse a Site List XML file, use the following steps:

1. Open **Group Policy Editor**.

2. Select **Computer Configuration > Administrative Templates > Windows Components > Internet Explorer**.

3. Double-click **Use the Enterprise Mode IE website list**.

4. Select **Enabled**.

5. Under **Options**, type the location of website list. You can use one of the following locations:

   a. (Recommended) HTTPS location: https://iemode/sites.xml

   b. Local network file: \\network\shares\sites.xml

   c. Local file: file:///c:/Users/<user>/Documents/sites.xml

6. Select **OK** or **Apply** to save these settings.

NEED MORE REVIEW? **USE IE MODE TO IMPROVE COMPATIBILITY**

To learn more about using and configuring Microsoft Edge in IE mode and the Enterprise Mode Site List, visit this Microsoft website article at *https://docs.microsoft.com/en-us/deployedge/edge-ie-mode*.

Configure Internet Explorer

Although Microsoft Edge is suitable for most users when browsing modern websites, Internet Explorer 11 is included to provide backward compatibility for websites that require features currently not supported in Microsoft Edge. Because your users might use both browsers, it is important to know how to configure both Microsoft Edge and Internet Explorer.

Internet Explorer contains a number of security and privacy features that can help make browsing safer. Specifically, the Protected Mode, InPrivate Browsing, and InPrivate Filtering features help maintain user privacy, whereas the Windows Defender SmartScreen helps guard against malicious websites and software. To help your users get the best from Internet Explorer, you must know how to configure these and other settings.

NOTE **DOWNLOAD INTERNET EXPLORER 11**

If you have removed Internet Explorer 11, you can download it from the Microsoft Store or from the download page at *https://docs.microsoft.com//troubleshoot/browsers/how-to-repair-or-reinstall-ie*.

To access Internet Explorer settings, open Internet Explorer and select the Tools menu (cog), as shown in Figure 1-31.

FIGURE 1-31 Accessing Internet Explorer settings

You can then choose from among the following options:

- **Manage Add-Ons** Enable enhancements to some websites, such as providing tool-bars and extensions, search providers, multimedia support, and enhanced content. Use this option to enable and disable add-ons.

- **Compatibility View Settings** Most websites render as intended in Internet Explorer 11, but some sites use design standards for earlier versions of Internet Explorer. If you encounter websites that do not render correctly, you can use Compatibility View set-tings to force Internet Explorer to render the website as if it was using an earlier version of Internet Explorer. To render a website using an earlier version of Internet Explorer, from the Compatibility View Settings dialog box, enter the name of the website and select Add.

EXAM TIP

You can display all intranet sites in Compatibility View by selecting the Display Intranet Sites In Compatibility View check box in the Compatibility View Settings dialog box.

- **Internet Options** To configure additional settings, select Internet Options. This opens the dialog box shown in Figure 1-32.

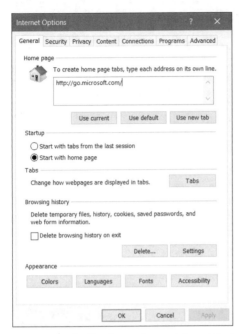

FIGURE 1-32 Configuring settings in Internet Explorer

The Internet Options dialog box has the following tabs:

- **General** Available options are:

  - **Home Page** Create home page tabs by entering addresses, each on its own line.

  - **Startup** Choose Start With Tabs From The Last Session or Start With Home Page.

  - **Change How Webpages Are Displayed In Tabs** Selecting the Tabs button opens the Tabbed Browsing Settings dialog box, where you can control how tabbed browsing behaves, such as warning you when multiple tabs are closed at once, showing previews for individual tabs in the taskbar, and showing you how to deal with pop-ups.

  - **Browsing History** This portion of the dialog box includes options to delete elements of browsing history, such as Temporary Internet Files, History, and Caches And Databases.

  - **Appearance** Four buttons—Colors, Languages, Fonts, and Accessibility—provide you with options for managing the appearance of websites.

- **Security** Available options are:

  - **Security Zone Settings** You can configure the four security zones' settings. The zones are Internet, Local Intranet, Trusted Sites, and Restricted Sites. You can add or remove websites from these zones and configure the security settings for each zone. The Internet Zone is the default zone for all websites and has medium-high security settings, which allows users to perform most tasks.

- **Enable Protected Mode**   Protected Mode makes it more difficult for malware to be downloaded, thereby helping to protect users from attack by running an IE process with greatly restricted privileges on Windows 10. It is enabled by default.
- **Privacy**   Available options are:
  - **Sites**   This option enables you to define cookie handling on a per-site basis.
  - **Advanced**   This option enables you to define whether to accept, block, or prompt for first-party and third-party cookies.
  - **Never Allow Websites To Request Your Physical Location**   Select this option if you want to prevent sites from requesting your physical location.
  - **Turn On Pop-up Blocker**   This setting is enabled by default. The Settings button enables you to configure per-website settings for notification pop-up handling.
  - **Disable Toolbars And Extensions When InPrivate Browsing Starts**
- **Content**   Available options are:
  - **Certificates**   This option enables you to view your certificates and trusted publishers.
  - **AutoComplete**   This option enables you to define autocomplete options for the address bar, forms, and usernames and passwords. You can also delete autocomplete history here.
  - **Feeds And Web Slices**   This option enables you to define the default schedule and frequency of when feeds and web slices from online content are updated.
- **Connections**   Available options are:
  - **Dial-Up And Virtual Private Network**   These settings are for connecting to the internet.
  - **LAN Settings**   This setting allows you to configure script settings and configure IE to use a web proxy server.
- **Programs**   Available options are:
  - **Define How Internet Explorer Opens**   This setting allows you to configure the default browser.
  - **Manage Add-Ons**   This setting allows you to enable or disable browser add-ons installed on your system.
  - **Configure HTML Editing**   This option allows you to choose the program that you want Internet Explorer to use for editing HTML files.
  - **Internet Programs**   This option allows you to select the programs you want to use for other internet services such as email.
  - **Manage File Associations**   This option allows you to select the file types that you want Internet Explorer to open by default.
- **Advanced**   Many options are available, enabling you to fine-tune Internet Explorer configuration and behavior. You can also reset Internet Explorer settings to their default condition.

Although you can manually configure these settings in Internet Explorer on each computer, you can also use more than 1,600 GPOs in an AD DS domain environment to configure the settings for computers at scale.

The GPO settings for Internet Explorer are located in the Computer Configuration\Policies\Administrative Templates\Windows Components\Internet Explorer node.

There are 11 child nodes within the main Internet Explorer node, as shown in Figure 1-33, including GPOs that control privacy, compatibility view, and security features. You can configure the same settings on the User Configuration node if necessary.

NEED MORE REVIEW? **GROUP POLICY AND INTERNET EXPLORER 11**

To review further details about the GPO settings available for Internet Explorer 11, refer to the Microsoft website at *https://docs.microsoft.com/internet-explorer/ie11-deploy-guide/group-policy-and-ie11.*

FIGURE 1-33 Internet Explorer Group Policy

Internet Explorer 11 will continue to receive security updates through its supported lifespan. Internet Explorer is a component of the operating system and follows the Lifecycle Policy of Windows 10. Internet Explorer 11 bugs will be evaluated by Microsoft on a case-by-case basis.

Microsoft recommends that users use Microsoft Edge as their default browser, and Microsoft supports Internet Explorer 11 for backward compatibility. The latest features and platform updates will only be available in Microsoft Edge.

Implement activation

Activation is a very important part of configuring and managing Microsoft products and remaining within the Microsoft Software License Terms.

In some environments, the activation process will be fully automated, or silent, and it is easy to overlook it. This section explores Windows 10 activation options and procedures that you need to understand.

Like most Microsoft products, Windows 10 requires activation. Activation verifies that your copy of Windows 10 is genuine and that it hasn't been used on more devices than the license terms allow. Only a valid product key can be used to activate Windows 10. Figure 1-34 shows the current activation status of a computer running Windows 10 Professional.

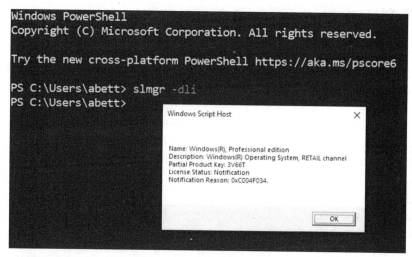

FIGURE 1-34 Viewing the activation status of Windows 10

You can activate Windows 10 in several ways—by using an internet-accessible service at Microsoft, by telephone, or by using bulk activation methods such as Key Management Service (KMS) and Active Directory–based activation. This section explores activation and the methods you can use to manage your organization's Windows 10 activation.

Select an activation method

To activate Windows 10, you might need a *product key*, a 25-character code that looks like this:

PRODUCT KEY: XXXXX-XXXXX-XXXXX-XXXXX-XXXXX

Not all Windows 10 installations require the use of a product key to activate, relying instead on a *digital license* (called a *digital entitlement* in Windows 10, Version 1511). A digital license is a method of activation in Windows 10 that doesn't require you to enter a product key; instead, digital licenses are connected to your Microsoft account. Once your PC is connected to the internet and you log into your Microsoft account, the activation takes place.

You must use a product key for activation when:

- You purchase Windows 10 from a retail store or authorized reseller, either as a physical product or as a digital download.
- You do not have a digital license.
- Your organization has a Microsoft volume licensing agreement for Windows 10.
- You purchase a new device on which Windows 10 is preinstalled.

You do not need a product key for activation and can rely on a digital license when:

- You upgrade to Windows 10 from an eligible device running a genuine copy of Windows 7 or Windows 8.1.
- You purchase Windows 10 from the Microsoft Store.
- You purchase Windows 10 Pro upgrade from the Microsoft Store.
- You use Windows 10, version 1803 or later on a device with a firmware-embedded activation key.
- You are a Windows Insider and upgrade to the newest Windows 10 Insider Preview build on an eligible device that was running an activated earlier version of Windows and Windows 10 Preview.

The method you use to activate Windows 10 is determined by a number of factors, including how you obtained Windows 10 and whether your organization has a volume license agreement in place with Microsoft. The following scenarios determine how you activate Windows 10:

- **Retail**   If you purchase Windows 10 from a retail store or from an authorized retailer, it should come with a unique product key, which can be found on a label inside the Windows 10 box. For a digital copy of Windows 10, you should have access to the product key, which may be stored in a digital locker accessible through the retailer's website. You can enter the key during or after installation to activate your copy of Windows 10.
- **OEM**   If you purchase a new computer on which Windows 10 is preinstalled, it comes with a product key, which is included with the device packaging or included as a card or on the Certificate of Authenticity (COA) attached to the device. You can activate Windows by using this product key.
- **Microsoft volume licensing**   Microsoft offers several volume licensing programs to suit different organizational sizes and needs. These programs support both Active Directory–based activation and KMS.

EXAM TIP

Retail versions of Windows 10 cannot be activated using volume licensing methods.

Volume Activation Services

For large organizations with many hundreds or even thousands of devices, using manual product key entry and activation is impractical; it is both error prone and time-consuming. For these reasons, Microsoft provides three methods for volume activation:

- **Key Management Service (KMS)**   You can use this Windows Server role service to activate Windows 10 in your organization's network. Client computers connect to the KMS server to activate, thereby negating the need to connect to Microsoft for activation. It is not necessary to dedicate a server computer to perform activation with the KMS role.

EXAM TIP

KMS is designed for organizations with either 25 (physical or virtual) client devices persistently connected to a network or organizations with five or more (physical or virtual) servers. KMS requires a minimum threshold of 25 computers before activation requests will be processed.

- **Active Directory–based activation**   A device running Windows 10 that is connected to your organization's domain network and that is using a generic volume license key (VLK) can use Active Directory–based activation. Periodically, the client must renew the license from the licensing service. Therefore, for the activation to remain valid, the client device must remain part of your organization's domain. As with KMS, you do not need to dedicate a server to the Active Directory–based activation role.

EXAM TIP

You cannot use Active Directory–based activation to activate devices running Windows 10 that are not members of your domain.

- **Multiple Activation Key**   Multiple Activation Key (MAK) uses special VLKs that can activate a specific number of devices running Windows 10. You can distribute MAKs as part of your organization's Windows 10 operating system image. This method is ideal for isolated client computers, which will benefit from a one-time activation using the hosted activation services provided by Microsoft.

To use either KMS or Active Directory–based activation to manage your volume activations, the Volume Activation Services server role must be running on a Windows Server 2016 R2 or Windows Server 2019 computer and be configured to use either KMS or Active Directory–based activation. You need to activate the role with Microsoft so that the service can activate devices. This step involves entering and validating a KMS host key with Microsoft, either online or by telephone.

An administrator can manage the organization's volume activations centrally using the Volume Activation Management Tool (VAMT) from a Windows 10 or Windows Server 2016 R2 computer. You can download the VAMT as part of the Windows Assessment and Deployment Kit (Windows ADK).

Activate Windows 10

If you are using one of the volume activation methods, you do not need to perform any tasks on your Windows 10–based devices because Windows 10 will automatically remain in an activated state while the volume license agreement is in place. However, if you are manually managing activation on Windows 10–based devices following installation, you must complete the following procedure:

1. Select **Start > Settings**.

2. Select **Update & Security > Activation > Change product key**.

3. In the **Enter a product key** dialog box, enter your 25-character product key.

4. On the **Activate Windows** page, select **Next**.

5. When prompted, select **Close**.

After you have activated Windows 10, you can view the activation status on the Activation tab of the Update & Security section of the Settings app. Also, you can view and manage the activation status of your Windows 10–based product by using the `slmgr` command. For example, Figure 1-34 showed the result of entering the `slmgr -dli` command. You can see that Windows 10 Pro is licensed properly.

Activate Windows 10 virtual machines

For Windows 10 virtual machines running on Windows 10, version 1803 or later versions, a new feature called Inherited Activation allows Windows 10 virtual machines to inherit an activation state from their Windows 10 hosts.

When a user creates a new Windows 10 virtual machine (VM) using a Windows 10 local host, the VM will automatically inherit the activation state from a host machine. Inherited Activation requires that both the host computer and the VM are running Windows 10, version 1803 or later and that the host computer has been activated using a Windows 10 E3/E5 or A3/A5 license.

Troubleshoot activation issues

When a device running Windows 10 is not activated, you are presented with a watermark on the lower-right corner of the screen requesting that you activate Windows. Additionally, you cannot personalize the device, such as changing wallpaper, accent colors, lock screen, themes, or sync settings between devices.

Unlike earlier versions of Windows, there is no grace period for how long you can use Windows 10 without activation. In the Windows 10 license agreement, users are authorized to use Windows 10 only if they are properly licensed and the software has been properly activated with a genuine product key or by another authorized method.

If you are having trouble activating Windows 10, you could try these actions to resolve common activation issues.

VOLUME LICENSE ACTIVATION RENEWAL

If you are using one of the volume activation methods, and your device falls out of activation, you should ensure that the device has network connectivity and that the user has signed onto the device successfully using their corporate credentials. If the activation process does not trigger automatically within two hours, there may be an issue with KMS.

Client computers that use KMS must have their activation status renewed at least once every 180 days. Clients achieve renewal by connecting to the KMS host located on the network. By default, devices will attempt to renew their activation every seven days following a reboot or restart of the KMS client service. If KMS activation fails, then the client will retry every two hours, and after 180 days have elapsed following activation, the device will fall out of activation.

If client devices are within the renewal window but fail to automatically activate (perhaps they are present on the network for only a short time), you can force a manual activation while the device is on the network by running or scripting the command `slmgr /ato` using administrative privileges.

CHECKING ACTIVATION STATUS

To check activation status in Windows 10, follow these steps:

1. Open the **Settings** app.
2. Select **Update & Security** and then select **Activation**.
3. View the activation status.
4. If Windows 10 isn't activated, select the **Troubleshoot** link, shown in Figure 1-35.

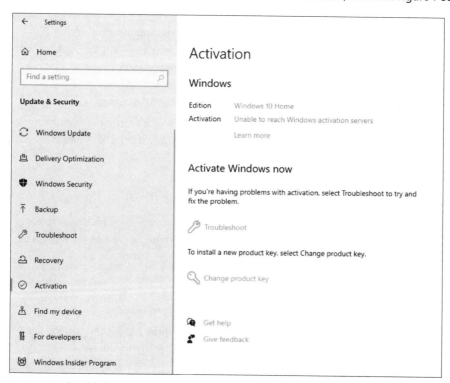

FIGURE 1-35 Troubleshoot activation

ACTIVATING WINDOWS 10 FOR THE FIRST TIME

Windows 10 comes preinstalled with most new Windows devices. These devices will automatically activate once the device is connected to the internet.

If you manually install Windows 10 on a device that has not previously had an activated copy of Windows 10 on it, you'll need to use a valid product key to activate the device. This scenario also covers if you install a different edition of Windows 10 that wasn't previously activated on the device. For example, if you install Windows 10 Pro on a device that had Windows 10 Home installed on it, then you will need to provide a valid Windows 10 Pro product key to activate the device.

ACTIVATING AFTER REINSTALLING WINDOWS 10

If you need to reinstall Windows 10, this could cause issues with your activation status depending on how Windows 10 was originally installed on your device.

If you bought Windows 10 from the Microsoft Store, or if you activated a free upgrade to Windows 10, then you have a digital license for the device.

As long as you reinstall the same edition of Windows 10 onto your device, you won't need a product key. If you're asked to enter a product key during reinstallation, you should skip this step. Windows 10 will automatically activate online after the installation is complete.

ACTIVATION ISSUES AFTER A HARDWARE CONFIGURATION CHANGE

If significant hardware changes are made to a device (such as replacing the motherboard), Windows 10 might fall out of activation. Devices running Windows 10, version 1607 or later that have been used with a Microsoft account will have a digital license linked to the device. If the activation error codes 0x803f7001 or 0xC004C008 appear on the Activation page of the Settings app, you should use the Activation troubleshooter to reactivate Windows.

If the motherboard was replaced under warranty—by the OEM, for example—then the device should reactivate automatically, or a replacement product key should have been provided.

> **NOTE FIRMWARE UPGRADE**
> Consider checking whether the motherboard manufacturer has a firmware update available. This update should be applied prior to installing Windows; otherwise, upgrading the firmware after activation might require the system to fall out of activation.

ACTIVATING REFURBISHED DEVICES RUNNING WINDOWS 10

A refurbished device running Windows 10 can be activated using the product key on the Certificate of Authenticity label attached to the device. Use the following procedure:

1. Open the **Settings** app.
2. Select **Update & Security** and then select **Activation**.

3. Select **Change product key**.

4. Enter the 25-character product key found on the Certificate of Authenticity and follow the instructions.

USE THE ACTIVATION TROUBLESHOOTER

The Activation troubleshooter is available for all users on the Activation tab in the Settings app. If the device has not been activated, running the troubleshooter can locate a digital license linked to the Microsoft account used on the computer and then prompt you to try activation again.

Sometimes when you run the Activation troubleshooter or attempt to activate a device the activation will fail, and an error code and message will be presented to the user.

COMMON ACTIVATION ERRORS

If you see an error code relating to Windows 10 activation, you can check the list of error codes in Table 1-13 and follow the suggested steps to resolve it. It is not necessary to remember the error codes for the exam, though it is useful to understand the various issues that can arise when activating Windows.

TABLE 1-13 Windows 10 activation errors

Error	Description
0xC004F211	Windows reported that the hardware of your device has changed. Use the Activation troubleshooter to reactivate Windows 10 after you make a hardware change or purchase a new Windows license.
0xC004F212, 0xC004F034, 0xC004F210, 0xC004E016	The product key does not match the installed edition of Windows 10. Reinstall the correct edition of Windows 10 or enter a different product key. You might also see this error if the current edition of Windows installed on the device doesn't match the edition of the digital license.
0xC004F213	Windows reported that no product key was found on your device. A digital license is associated with the device hardware, but this is no longer available if the hardware of the device has changed. Use the Activation troubleshooter to reactivate Windows 10 after you make a hardware change or purchase a new Windows license.
0x803f7001 or 0x800704cF	A valid Windows 10 license couldn't be found to activate Windows 10. If you have a valid product key, select Change Product Key, and then enter the 25-character product key. If you don't have a valid product key, you will need to purchase a new Windows license.
0xC004C060, 0xC004C4A2, 0xC004C4A2, 0x803FA067L, 0xC004C001, 0xC004C004, 0xC004F004, 0xC004C007, 0xC004F005, 0xC004C00F, 0xC004C010, 0xC004C00E, 0xC004C4A4, 0xC004C4A5, 0xC004B001, 0xC004F010, 0xC004F050	The product key entered can't be used to activate Windows. Enter a different product key or buy a new product key. The activation servers were busy; wait a while and then select Activate. If you upgraded to Windows 10 using the free upgrade offer, Windows 10 should automatically be activated if you didn't make any significant hardware changes to your device (such as replacing the motherboard). If you continue to have problems with activation, contact customer support.
0xC004C003	The Windows 10 product key entered isn't valid. Product keys are unique; if a key has already been used, it's marked as not valid.

Error	Description
0xC004FC03	If you're not connected to the internet or your firewall settings are preventing Windows from completing the activation process online, Windows will not be able to activate. You could try to activate Windows by phone.
0xC004E028	This error is shown if a device is already in the process of activation. Wait for the first request to complete.
0x8007267C	This error appears if the device is not connected to the internet or the activation server is temporarily unavailable.
0xD0000272, 0xC0000272, 0xc004C012, 0xC004C013, 0xC004C014	If the activation server is temporarily unavailable, Windows will automatically be activated when the service comes back online.
0xC004C008, 0xC004C770, 0x803FA071	The product key has already been used on another PC, or it's being used on more PCs than the Microsoft Software License Terms allow.
0xC004F00F	You might see this error if a product key for the Enterprise edition of Windows is used to activate Windows 10 Home or Windows 10 Pro.
0xC004C020	A Volume License has been used on more PCs than the Microsoft Software License Terms allow.
0x8007232B, 0xC004F074, 0xC004F038, 0x8007007B	A product key for the Enterprise edition of Windows has been used to activate Windows 10 Home or Windows 10 Pro, or a work device is trying to activate, but the device is not connected to the workplace's network.
0x80072F8F	The date and time for the PC is incorrect, or Windows has trouble connecting to the online activation service and can't verify your product key. Use the network troubleshooter to identify and repair any network problems.
0xC004E003	If third-party software has changed system files, then Windows activation may fail. Restore the system files back to an earlier point in time and try to activate again.
0x80004005	Windows activation has failed. Use the Activation troubleshooter, and if this doesn't work, you might need to reset your PC.
0x87e10bc6	An error occurred with the activation server or licensing service. Wait a few minutes, try again, and then use the Activation troubleshooter. Alternatively, launch the Microsoft Store app and if the Microsoft Store app shows there was a problem, select Try Again, which should resolve the issue.

> **NOTE ACTIVATE WINDOWS BY PHONE**
>
> Sometimes, you will not be able to connect to the internet to complete the activation process. In that case, you can activate Windows 10 by phone. To find your local freephone telephone number, enter **SLUI 04** in the search box on the taskbar and select the SLUI 04 command. Select your country and then use the telephone number and installation ID provided to access the automated phone system to activate Windows. Phone activation cannot be used for Windows 10 Pro, Edu, or Windows 10 Pro for Workstations editions.

Configure mobility settings

For users of mobile devices such as the Surface range of Windows 10 tablets and laptops, a priority is to be able to conserve battery life so that extended device use is possible. Mobile devices are often used away from the office or home environment, and it is important to know how to configure power settings in Windows 10 to meet your users' needs.

Mobile devices can be used to display information, such as PowerPoint presentations during meetings, and enabling the presentation settings within Windows 10 can configure the device for a presentation and reduce distractions and interruptions.

Configure basic power options

You can control Windows 10 power settings in several ways. On a mobile device, you can configure basic power options by using the Power & Sleep tab in the System Settings app, as shown in Figure 1-36.

On the Power & Sleep tab, you can configure the following options:

- **Screen**   Available options are:
    - **On battery power, turn off after**   Select a value or choose Never.
    - **When plugged in, turn off after**   Select a value or choose Never.
- **Sleep**   Available options are:
    - **On battery power, PC goes to sleep after**   Select a value or choose Never.
    - **When plugged in, PC goes to sleep after**   Select a value or choose Never.

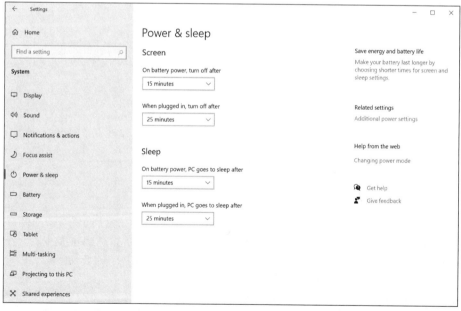

FIGURE 1-36 Power & Sleep options

You can configure additional power options by selecting the Battery tab, as shown in Figure 1-37, and setting the following options:

- **Overview** View estimated battery time remaining.
- **Battery saver** Configure when Battery Saver is enabled, implement Battery Saver until the next charge, and configure lower screen brightness while the device is using Battery Saver.
- **Battery usage per app** View a report showing battery usage over the preceding 24 hours or one week.

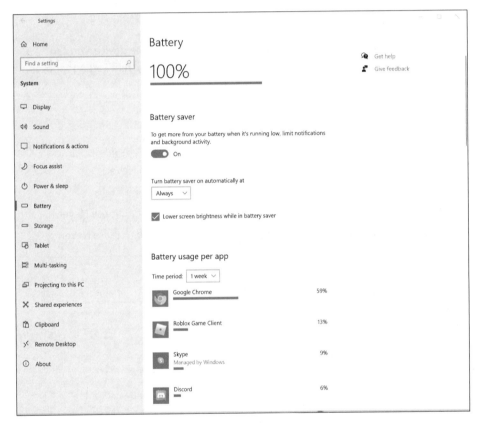

FIGURE 1-37 Battery options

Configure power plans

In addition to the battery settings available within the Settings app, Windows 10 provides access to configure a power plan. By default on Windows 10, version 1709 (Fall Creators Update), you are shown only the Balanced power plan.

Previous versions of Windows 10 offered the following plans:

- Power Saver
- Balanced

- High Performance
- Ultimate Performance

You can access the power plan settings from the Settings app by selecting System > Power & Sleep, and then selecting the Additional Power Settings link.

You can create a new power plan by selecting Create A Power Plan and then configuring basic options, such as whether your device will prompt you for a password when it wakes up, and what the power buttons and lid do on your computer. To reconfigure a plan, select Change Plan Settings. In the settings options, you can also choose Change Advanced Power Settings to configure detailed plan settings.

WINDOWS 10 PRO FOR WORKSTATIONS

If you're running Windows 10 Pro for Workstations, there is an additional Ultimate Performance power plan scheme available. This plan is intended to be used on high-end workstation devices that demand increased performance. The policy implements fine-grained power management techniques that allow devices to run at maximum performance by removing the power management, performance, and efficiency trade-offs that are normally present in Windows 10.

Unless you are using the Windows 10 Pro for Workstations edition, the Ultimate Performance power plan will be hidden in Power Options. The plan is also not available on battery-powered devices.

CONFIGURE POWER SETTINGS

You can exert more granular control over your computer's power settings by using the Additional Power Settings link in the Settings app or by opening the Power Options item in Control Panel. You can switch power plans, and you can also configure these options:

- **Choose What The Power Buttons Do**   This option enables you to specify the actions to be taken when the power button on the device is pressed.
- **Choose What Closing The Lid Does**   This option enables you to specify the actions to be taken when the device lid is closed.
- **Create A Power Plan**   This option enables you to create a new device power plan with custom settings.
- **Change When The Computer Sleeps**   This option enables you to specify the idle time delay before the system automatically puts the device into sleep mode.

If you aren't already familiar with these features, take some time now to explore them. Be sure to create your own personal power plan by using the Create A Power Plan option because you might see something about that on the exam. Additionally, you'll need to know how to monitor battery usage from the Notification area of the taskbar and how to change common mobility settings, such as the power plan type and display brightness.

USING POWERCFG.EXE

Powercfg.exe is a command-line tool you can use to configure and manage power settings. Using Powercfg.exe, you can view the power plans available and export power plans. Powercfg.exe can be useful when configuring a batch of devices, each with the same hardware specifications, such as a rollout of new laptops. You would create a custom power plan on one device, and then export the power management plan to a file using Powercfg.exe. You would then import the plan to the other devices using either Powercfg.exe or Group Policy.

To get a list of the available power plans using this command, enter `powercfg.exe list` at a command prompt. If you haven't yet created any custom plans, you'll only see the default plan in Windows 10, as shown in Figure 1-38. Choose the plan to export and note the GUID value. To export the policy, open an elevated command prompt, and run `powercfg.exe export power.pow` **GUID** (where the GUID value used is the plan that you want to export). The plan that is enabled has an * character at the end of the scheme.

```
C:\WINDOWS\system32\cmd.exe - cmd

Microsoft Windows [Version 10.0.19042.804]
(c) 2020 Microsoft Corporation. All rights reserved.

C:\Users\tommy>powercfg.exe list

Existing Power Schemes (* Active)
-----------------------------------
Power Scheme GUID: 381b4222-f694-41f0-9685-ff5bb260df2e  (Balanced) *

C:\Users\tommy>
```

FIGURE 1-38 Windows 10 power plan(s), as shown by Powercfg.exe

---

***NEED MORE REVIEW?* POWERCFG COMMAND-LINE OPTIONS**

For more information about Powercfg.exe command-line options, visit *https://docs.microsoft. com/windows-hardware/design/device-experiences/powercfg-command-line-options*.

There are some other parameters you can use with Powercfg.exe. You should review these so that you are familiar with them.

- `changename` Modifies the name of a power scheme and optionally, its description
- `-delete` Deletes the power scheme with the specified GUID
- `-setactive` Makes the specified power scheme active on the system
- `/deviceenablewake` and `/devicedisablewake` Enables or disables a device from waking the system from a sleep state
- `/systempowerreport` Generates a diagnostic system power transition report

- **/batteryreport** Generates a report of battery usage characteristics over the lifetime of the system

Some of the modern reports, such as the battery usage or system power reports, are generated in HTML format and provide a huge amount of detail, which is invaluable if you are troubleshooting issues with battery life or device power consumption.

CREATING POWER POLICIES

You can use Group Policy to set policies related to the available power plans. Use the Group Policy Management Editor to navigate to Computer Configuration\Administrative Templates\System\Power Management. When you expand Power Management in the left pane, you can see the additional containers: Button Settings, Energy Saver Settings, Hard Disk Settings, Notification Settings, Power Throttling Settings, Sleep Settings, and Video And Display Settings. In the right pane, you can see two options: Specify A Custom Active Power Plan and Select An Active Power Plan, as shown in Figure 1-39. For a custom power plan, you need to supply the GUID from the power plan.

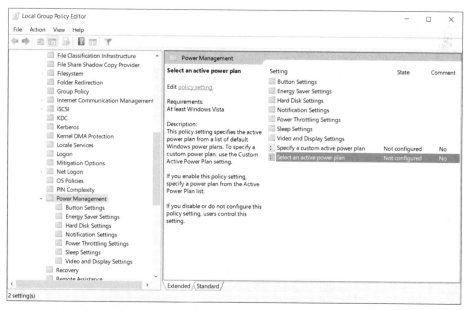

FIGURE 1-39 The Power Management node in the Local Group Policy Editor

When you select one of the seven nodes under Power Management, more options appear. You can control every aspect of power management here. For instance, in the Sleep Settings node, you can configure, enable, and disable the following (and more):

- **Specify The System Sleep Timeout (Plugged In)** Enables you to specify the period of inactivity before the system is put into sleep mode while plugged into a power outlet
- **Specify The System Sleep Timeout (On Battery)** Enables you to specify the period of inactivity before the system is put into sleep mode while running on battery power

- **Require A Password When The Computer Wakes (Plugged In)** Specifies whether the user is prompted for a password when the system resumes from sleep while plugged into a power outlet

- **Require A Password When The Computer Wakes (On Battery)** Specifies whether the user is prompted for a password when the system resumes from sleep while running on battery power

- **Allow Standby States (S1 S3) When Sleeping (Plugged In)** Specifies whether a device can use standby states other than hibernate when putting the computer in a sleep state while plugged into a power outlet

- **Allow Standby States (S1 S3) When Sleeping (On Battery)** Specifies whether a device is able to use standby states other than hibernate when putting the computer in a sleep state while running on battery power

You should review these policies in each node to familiarize yourself with the various options available.

VIEWING PROCESS POWER USAGE

A new feature within Task Manager allows you to view the instantaneous power usage of apps and services using your device's power.

Task Manager now includes two new columns in the Processes tab, as displayed in Figure 1-40, to show the energy impact of the running process on your system. You can use this information to determine the levels of power that apps and services are using. Task Manager considers the processor, graphics, and disk drive power when calculating power usage. Two columns are available, as follows:

Power Usage Provides an instantaneous view of apps and services using power

Power Usage Trend Provides a power usage trend over the previous two minutes for running apps and services

FIGURE 1-40 View Process Power Usage with Task Manager

Using Task Manager, you can also see if a process has been suspended. To view suspended apps, look in the Status column of the Processes tab for a leaf icon. In Figure 1-40, you can see that the Your Phone app has been suspended. When the cursor is hovered over the leaf icon next to Microsoft Edge, a tooltip describing the status is displayed.

Configure presentation settings

Windows 10 includes a useful utility called the Windows Mobility Center, which can be used to configure various mobility settings, all from one location. Depending on your system, some or all of the following settings, shown in Figure 1-41, will be available on your mobile device:

- **Brightness**   Enables you to adjust the brightness of your display.
- **Volume**   Enables you to adjust the speaker volume of your device; also, you can select the Mute check box to silence the speaker.
- **Battery Status**   Lets you view how much charge is remaining on your battery and change the active power plan.
- **Screen Orientation**   Lets you change the orientation of your device screen from portrait to landscape, and vice versa.
- **External Display**   Enables connection of an additional monitor to your device.
- **Sync Center**   Enables you to sync with external data sources, such as Offline Files.
- **Presentation Settings**   Lets you turn on presentation settings during a presentation. Enabling presentation settings will temporarily have the following effects:
    - Disables pop-ups and notifications area pop-ups (such as from Outlook)
    - Prevents Windows from going into sleep mode
    - Prevents Windows from turning the screen off
    - Uses the display background and volume settings defined in the Presentation Settings, as shown in Figure 1-41

The Windows Mobility Center is only available on mobile devices, such as laptops and tablets.

FIGURE 1-41 Windows Mobility Center

The Presentation Settings utility, as shown in Figure 1-42, can be used in association with the Windows Mobility Center to configure turning off the screen saver, controlling the volume, and selecting a background image to be displayed when you give a presentation.

You can access the Presentation Settings utility on a mobile device by selecting the Presentation Settings icon or by using these steps:

1. Select **Start** and search for **Presentation Settings**.

2. In the search results, select **Adjust settings before giving a presentation**.

3. The **Presentation Settings** utility appears, as shown in Figure 1-42.

FIGURE 1-42 Adjust settings before giving a presentation

Configure printers and external devices

To function properly, hardware requires special software designed for Windows 10 to communicate with it. This software is referred to as a *device driver*. When Windows 10 detects new hardware, the system automatically attempts to install one of the built-in drivers included as part of the operating system. The printer drivers are provided in the Windows 10 Driver Store, or you can use the drivers provided by the OEM, or you can download drivers through Windows Update. A common reason for a computer to fail to start, or to start with errors, is because a device driver is faulty or corrupted.

Install devices

New and updated hardware device drivers are regularly submitted to Microsoft by equipment vendors for testing and cataloging. As part of Windows Update, Windows 10 automatically detects the presence of new device drivers, downloads them, and installs them.

New hardware is typically installed automatically when it's added to Windows 10; the operating system detects and identifies the new hardware through the Plug and Play feature. Windows 10 supports new hardware connected through a variety of connection methods, including USB, Wi-Fi, and Bluetooth. In addition to backward compatibility for existing and earlier hardware, newer technologies, such as near-field communication (NFC) and Miracast for wireless displays, have built-in support in Windows 10.

For advanced users or for managing or troubleshooting a hardware device issue, you can use Device Manager. Device Manager provides information about each device, such as the device type, device status, manufacturer, device-specific properties, and device driver information.

There are multiple ways to load the Device Manager, including:

- Right-selecting the Start button and selecting Device Manager
- Entering **Device Manager** in Search
- Opening Control Panel, selecting Hardware And Sound, and then selecting Device Manager

The Device Manager default view (devices by type) is shown in Figure 1-43.

You can expand and explore each node in Device Manager and then select a device. All devices have properties, and you can view them by right-selecting the desired device and selecting **Properties**. The Properties dialog box for a device is shown in Figure 1-44.

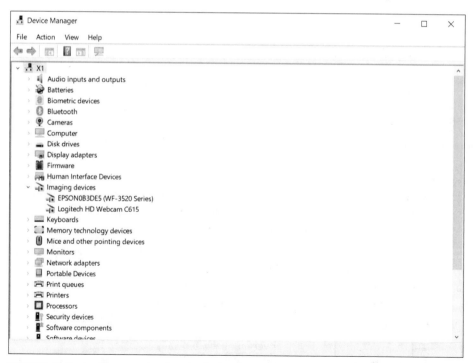

FIGURE 1-43 Device Manager showing the devices by type view

If you added a new peripheral and Windows 10 does not immediately recognize it, first check that the device is connected properly and that no cables are damaged. You should ensure that the external device is powered on and not in sleep or standby mode. You can also open Device Manager and launch the Scan For Hardware Changes Wizard from the Action menu, which will locate previously undetected hardware and then configure it for you.

FIGURE 1-44 Device Properties

Update Device Drivers

Most computers that you'll work with have different hardware components, such as motherboards, disk controllers, graphics cards, and network adapters. Fortunately, Windows 10 is designed to work with an extensive list of hardware devices, and it benefits from Plug and Play, which tries to detect new devices automatically and then installs the correct driver software. If Windows has a problem with a device, you must troubleshoot the cause. Troubleshooting can involve locating the correct or updated device drivers and installing them.

Windows 10 automatically attempts to install a device driver, and if one is not available locally, it attempts to locate one through Windows Update. For most systems, devices and their associated drivers remain constant and require no further administrative effort. In the following instances, you might need to update, disable, or reinstate a previous driver:

- Windows 10 detects that a newer driver is available through Windows Update.
- You want to install a newer device driver manually, typically obtained from the manufacturer's website.

- The device is not performing or functioning correctly with the current driver.
- A new or beta version of a driver is causing stability issues.

To update a specific driver, select the device in Device Manager and select Update Driver from the Action menu.

Windows 10 offers you two choices for updating the driver:

- Search Automatically For Drivers
- Browse My Computer For Drivers

Typically, users allow Windows to locate, download, and install an updated device driver automatically if one is available through Windows Update. This is the default method.

If you have the installation media that came with the hardware, you can use the browse feature to locate the correct driver. The Windows 10 Update Driver Software Wizard can automatically search through the subfolders in the media and locate all the relevant drivers for the device.

If you have already downloaded a specific device driver from the manufacturer, such as a video driver from NVIDIA, you might need to run the driver installation wizard included in the download files, which includes additional software besides the device driver.

If Windows determines that the current driver is the most up-to-date or best driver available, you can confirm the version number of the driver by viewing the properties of the driver in Device Manager. If you have a more recent driver that you want to use, you must manually uninstall the current driver and then manually install the more recent driver.

Remove an individual driver update

Sometimes it is important to remove a device driver completely from the system. It might be corrupted or incompatible with your system. If Windows determines that the driver is valid and up-to-date, it is impossible to use another device driver while the current driver is present. To uninstall an unwanted device driver, use the following steps:

1. Open **Device Manager**.
2. Locate the device with the problem driver, right-select it, and choose **Uninstall device**.
3. In the **Uninstall device** dialog box, select **Uninstall**.

If the item relates to an unwanted Windows Update, use the following steps:

1. Open **Settings**, select **Update and Security**, and on the **Windows Update** tab, select **View update history**.
2. Select **Uninstall updates**. The **Installed updates** page appears, and you should locate and uninstall the unwanted update by selecting it from the list and then selecting **Uninstall**.

If the driver will not uninstall, try restarting the computer and attempting the procedure again. Only as a last resort should you try to delete the software manually. You can use the

PnPUtil.exe command-line tool and remove the INF files that are associated with the device as shown:

```
PnPUtil.exe -a -d <path to the driver> \<drivername>.inf
```

> **NOTE** **DRIVER INSTALLATION AND REMOVAL ARE ADMINISTRATIVE FUNCTIONS**
>
> You must use administrative privileges to install or uninstall a device or driver package by using Device Manager.

Because different hardware types have different functions and features, review the tabs on the Properties screen. Not all devices have the same tabs, and some devices do not offer the ability to view or modify the device driver.

Configure and manage printers

Printers offer the ability to print documents, pictures, webpages, and much more. You need to understand how to install a printer and configure it for use by the Windows 10 user. When you connect a modern printer via USB directly to a device, Windows 10 will automatically discover and download the most appropriate driver. For a printer that is required to be shared from the Windows 10 device or attached directly to the network, additional configuration may be required to enable other devices to print to it.

Most modern printing devices support Plug and Play, but a device that offers wireless or network-attached printing must be configured using the Add Printer Wizard or the specialist software provided with the printer.

Windows 10 includes an optional Print Management app to manage printers when Windows 10 acts as a print server. Most users will use the Printers & Scanners options in the Settings app, which provide basic printer management such as Add, Remove, and Set As Default Printer.

You still have previous printer tools in the Devices And Printers section of Control Panel or from the link at the bottom of the Printers & Scanners options in the Settings app. The Devices And Printers Control Panel item is the same interface as in previous versions of Windows. This section focuses on the new features relating to printing with Windows 10.

Manage printers by using Print Management

The Print Management console is available for you to manage your print devices from a single management console. Print devices connected to your PC can be shared, and you can manage the properties of the device. If you are using a Windows 10 Pro and Enterprise edition version, you will need to add the Print Management Microsoft Management Console (MMC), displayed in Figure 1-45, using the following steps:

1. Select the Windows key+R to launch the **Run** dialog.

2. In the **Run** dialog box, type **printmanagement.msc** and press Enter to open the **Print Management** console.

If Print Management fails to open and you receive an error message, that means you must add the Print Management Console feature via the Optional Features applet in the Settings app as follows:

1. Open the **Settings** app.
2. Select **Apps**.
3. Select **Optional features**.
4. To add a feature, select the **+Add a feature** link at the top of the page.
5. On the **Add an optional feature** page, select **Print Management Console**.
6. Select **Install**.

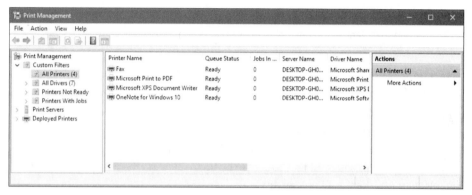

FIGURE 1-45 Managing printers

The Print Management console offers you a single location to perform the following printer-related management tasks:

- Add and delete print devices
- View printers and print servers
- Add and remove print servers
- Add and manage print drivers
- Deploy printers using Group Policy
- Open and manage printer queues
- View and modify status of printers
- Use the filter feature to view printers based on filters

If you right-select a printer, you are presented with a list of some action items that can be performed on the selected printer. These include the following tasks:

- Open Printer Queue
- Pause Printing
- Deploy With Group Policy
- Set Printing Defaults

- Manage Sharing
- Print Test Page
- Enable Branch Office Direct Printing
- Properties
- Delete
- Rename
- Help

> **NOTE REMOTE PRINTERS**
>
> You can use the Print Management console to manage both local and remote printers. Devices And Printers in Control Panel can only manage locally connected printers.

Add and remove print servers and printers

The Print Management console shows your local Windows 10–based printing devices. You can configure the console to manage other Windows-based print servers that are available on your network if you have the appropriate permissions to manage. To add other print servers within Print Management, you must first add them by right-selecting the Print Servers node and then selecting Add/Remove Print Servers.

In addition to managing other print servers, you can add or delete printers locally or remotely on any print server that is added to the Print Management console. You add printers by using Network Printer Installation Wizard, which is similar to the Add Printer Wizard in Devices and Printers.

The Network Printer Installation Wizard enables you to:

- Scan the local subnet for network printers
- Add a TCP/IP or Web Services for Devices (WSD) printer by IP address or host name
- Add a new printer by using an existing port
- Create a new port and add a new printer

Understand Type 4 printer drivers

To simplify and reduce the complexity of printer drivers, Microsoft uses the new Type 4 printer driver model for Windows 10.

The Type 4 printer driver model allows printer manufacturers to create a single Print Class Driver that supports similar printing features and languages that are common to a large number of printer models and across common printing languages such as PCL, PostScript, and XPS.

Unlike Type 3 drivers, Type 4 drivers are not supplied and downloaded from a print server on demand.

The Type 4 printer driver model simplifies driver operations with the following benefits:

- Sharing a printer does not require adding additional drivers that match the client architecture.
- Type 4 drivers support multiple printer models.
- Driver packages are small and install quickly.
- OEMs can separate the printer driver from the printer software.

> **NEED MORE REVIEW?**   **V4 PRINTER DRIVER**
>
> For more information about Type 4 printer drivers, visit *https://docs.microsoft.com/en-us/windows-hardware/drivers/print/v4-printer-driver*.

Manage printers by using Windows PowerShell

More than 20 Windows PowerShell cmdlets can be used to manage printers. Some of the most common cmdlets are shown in Table 1-14.

TABLE 1-14 Windows PowerShell printer cmdlets

Cmdlet	Description
Add-Printer	Adds a printer to the specified computer
Add-PrinterDriver	Installs a printer driver on the specified computer
Add-PrinterPort	Installs a printer port on the specified computer
Get-PrintConfiguration	Gets the configuration information of a printer
Get-Printer	Retrieves a list of printers installed on a computer
Get-PrinterDriver	Retrieves the list of printer drivers installed on the specified computer
Get-PrinterPort	Retrieves a list of printer ports installed on the specified computer
Get-PrinterProperty	Retrieves printer properties for the specified printer
Remove-Printer	Removes a printer from the specified computer
Remove-PrinterDriver	Deletes printer drivers from the specified computer
Remove-PrintJob	Removes a print job on the specified printer
Rename-Printer	Renames the specified printer
Restart-PrintJob	Restarts a print job on the specified printer
Resume-PrintJob	Resumes a suspended print job

Cmdlet	Description
Set-PrintConfiguration	Sets the configuration information for the specified printer
Set-Printer	Updates the configuration of an existing printer
Set-PrinterProperty	Modifies the printer properties for the specified printer

To list all the available cmdlets, enter the following command into a Windows PowerShell console:

```
Get-Command -Module PrintManagement
```

Configure Windows 10 by using provisioning packages

You saw in the initial deployment of Windows 10 that you can use the Windows Configuration Designer tool to create provisioning packages with specific configurations and settings. The Windows Configuration Designer is a component of the Windows 10 ADK. This tool can also be used after deployment to configure Windows 10 without the need for installing a new image. This dynamic provisioning can be useful in small to mid-sized organizations and bring-your-own-device (BYOD) scenarios, which may not use more complex tools such as MDT, Configuration Manager, or Microsoft Intune.

To create a provisioning package that contains the collection of apps and settings customized for your deployment, you use the Windows Configuration Designer tool. The package is then applied to devices. Typical examples of these customizations include:

- Changing the Windows edition from Professional to Enterprise

- Configuring VPN and Wi-Fi profiles

- Enrolling devices in Microsoft Intune

- Installation of modern applications (Universal Windows Platform apps using the file extension .appx)

The Windows Configuration Designer is wizard driven and allows you to create the provisioning packages in a PPKG file format. The PPKG files created by the Windows Configuration Designer contain the desired customizations and can be applied to Windows 10 either during or after the initial deployment has taken place.

> **NOTE** **INSTALL WINDOWS CONFIGURATION DESIGNER**
> You can install the Windows Configuration Designer app from the Microsoft Store. To install Windows Configuration Designer on older operating systems or in languages other than English, you need to install it from the Windows Assessment and Deployment Kit (ADK) for Windows 10 from here: *https://docs.microsoft.com/en-us/windows/configuration/provisioning-packages/provisioning-install-icd*.

To create a new provisioning package, use the following steps:

1. Open **Windows Configuration Designer**.

2. On the **Start** page, as shown in Figure 1-46, choose your desired wizard-based option.

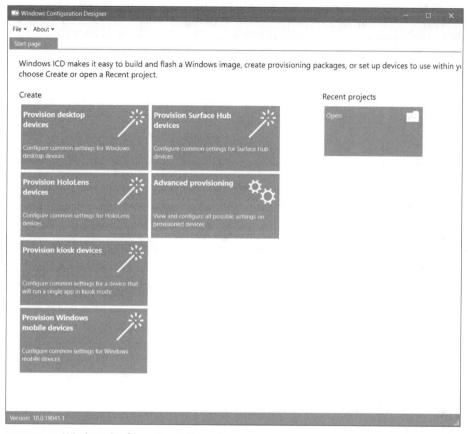

FIGURE 1-46 Windows Configuration Designer home screen

3. Select **Advanced Provisioning** to configure all the available runtime settings.

4. Enter a name for your project, and then select **Next**.

5. Select the settings you want to configure, based on the type of device, and then select **Next**.

6. On the **Import a provisioning package (optional)** page, you can select **Finish** to create your project, or browse to and select an existing provisioning package to import to your project, and then select **Finish**.

7. In the **Available customizations** pane, you can configure settings for the package.

Configure Microsoft Store settings

The Microsoft Store is an online portal for acquiring Universal Windows apps. The Windows apps run in resizable windows similar to traditional desktop apps and typically consume less memory and processing demands. You need to know how to manage user access to the Microsoft Store to control the installation and use of these applications. Organizations can also use the Microsoft Store for Business, which enables enterprises to create their own private portal that contains preapproved and custom applications.

Universal Windows apps

The Microsoft Store allows you to access and install Universal Windows apps on all editions of Windows 10. In addition to the memory and processing benefits, the apps can be updated seamlessly and automatically (though you can modify this behavior). Each app installation installs in the background and creates a shortcut in the user's Start menu under All Apps.

Users with multiple devices can install each Microsoft Store app up to 10 times. After 10 instances, the user will receive a prompt to remove an application from one of their devices.

In Windows 10 version 20H2, the list of provisioned apps includes the following:

- **Alarms & Clock**   Shows world time and acts as an alarm, stopwatch, and timer
- **Calculator**   Includes a programmer mode for binary, octal, and hexadecimal values, along with common standard and scientific modes, and a converter for measurements
- **Calendar**   Keeps track of appointments and other events
- **Camera**   Captures still images and video
- **Connect**   Enables you to use your computer as an extended screen from your phone or other device
- **Cortana**   Is a digital personal assistant
- **Feedback Hub**   Enables you to share bug reports and suggestions with the Windows development team
- **Get Help**   Puts you in touch with Microsoft's Virtual Agent for automated troubleshooting
- **Groove Music**   Is a music player
- **Mail**   Creates, sends, receives, and manages email
- **Maps**   Displays maps and aerial photos along with directions between points
- **Mixed Reality Portal**   Features a 3D environment to explore and customize with application shortcuts and virtual desktops
- **Microsoft Edge**   Is the modern web browser in Windows 10
- **Microsoft Solitaire Collection**   Includes solo card games and online challenges and tournaments
- **Movies & TV**   Plays videos that you create, purchase, or rent
- **Microsoft News**   Provides headlines and links for current news on subjects

- **OneDrive** Manages synchronization with your OneDrive cloud storage
- **Office** Provides details about your Office 365 subscription and lists Office files that you have recently worked with
- **OneNote** Is an app for creating, storing, and managing notes
- **Paint 3D** Is a 3D version of the classic Paint app
- **Photos** Stores, organizes, and displays your collection of pictures
- **Skype** Is an app for communicating with others via text message or videoconferencing
- **Snip & Sketch** Is a tool for capturing and editing screen images to replace the Snipping tool, which is still included
- **Sticky Notes** Provides a place to store notes
- **Tips** Offers videos and other instructional material about Windows 10
- **Video Editor** Allows you to create new videos
- **Voice Recorder** Captures notes in audible form
- **Weather** Displays current conditions and detailed forecasts for locations around the world
- **Xbox Game Bar and Xbox Console Companion** Connects you to the world of computer gaming
- **Your Phone** Connects your Windows 10 device to your Android device

Universal Windows apps are stored in a hidden folder, %ProgramFiles%\WindowsApps. You can view this folder, but it is locked so that only Microsoft Store or the Windows System account can view, run, or modify its contents. Each app is located within a subfolder, such as Microsoft.WindowsCalculator_10.2101.10.0_x64__8wekyb3d8bbwe for the built-in Calculator app.

Microsoft Store vs. Microsoft Store for Business

The Microsoft Store for Business allows enterprises to customize a store for their staff to access a curated list of apps. Administrators can purchase, approve, and distribute applications to their staff. In addition to purchasing apps, administrators can upload and make available any Universal Windows apps that will appear in the Microsoft Store app for users.

There are some differences between the Microsoft Store and the Microsoft Store for Business, as shown in Table 1.15.

TABLE 1-15 Microsoft Store vs. Microsoft Store for Business

Microsoft Store	Microsoft Store for Business
Purchasing requires a Microsoft account.	Purchasing requires an Azure AD account.
Each user purchases their own license for an application.	An administrator can purchase multiple application licenses.

Microsoft Store	Microsoft Store for Business
You can deploy applications only through the Microsoft Store.	You can deploy applications through the Microsoft Store and by using deployment tools.
The store contains Universal Windows apps only.	The store contains Universal Windows apps, desktop apps, and Android apps.
Available in all Windows 10 editions.	The store is available only in Windows 10 Pro, Enterprise, and Education editions.

You can disable user access to the Microsoft Store by modifying the registry or by using Group Policy. The steps for using Group Policy are as follows:

1. Open the **Local Group Policy Editor**.

2. In the left pane of the **Local Group Policy Editor**, navigate to Computer Configuration\ Administrative Templates\Windows Components\Store.

3. In the right pane of **Store in Local Group Policy Editor**, select **Turn off the store application** or **Disable all apps from the Microsoft Store**.

4. Configure the enabled setting in the policy to prevent access the Microsoft Store.

5. Close the **Local Group Policy Editor**.

Configure application settings

Universal Windows apps that are part of Windows 10 are built using a common set of development UI guidelines. This allows for a consistent appearance and customization. For all Universal Windows apps, you can view the various app settings in the Settings app.

Examples of options that are available in an app's settings include:

- **Configuration options**   Affect the behavior of the app, such as choosing between Celsius or Fahrenheit as default units for temperature in a weather app

- **Changing account settings**   Settings for notifications or accessibility options in a mail app, for example

- **User's preferences**   Settings for sound effects or color themes, for example

- **App information**   Settings such as privacy policy, help, app version, or copyright information

In the Groove Music app, for example, the settings are accessible by selecting the cog icon in the bottom-left corner, as shown in Figure 1-47. Various settings are included with the app that use the consistent appearance available with all Universal Windows apps.

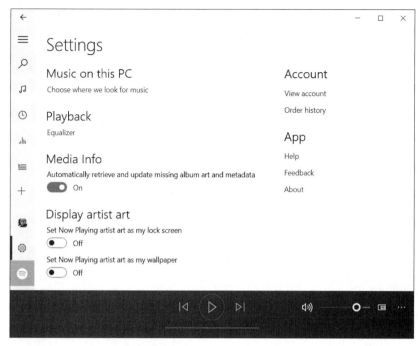

FIGURE 1-47   Groove app settings page

In the Apps section of the Settings app, you have additional settings that you can configure for installed apps. On the Apps & Features page of the Settings app, you can select an app and configure the advanced options. For the Groove music app, the advanced options allow you to configure the following settings:

- **App Permissions**   Allow the app to run in the background.
- **Defaults**   Select which apps to use as the default app.
- **Terminate**   Immediately terminate the app and its related processes.
- **Reset**   Delete all of the app's data and reset the app to its defaults.
- **Uninstall**   Remove the app and its settings from Windows 10.
- **App Add-ons & Downloadable Content**   List any add-ons that are installed for the app.

In the Default Apps section of the Settings app, you can select which apps you want to use for common operations such as listening to music, viewing pictures, checking mail, and accessing the internet.

To modify an app, select the app icon and then select your preferred default app from the list presented, as shown in Figure 1-48, or choose the option Look For An App In The Microsoft Store and then install a new app.

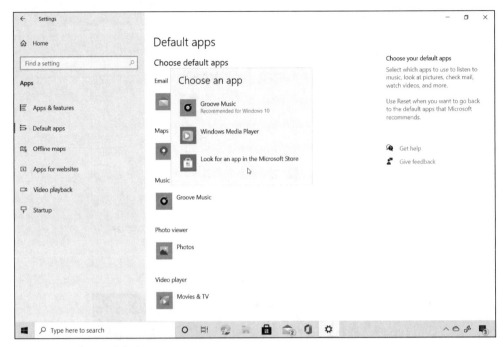

FIGURE 1-48 Choose default apps

Configure and manage services

Services are essential to the smooth operation of Windows 10. They perform functions that support other apps. Most services operate at a low level and are not visible to the user; they can even run when no user is signed in. You can view the account that a service uses, such as the Local System account (which has elevated privileges), or a user account, within the Services console.

You need to know how to view installed services, as well as start, stop, and configure them.

View Services console

The tool for viewing the services running on your computer is the Services console, though you can also view running services by using Task Manager. Launching the Services snap-in (Services.msc), as shown in Figure 1-49, with administrator privileges allows you to gain full functionality in the Services console, where you can view service settings, and start or stop services, change the startup type, and make other configuration changes.

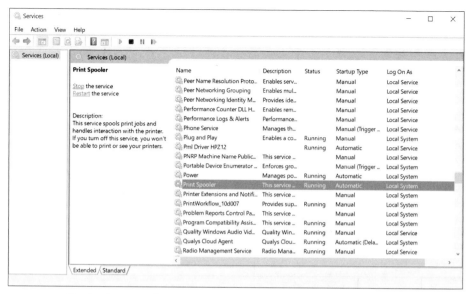

FIGURE 1-49 The Services console

To the left of the list of services is a pane that displays Extended and Standard views. You can select the tab at the bottom of the window to show the extended view, which provides descriptive information of the selected service and includes links for starting, stopping, or pausing the selected service.

Most essential services are configured by Windows to start automatically when your device starts and will be stopped as part of the shutdown process. If you browse the list of services, some are set with the Automatic (Delayed Start) option, which starts the service 2 minutes after the startup completes. This is useful for smoothing the startup process by preventing congestion for system resources during the first few minutes of startup. An additional option is Trigger Start, which allows Windows to run or stop a service as needed in response to other events, such as not running the service unless you enable another service first.

If you are troubleshooting system resources such as memory or other performance issues, you can also stop and restart a service manually. A common example for stopping a service is because it isn't working properly. For example, if print jobs get stuck in the print queue, you can easily stop and then restart the Print Spooler service, which will often resolve the issue.

Configuring services

In addition to stopping or starting a service, you can review or modify the way a service starts up and what happens if it doesn't start properly. In the Services console, open the service's properties by double-clicking the service, as displayed in Figure 1-50.

FIGURE 1-50 Print Spooler Properties

On the General tab, you specify the startup type:

- **Automatic (Delayed Start)** The service starts shortly after the device starts.
- **Automatic** The service starts when the computer starts.
- **Manual** The service doesn't start automatically at startup; it can be started by a user, a program, or a dependent service.
- **Disabled** The service can't be started.

There are additional startup options on the Log On tab of the Properties dialog box that allow you to specify a sign-in account other than the Local System account.

If you need to configure a Trigger Start option, you will have to configure this using the SC (Sc.exe) command-line program, which communicates with the Service Control Manager.

Recovering services

When services stop working or "fail over," they can be configured to perform an automatic action, such as restart. Services may stop for various reasons, such as a driver error, network outage, or performance bottleneck. The settings on the Recovery tab of the Properties dialog box allow the service recovery settings to be configured and affect what happens if a service fails.

You can perform a different action the first time a service fails and on the second or subsequent failures. The Recovery tab enables you to assign the following responses:

- **Take No Action** The service enters the stop state and the stoppage is entered in the event log.

- **Restart The Service**   The device waits for the time specified in the Restart Service After box and then tries to start the service.
- **Run A Program**   The device runs the app you specify in the Run Program section.
- **Restart The Computer**   This option restarts the device. Once the option is enabled, you can configure additional settings in the Restart Computer Options, such as specifying a message to be broadcast to users warning them of the impending shutdown.

Service dependencies

Services often work with other services, and therefore, if a service stops working, it can have a cascading effect on other services that depend on the functions of the stopped service. You can view the effect of dependent services by attempting to start a service that depends on other services; the dependent services will be started. Similarly, if you stop a service upon which others are dependent, these other services will also be stopped. The dependency information is available on the Dependencies tab of a service's Properties dialog box.

Viewing services from Task Manager

In Task Manager, the status of a service is available on the Services tab. You can also right-select any service to open a context menu and start, stop, or restart the service. The context menu also allows you to open the Services console, or you can select the Open Services link at the bottom of Task Manager.

You can also display a running service with its process identifier (PID) and then view other programs and services being run under that PID. Only running services will display a PID, as shown in Figure 1-51.

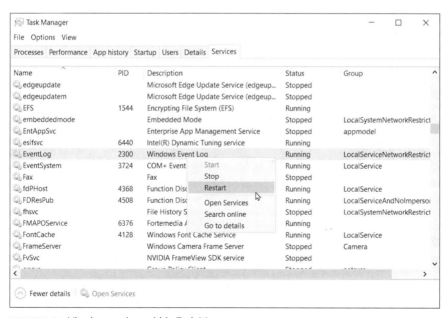

FIGURE 1-51   Viewing services within Task Manager

Right-selecting one of the services allows you to stop or restart the service. You can also select Go To Details from the context menu to open the Details tab in Task Manager with the particular process (typically, Svchost.exe) highlighted that uses the same PID.

Another method of retrieving a list of services is to use PowerShell. Here, you would use the Get-Service cmdlet, which lists all services on a device. You can refine the PowerShell command to list only running services as in the following example:

```
Get-Service | Where-Object {$_.Status -eq "Running"}
```

The following example shows how to start the Application Identity service by using the –Name parameter:

```
Start-Service -Name "Application Identity"
```

Chapter summary

- Windows 10 is available in many editions, including Windows 10 Home, Windows 10 Pro, Windows 10 Pro for Workstations, Windows 10 Enterprise, and Windows 10 Education.
- Windows 10 in S mode is a special edition of Windows 10 that is a limited, locked-down version of the operating system.
- Some features of Windows 10 require special hardware or additional configuration, such as biometric sensors or TPM.
- You cannot perform an in-place upgrade from a 32-bit version of Windows to the 64-bit version of Windows 10.
- There are multiple methods of implementing Windows 10, including performing clean installations and upgrading a prior version of Windows.
- You can choose between three upgrade strategies: in-place, side-by-side, and wipe-and-load.
- You can use a number of tools in Windows ADK, including the Windows Configuration Designer, to customize and distribute Windows 10 settings for deployment throughout your organization.
- Windows Configuration Designer generates provisioning packages with the .ppkg file extension that can customize Windows 10.
- You can migrate user and application settings from one device to another by using the USMT.
- USMT uses ScanState and LoadState to migrate data and can use compression or encryption during the migration process.
- Windows 10 can be configured with additional language features, including the display language, text-to-speech, speech recognition, and handwriting support.

- You can use the Lpksetup command-line tool to implement silent-mode language pack installations.

- Windows 10 requires activation, which can be performed manually or automatically.

- Microsoft provides a number of ways to manage Windows 10 volume activation.

- Microsoft provides the Activation Troubleshooter, which can identify issues experienced with activating Windows 10.

- Windows Hello is a two-factor biometric authentication mechanism built into Windows 10.

- Dynamic Lock enables you to pair a Bluetooth device, such as an Android smartphone, to your Windows 10 device, which will automatically lock the device when the Bluetooth device is moved away from the PC.

- You can customize the Start menu, desktop, taskbar, and notification settings individually or by using Group Policy, provisioning packages, or mobile device management.

- Customizing the Start layout using XML templates and GPOs requires Windows 10 Pro, Windows 10 Enterprise, or Windows 10 Education.

- Microsoft Edge is a cross-platform web browser for Windows 10 that supports touch devices, inking, reading mode, and secure browsing.

- Microsoft Edge is the recommended web browser for Windows 10 and includes many features not available with Internet Explorer, including kiosk mode, collections, and extensions.

- Microsoft Edge kiosk mode allows Microsoft Edge to display a specific site in full-screen mode as used in digital/interactive signage or for public browsing.

- IE mode on Microsoft Edge allows you to specify Microsoft Edge as the default browser and allows selected websites to open in Edge using the Trident MSHTML engine from Internet Explorer 11.

- You can install both local and network printers and manage them using the Print Management console.

- You can configure Windows 10 settings using provisioning packages created in the Windows Configuration Designer.

- The Microsoft Store allows you to download Universal Windows apps and provision a Microsoft Store for Business portal for your staff to download curated apps.

- Windows 10 provides several ways to manage power settings, including creating custom power policies, thereby extending the battery life of your users' devices.

- Desktop computers running Windows 10 Pro for Workstations can use the Ultimate Performance power plan scheme, which enables the device to run at maximum performance.

- You can import and export power plans by using the Powercfg.exe command-line tool.
- You can identify the status of services within the Services console and Task Manager and configure their startup behavior.

Thought experiment

In these thought experiments, demonstrate your skills and knowledge of the topics covered in this chapter. You can find the answers to these thought experiments in the next section.

Scenario 1

Adatum has 2,000 workstations running Windows 8.1. The company plans to implement Windows 10. Adatum management wants to minimize the effects of the changes and it intends to roll out the new operating system over a weekend. All computers are less than two years old and must be running Windows 10 Enterprise at the end of the project.

As a consultant for Adatum, answer the following questions:

1. What is the most appropriate method for Adatum to implement Windows 10?
2. How can you reassure management whether devices meet the minimum system requirements?
3. What deployment method could you use to minimize the disruption to Adatum employees?
4. How would you plan to activate the devices once they are running Windows 10?

Scenario 2

Adatum has recently implemented Microsoft 365 Business with all devices using Windows 10 Pro. The company has a head office with 200 people using desktop computers, a branch office where 25 members of the design team work, and a remote salesforce of 50 people. Each member of the sales team uses a Surface Pro device. Adatum is concerned about security, especially on the mobile devices.

Members of the sales and finance teams need to access the Adatum intranet to produce quotes and manage sales orders. The intranet does not display properly using Microsoft Edge.

Answer the following questions to address Adatum concerns:

1. What sign-on method would you recommend for the mobile devices?
2. What encryption technology could you implement on the mobile devices?
3. How would you recommend the sales and finance team access the Adatum intranet website?
4. How would you enable the Ultimate Performance power plan on the design team desktop computers?

Thought experiment answers

This section provides the solutions for the tasks included in the Thought Experiment section.

Scenario 1

1. An in-place upgrade from Windows 8.1 directly to Windows 10 is supported and recommended by Microsoft and could be performed in the specified time window.

2. Because all devices are less than two years old and currently run Windows 8.1, they already meet the minimum system requirements for running Windows 10.

3. Upgrading the devices directly to Windows 10 by using an in-place upgrade ensures that all user and application settings will be preserved. This approach offers the least disruption to the users.

4. All devices would be automatically activated using the digital license present on the device if they were previously running a genuine version of Windows 8.1.

Scenario 2

1. The Surface Pro devices should be configured to use Windows Hello, with users providing either facial recognition or their Microsoft 365 usernames and passwords for sign-in.

2. The Surface Pro devices are running Window 10 Pro and should be configured to use BitLocker Drive Encryption.

3. Adatum could implement Enterprise Mode so that the Adatum intranet website opens automatically in Internet Explorer 11. All other websites would be opened in Microsoft Edge by default.

4. The design team desktop computers would need to be upgraded to Windows 10 Pro for Workstations for them to use the Ultimate Performance power plan.

Manage devices and data

The MD-100 Windows 10 exam focuses on how to manage devices within an enterprise environment, by using a Microsoft 365 subscription, for example. Once you have installed or upgraded devices with Windows 10, you need to know how to join devices to Azure Active Directory. Organizations that do not use the cloud use Active Directory Domain Services, and you must manage both users and devices.

Devices are managed using local or Group Policy, and you have to implement and troubleshoot these policies. To ensure that data and devices remain safe, you must know how to configure Windows security and use Windows Defender Firewall and Windows Defender Antivirus to safeguard Windows 10.

Skills covered in this chapter:

- Skill 2.1: Manage local users, local groups, and devices
- Skill 2.2: Configure devices by using local policies
- Skill 2.3: Manage Windows security

Skill 2.1: Manage local users, local groups, and devices

In this skill, you will review how to manage local users and local groups on Windows 10 devices. If you have experience with an earlier version of Windows, you might be familiar with configuring local users and local groups, as these operations are largely unchanged. Before you use Windows 10 on a device, you must sign in with the credentials for a user account. In an enterprise environment, the device and the user are often used to provide, control, and audit access to resources. Groups may be used for simplifying administration, allowing entities to share a common function or role or require the same set of privileges. You need to understand how local users, local groups, and devices form a key component in Windows security.

Manage local users

A user account is required to log on to a Windows 10 computer, and to secure the device, it should have a password. You need to understand the default user accounts that are created automatically when you install Windows 10 and how to create new user accounts so that users can log on to machines and access resources. In this skill, you will focus on local accounts that are created and operate only on the local device.

Configure local accounts

Local accounts, as the name suggests, exist in the local accounts database on your Windows 10 device; they can only be granted access to local resources and, where granted, exercise administrative rights and privileges on the local computer.

When you first install Windows 10, you are prompted to sign in using a Microsoft account or a Work Account, such as a Microsoft 365 account that is connected to Azure Active Directory. If neither of these options is available or suits your requirements, you can choose an offline account and create a local account to sign in. Thereafter, you can create additional local user accounts as your needs dictate.

Default accounts

In Windows 10, there are three default local user accounts on the computer in the trusted identity store. This is a secure list of users and groups and is stored locally as the Security Accounts Manager (SAM) database in the registry. The three accounts are the Administrator account, the Default Account, and the Guest account.

The default Administrator account cannot be deleted or locked out, but it can be renamed or disabled. When the default administrator account is enabled, it requires a strong password. Another local account called the HelpAssistant account is created and enabled when a Windows Remote Assistance session is run. The HelpAssistant account provides limited access to the computer to the person who provides remote assistance. The HelpAssistant account is automatically deleted if there are no Remote Assistance requests pending.

When you install Windows 10 using a local account, you can create additional user accounts and give these accounts any name that is valid. To be valid, the username

- Must be from 1 to 20 characters
- Must be unique among all the other user and group names stored on the computer
- Cannot contain any of the following characters: / \ [ ] : ; | = , + ? < > " @
- Cannot consist exclusively of periods or spaces

The initial user account created at installation is a member of the local Administrators group and therefore can perform any local management task on the device. You can view the installed accounts, including the default accounts, by using the Computer Management console, as shown in Figure 2-1. If you cannot find the Local Users And Groups section within Computer Management, then you are probably running Windows 10 Home Edition, which does not have the Local Users And Groups Microsoft Management Console (MMC) snap-in.

You can also use the net user command and the **get-wmiobject -class win32_useraccount** Windows PowerShell cmdlet to list the local user accounts on a device.

EXAM TIP

In Windows 10 Home edition, you must use the User Accounts applet in Control Panel, and you cannot create or manage groups since the Local Users And Groups Console snap-in is not present.

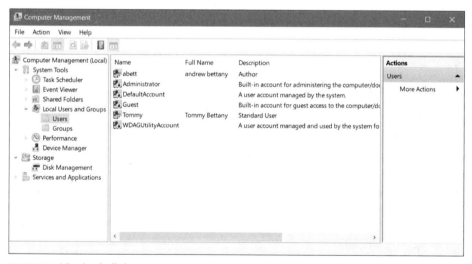

FIGURE 2-1 Viewing built-in user accounts

Manage local user accounts

You can manage local user accounts by using Computer Management (except with Windows 10 Home edition), Control Panel, the Settings app, and Windows PowerShell.

USING COMPUTER MANAGEMENT

To manage user accounts by using Computer Management, right-click **Start** and then select **Computer Management**. Expand the Local Users and Groups node and then select **Users**. To create a new user, right-click the **Users** node and select **New User.**

In the **New User** dialog box, configure the following properties, as shown in Figure 2-2, and then select **Create**.

FIGURE 2-2 Adding a user with Computer Management

- User Name
- Full Name
- Password
- User Must Change Password At Next Logon
- User Cannot Change Password
- Password Never Expires
- Account Is Disabled

After you have added the new user account, you can modify more advanced properties by double-clicking the user account. On the General tab, you can change the user's full name and description and password-related options. On the Member Of tab, you can add the user to groups or remove the user from groups. The Profile tab, shown in Figure 2-3, enables you to modify the following properties:

- **Profile Path**   This is the path to the location of a user's desktop profile. The profile stores the user's desktop settings, such as color scheme, desktop wallpaper, and app settings (including the settings stored for the user in the registry). By default, each user who signs in has a profile folder created automatically in the C:\Users*Username* folder. You can define another location here, and you can use a Universal Naming Convention (UNC) name in the form of *Server**Share**Folder*.

- **Logon Script**   This is the name of a logon script that processes each time a user signs in. Typically, this will be a BAT or CMD file. You might include commands that map network drives or load apps in this script file. Assigning logon scripts in this way is not usually done. Instead, Group Policy Objects (GPOs) are used to assign logon and startup scripts for domain user accounts.

- **Home Folder**   This is a personal storage area where users can save their personal documents. By default, users are assigned subfolders within the C:\Users*Username* folder for this purpose. However, you can use either of the following two properties to specify an alternate location:

  - **Local Path**   A local filesystem path for storage of the user's personal files. This is entered in the format of a local drive and folder path.

  - **Connect**   A network location mapped to the specified drive letter. This is entered in the format of a UNC name.

FIGURE 2-3 Modifying the profile properties for a user

USING CONTROL PANEL

You can also manage user accounts by opening Control Panel, clicking User Accounts, and then clicking User Accounts again. From here, you can do the following:

- **Make changes to my account in PC settings**   Launches the Settings app to enable you to make user account changes

- **Change your account type**   Enables you to switch between Standard and Administrator account types

- **Manage another account**   Enables you to manage other user accounts on this computer

- **Change User Account Control settings**   Launches the User Account Control Settings dialog box from Control Panel

If you are an administrator and you select another local user, you can perform these tasks:

- **Change the account name** Enables you to change your account name.

- **Change the password** Lets you change the password for the user and provide a password hint

- **Change your account type** Enables you to switch between Standard and Administrator account types

- **Delete the account** Allows you to delete the user account and optionally any files associated with their account

- **Manage another account** Enables you to manage other user accounts on this computer

You cannot add new accounts from Control Panel. If you want to add a new local account, use Computer Management, Windows PowerShell, or Add A Family Member in the Family And Other Users section of the Settings app.

USING THE SETTINGS APP

The preferred way to manage local accounts in Windows 10 is by using the Settings app. From Settings, select Accounts. As shown in Figure 2-4, on the Your Info tab, you can modify your account settings, including these:

- **Sign in with a Microsoft account instead** You can sign out and sign in using a Microsoft account.

- **Create your picture** You can browse for an image or take a selfie if your device has a webcam.

- **Creating a Microsoft account** You can create a new Microsoft account using this option.

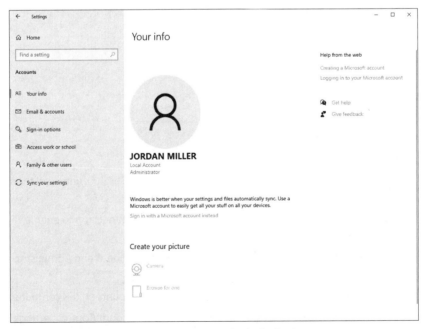

FIGURE 2-4 Modifying your user account properties in the Settings app

If you need to add a new local user account, select the Family & Other Users section and then select Add Someone Else To This PC.

Windows 10 requires you to then enter that person's email address, typically the address they use to sign in to Office 365, OneDrive, Skype, Xbox, or Outlook.com.

If you do not have the recipient's email address, you can still add a local account by using the following procedure:

1. In the **Settings** app, select **Accounts**.

2. On the **Family & other users** tab, under **Other users**, select **Add someone else to this PC**.

3. In the **How will this person sign in** dialog box, select **I don't have this person's sign-in information**.

4. In the **Create account** dialog box, select **Add a user without a Microsoft account**.

5. On the **Create an account for this PC** page, type the username, enter a new password twice, provide answers to the three security questions, and then select **Next** to create the local account. The account is listed under **Other users**.

USING WINDOWS POWERSHELL

You can view local user accounts using Windows PowerShell, but to add or modify local accounts, you will need to run the cmdlets with elevated privileges.

You can use the following cmdlets to manage local user accounts:

- **Get-LocalUser** Gets local user accounts
- **New-LocalUser** Creates a local user account
- **Remove-LocalUser** Deletes a local user account
- **Rename-LocalUser** Renames a local user account
- **Disable-LocalUser** Disables a local user account
- **Enable-LocalUser** Enables a local user account
- **Set-LocalUser** Modifies a local user account

For example, to add a new local user account called User 03 with a password, run the following cmdlets:

```
$Password = Read-Host -AsSecureString
<<Enter Password>>
New-LocalUser "User03" -Password $Password -FullName "Third User" -Description "User 3"
```

> **NEED MORE REVIEW?**   **LOCAL ACCOUNTS CMDLETS**
>
> To review further details about using Windows PowerShell to manage local accounts, refer to the Microsoft PowerShell reference at *https://docs.microsoft.com/powershell/module/microsoft.powershell.localaccounts/?view=powershell-5.1*.

Manage local groups

There are several built-in groups with Windows 10, which provide an easy way for users to be granted the same permissions and rights as other group members. Assigning permissions to groups is usually more efficient than applying them to individual users.

You use the Computer Management console, or if you are an administrator, you can create a custom Microsoft Management Console (MMC) and add the Local Users And Groups snap-in, as shown in Figure 2-5, to create and manage local groups.

FIGURE 2-5 Default groups in Windows 10

In Figure 2-5, you can see the default built-in local groups (such as Administrators and Device Owners) and a description for each. These built-in groups already have the necessary permissions associated to them to accomplish specific tasks.

If you select the Users or Administrators group, you should see members that you recognize. Administrators have complete and unrestricted access to the computer, whereas users are unable to make accidental or intentional systemwide changes, but they can run most applications that have already been installed on a device.

Built-in local groups

You can add your own groups, change group membership, rename groups, and delete groups. It is best practice to use the built-in groups wherever possible because they already have the appropriate permissions and are familiar to other administrators. Some built-in local groups are special groups that the Windows 10 system requires (and cannot be managed).

Some of the local groups created on Windows 10 devices, together with their uses, are shown in Table 2-1.

TABLE 2-1 Built-in local groups

Local Group	Description
Access Control Assistance Operators	Members of this group can remotely query authorization attributes and permissions for resources on the computer.
Administrators	The Administrators group has full permissions and privileges on a Windows 10 device. Members can manage all the objects on the computer. The Administrator and initial user accounts are members of the Administrators local group.
Backup Operators	Backup Operators group members have permissions to back up and restore the file system regardless of any NTFS permissions. Backup Operators can access the file system only through the Backup utility.
Cryptographic Operators	The Cryptographic Operators group has access to perform cryptographic operations on the computer.
Device Owners	Members of this group can change systemwide settings to the computer.
Distributed COM Users	The Distributed COM Users group can launch and run Distributed COM objects on the computer.
Event Log Readers	Event Log Readers group members can read the event log on the local computer.
Guests	The Guests group has very limited access to the computer. In most cases, administrators disable guest access because guest access can pose a potential security risk; instead, most administrators prefer to create specific users. By default, the Guest user account is a member of the Guests local group.
Hyper-V Administrators	Members of this group have complete and unrestricted access to all features of Hyper-V if this feature has been installed.
IIS_IUSRS	The IIS_IUSRS group is used by Internet Information Services (IIS). By default, the NT AUTHORITY\IUSR user account, used by IIS, is a member of the IIS_IUSRS group.
Network Configuration Operators	Members of the Network Configuration Operators group can manage the computer's network configuration.
Performance Log Users	The Performance Log Users group can access and schedule logging of performance counters and create and manage trace counters on a device.
Performance Monitor Users	The Performance Monitor Users group can access and view performance counter information on a device. Members of this group can access performance counters both locally and remotely.
Power Users	The Power Users group is included in Windows 10 for backward compatibility only. Power Users was a group used on computers running Windows XP and granted members limited administrative rights.
Remote Desktop Users	The Remote Desktop Users group members can log on remotely using the Remote Desktop service.
Remote Management Users	Members of this group can access WMI resources over management protocols (such as WS-Management via the Windows Remote Management service). This applies only to WMI namespaces that grant access to the user.
Replicator	The Replicator group supports directory replication, which is a feature used by domain controllers.

Local Group	Description
System Managed Accounts Group	Members of this group are managed by the system.
Users	The Users group is used for end users who require very limited system access. On a fresh copy of Windows 10, members of the Users group are unable to compromise the operating system or program files. By default, all users who have been created on a device, except Guest users, are members of the Users local group.

As Table 2-1 shows, Administrators group members have full permissions and privileges on a Windows 10 device. A member of the Administrators local group can perform the following tasks:

- Access any data on the computer
- Assign and manage user rights
- Back up and restore all data
- Configure audit policies
- Configure password policies
- Configure services
- Create administrative accounts
- Create administrative shares
- Increase and manage disk quotas
- Install and configure hardware device drivers
- Install applications that modify the Windows system files
- Install the operating system
- Install Windows updates, service packs, and hot fixes
- Manage disk properties, including formatting hard drives
- Manage security logs
- Modify groups and accounts that have been created by other users
- Modify systemwide environment variables
- Perform a system restore
- Reenable locked-out and disabled user accounts
- Remotely access the registry
- Remotely shut down the system
- Stop or start any service
- Upgrade the operating system

Create and delete groups

Only members of the Administrators group can manage users and groups. When creating a new group, keep in mind that the group name has to be unique on the local computer and cannot be the same as a local username that exists on the computer.

You should make the group name descriptive, and wherever possible, you include a description of the new group's function. Group names can have up to 256 characters in length and include alphanumeric characters such as spaces, but the backslash (\) is not allowed.

To create a new group, follow these steps:

1. Right-click **Start** and select **Computer Management**.

2. Open the **Local Users and Groups** console.

3. Right-click the **Groups** folder and select **New Group** from the context menu.

4. In the **New Group** dialog box, enter the group name. (Optionally, you can enter a description for this group.)

5. To add group members, select the **Add** button.

6. In the **Select Users** dialog box, type the username, then select **OK**. In the **New Group** dialog box, you will see that the user has been added to the group.

7. To create the new group, select the **Create** button.

To delete a group from the Local Users And Groups console in Computer Management, right-click the group name and choose Delete from the context menu. You will see a warning that deleting a group cannot be undone, and you should select the Yes button to confirm the deletion of the group.

When a group is deleted, all permissions assignments that have been specified for the group will be lost.

Special identity groups

Several special identity groups (sometimes known as special groups) are used by the system or by administrators to allocate access to resources. Membership in special groups is automatic, based on criteria, and you cannot manage special groups through the Local Users And Groups console. Table 2-2 describes the special identity groups that are built into Windows 10.

TABLE 2-2 Built-in special identity groups

Special Identity Group	Description
Anonymous Logon	When a user accesses the computer through an anonymous logon, such as via special accounts created for anonymous access to Windows 10 services, they become members of the Anonymous Logon group.
Authenticated Users	This is a useful group because it includes all users who access Windows 10 using a valid username and password.
Batch	This group includes users who log on as a batch job operator to run a batch job.
Creator Owner	The Creator Owner is the account that created or took ownership of an object, such as a file, folder, printer, or print job. Members of the Creator Owner group have special administrator-level permissions to the resources over which they have ownership.
Dialup	This group includes users who log on to the network from a dial-up connection.

Special Identity Group	Description
Everyone	This group includes anyone who accesses the computer. This includes all users, including Guest accounts and all users that are within a domain or trusted domains. Members of the Anonymous Logon group are not included as a part of the Everyone group.
Interactive	This group includes all users who use the computer's resources locally and those who are not using the computer's resources remotely via a network connection.
Network	This group includes users who access the computer's resources over a network connection.
Service	This group includes users who log on as a user account that is used to run a service.
System	When Windows 10 needs to access internal functions, it can perform actions as a system user. The process being accessed by the operating system becomes a member of the System group.
Terminal Server User	This group includes users who log on through Terminal Server applications.

Manage users, groups, and devices in Active Directory Domain Services

Once a network grows larger than a few computers, companies and enterprises configure networks as a domain or directory. A large network is managed by using a domain. On-premises environments will use Active Directory Domain Services (AD DS) and cloud-based environments use Azure Active Directory (Azure AD). Using both on-premises and cloud resources is referred to as a *hybrid model*. Both directory services are responsible for identity-related management. User and device information is stored in a directory, which creates a logical, hierarchical organization of information, represented as objects.

Users are aware that they are part of an Active Directory domain because they will access shared resources by signing into their device using a domain username and password such as user@contoso.com rather than a local or Microsoft account.

AD DS can store millions of objects that can be managed and controlled. Objects typically include shared resources such as servers, volumes, printers, and the network user and computer accounts. AD DS also simplifies the administration of user accounts and stores information about them, such as names, passwords, phone numbers, or information about a computer, like the device name or the last user logged on.

One or more Windows servers can be configured with the domain controller role, which then stores the directory and allows administrators to manage AD DS objects using a console app, such as Active Directory Administrative Center (ADAC).

You will learn later in this chapter how user or computer objects' properties can also be configured by using local policies or managed at scale by using Group Policy Objects. Computers that are managed by Active Directory are referred to as *domain joined*.

Use Active Directory users

Within Active Directory (AD), there are two primary objects that you need to know: user accounts and computer accounts. These are two forms of common security principals held in AD, and they allow you to manage the account and control access to resources by the entity (a person or a computer). Within a domain you will create domain user accounts for the person in most scenarios. A domain user will use their domain username and password to sign in to any device on the domain-based network (with the correct permissions). This approach allows administrators to centrally manage user accounts across an organization rather than on each individual device, as with a workgroup environment.

Use Active Directory groups

Active Directory groups allow you to collect user accounts, computer accounts, and other groups into units that can be managed. By controlling groups of objects, administrators can manage permissions to resources at scale. It is best practice for users and other objects to be added to a group and then permissions set at the group level, rather than at the user or computer object level. This way, if a specific user or computer account joins or leaves the organization, the group membership can be dynamically updated by Active Directory. A huge amount of time and effort is therefore saved every time a personnel change occurs.

Two types of groups are available in Active Directory:

- **Distribution groups**   Used to create email distribution lists used by email applications, such as Exchange Server, to send emails to the group membership. It is not possible to configure security permissions on distribution groups.

- **Security groups**   Used to assign rights and permissions to objects within the group.

User rights are assigned to a security group to determine what members of that group can do using their user account. For example, you may want to add a user to the Backup Operators group in Active Directory. The user will then be granted the ability to back up and restore files and directories that are located on each file server or domain controller in the domain.

Permissions are assigned to the shared resource. Best practice is to assign the permissions to a security group and allow AD to determine who can access the resource and the level of access whenever the resource is accessed. The level of access can be fine-tuned using access control entries (ACEs), such as Full Control or Read, which are stored in the discretionary access control list (DACL) for each resource. The DACL defines the permissions on resources and objects such as file shares or printers.

Active Directory default security groups

You can use several built-in groups with Active Directory. Some commonly used security groups are shown in Table 2-3.

TABLE 2-3 Built-in Active Directory security groups

AD Security Group	Description
DnsAdmins	Members of this group have administrative access to the DNS Server service.
Domain Admins	Domain Admins are the designated administrators of the domain. Present on every domain-joined computer within the local Administrators group. Receives rights and permissions granted to the local Administrators group and to the domain's Administrators group.
Domain Computers	All computers and servers that are joined to the domain are members of this group.
Domain Users	All users in the domain.
Enterprise Admins	Enterprise Admins have permissions to change forest-wide configuration settings. Enterprise Admins are members of the domain's Administrators group and receive rights and permissions granted to that group.
IIS_IUSRS	The IIS_IUSRS group is used by Internet Information Services (IIS). By default, the NT AUTHORITY\IUSR user account, used by IIS, is a member of the IIS_IUSRS group.
Print Operators	Members can administer domain-based printers.
Remote Desktop Users	The Remote Desktop Users group members can log on remotely using the Remote Desktop service.

Understand Active Directory

A detailed knowledge of Windows Server and AD DS is outside the scope of the MD-100 exam, but you should know the difference between an on-premises environment and a cloud-based one. Active Directory Domain Services (AD DS), commonly referred to as Active Directory (AD), is a role of associated services that are installed on physical or virtual Windows servers. Simply hosting a Windows Server running the AD DS role on an Azure-based virtual machine is an example of a "lift and shift" deployment to the cloud running AD DS and does not provide an Azure Active Directory (Azure AD) environment.

Windows Server installed with the AD DS role is a complex environment that has benefited organizations for over 20 years and, as such, has many legacy components necessary to support AD feature backward compatibility. In addition to the directory service, technologies are often provisioned when you add the AD DS role to a Windows server, including:

- Active Directory Certificate Services (AD CS)
- Active Directory Lightweight Directory Services (AD LDS)
- Active Directory Federation Services (AD FS)
- Active Directory Rights Management Services (AD RMS)

Active Directory Domain Services has the following characteristics (which are not shared by Azure AD):

- AD DS is a true directory service, with a hierarchical X.500-based structure.
- AD DS uses Domain Name System (DNS) for locating resources.

- You can query and manage AD DS using Lightweight Directory Access Protocol (LDAP).
- The Kerberos protocol is primarily used for AD DS authentication.
- Computer objects represent computers that join an Active Directory domain.
- You can manage objects stored in the directory using organizational units (OUs) and Group Policy Objects (GPOs).
- You can establish trusts between domains for delegated management.

Manage devices in directories

Microsoft has designed Windows 10 to be managed using cloud-based tools such as Microsoft Intune for remote device management. As more businesses migrate away from traditional on-premises domain environments to the cloud, you will need to understand how to configure devices to register them in Azure Active Directory.

In this section, you will learn how to register a device so that it can be managed by a business or a school using cloud-based services. You will see how to enable Device Registration and the process of joining devices to Azure Active Directory.

Understand device management

Once devices are managed by Azure Active Directory (Azure AD), you can ensure that your users are accessing your corporate resources from devices that meet your standards for security and compliance. To protect devices and resources using Azure AD, users must be allowed to have their Windows 10 devices managed by Azure AD.

Azure AD is a cloud-based identity authentication and authorization service that enables your users to enjoy the benefits of single sign-on (SSO) for cloud-based applications, such as Office 365. Users can easily join their devices to your organization's Azure AD once you have enabled device joining in the Azure Active Directory Admin Center.

When you are joining devices to an on-premises domain environment, the types of devices that you can join to the domain are quite restrictive; devices, for example, must be running a supported operating system. This means that any users who have devices running Windows 10 Home editions cannot join the company's on-premises domain. However, Azure AD is less restrictive in this respect; you can add to Azure AD almost any tablet, laptop, smartphone, and desktop computer running a variety of platforms. When you enable users to add their devices to Azure AD, you will manage their enrolled devices by using a mobile device management solution, such as Microsoft Intune, which allows you to manage and provision your users' devices.

Devices can be managed by Azure AD using two methods:

- Joining a device to Azure AD
- Registering a device to Azure AD

AZURE AD–JOINED DEVICE

Joining a Windows 10 device to Azure AD is like registering a device with Azure AD, but it allows enhanced management capabilities. Once a device has been joined to Azure AD, the local state of a device changes to enable your users to sign into the device using the work or school account instead of a personal account.

An enterprise will typically join its owned devices to Azure AD to allow for cloud-based management of the devices and to grant access to corporate apps and resources.

> **NOTE BULK-JOIN DEVICES TO AZURE AD**
>
> Bulk joining of devices to Azure AD and Windows Autopilot deployment are outside the scope of the MD-100 Windows 10 exam, though you should expect to find these topics covered in the MD-101 Managing Modern Desktops exam.

Organizations of any size can deploy Azure AD Join. Azure AD Join works well in a cloud-only (no on-premises infrastructure) environment. When Azure AD Join is implemented in a hybrid environment, users gain access to both cloud and on-premises apps and resources.

Azure AD–joined devices allow your users to access the following benefits:

- **Single-Sign-On (SSO)** Allows users simplified access to Azure managed SaaS apps, services, and work resources.
- **Enterprise-compliant roaming** User settings can be kept in sync across joined devices using their Azure AD–joined devices (without the need to sign in using a Microsoft account).
- **Access to Microsoft Store for Business** Users can access a Microsoft Store populated with apps chosen by your organization.
- **Windows Hello** Devices can be secured using the enterprise features of Windows Hello.
- **Restriction of access** Devices will only be able to access apps that meet the organizational compliance policy.
- **Seamless access to on-premises resources** Hybrid Azure AD–joined devices can access on-premises resources when connected to the domain network.

Organizations that already have Microsoft 365 or other SaaS apps integrated with Azure AD have the necessary components in place to have devices managed in Azure AD instead of being managed in Active Directory.

AZURE AD–REGISTERED DEVICES

Once a device is registered into management, it is "known" to Azure AD, and information relating to the device is stored in Azure AD. Effectively, the device is given an identity with Azure AD. You can create conditional access rules to determine whether access to resources from your devices will be granted.

Azure AD–registered devices enable users to use personally owned devices to access your organization's resources in a controlled manner. Azure AD supports bring-your-own-device (BYOD) scenarios for several types of devices, including devices running Windows 10, iOS, Android, and macOS.

With an Azure AD–registered device, the user will gain access to resources using a work or school Azure AD account at the time they access the resources. All corporate data and apps will be kept completely separated from the personal data and apps on the device. If the personal computer, tablet, or phone that is registered with Azure AD does not meet your corporate standards for security and compliance—for example, if a device is not running a supported version of the operating system, or it has been jail broken—then access to the resource will be denied.

Device Registration enables you to facilitate an SSO experience for users, removing the need for them to repeatedly enter credentials to access resources.

The main reasons to implement Device Registration are:

- To enable access to corporate resources from non-domain joined or personally owned devices

- To enable SSO for specific apps and/or resources managed by Azure AD

After you enable Device Registration, users can register and enroll their devices in your organizational tenant. After they have enrolled their devices:

- Enrolled devices are associated with a specific user account in Azure AD.

- A device object is created in Azure AD to represent the physical device and its associated user account.

- A user certificate is installed on the user's device.

Configure device management

Device management requires configuration to ensure that when your users attempt Device Registration, the process will not fail. By default, the setting is enabled, and it allows all Windows 10 devices that present valid credentials to be managed by your Azure AD.

The Azure portal provides a cloud-based location to manage your devices. To allow registration of devices into Azure AD, follow these steps:

1. Sign in as an administrator to the Azure portal at *https://portal.azure.com*.

2. On the left navigation bar, select **Azure Active Directory**.

3. In the **Manage** section, select **Devices**.

4. Select **Device settings**.

5. On the **Device settings** blade, ensure that **Users may join devices to Azure AD** is set to **All**, as shown in Figure 2-6. If you choose **Selected**, then select the **Selected** link and choose the users who can join Azure AD. You can select both individual users and groups of users.

6. Select **Save**.

FIGURE 2-6 Enabling Azure AD join

Within the Azure AD portal, you can fine-tune the process of registering and joining devices by configuring the device settings as listed in Table 2-4.

TABLE 2-4 Azure AD device configuration settings

Device Setting	Description
Users May Join Devices To Azure AD	The default is All. The Selected option allows you to select users who can join Windows 10 devices to Azure AD.
Users May Register Their Devices With Azure AD	Required to allow devices to be registered with Azure AD by users. Options include the following: ■ **None** Prevents devices from being registered with Azure AD. ■ **All** Automatically configured if Enrollment with Microsoft Intune or Mobile Device Management (MDM) for Office 365 is configured as they require Device Registration.
Additional Local Administrators On Azure AD Joined Devices	You can assign the users who are granted local administrator rights on a device and added to the Device Administrators role in Azure AD. By default, global administrators in Azure AD and device owners are granted local administrator rights. Requires an Azure AD Premium license.
Devices To Be Azure AD Joined Or Azure AD Registered Require Multi-Factor Authentication	Choose whether users are required to use multifactor authentication to join their devices to Azure AD. The default setting is No. This setting is only applicable to Azure AD Join on Windows 10 and BYOD registration for Windows 10, iOS, and Android. This setting does not apply to hybrid Azure AD–joined devices, Azure AD–joined VMs in Azure, and Azure AD–joined devices using Windows Autopilot self-deployment mode.
Maximum Number Of Devices Per User	By default, all users can have a maximum of 50 devices in Azure AD. Once this quota is reached, they are not able to add additional devices until one or more of the existing devices are removed. The device quota is across both Azure AD–joined and Azure AD–registered devices.
Enterprise State Roaming	You can configure the Enterprise State Roaming settings for specific users or groups. With Azure AD Premium, you can select a subset of your users and enable this feature for them. Without Azure AD Premium, you can only configure Enterprise State Roaming for all users at once.

DEVICE MANAGEMENT TASKS

Once devices have been registered or joined to Azure AD, they appear in the list within the All Devices section of the Azure Active Directory Admin Center. Devices managed by another management authority, such as Microsoft Intune, are also listed.

To locate a device, you can search using the device name or device ID. Once you have located a device, you can perform additional device management tasks, including the following:

- **Update devices** You can enable or disable devices. You need to be a global administrator in Azure AD to perform this task, which prevents a device from being able to authenticate with Azure AD and thus prevents the device from accessing any Azure AD resources.

- **Delete devices** When a device is retired, or it no longer requires access to your corporate resources, it should be deleted in Azure AD. Deleting a device requires you to be a global administrator in Azure AD or an Intune administrator. Once deleted, all details stored in Azure AD relating to the device—for example, BitLocker keys for Windows devices—are removed. If a device is managed elsewhere, such as in Microsoft Intune, you should ensure that the device has been wiped before deleting the device in Azure AD.

- **View device ID** Each device has a unique device ID that can be used to search for the device; the unique device ID can be used as a reference if you need to use PowerShell during a troubleshooting task.

- **View device BitLocker key** Windows devices managed by Azure AD can have their BitLocker recovery keys stored in Azure AD. You can access this key if the encrypted drive needs to be recovered. To view or copy the BitLocker keys, you need to be the owner of the device or have one of the following roles assigned: Global Administrator, Help desk Administrator, Security Administrator, Security Reader, or Intune Service Administrator.

> **NOTE USE POWERSHELL TO BACK UP THE BITLOCKER RECOVERY KEY TO AZURE AD**
>
> For Azure AD–joined computers, the BitLocker recovery password should be stored in Azure AD. You can use the PowerShell cmdlets Add-BitLockerKeyProtector, Get-BitLockerVolume, and BackupToAAD-BitLockerKeyProtector to add a recovery password and back it up to Azure AD before enabling BitLocker.

Connect devices to Azure AD

Once the prerequisites have been configured to allow the Device Registration service to take place, you are able to connect devices to Azure AD.

There are three ways to connect a Windows 10 device to Azure AD:

- Joining a new Windows 10 device to Azure AD
- Joining an existing Windows 10 device to Azure AD
- Registering a Windows 10 device to Azure AD

In this section, you will learn the steps required for each method of connecting Windows 10 to Azure AD.

JOIN A NEW WINDOWS 10 DEVICE TO AZURE AD

In this method, we will take a new Windows 10 device and join the device to Azure AD during the first-run experience. The device could have been previously prepared using an enterprise deployment method, or it could have been distributed by the original equipment manufacturer (OEM) directly to your employees.

If the device is running either Windows 10 Professional or Windows 10 Enterprise, the first-run experience will present the setup process for company-owned devices.

> **NOTE** **JOINING A DEVICE TO ACTIVE DIRECTORY DURING THE FIRST-RUN EXPERIENCE**
> Joining an on-premises Active Directory domain is supported in Windows 10 during the Windows Out-of-Box Experience (OOBE). If you need to join a computer to an AD domain, during setup you should choose the option Set Up For An Organization and then select the Domain Join Instead link. You then need to set up the device with a local account and join the domain from the Settings app on your computer. For the MD-100 Windows 10 exam, you should expect that devices will be cloud- or hybrid cloud–enabled.

To join a new Windows 10 device to Azure AD during the first-run experience, use the following steps:

1. Start the new device and allow the setup process.
2. On the **Let's start with region. Is this right?** page, select the regional setting that you need and select **Yes**.
3. On the **Is this the right keyboard layout?** page, select the keyboard layout settings and select **Yes**.
4. On the **Want to add a second keyboard layout?** page, add a layout or select **Skip**.
5. The computer should automatically connect to the internet, but it if it does not, you will be presented with the **Let's connect you to a network** page, where you can select a network connection.

6. On the **How would you like to set up?** page, choose **Set up for an organization** and select **Next**.

7. On the **Sign in with Microsoft** page, enter your organization or school account and password and select **Next**.

8. On the **Choose privacy settings for your device**, choose the settings and select **Accept**.

9. On the **Use Windows Hello with your account** page, select **OK**.

10. On the **More information required** page, select **Next**, provide the additional security verification information, and select **Next** again.

11. Depending on organizational settings, your users might be prompted to set up MFA. On the **Keep your account secure** page, select **Next** and set up the Microsoft Authenticator.

12. Depending on organizational settings, your users might be prompted to set up Windows Hello. By default, they will be prompted to set up a PIN. When prompted to set up a PIN, select **Set up PIN**. You should now be automatically signed in to the device, joined to your organization or school Azure AD tenant, and presented with the desktop.

JOIN AN EXISTING WINDOWS 10 DEVICE TO AZURE AD

In this method, we will take an existing Windows 10 device and join it to Azure AD. You can join a Windows 10 device to Azure AD at any time. Use the following procedure to join the device:

1. Open the **Settings** app and then select **Accounts**.

2. In **Accounts**, select the **Access work or school** tab.

3. Select **Connect**.

4. On the **Set up a work or school account** page, under **Alternate actions**, select **Join this device to Azure Active Directory**, as shown in Figure 2-7.

5. On the **Microsoft account** page, enter your email address and select **Next**.

6. On the **Enter password** page, enter your password and select **Sign In**.

7. On the **Make sure this is your organization** page, confirm that the details on screen are correct and select **Join**.

8. On the **You're all set!** page, select **Done**.

9. To verify that your device is connected to your organization or school, check that your Azure AD email address is listed under the **Connect** button, indicating that it is connected to Azure AD.

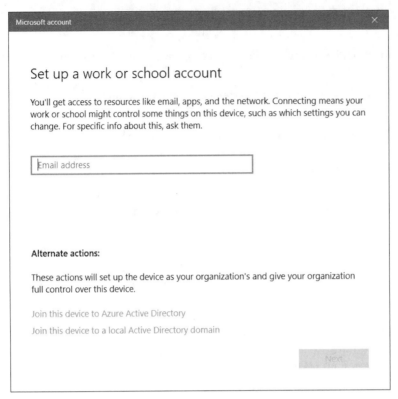

FIGURE 2-7 Joining a device to Azure AD

If you have access to the Azure Active Directory portal, then you can validate that the device is joined to Azure AD by following these steps:

1. Sign in as an administrator to the Azure portal at *https://portal.azure.com*.

2. On the left navigation bar, select **Azure Active Directory**.

3. In the Manage section, select **Devices > All devices**.

4. Verify that the device is listed, as shown in Figure 2-8.

FIGURE 2-8 Viewing All Devices in Azure AD

REGISTER DEVICES TO AZURE AD

You connect a Windows 10 device to Azure Active Directory using the Add Work Or School Account feature found in the Settings app. Device Registration is used to allow devices to be known by both Azure AD and MDM solutions.

In this method, we will take an existing Windows 10 device and register it to Azure AD. Use the following procedure to register the device:

1. Open the **Settings** app and then select **Accounts**.

2. In **Accounts**, select the **Access work or school** tab.

3. Select **Connect**.

4. On the **Set up a work or school account** page, enter your work or school email address, select **Next**, and complete the wizard.

To verify that a device is registered to your organization or school Azure AD tenant, users can use these steps:

1. Open the **Settings** app and then select **Accounts**.

2. In **Accounts**, select the **Access work or school** tab.

3. On the **Access work or school** page, verify that your organization or school Azure AD email address is listed under the **Connect** button.

> *NOTE* **REGISTER BYO DEVICES TO AZURE AD**
>
> You can register a personally owned device with Azure AD using the Set Up A Work Or School Account Wizard. Personal devices are then known to Azure AD but are not fully managed by the organization.

Enroll devices into Microsoft 365

Microsoft 365 is a bundled subscription that includes Office 365, Windows 10, and Enterprise Mobility + Security. Microsoft 365 comes in three primary bundles:

- **Microsoft 365 Business Premium**   For small and medium-sized organizations up to 300 users

- **Microsoft 365 Enterprise**   For organizations of any size

- **Microsoft 365 Education**   For educational establishments

With Microsoft 365, you use Azure Active Directory for your identity and authentication requirements, and you can (and should) enroll Windows 10 into device management so that your users can gain access to corporate resources. Once devices are joined to your Microsoft 365 tenant, Windows 10 becomes fully integrated with the cloud-based services offered by

Office 365 and Enterprise Mobility + Security. Microsoft 365 supports other platforms, including Android and iOS, which can also be managed as mobile devices. However, only Windows 10 devices can be joined to Azure AD.

> **NOTE** **MICROSOFT 365 BUSINESS PREMIUM DOES NOT INCLUDE WINDOWS 10**
>
> The Microsoft 365 Business Premium subscription includes Office 365 Business and Enterprise Mobility + Security, but it does not include Windows 10. However, the Microsoft 365 Business Premium subscription does allow businesses to upgrade their existing Windows 7 Professional, Windows 8 Pro, or Windows 8.1 Pro devices to Windows 10 Pro. Windows 10 Pro is then provided with a Windows 10 Business license, which enables businesses to use the set of cloud services and device management capabilities included with Microsoft 365 Business Premium.

ENROLL DEVICES INTO MICROSOFT 365 BUSINESS

When you enroll Windows devices into Microsoft 365 Business, they must be running Windows 10 Pro, version 1703 (Creators Update) or later. If you have any Windows devices running Windows 7 Professional, Windows 8 Pro, or Windows 8.1 Pro, the Microsoft 365 Business subscription entitles you to upgrade them to Windows 10 Pro.

Microsoft 365 Business includes a set of device-management capabilities powered by Microsoft Endpoint Manager. Microsoft 365 Business offers organizations a simplified management console that provides access to a limited number of device management tasks, including the following:

- Deploy Windows with Autopilot
- Remove company data
- Factory reset
- Manage office deployment

To enroll a brand-new device running Windows 10 Pro into Microsoft 365 Business, known as a "user-driven enrollment," follow these steps:

1. Go through Windows 10 device setup until you get to the **How would you like to set up?** page, as shown in Figure 2-9.

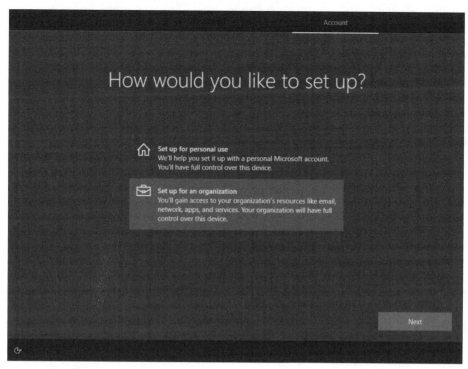

FIGURE 2-9 Windows 10 device setup

2. Choose **Set up for an organization** and then enter your username and password for your Microsoft 365 Business Premium subscription (the new user account, not the tenant admin account).

3. Complete the remainder of the Windows 10 device setup.

4. The device will be registered and joined to your organization's Azure AD, and you will be presented with the desktop. You can verify the device is connected to Azure AD by opening the **Settings** app and clicking **Accounts**.

5. On the **Your Info** page, select **Access Work or School**.

6. You should see that the device is connected to your organization. Select your organization name to show the **Info** and **Disconnect** buttons.

7. Select **Info** to see that your device is managed by your organization and to view your device sync status.

8. To verify that the device has been granted a Windows 10 Business license, select the **Home** icon, select **System**, and then select **About**.

9. In the **Windows specifications** section, the Windows Edition shows Windows 10 Business, as shown in Figure 2-10.

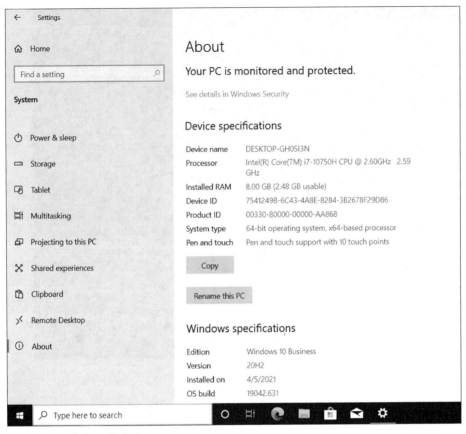

FIGURE 2-10 Windows 10 device setup

Although there is no link to Microsoft Intune within the Microsoft 365 Business Admin Center, the subscription includes the use of the full MDM capabilities for iOS, Android, macOS, and other cross-platform device management. To access the Microsoft Endpoint Manager admin center, launch a browser and sign in with your Microsoft 365 Business Premium credentials at *https://endpoint.microsoft.com*.

To access Intune App Protection in the Azure portal and view the app protection settings for managed Windows 10, Android, and iOS devices, follow these steps:

1. Sign in to the Microsoft Endpoint Manager admin center at *https://endpoint.microsoft. com* with your Microsoft 365 Business admin credentials.

2. In the left navigation bar, select **Apps**.

3. In the **Apps** blade, select **App protection policies**.

4. You can now select **Create policy** from the menu and configure **App Protection Policies**.

ENROLL DEVICES INTO MICROSOFT 365 ENTERPRISE

Microsoft 365 Enterprise plans can be chosen by larger organizations with more than 300 users or businesses of any size that require access to the increased levels of compliance and security management over Microsoft 365 Business Premium.

The Microsoft 365 Enterprise solution includes additional functionality, such as business intelligence, analytics tools, and access to the Microsoft Endpoint Manager from the Microsoft 365 Admin Center for device and app management.

When enrolling devices into Microsoft 365 Enterprise, those devices must be running Windows 10 Enterprise, version 1703 (Creators Update) or later. Devices running an earlier version of Windows can be upgraded to Windows 10 Enterprise as part of the Microsoft 365 Enterprise licensing.

Users can perform an Azure AD join using the user-driven enrollment method shown in the previous section to enroll their devices into management. Enrollment can happen during Out-of-Box Experience (OOBE) or after a Windows profile has already been set up. To enroll a device once a user has already set up a Windows user profile, follow the steps outlined in the "Join a new Windows 10 device to Azure AD" section of this skill.

If you want to enroll a large number of devices in an enterprise scenario, you can use the Device Enrollment Manager (DEM) account in Microsoft Intune. The DEM is a special account in Microsoft Endpoint Manager that allows you to enroll up to a maximum of 1,000 devices. (By default, standard users can manage and enroll up to five devices.) For security reasons, the DEM user should not also be an Intune administrator. Each enrolled device will require a single Intune license, but the DEM user does not require an Intune license. You can have a maximum of 150 DEM accounts in Microsoft Intune.

By default, there is no device enrollment account user present in Microsoft Intune. You can create a device enrollment account by performing the following steps:

1. Sign in to the Microsoft Endpoint Manager admin center at *https://endpoint.microsoft.com* with your Microsoft 365 Enterprise admin credentials.

2. In the left navigation bar, select **Devices**, and then under **Device enrollment**, choose **Enroll devices**.

3. In the left navigation bar, select **Device enrollment managers**.

4. Select **Add**.

5. On the **Add user** blade, enter the username for the DEM user and select **Add**. The user is promoted to the DEM role.

6. Close the **Add user** blade.

7. The **Device enrollment managers** list now contains the new user, as shown in Figure 2-11.

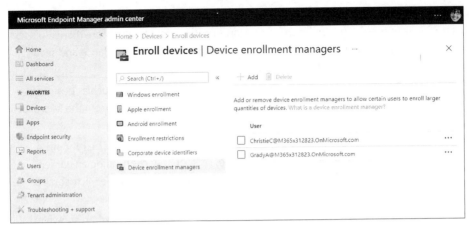

FIGURE 2-11 List of Device Enrollment Managers

> **NEED MORE REVIEW?**   **ENROLL DEVICES USING DEVICE ENROLLMENT MANAGER**
>
> For more information on the DEM in Microsoft Intune, including example scenarios and limitations of devices that are enrolled with a DEM account, visit *https://docs.microsoft.com/ intune/device-enrollment-manager-enroll.*

View and manage devices in Microsoft 365

Microsoft 365 Business Premium subscription administrators can manage their enrolled devices directly from the Microsoft 365 Admin Center screen using the Enroll Devices tile, as shown in Figure 2-12. On the Microsoft 365 Admin Center portal screen, both the Device Enrollment link on the Enroll Devices tile and the Endpoint Manager option (under Admin Centers) will open the stand-alone Microsoft Endpoint Manager admin center This portal can also be accessed at *https://endpoint.microsoft.com/#home.*

You can perform the following device-related actions on devices from within the Devices section on the navigation bar:

- **Active Devices**   Includes viewing device details and managing device actions such as Factory Reset, Remove Company Data, and Remove Device.
- **AutoPilot**   Includes adding new devices to be deployed with the Windows AutoPilot service and managing Windows AutoPilot profiles that can be applied to devices.
- **Policies**   Includes managing existing policies and assigning policies to groups; adding new application policies to Android, iOS, and Windows 10 devices; and adding new device configuration policies to Windows 10 devices.

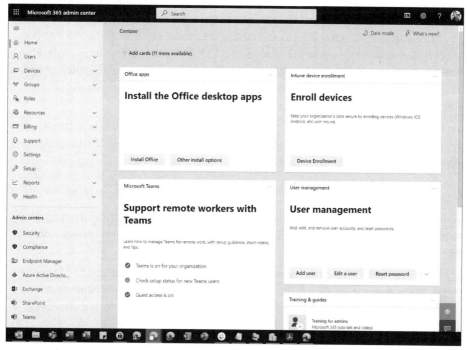

FIGURE 2-12 Microsoft 365 Business Admin portal Home screen

Organizations with a Microsoft 365 Enterprise subscription cannot view or manage devices from the Microsoft 365 Enterprise Admin Center and will need to use the following locations:

- **Azure Active Directory** *https://aad.portal.azure.com*
- **Microsoft Endpoint Manager admin center** *https://endpoint.microsoft.com*

From these views, you can manage and interact with the devices enrolled in your Azure AD tenant, including retiring or wiping a device. Also, you can perform remote tasks, such as retiring, wiping, or restarting the device, as shown in Figure 2-13.

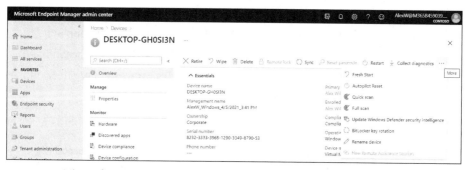

FIGURE 2-13 Microsoft Endpoint Manager Admin Center

Configure sign-in options

After you have activated Windows 10, you can customize the user interface. In some respects, the Windows 10 user interface is familiar to users of Windows 7. It has a Start menu, a desktop, and a taskbar. These things all appear in Windows 7. However, because Windows 10 is designed to work across a variety of device types, including phones, tablets, and traditional desktop computers, it provides additional ways for users to interact.

As an IT pro, you must understand how to customize the Windows 10 user interface, including Start, taskbar, desktop, and notification settings. This enables you to ensure that the operating system interface meets the needs of the users in your organization.

Configure Microsoft accounts

A Microsoft account (previously called Windows Live ID) provides you with an identity that you can use to securely sign in on multiple devices and access cloud services. You can also use the account to synchronize your personal settings between your Windows-based devices.

If Windows 10 detects an internet connection during setup, you are prompted to specify your Microsoft account details, though you can skip this step and create a local account instead. You can link your Microsoft account to a local or AD DS domain account after setup is complete.

Microsoft accounts are primarily for consumer use. Domain users can benefit by using their personal Microsoft accounts in your enterprise, though there are no methods provided by Microsoft to provision Microsoft accounts within an enterprise. After you connect your Microsoft account to Windows 10, you can:

- Access and share photos, documents, and other files from sites such as OneDrive, Outlook.com, Facebook, and Flickr.
- Integrate social media services; contact information and status for your users' friends and associates are automatically obtained from sites such as Hotmail, Outlook, Facebook, Twitter, and LinkedIn.
- Download and install Microsoft Store apps.
- Perform app synchronization with Microsoft Store apps. After user sign-in, when an app is installed, any user-specific settings are automatically downloaded and applied.
- Sync your app settings between devices that are linked to your Microsoft account.
- Use single sign-on with credentials roaming across any devices running Windows 10, Windows 8.1, Windows 8, or Windows RT.

EXAM TIP

You can browse the Microsoft Store even if you do not sign in using a Microsoft account. However, you cannot install Store apps without using a Microsoft account.

If Microsoft accounts are allowed in an enterprise environment, you should note that only the owner of the Microsoft account is able to change the password. A user can perform a password reset in the Microsoft account sign-in portal at *https://account.microsoft.com*.

SIGNING UP FOR A MICROSOFT ACCOUNT

To sign up for a Microsoft account, use the following procedure:

1. Open a web browser and navigate to *https://signup.live.com*.

2. To use your own email address for your Microsoft account, enter it in the web form; otherwise, provide a telephone number to verify that you are not a robot.

3. To create a new Hotmail or Outlook.com account, select **Get A New Email Address** and then complete the email address line, specifying whether you want a Hotmail or Outlook suffix.

4. Select **Tab** to verify that the name you entered is available.

5. Complete the rest of the form and then agree to the privacy statement by selecting **I Accept**.

After you have created your Microsoft account, you can connect it to your local or domain account and access cloud services.

CONNECTING YOUR MICROSOFT ACCOUNT TO YOUR DEVICE

To connect your Microsoft account to your local or domain user account, use the following procedure:

1. Sign in with your local account.

2. Open the **Settings** app and select **Accounts**.

3. On the **Your Info** page, select **Sign in with a Microsoft account instead**.

4. On the **Make it yours** page, enter the email address and then select **Sign in**.

5. On the **Enter password** page, enter the password associated with your Microsoft account and select **Sign in**.

6. If prompted, enter your local account password to verify your local identity and select **Next**.

7. The device will now use your Microsoft account to log on. If you want to add additional Microsoft accounts to Windows 10, you can use the **Add a Microsoft account** option found on the **Email & accounts** tab of the **Accounts** page in the **Settings** app.

NEED MORE REVIEW? **SETTING UP MICROSOFT ACCOUNTS ON DEVICES**

For more information about setting up Microsoft accounts on devices, refer to the Microsoft website at *https://account.microsoft.com/account/connect-devices*.

Within an enterprise, you may want to prevent users from associating their Microsoft accounts with a device and block users from accessing cloud resources using their Microsoft accounts.

You can configure Microsoft account restrictions using two GPOs:

- **Block all consumer Microsoft account user authentication**   This setting can prevent users from using Microsoft accounts for authentication for applications or services. Any application or service that has already been authenticated will not be affected by this setting until the authentication cache expires. We recommend that you enable this setting before any user signs in to a device to prevent cached tokens from being present. This GPO is located at Computer Configuration\Administrative Templates\Windows Components\Microsoft account.

- **Accounts: Block Microsoft accounts**   This setting prevents users from adding a Microsoft account within the Settings app. There are two options: Users Can't Add Microsoft Accounts and Users Can't Add Or Log On With Microsoft Accounts. This GPO is located at Computer Configuration\Windows Settings\Security Settings\Local Policies\Security Options.

Understand multifactor authentication

Traditional computer authentication is based on users providing a name and a password. This allows an authentication authority to validate the exchange and grant access. Although password-based authentication is acceptable in many circumstances, Windows 10 provides a number of additional, more secure methods for users to authenticate with their devices, including multifactor authentication (also referred to as two-factor authentication).

Multifactor authentication is based on the principle that users who wish to authenticate must have two (or more) things with which to identify themselves. Specifically, they must have knowledge of something, they must be in possession of something, and they must be something. For example, a user might know a password, possess a security token (in the form of a digital certificate), and be able to prove who they are with biometrics, such as fingerprints.

EXPLORE BIOMETRICS

Biometrics, like a fingerprint, provides more secure and, often, more convenient methods for both users and administrators to be identified and verified. Windows 10 includes native support for biometrics through the Windows Biometric Framework (WBF), and when used as part of a multifactor authentication plan, biometrics is increasingly replacing passwords in modern workplaces.

Biometric information is obtained from the individual and stored as a biometric sample, which is then securely saved in a template and mapped to a specific user. To capture a person's fingerprint, you can use a fingerprint reader (you "enroll" the user when configuring this). Also, you can use a person's face, her retina, or even her voice. The Windows Biometric service can be extended to also include behavioral traits such as body gait and typing rhythm.

Windows includes several Group Policy settings related to biometrics, as shown in Figure 2-14, that you can use to allow or block the use of biometrics from your devices. You can find Group

Policy Objects here: Computer Configuration\Administrative Templates\Windows Components\
Biometrics.

FIGURE 2-14 Biometrics Group Policy settings

Configure Windows Hello and Windows Hello for Business

Windows Hello is a two-factor biometric authentication mechanism built into Windows 10,
and it is unique to the device on which it is set up. Windows Hello allows users to unlock their
devices by using facial recognition, fingerprint scanning, or a PIN.

Windows Hello for Business is the enterprise implementation of Windows Hello and allows
users to authenticate to an Active Directory or Azure Active Directory account, and it enables
them to access network resources. Administrators can configure Windows Hello for Business
using Group Policy or mobile device management (MDM) policy and use asymmetric (public/
private key) or certificate-based authentication.

Windows Hello provides the following benefits:

- Strong passwords can be difficult to remember, and users often reuse passwords on
  multiple sites, which reduces security. Windows Hello allows them to authenticate using
  their biometric data.

- Passwords are vulnerable to replay attacks, and server breaches can expose password-
  based credentials.

- Passwords offer less security because users can inadvertently expose their passwords as a result of phishing attacks.

- Windows Hello helps protect against credential theft. Because a malicious person must have both the device and the biometric information or PIN, it becomes more difficult to hack the authentication process.

- Windows Hello can be used both in cloud-only and hybrid deployment scenarios.

- Windows Hello logs you into your devices three times faster than a password.

If you want to implement Windows Hello, your devices must be equipped with the appropriate hardware. For example, facial recognition requires that you use special cameras that see in infrared (IR) light. These can be external cameras or cameras incorporated into the device. The cameras can reliably tell the difference between a photograph or scan and a living person. For fingerprint recognition, your devices must be equipped with fingerprint readers, which can be external or integrated into laptops or USB keyboards.

If you have previously experienced poor reliability from legacy fingerprint readers, you should review the current generation of sensors, which offer significantly better reliability and are less error-prone.

After you have installed the necessary hardware devices, you can set up Windows Hello by openings Settings, selecting Accounts, and then, on the Sign-In Options page, under Windows Hello, reviewing the options for face or fingerprint. If you do not have Windows Hello–supported hardware, the Windows Hello section does not appear on the Sign-In Options page.

To configure Windows Hello, follow these steps:

1. Open the **Settings** app and select **Accounts**.
2. On the **Accounts** page, select **Sign-in options**.
3. Under **Windows Hello Face**, select **Set up**.
4. Select **Get started** on the **Windows Hello setup** page.
5. Enter your PIN or password to verify your identity.
6. Allow Windows Hello to capture your facial features, as shown in Figure 2-15.
7. Once Windows Hello has captured your facial features, you are presented with an **All Set!** message and you can close the **Windows Hello setup** page.

Users can use Windows Hello for a convenient and secure sign-in method that is tied to the device on which it is set up.

Enterprises that want to enable Windows Hello can configure and manage Windows Hello for Business. Windows Hello for Business uses key-based or certificate-based authentication for users by using Group Policy or MDM policy, or a mixture of both methods.

NEED MORE REVIEW? **WINDOWS HELLO BIOMETRICS IN THE ENTERPRISE**

To review further details about using Windows Hello in the enterprise, refer to the Microsoft website at *https://docs.microsoft.com/windows/access-protection/hello-for-business/hello-biometrics-in-enterprise.*

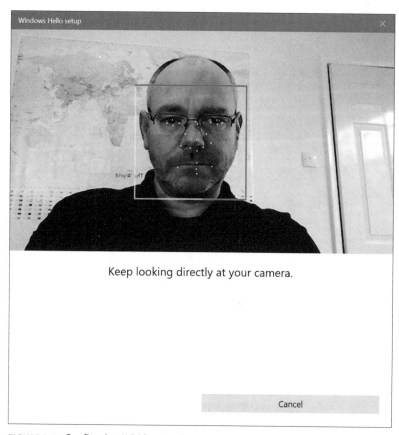

Keep looking directly at your camera.

Cancel

FIGURE 2-15 Configuring Windows Hello

Configure PIN

To avoid authentication with passwords, Microsoft provides an authentication method that uses a PIN. When you set up Windows Hello, you're asked to create a PIN first. This PIN enables you to sign in using the PIN as an alternative to when you can't use your preferred biometric because of an injury or because the sensor is unavailable or not working properly. The PIN provides the same level of protection as Windows Hello.

Windows Hello PIN provides secure authentication without sending a password to an authenticating authority, such as Azure AD or an AD DS domain controller. Windows Hello for Business provides enterprises with compliance with the new FIDO 2.0 (Fast IDentity Online) framework for end-to-end multifactor authentication.

Within a domain environment, a user cannot use a PIN on its own (known as a convenience PIN). You will see from the user interface shown in Figure 2-16 that the PIN settings are known as the Windows Hello PIN. A user must first configure Windows Hello and already be signed in using a local account, a domain account, a Microsoft account, or an Azure AD account. The user is then able to set up PIN authentication that is associated with the credential for the account.

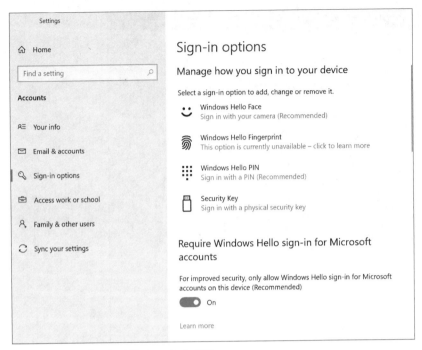

FIGURE 2-16 Configuring Windows Hello PIN

After a user has completed the registration process, Windows Hello for Business generates a new public-private key pair on the device known as a *protector key*. If installed on the device, the Trusted Platform Module (TPM) generates and stores this protector key; if the device does not have a TPM, Windows encrypts the protector key and stores it on the file system. Windows Hello for Business also generates an administrative key that is used to reset credentials if necessary.

> **NOTE PAIRING OF CREDENTIALS AND DEVICES**
>
> Windows Hello for Business pairs a specific device and a user credential. Consequently, the PIN the user chooses is associated only with the signed-in account and that specific device.

The user now has a PIN defined on the device and an associated protector key for that PIN gesture. The user can now securely sign in to their device using the PIN and then add support for a biometric gesture as an alternative for the PIN. The *gesture* can be facial recognition, iris scanning, or fingerprint recognition, depending on available hardware in the device. When a user adds a biometric gesture, it follows the same basic sequence as mentioned in the previous section. The user authenticates to the system by using the PIN and then registers the new biometric. Windows generates a unique key pair and stores it securely. The user can then sign in using the PIN or a biometric gesture.

NEED MORE REVIEW? **WINDOWS HELLO FOR BUSINESS**

To review further details about deploying Windows Hello for Business within an enterprise environment, refer to the Microsoft website at *https://docs.microsoft.com/windows/security/ identity-protection/hello-for-business/hello-identity-verification*.

You can use MDM policies or GPOs to configure settings for Windows Hello for Business in your organization. For example, you can configure a policy that enables or disables the use of biometrics on devices affected by the policy.

NOTE **ENHANCING THE SECURITY OF A PIN**

When we think of a PIN, we generally think of ATMs and four-digit PINs. For securing Windows 10 with Windows Hello for Business, you can significantly increase the level of security by imposing rules on PINs so that, for example, a PIN can require or block special characters, uppercase characters, lowercase characters, and digits. Something like t496A? could be a complex Windows Hello PIN. The maximum length that can be set is 127 characters.

To configure Windows Hello for Business in your organization, you use the appropriate GPOs within the following location:

Computer Configuration\Policies\Administrative Templates\Windows Components\ Windows Hello for Business

To configure PIN complexity with Windows 10 (with and without Windows Hello for Business), you can use the eight PIN Complexity Group Policy settings, which allow you to control PIN creation and management.

These policy settings can be deployed to computers or users. If you deploy settings to both, then the user policy settings have precedence over computer policy settings and GPO conflict resolution is based on the last applied policy. The policy settings included are:

- Require digits
- Require lowercase letters
- Maximum PIN length
- Minimum PIN length
- Expiration
- History
- Require special characters
- Require uppercase letters

In Windows 10, version 1703 and later, the PIN complexity Group Policy settings are located at Administrative Templates\System\PIN Complexity under both the Computer and User Configuration nodes.

If an organization is not using Windows Hello for Business, they can still use the option to set a convenience PIN. A convenience PIN is very different from a Windows Hello for Business PIN because it is merely a wrapper for the user's domain password. This means that the user's password is cached and replaced by Windows when signing in with a convenience PIN.

Since the Anniversary release (Windows 10, version 1607), the option to allow a convenience PIN is disabled by default for domain-joined clients. To modify the option to sign in with the convenience PIN, you can use the Turn On Convenience PIN Sign-In GPO at Group Policy\Computer Configuration\Administrative Templates\System\Logon.

Configure picture password

A picture password is another way to sign in to a computer. This feature does not use Windows Hello or Windows Hello for Business, and therefore, it is not available to be used within a domain-based environment.

You sign in to a touch-enabled device by using a series of three movements consisting of lines, circles, and/or taps. You can pick any picture you want and provide a convenient method of signing in to touch-enabled, stand-alone devices. Picture password combinations are limitless because the pictures that can be used are limitless. Although picture passwords are considered more secure for stand-alone computers than typing a four-digit PIN, a hacker may be able to guess their way into a device by holding the screen up to a light to see where most of the gestures are (by following the smudges on the screen). This is especially true if the user touches the screen only to input the password and rarely uses touch for anything else.

To create a picture password, follow these steps:

1. Open the **Settings** app and select **Accounts**.
2. Select **Sign-in options**.
3. Under **Picture password**, select **Add**.
4. Enter your current account password and select **Choose picture** to browse to and select the picture to use.
5. Adjust the position of the picture and select **Use this picture**.
6. Draw three gestures directly on your screen. Remember that the size, position, and direction of the gestures are stored as part of the picture password.
7. You are prompted to repeat your gestures. If your repeated gestures match, select **Finish**.

There is only one GPO relating to this feature. To disable Picture Password using Local Group Policy, you can use the Turn Off Picture Password Sign-In GPO in the following location:

Computer Configuration\Administrative Templates\System\Logon

Configure Dynamic Lock

Users with smartphones can take advantage of Dynamic Lock, which was introduced with the Creators Update for Windows 10. Dynamic Lock allows users to automatically lock their devices whenever they are not using them. (As of this writing, the iPhone does not support this feature.)

The Dynamic Lock feature relies on a Bluetooth link between your PC and the paired smartphone.

To configure Windows 10 Dynamic Lock, use the following steps:

1. Open the **Settings** app and select **Accounts**.

2. Select **Sign-in options** and scroll to **Dynamic lock.**

3. Select **Allow Windows to detect when you're away and automatically lock the device**.

4. Select **Bluetooth & other devices**.

5. Add your smartphone using Bluetooth and pair it.

6. Return to the **Dynamic lock** page and you should see your connected phone, as shown in Figure 2-17. Your device will be automatically locked whenever Windows detects that your connected smartphone has moved away from your desk for 30 seconds.

You can configure Dynamic Lock functionality for your devices using the Configure Dynamic Lock Factors GPO. You can locate the policy setting at Computer Configuration\Administrative Templates\Windows Components\Windows Hello for Business.

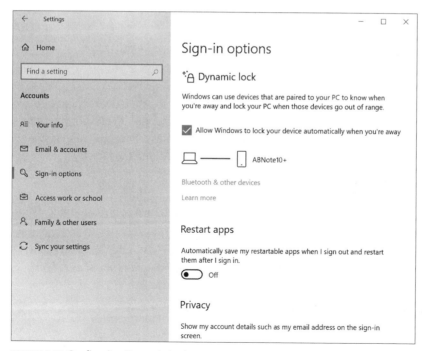

FIGURE 2-17 Configuring Dynamic Lock

Skill 2.2: Configure devices by using local policies

In this skill section, you review how the Windows 10 registry can be used to configure computer settings that may not be available within the Settings app or Control Panel.

Group Policy is a key technology designed to help manage and control how users use Windows 10–based computers. Local Group Policy is the local implementation of these policies, and you need to understand how to configure local settings on your computer using policies.

Finally, in this skill, you will review how to troubleshoot group policies on a computer to identify what policies are effective and how to resolve issues. Some of the tools used to fix policy issues on a local computer can be directly applied to domain-joined devices, and this knowledge is valuable if you must apply the same type of settings to thousands of computers in a domain environment.

> **This skill covers how to**
> - Configure local registry
> - Implement local policy
> - Configure Windows 10 settings by using Group Policy
> - Troubleshoot group policies on devices

Configure local registry

All settings within Windows 10 are ultimately stored in the Windows Registry. This is a database that contains details of all Windows settings, installed software, device drivers, and much more. Without the registry, Windows would not work.

Every reference to working the registry always stipulates that you should take great care when working with or editing the registry. An incorrect registry change can prevent your system from booting and can result in you needing to completely reinstall the operating system. You should always take care and create a system backup before editing the registry.

Understand the registry structure

The registry is a database that is split into multiple separate files known as hives, together with associated log and other support files.

You can find the registry files located in %systemroot%\System32\Config\, though you will need to be an administrator to access this folder. Within this system folder, you should find several binary format "files" that the registry uses:

- SAM (Security Accounts Manager used to store local passwords)
- SECURITY
- SOFTWARE

- SYSTEM
- DEFAULT
- USERDIFF (used only for Windows upgrades)

In addition to the system files, the user-specific settings stored within the user profile are loaded into system memory when a user signs in. These registry files are located in the following locations:

- %userprofile%\ntuser.dat
- %userprofile%\AppData\Local\Microsoft\Windows\UsrClass.dat

Other notable registry files include the Boot Configuration Data (BCD) store, which stores its own file on the boot drive. The local services are located in %SystemRoot%\ServiceProfiles\LocalService and network services are stored in %SystemRoot%\ServiceProfiles\NetworkService.

The vast majority of changes to the hive files are made automatically by Windows whenever you install an application or change a setting or configuration by using the Settings app or Control Panel,

The main hives, or subtrees, that store settings for Windows 10 are shown in Table 2-5.

TABLE 2-5 Registry hives

Hive	Description
HKEY_CLASSES_ROOT	This hive relates to file association information relating to applications installed in the device. For example, it defines that the application for DOCX files is Microsoft Word. This hive contains application information derived from the settings that are stored in the HKEY_LOCAL_MACHINE\Software\Classes and HKEY_CURRENT_USER\Software\Classes hives.
HKEY_CURRENT_USER	This hive contains information for the signed-in user. Personalized settings such as background image, Windows color scheme, and font settings are stored in this hive.
HKEY_LOCAL_MACHINE	This hive stores computer-related configuration settings.
HKEY_USERS	This hive contains user-related configuration settings for all users who have signed in locally to the computer, including the currently signed-in user. The HKEY_CURRENT_USER hive is a subkey of HKEY_USERS. Edits to this hive will affect the user settings for the currently signed-in user.
HKEY_CURRENT_CONFIG	This hive contains current hardware profile information for the local computer.

Should you need to make a manual change, create a new entry, or modify an existing registry entry, these will typically take place in the following two hives:

- HKEY_LOCAL_MACHINE
- HKEY_CURRENT_USER

The primary tool for managing and editing the registry is the built-in registry editor.

Within the hives, settings containing values are stored in subtrees, keys, and subkeys. The hierarchical nature of the registry makes it easy to locate a registry value. Here is an example of a key, subkeys, and value:

`Computer\HKEY_CURRENT_USER\Control Panel\Mouse`

This key holds many subkeys, which Windows uses to store settings for the mouse.

The mouse settings can be modified in the registry, as shown in Figure 2-18, or by using the Mouse item within Control Panel. If you enable mouse pointer trails in Control Panel, the registry subkey for MouseTrails is modified to have a value of 7.

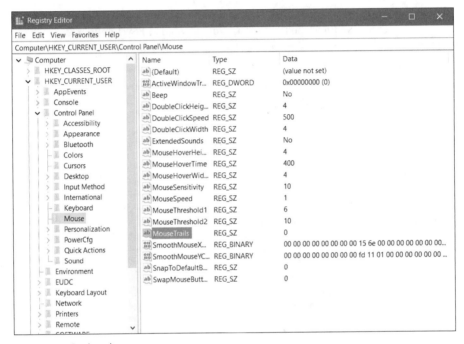

FIGURE 2-18 Registry keys

Values are stored within each key and subkey that are used to configure the operating system. Several value types are used to store information such as numerical data, text, and variables such as file paths. Often a value is empty or not defined, as shown in the (Default) subkey in Figure 2-18, which shows (value not set). Table 2-6 lists common types of registry values.

TABLE 2-6 Registry value types

Value Type	Data Type	Description
REG_BINARY	Binary	Raw binary data. Values are normally displayed in hexadecimal format. Hardware information is often stored in these values.
REG_DWORD	DWORD	4-byte numbers (a 32-bit integer). Device-driver and service-related values are stored in these values.

Value Type	Data Type	Description
REG_SZ	String	A fixed-length text string. Most of the values listed in the \HKEY_CURRENT_USER\Control Panel\Mouse keys are REG_SZ values.
REG_EXPAND_SZ	Expandable string	A variable length text string. Windows uses REG_EXPAND_SZ values to contain variables, such as file system paths.
REG_MULTI_SZ	Multiple strings	Multiple string values. These values are typically used when multiple values are required.

Understand the Registry Editor

The built-in Registry Editor (Regedit.exe) allows you to view, search, and modify the registry's contents. Some common tasks that administrators can perform using the Registry Editor tool are as follows:

- Search the registry for a value, value name, subkey, or key
- Create, delete, and modify keys, subkeys, and values
- Import entries into the registry from an external (REG) file
- Export entries from the registry into an external (REG) file
- Back up the entire registry
- Manage the HKEY_LOCAL_MACHINE and HKEY_USERS registry hives on a remote computer

You can also import registry keys and values directly into the registry using a text file with the .reg extension.

All REG files will use the following syntax for Registry Editor to understand them:

```
Windows Registry Editor Version 5.00
[<Hive name>\<Key name>\<Subkey name>]
"Value name"=<Value type>:<Value data>
```

Because REG files are associated with the registry, executing a REG file will merge it with—or import it to—the local Windows Registry. The contents of the REG file will add, delete, or modify one or more keys or values in the registry. Depending on the changes contained within the REG file, you might need to restart your computer after the changes have been made.

You can also use the Import option on the File menu within the Registry Editor to import the settings, or you can use the command line with a script similar to the following example:

```
regedit /s C:\\Registry\\regsetting.reg \> nul
```

Use PowerShell to manage registry settings

The registry can be accessed directly using Windows PowerShell. The registry provider within PowerShell displays the registry like a file system, displaying the keys and subkeys as subfolders within a registry hive.

Windows PowerShell uses the abbreviated form of the hive nomenclature where the HKEY_LOCAL_MACHINE hive becomes HKLM and HKEY_LOCAL_USER becomes HKLU.

To view the registry using Windows PowerShell, open an elevated Windows PowerShell command prompt and then type the following, pressing Enter after each line:

```
Get-ChildItem -Path hklm:
Dir
```

You can also obtain a richer output by using this PowerShell command:

```
Get-Childitem -ErrorAction SilentlyContinue | Format-Table Name, SubKeyCount, ValueCount
-AutoSize
```

To create a new registry key, you can first use the Set-Location cmdlet to change to the appropriate registry subtree and key as shown here:

```
Set-Location "HKCU:\Software"
```

Alternatively, you can use the full path to the registry key in the cmdlet as follows:

```
New-Item -Path HKCU:\Software -Name "Demonstration" -Force
```

Use the following cmdlet to assign the new registry key a value of "demo":

```
Set-Item -Path HKCU:\Software\Demonstration -Value "demo"
```

To validate that the key value has been stored correctly, view the key in the registry, or enter the following:

```
Get-Item -Path HKCU:\Software\Demonstration
```

Implement local policy

Local Security Policy allows you to configure various security policies on a local computer. The computer may or may not be domain joined. When used in a domain-based environment, local policies can be used to affect all computers in the domain. Only the Windows 10 Pro, Enterprise, and Education editions provide access to the Local Security Policy console. For Windows 10 Home edition, the settings and rights are predefined and unchangeable.

With Local Security Policy, you create rules so that you can manage users' computers. You can apply configuration settings that can affect a single device when deployed using the Local Group Policy Editor. When settings are configured using Group Policy within a domain environment, the settings can be deployed from one to thousands of targeted devices. When a policy has been configured, standard users cannot modify a managed policy setting.

Local Security Policy is a subset of the Local Group Policy Object Editor (gpedit.msc). You can see the same settings by using the dedicated tool called Local Security Policy Editor, as shown in Figure 2-19. To launch the tool, follow these instructions:

1. Log on to Windows 10 with administrative privileges.

2. Select **Start** and search for **Secpol.msc**.

3. Select the **Secpol.msc** link to open the **Local Security Policy** editor.

4. Expand both **Account Policies** and **Local Policies**.

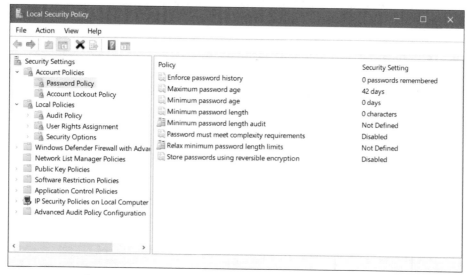

FIGURE 2-19 Local Security Policy

Within Local Security Policy, you can find the following sections:

- **Account Policies**   These include local account Password Policy and Account Lockout Policy. These allow you to configure the device password history, maximum and minimum password age, password complexity, and password length. You can also configure what action will be taken when a user enters an incorrect password during logon.

- **Local Policies**   These include Audit Policy, User Rights Assignment, and Security Options, and they allow you to enable/disable auditing, configure user rights (including the ability to log on locally to the device), access the computer from the network, and have the right to shut down the system. In this section, you will also find settings to configure many security settings, such as interactive logon settings, User Account Control settings, and shutdown settings.

- **Windows Defender Firewall With Advanced Security**   These are used to configure the local firewall settings.

- **Network List Manager Policies**   These enable you to configure whether users can configure new network properties, including the network name, location, and icon.

- **Public Key Policies**   These allow you to configure settings for Certificate Auto-Enrollment and the Encrypting File System (EFS) Data Recovery Agents.

- **Software Restrictions Policies**   These are used to identify and control which applications can run on the local computer.

- **Application Control Policies**   These are used to configure AppLocker.

- **IP Security Policies on Local Computer** These allow you to create, manage, and assign IPsec policies.
- **Advanced Audit Policy Configuration** These allow you to provide additional fine-tuning and control when using audit policies.

Configure a password policy

On a local device, if you want to ensure that all users use secure passwords and that the passwords are changed after a set number of days, you can configure a password policy as follows:

1. Log on to Windows 10 with administrative privileges.
2. Select **Start** and search for **Secpol.msc**.
3. Select the **Secpol.msc** link to open the **Local Security Policy** editor.
4. Expand **Account Policies** and select **Password Policy**.
5. Select **Enforce password history**. You can now enter a value that represents the number of unique new passwords that a user account must have used before an old password can be reused.
6. Enter **5** and select **OK** to set this policy.
7. Double-click **Maximum password age**. The default setting is 42, which allows a user to use their password over a 42-day period before they are forced to change it. The best practice is to have passwords expire every 30 to 90 days.
8. Enter **90** and select **OK**.
9. Double-click **Minimum password age**. The default setting is 0 days, which allows users to change their passwords whenever they like. A setting of 14 days prevents users from changing their password in rapid succession to bypass the password history setting.
10. Enter **14** and select **OK**.
11. Double-click **Minimum password length**. The default is set to 0 characters. A setting of 8 would require that a password must be at least 8 characters long.
12. Enter **8** and select **OK**.
13. Double-click **Password must meet complexity requirements**. This setting is disabled by default. Once set to enabled, all passwords need to be complex.
14. Double-click **Store passwords using reversible encryption**. The default is disabled. If you enable this policy, all passwords are stored in a way that all applications are able access the password, which also makes them vulnerable to hackers to access.
15. Close the **Local Security Policy** editor.

The changes relating to local passwords become effective immediately once the policy is configured. Users with existing passwords can continue to use them until they need to be changed. The next time a user changes their password, the new password will need to conform with the settings in the Password Policy.

Configure an account lockout policy

When you implement a strong password policy, it is recommended that you also configure an account lockout policy, which helps to protect accounts from password-cracking tools, which can attempt thousands of different passwords every hour in the hope that they succeed. Within a local environment, even an employee can try to guess a password to gain access to a system.

This brute-force attack on a system cannot be prevented. However, you can implement measures within the account lockout policy that monitor incorrect attempts to log in to a local device. If a brute-force attack is suspected (for example, five incorrect passwords are entered in quick succession), then the account can be locked for a period of time.

To define that lockout policy, use the following steps:

1. Log on to Windows 10 with administrative privileges.
2. Select **Start** and search for **Secpol.msc**.
3. Select the **Secpol.msc** link to open the **Local Security Policy** editor.
4. Expand **Account Policies** and select **Account Lockout Policy**.
5. Double-click **Account lockout threshold**, enter **3**, and select **OK**.
6. When the **Account lockout threshold** has been set, Windows suggests two other settings:

    - **Account lockout duration**   This setting specifies how long, in minutes, the user account will remain locked once the threshold has been reached.

    - **Reset account lockout counter after**   This setting specifies how long, in minutes, before the count of incorrect passwords entered is set back to 0.

7. Leave these settings as recommended and select **OK**.

Configure local policy

Local policies are used to control users once they have logged on and gained access to a system. You can configure policies that implement auditing, specify user rights, and set security options.

Audit policy

Audit policies are used to track specified user actions on a device. These actions are recorded as a success or a failure, such as accessing a file or being blocked from printing a document. Auditing is costly because system resources are required to constantly monitor a system and record actions to the audit logs. Audit settings can generate many log items, and this may impede a computer's performance. Therefore, you should use auditing on selective actions and turn off the feature when it is no longer required.

Auditing allows you to create a history of specific tasks and actions, such as file access (Audit Object Access policy), user account deletion (Audit Account Management) or successful logon attempts (Audit Account Logon Events). Often, auditing is used to identify security violations that arise; security violations could include, for example, when users attempt to access system management tasks or files within File Explorer for which they do not have permission. In this example, failed attempts to access resources will be logged in the audit log, with details of the user account, time, and details of the resources for which access was denied because of insufficient privileges.

Configuring audit policy involves three components:

- Enable auditing within Local Policies for success or failure (or both) for specific events or actions.
- For object access, such as file system files and folders, enable auditing on the objects to be audited.
- Use Event Viewer to view the results of the audit in the security log.

To view the various settings that can be configured using audit policy, view the audit policy options in Table 2-7.

TABLE 2-7 Audit policy options

Policy Description	Description
Audit Account Logon Events	Tracks user logon activity on their local device or to a domain (if domain auditing is enabled).
Audit Account Management	Tracks user and group account management, including creation, deletion, and password changes.
Audit Directory Service Access	Tracks access to Active Directory objects by a user within a domain.
Audit Logon Events	Audits events related to local account activity, such as running a logon script, accessing a member server, or using a device that uses a local account to generate a logon event.
Audit Object Access	Enables auditing of access to the file system and registry objects, including files, folders, printers, hives, and values.

Policy Description	Description
Audit Policy Change	Tracks any changes to user rights assignment policies, audit policies, or trust policies, such as assigning, removing, creating, changing, starting, or stopping policies.
Audit Privilege Use	Tracks each instance of when a user exercises a user right that has been assigned to their user account.
Audit Process Tracking	Tracks events when a program is activated, when a new process is created or exited, or if a user attempts to install a service.
Audit System Events	Tracks system events, such as when a user shuts down or restarts their computer and when an event occurs that affects either the system security or the security log.

To configure an audit policy to monitor account logon events, use these steps:

1. Log on to Windows 10 with administrative privileges.

2. Select **Start** and search for **Secpol.msc**.

3. Select the **Secpol.msc** link to open the **Local Security Policy** editor.

4. Expand **Local Policies** and select **Audit Policy**.

5. Double-click the **Audit account logon events** policy and select **Success** and **Failure**.

6. Select **OK**.

7. Log off the device and attempt to log back on as an administrator, but use an incorrect password. Allow the logon to fail.

8. Log on as an administrator using the correct password.

9. Select **Start** and search for **Event Viewer**.

10. Select the **Event Viewer** app to open the **Event Viewer**.

11. Expand **Windows Logs** and select the **Security Log**. You should see the audited events listed with an Event ID of 4624 and a **Task Category** of **Logon**, as shown in Figure 2-20.

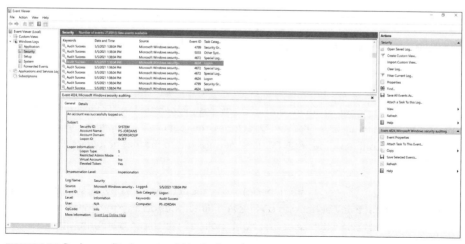

FIGURE 2-20 Review audited events within the Security Log

User rights assignment

The user rights policies are used to determine what rights a user or group of users have on a device. Often, there is confusion between rights and permissions, and you should be clear that user rights, or privileges, apply to the system and relate to activities or tasks that the user can perform.

Here are some of the activities that you can grant to a user:

- Add Workstations To Domain
- Allow Log On Locally
- Allow Log On Through Remote Desktop Services
- Back Up Files And Directories
- Change The System Time
- Deny Log On Locally
- Shut Down The System
- Take Ownership Of Files Or Other Objects

To configure a user to have the right to perform a backup of a device, use the following steps:

1. Log on to Windows 10 with administrative privileges.
2. Select **Start** and search for **Secpol.msc**.
3. Select the **Secpol.msc** link to open the **Local Security Policy** editor.
4. Expand **Local Policies** and select **User Rights Assignment**.
5. Double-click the user right **Back up files and directories**.
6. Select **Add User or Group**. The **Select Users or Groups** dialog box appears.
7. Enter the name of the user or group to which you want to grant the right or select the **Advanced** button and then select **Find Now**. Select the user or group of users within the list.
8. Select **OK**.
9. Select **OK** in the **Select Users or Groups** dialog box.
10. In the **Back Up Files and Directories** properties dialog box, select **OK**.

> **NOTE   USER RIGHTS ASSIGNMENT**
>
> A user may be given a right that could contradict any existing permissions. For example, if a user is given the right to Back Up Files And Directories, the user can back up files and folders even if the user does not have specific NTFS-level permissions to the files or folders.

Remember, a right authorizes a user to perform specific actions on a device, such as logging on to a computer interactively or backing up files and directories on a system. Before leaving this section, you should review the list of user rights policies, which can be found within the User Rights Assignment node of the Local Policies.

Security Options

The Security Options section of the local policies includes many options, which are used to allow or restrict activities on the device.

Here are some of the activities that you can configure with Security Options:

- **Accounts** Block Microsoft Accounts
- **Interactive Logon** Do Not Require CTRL+ALT+DEL
- **Interactive Logon** Don't Display Username At Sign-In
- **User Account Control** Admin Approval Mode For Built-In Administrator Account

Nearly all the several dozen settings have their default settings set to Not Defined. Once configured, a setting can have the following statuses:

- **Enabled** or **Disabled**
- **Text entry** (For example, a user account name, or a system path)
- **Value** (For example, the number of previous logons to cache for when a domain controller is not available)

One area of the Security Options that you should pay attention to is the User Account Control (UAC) settings. We will cover UAC in detail in the next skill, but you should note that you can configure UAC using policy settings in this area of Local Policy.

EXAM TIP

For the exam, you should know how to set local group policies and understand the purpose of account policies and local policies. Work through the examples showing how to configure password policies and account lockout policies. Review the various audit policies, user rights assignments, and security options that are available.

Configure Windows 10 settings by using Group Policy

Generally, when we refer to Group Policy, we are referring to Group Policy Objects (GPO) containing GPO settings that are created by IT administrators and pushed over the network to affect devices within a domain environment. Local policy, or Local Group Policy, refers to policy settings that are locally administered and configured.

Within a managed environment, IT administrators can control nearly any setting on a device using policy. When AD DS is installed on one or more Windows servers with the domain controller role, administrators can centrally manage AD DS objects using a console app, such as Active Directory Administrative Center on Windows Server. Centrally managing Group Policy allows for easier and more efficient management of the settings, as well as the ability to manage devices at scale.

Devices that are managed by Active Directory are commonly referred to as domain-joined. User accounts that are managed by AD are often referred to as domain users, and their domain username or LDAP username is used when they sign on to their device to access resources.

Group Policy settings

When you configure a Group Policy setting, you are configuring a specific change to apply to an object (something configurable such as a device, a user, or a printer) that is held within AD DS. Group Policy has thousands of configurable settings. Nearly every aspect of Windows 10 can be modified by Group Policy, such as the Edge browser, the firewall, users' rights, and security settings. Group Policy also allows IT administrators to configure settings in older versions of Windows Server and Windows operating systems, and therefore the number of GPOs has grown with each new version of Windows. Only settings that are compatible with the device receiving the policy will be applied, and if a device is configured with an older Group Policy setting, then the Group Policy setting will be ignored.

Most Group Policy settings have three states that can be configured:

- **Not Configured** The GPO does not modify the existing configuration of the setting for the user or computer.
- **Enabled** The GPO applies the policy setting.
- **Disabled** The GPO reverses the policy setting.

By default, most Group Policy settings are set to Not Configured.

Group Policy Management Editor

The Group Policy Management Editor is the tool that enables you to view and configure the individual Group Policy settings on a Windows 10 device. GPOs are organized in a hierarchy as shown here:

Computer Configuration Settings These settings modify the HKEY_LOCAL_MACHINE hive of the registry.

User Configuration Settings These settings modify the HKEY_CURRENT_USER hive of the registry.

These top-level settings each have three areas of configuration, as described in Table 2-8.

TABLE 2-8 Group Policy settings structure

Section	Description
Software Settings	Contains software settings that can be deployed to either the user or the device. Software that deploys or publishes to a user is specific to that user. Software that deploys to a device is available to all users of that device.
Windows Settings	Contains startup and shutdown script settings and printer settings for both the user and the device, and password policies and firewall settings for the device only.
Administrative Templates	Contains hundreds of settings that modify the Windows operating system to control various aspects of the user and computer environment. New administrative templates can be downloaded from vendors or Microsoft and then imported to expand the number of GPOs available on a device.

IT administrators use the Group Policy Management Console to the configure GPOs that are then managed by AD DS. An IT administrator or local administrator can manage individual devices using the Local Group Policy Editor. To open the Local Group Policy Editor, follow these steps:

1. Select **Start** and enter **gpedit.msc.**

2. Select **Edit Group Policy** to launch the **Local Group Policy** editor.

Even if a device is managed using GPOs within an AD DS environment, each device will also have the default local policy. This local GPO is the least influential of all GPOs and any settings can be overwritten by GPOs that are created at higher levels within the environment such as a site, domain, or organizational unit (OU). You should be careful when using GPOs because misconfiguring a GPO can lock you out of specific apps or even the device itself.

Troubleshoot Group Policies on devices

Diving deep into Group Policy would double the size of this book, but you should understand how to perform basic troubleshooting of Group Policies on Windows 10 devices.

Sometime a Group Policy can fail to be applied successfully. There can be many reasons for these failures, including incorrect GPO settings, poor network connection, or failure of the Group Policy Client service.

Troubleshooting tools

You can use many tools to investigate GPO-related issues, including the Resultant Set of Policy (RSoP.msc) tool within the GUI and Group Policy Result (GPResult) from the command line.

CONNECTION ISSUES

- There are several preliminary troubleshooting areas that you should verify before proceeding to use the specialist GPO tools. These relate to the essential services, network connection, and time synchronization:

- **Group Policy Client Service**   Before troubleshooting Group Policy, you should verify the status of the required services for the GPO. Check that the Group Policy Client service has the status of Running or Automatic within the Services utility.

- **Network Connection**   Verify the network connection and configuration. This can be achieved by running the Network Adapter troubleshooter within the Settings app to find and fix issues automatically. Without a reliable network connection, your device will not be able to connect to the domain controller and obtain Group Policy.

- **Time**   The device time needs to be within five minutes of the time on the server. If there is more than a five-minute time difference, then problems with Active Directory synchronization can occur, which can then affect GPO delivery.

RESULTANT SET OF POLICY TOOL

The Resultant Set of Policy (RSoP) tool is a diagnostic tool that is used to check and trouble-shoot Group Policy settings. RSoP is built into Windows 10 and can be used to view the policies being applied to users and devices, and it can identify where the policy settings are coming from. It can also be used to simulate GPO settings for planning purposes.

There are two modes in which RsoP can be run: Logging Mode and Planning Mode.

- **Logging Mode**   Generates a report on policy settings for users and computers and is used to verify and troubleshoot Group Policy settings.
- **Planning Mode**   Used for "what if" scenarios, such as: If a user or computer is moved to a different Active Directory AD group, will they still receive the expected GPOs?

To run RSoP to determine computer and user policy settings, perform these steps:

1. Log on to Windows 10 with administrative privileges.
2. Select **Start** and enter **rsop.msc**.
3. Select the **rsop.msc** link to open the **Resultant Set of Policy** tool.
4. RSoP will run and generate a report for the user and computer policy settings.
5. Review the policy settings that have been applied to the system by any Group Policy Objects that are in effect.
6. To verify that the policies that you have linked are being applied, you should compare the system results to those that are expected.

To simulate GPO policy settings, you can use the planning mode of the Resultant Set of Policy tool. You would open the RSoP tool from Microsoft Management Console and add the Resultant Set Of Policy snap-in, follow the wizard, and select Generate RSoP Data while in Planning Mode.

GPRESULT

The GPResult command-line tool provides a powerful method of verifying what Group Policy Objects are applied to a user or computer. The tool creates a report that displays the GPOs that have been applied to a system and separates the results into the user and computer settings.

Follow these steps to display all GPOs that have been applied to a system:

1. Log on to Windows 10 with administrative privileges.
2. Right-click **Start** and select **Windows PowerShell (Admin)**.
3. Confirm the **User Account Control** warning, if prompted.
4. Type **gpresult /r** and press **Enter**. You should see the RSoP data for your logged-in user and device.

The output of the `gpresult /r` command will display information such as the following:

- The applied GPO(s) name(s)
- Order of GPO application
- GPO details and the last time Group Policy was applied
- Domain and domain functional level

- Which domain controller issued the GPO
- Network speed link threshold
- Which security groups the user and computer are a member of
- Details of GPO filtering

You can fine-tune the report to select only the user or computer GPOs by limiting the command scope as follows:

- If you don't want to see both user and computer GPOs, then you can use the scope option to specify a user or computer.
- To display GPOs applied to a specific user:

```
gpresult /r /scope:user
```

- To display GPOs applied to a specific computer:

```
gpresult /r /scope:computer
```

- To display GPOs applied on a remote computer, you can use this command:

```
gpresult /s Laptop123 /r
```

- To generate an HTML report of the GPResult, as shown in Figure 2-21, you can use this command:

```
gpresult /h c:\GPOreport.html
```

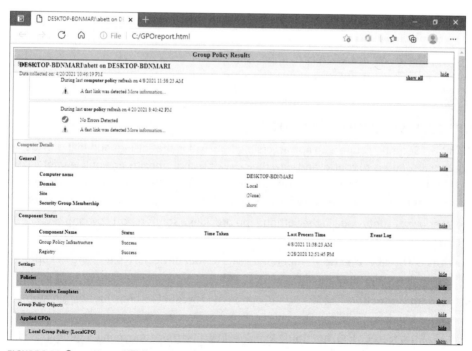

FIGURE 2-21 Generate an HTML report using GPResult

Skill 2.3: Manage Windows Security

In this skill section, you review how to keep Windows 10 secure by using features built into Windows. Devices and users need to be protected while online, and they rely on the built-in defense features, which provide resilience against ever-increasing threats.

You will review the Windows Security features and options that help maintain your device's health and manage threat-protection settings.

You will also review how to use User Account Control (UAC) to help you control administrative privilege elevation in Windows 10 to reduce security risks.

Windows Defender Firewall provides a significant security barrier that helps isolate and protect Windows from external threats, and you will need to understand how to configure and maintain the firewall.

Finally, you need to understand the various encryption methods available with Windows 10 and when to use Encrypting File System (EFS) and BitLocker.

> **This skill covers how to**
> - Configure Windows Security
> - Configure User Account Control
> - Configure Windows Defender Firewall
> - Implement encryption
> - Configure BitLocker
> - Configure Windows Defender Antivirus

Configure Windows Security

The Windows Security feature is an app accessible from within the Settings app that provides a single portal for users to control and view their device security, health, and online safety. The Windows Security section within the Settings app, as shown in Figure 2-22, contains an overview of the status of Windows security features, as well as links to other settings and support.

The Windows Security page in the Settings app provides a status report covering seven areas of security:

- **Virus & Threat Protection**   Monitor threats to your device, run scans, and get updates to help detect the latest threats.
- **Account Protection**   Access sign-in options and account settings, including features such as Windows Hello and Dynamic Lock.
- **Firewall & Network Protection**   Manage firewall settings and monitor network and internet connections.

- **App & Browser Control** Review and update settings for Windows Defender Smart-Screen and configure exploit protection settings.
- **Device Security** Review built-in security options that use virtualization-based security to help protect your device from attacks by malicious software.
- **Device Performance & Health** View the status information about your device's performance health.
- **Family Options** Use features, such as Parental Controls, that allow you to keep track of your kids' online activity.

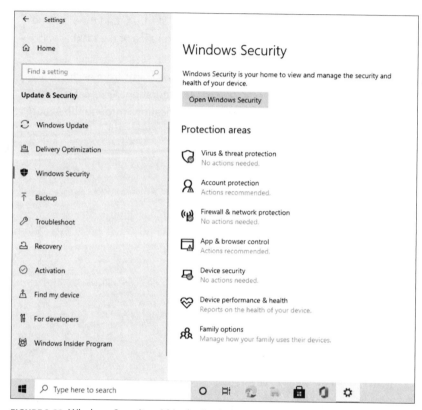

FIGURE 2-22 Windows Security within the Settings app

From the summary portal, you can review the color-coded status icons, which indicate the level of safety of the system:

- **Green tick** The device is sufficiently protected, and there aren't any recommended actions.
- **Yellow exclamation** There is a safety recommendation that should be reviewed.
- **Red warning** This is a warning indicating that something needs immediate attention.

From within the Settings app, you can launch the individual security elements, or launch the stand-alone Windows Security app by clicking the Open Windows Security button, shown previously in Figure 2-22.

> **NOTE WINDOWS DEFENDER SECURITY CENTER**
>
> In previous versions of Windows 10, Windows Security is called Windows Defender Security Center.

When a Windows Security item requires action from the user, like updating the virus and threat protection definitions, the shield icon within the notification area of the taskbar will show a red cross to indicate action is required.

The Windows Security app, as shown in Figure 2-23, collects the status from each of the included security features and allows you to perform some configuration. As updates are collated by the Windows Security app, they will also trigger notifications through the Action Center.

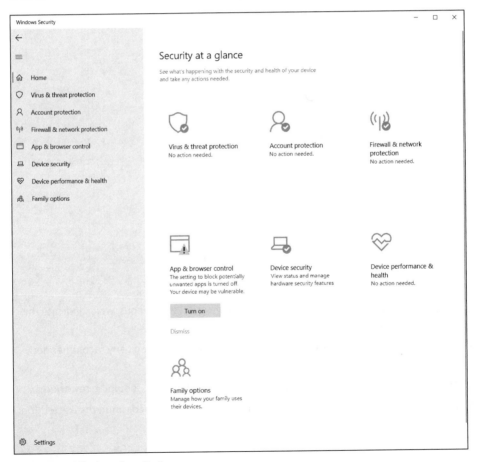

FIGURE 2-23 Windows Security App

It is possible to customize the view of the Windows Security app. Administrators can add support information about your organization in a contact card to the Windows Security app, and admins can hide entire sections of the app by using Group Policy. Hidden sections will not appear on the home page of the Windows Security app, and their icons will not be shown on the navigation bar on the side of the app.

NEED MORE REVIEW?   **THE WINDOWS SECURITY APP**

To review further details about configuring the Windows Security app, refer to the Microsoft website at *https://docs.microsoft.com/windows/security/threat-protection/ windows-defender-security-center/windows-defender-security-center*.

Configure User Account Control

Once a user has gained access to the operating system following successful sign-on, the Windows 10 feature called *User Account Control* (UAC) prevents unauthorized changes to the system.

Systems that suffer from malware attacks can easily be compromised if the malware can effectively use administrative access and wreak havoc on the system. This creates extra work for the help desk, increases support costs, and reduces productivity. UAC has been very successful in preventing users and malware from using administrative credentials to harm a system.

Beginning with Windows 10, administrators no longer have "always on" full access to the system. Rather than enabling administrators to implement systemwide changes, UAC presents administrators with a challenge pop-up prompt to force them to confirm their actions. Similarly, a standard user who attempts to change system settings will receive a UAC prompt, which requires administrative credentials to be provided. If the proper admin credentials are not provided, the user is denied the ability to make the requested changes.

Since the introduction of UAC in Microsoft Vista, Microsoft has fine-tuned the UAC process with the aim of making the use of UAC less frustrating for all users by reducing the number of application and system tasks that require elevation.

UAC offers various layers of protection, with the UAC prompt being the most visible to the user. The following features complement UAC:

- File and Registry Redirection
- Installer Detection
- UAC prompt
- ActiveX Installer Service
- Secure Desktop
- Application Information Service

Standard users

Except for administrators, all users are standard users with few privileges and limited ability to make changes to the system, such as installing software or modifying the date and time. Standard user accounts are described as "operating with least privilege." Here is a list of system tasks that a standard user can perform:

- Change the desktop background and modify display settings
- View firewall settings
- Change the time zone
- Add a printer
- Change their own user account password
- Configure accessibility options
- Configure power options
- Connect to a wireless or LAN connection
- Install drivers, either from Windows Update or those that are supplied with Windows 10
- Install updates by using Windows Update
- Use Remote Desktop to connect to another computer
- Pair and configure a Bluetooth device with the device
- Perform other troubleshooting, network diagnostic, and repair tasks
- Play CD/DVD media
- Restore own files from File History
- View most settings, although elevated permissions will be required when attempting to change Windows settings

UAC prevents you from making unauthorized or hidden (possibly malware-initiated) changes to your system that require administrator-level permissions. A UAC elevation prompt is displayed to notify you, as follows:

- **Prompt For Consent** This is displayed to administrators in Admin Approval Mode whenever an administrative task is requested. Select Yes to continue if you consent.
- **Prompt For Credentials** This is displayed if you are a standard user attempting to perform an administrative task. An administrator needs to enter their password into the UAC prompt to continue.

When an administrator provides permissions to a standard user via a UAC prompt, the permissions are only temporarily operative, and the permissions are returned to a standard user level once the isolated task has finished.

Standard users can become frustrated when they are presented with the UAC prompt, and Microsoft has reduced the frequency and necessity for elevation. Following are some common scenarios wherein a standard user would be prompted by UAC to provide administrative privileges. You will see that they are not necessarily daily tasks for most users:

- Add or remove a user account
- Browse to another user's directory
- Change user account types
- Change Windows Defender Firewall settings
- Configure Windows Update settings
- Install a driver for a device not included in Windows or Windows Update
- Install ActiveX controls
- Install or uninstall applications
- Modify UAC settings
- Move or copy files to the Program Files or Windows folders
- Restore system backup files
- Schedule automated tasks

Administrative users

Administrative users need to be limited to authorized personnel within the organization. In addition to the ability to perform all tasks that a standard user can perform, they have the following far-reaching permissions:

- Read/Write/Change permissions for all resources
- All Windows permissions

From this, it looks as if administrators have considerable power, which can potentially be hijacked by malware. Thankfully, by default, administrators are still challenged with the UAC prompt, which pops up when they perform a task that requires administrative permissions. However, they are not required to reenter their administrative credentials. This is known as Admin Approval Mode.

A user who signs on to a system with administrative permissions will be granted two tokens:

- The first token enables them to operate as a standard user.
- The second token can be used when the administrator performs a task that requires administrative permissions.

Just as with the standard user, after the task is completed using elevated status, the account reverts to a standard-user privilege.

Types of elevation prompts

UAC has four types of dialog boxes, as shown in Table 2-9. The Description column explains how users need to respond to the prompt.

TABLE 2-9 UAC elevation prompts

Type of Elevation Prompt	Description
A Windows 10 setting or feature needs your permission to start.	This item has a valid digital signature that verifies that Microsoft is the publisher of this item, and it is usually safe to use the application.
A non-Windows 10 application needs your permission to start.	This application has a valid digital signature, and it is usually safe to use the application.
An application with an unknown publisher needs your permission to start.	This application does not have a valid digital signature from its publisher. Use extra caution and verify that the application is safe before using. Search the internet for the program's name to determine whether it is a known trustworthy application or malware.
You have been blocked by your system administrator from running this application.	This application has been blocked because it is known to be untrusted. To run this application, you need to contact your system administrator to remove the restriction, if appropriate.

Within large organizations, nearly all users will be configured to sign in to their computer with a standard user account. On a managed system that has been provisioned and deployed by the IT department, standard user accounts should have little need to contact the help desk regarding UAC issues. They can browse the internet, send email, and use applications without an administrator account. Home users and small businesses that lack a centralized IT resource to provision and manage their devices are often found to use administrative user accounts.

As with previous versions of Windows, an administrator can determine when the UAC feature will notify you if changes are attempted on your computer.

To configure UAC, use the following procedure.

1. Log on to Windows 10 with administrative privileges.

2. Select **Start** and enter **UAC**.

3. Select **Change User Account Control Settings** to be shown the **User Account Control Settings** screen where you can adjust the UAC settings, as shown in Figure 2-24.

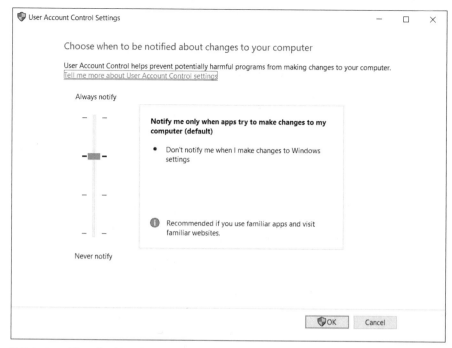

FIGURE 2-24 Changing User Account Control Settings

You need to review the information in this dialog box by moving the slider to each position in order to determine how the UAC feature will behave with each setting. The default is Notify Me Only When Applications Try To Make Changes To My Computer.

Table 2-10 shows the four settings that enable customization of the elevation prompt experience.

TABLE 2-10 User Account Control Settings

Prompt	Description
Never notify	UAC prompting is disabled.
Notify me only when applications try to make changes to my computer (do not dim my desktop)	When an application makes a change, a UAC prompt appears. However, if the user makes a change to system settings, the UAC prompt is not displayed. The desktop does not dim.
Notify me only when applications try to make changes to my computer (default)	When an application makes a change, a UAC prompt appears. However, if the user makes a change to system settings, the UAC prompt is not displayed. Secure desktop feature is active.
Always notify	The user is always prompted when changes are made to the computer by applications or by the user.

The settings enable changes to the UAC prompting behavior only, and do not elevate the status of the underlying user account.

> **NEED MORE REVIEW?** **USER ACCOUNT CONTROL**
>
> To review further details about configuring UAC, refer to the Microsoft website at *https://docs.microsoft.com/windows/security/identity-protection/user-account-control/user-account-control-overview.*

In addition to the UAC settings within the GUI, there are many more UAC security settings that can be configured via Group Policy. These can be found here: Computer Configuration\Windows Settings\Security Settings\Local Policies\Security Options.

EXAM TIP

You need to take time to review the UAC settings configurable by Group Policy, with attention to the settings that feature Admin Approval Mode.

Secure Desktop

When UAC prompts the user for consent or elevated credentials, it first switches to a feature called Secure Desktop, which focuses only on the UAC prompt. In addition, Secure Desktop prevents other applications (including malware) from interacting with the user or influencing the user response to the UAC prompt.

While it is possible for malware to generate a screen that imitates the look of Secure Desktop (and even re-create the visual UAC prompt), it is not possible for malware to actually provide UAC with the correct credentials. If a system was infected with malware, it could try to bypass the UAC security setting—using a bogus credential prompt to harvest usernames and passwords from unsuspecting users—and then use these credentials on genuine UAC prompts. Therefore, it is important that administrators are vigilant against potential malware attacks, and all devices are set to ensure that their malware protection is configured to automatically update.

> **NOTE** **UAC INTEGRATION WITH THE ANTIMALWARE SCAN INTERFACE**
>
> The Antimalware Scan Interface (AMSI) enables Windows applications and services to integrate with antimalware products on a device. If the AMSI detects malware behind the UAC elevation request, the admin privilege is blocked.

Configure Windows Defender Firewall

After you connect a computer to a network, you might expose the computer to security risks. To mitigate these possible risks, you can implement several network security features in Windows 10, including Windows Defender Firewall.

Windows Defender Firewall blocks or allows network traffic based on the properties of that traffic. You can configure how Windows Defender Firewall controls the flow of network traffic by using configurable rules. In addition to blocking or allowing network traffic, Windows Defender Firewall can filter traffic, implement authentication, and apply encryption to this filtered traffic.

The way in which you configure Windows Defender Firewall and your network location profiles can have a significant effect on file and printer sharing, and it can affect the discoverability of your device on connected networks.

Configure Firewall & Network Protection

Within the Windows Security app is the Firewall & Network Protection page. This page provides a unified interface for accessing firewall and network protection features, and it consolidates several firewall-related components that are found within the Windows Defender Firewall in Control Panel.

To access the Firewall & Network Protection page as shown in Figure 2-25, open Windows Security, and on the Home tab, select Firewall & Network Protection.

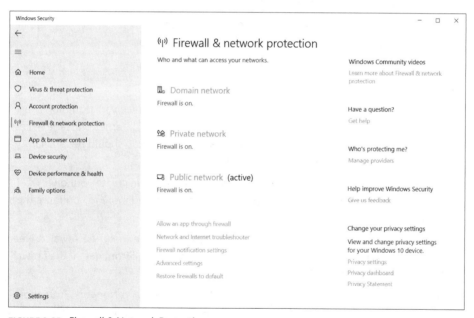

FIGURE 2-25 Firewall & Network Protection

On the Firewall & Network Protection page, you can view the current Windows Defender Firewall status and access links to enable you to configure firewall behavior. Much of the functionality is duplicated between the Firewall & Network Protection page and Windows Defender Firewall. You can choose to perform the configuration and monitoring task outlined in this chapter using either tool. Eventually, the Windows Defender Firewall located within Control Panel will be deprecated.

Manage and monitor Windows Defender Firewall

Windows Defender Firewall is a software-based firewall built into Windows 10 that creates a virtual barrier between a computer and the network to which it is connected. Windows Defender Firewall protects the computer from unwanted incoming traffic and protects the network from unwanted outgoing traffic.

To access the Windows Defender Firewall, select Start, enter **Firewall**, and then select Windows Defender Firewall.

A firewall allows specific types of data to enter and exit the computer while blocking other data; settings are configured by default (but they can be changed). This type of protection is called *filtering*. The filters are generally based on IP addresses, ports, and protocols. A description for each filter type includes the following:

- **IP addresses** are assigned to every computer and network resource connected directly to the network. The firewall can block or allow traffic based on an IP address of a resource (or a scope of addresses).

- **Port numbers** identify the application that is running on the computer. For example:

  - Port 21 is associated with the File Transfer Protocol (FTP).

  - Port 25 is associated with Simple Mail Transfer Protocol (SMTP).

  - Port 53 is associated with DNS.

  - Port 80 is associated with Hypertext Transfer Protocol (HTTP).

  - Port 443 is associated with HTTPS (HTTP Secure).

- **Protocols** are used to define the type of packet being sent or received. Common protocols are TCP, Telnet, FTP, HTTP, Post Office Protocol 3 (POP3), Internet Message Access Protocol (IMAP), HTTPS, and User Datagram Protocol (UDP). (You should be familiar with the most common protocols before taking the exam.)

Although many rules are already configured for the firewall, you can create your own inbound and outbound rules based on ports, protocols, programs, and more to configure the firewall to suit your exact needs.

You can monitor the state of the Windows Defender Firewall from either the Firewall & Network Protection area or the Windows Defender Firewall. It's easy to tell from here if the firewall is on or off and whether it is the active network.

To make basic changes to the state of the firewall within the Firewall & Network Protection area, select the network and choose to turn the Windows Defender Firewall on or off. In the left pane of Windows Defender Firewall, select Turn Windows Defender Firewall On Or Off. From there, you can change settings for both private and public networks. There are two options for each:

- **Turn on Windows Defender Firewall** (selected by default)

  - **Block all incoming connections, including those in the list of allowed apps**

  - **Notify me when Windows Defender Firewall blocks a new app** (selected by default)

- **Turn off Windows Defender Firewall (not recommended)**

You can also use the links on the page to allow an app or feature through the firewall and the links to the advanced settings options.

Allow an app through the Windows Defender Firewall

Some data generated with and by specific apps is already allowed to pass through the Windows Defender Firewall. You can see the list of which apps are allowed by clicking Allow An App Or Feature Through Windows Defender Firewall in the left pane of the Windows Defender Firewall window in Control Panel. As you scroll through the list, you'll see many apps (some you recognize and some you don't), including Candy Crush Saga, Cortana, Groove Music, and of course, Microsoft Edge.

You can modify which firewall profile apps can use by selecting the Change Settings button and providing administrator approval to the UAC prompt. The list will be editable. You will notice from the list that not all apps listed are enabled by default, including Windows Media Player Netlogon Service, Windows Remote Management, and Remote Shutdown. The list of apps and settings may vary depending on your existing configurations.

If you don't see the app you want to allow or block, select Allow Another App. You can then browse to the app executable and select the app from the list of applications in the Add An App dialog box, as shown Figure 2-26. You can configure the app to allow or stop it from communicating through the appropriate network profile by selecting the network type option in the dialog box. For existing apps, you can choose the network profile within the Allow An App Or Feature Through Windows Defender Firewall dialog box. There are two options for each app: Private and Public.

FIGURE 2-26 Adding an app through Windows Defender Firewall

You can also configure Windows Defender Firewall by using either the command-line tool Netsh.exe or by using Windows PowerShell. For example, to configure an app exception in Windows Defender Firewall with Netsh.exe, run the following command:

```
netsh firewall add allowedprogram C:\Program Files (x86)\MyApp\MyApp.exe
"My Application" ENABLE
```

> **NEED MORE REVIEW?** **USING NETSH.EXE TO CONFIGURE WINDOWS DEFENDER FIREWALL**
>
> To find out more about controlling Windows Defender Firewall with Netsh.exe, refer to the Microsoft Support website at *https://support.microsoft.com/kb/947709*.

There are a significant number of Windows PowerShell cmdlets that you can use to configure and control Windows Defender Firewall. For example, to allow a new app through the firewall, you can use the following command:

```
New-NetFirewallRule -DisplayName "Allow MyApp" -Direction Inbound -Program "C:\Program
Files (x86)\MyApp\MyApp.exe" -RemoteAddress LocalSubnet -Action Allow
```

> **NEED MORE REVIEW?** **USING WINDOWS POWERSHELL TO CONFIGURE WINDOWS DEFENDER FIREWALL**
>
> To find out more about controlling Windows Defender Firewall with Windows PowerShell, refer to the Microsoft Support website at *https://docs.microsoft.com/en-us/powershell/module/netsecurity/?view=win10-ps*.

Configure Windows Defender Firewall with Advanced Security

Although you can configure a few options in the main Windows Defender Firewall window, you can perform more advanced firewall configurations by using the Windows Defender Firewall With Advanced Security management console snap-in, as shown in Figure 2-27. To access the snap-in, from Windows Defender Firewall, select the Advanced Settings link on the Firewall & Network Protection page within Windows Security or from the Windows Defender Firewall.

The Windows Defender Firewall With Advanced Security configuration is presented differently. Traffic flow is controlled by rules, and there is a Monitoring node for viewing the current status and behavior of configured rules.

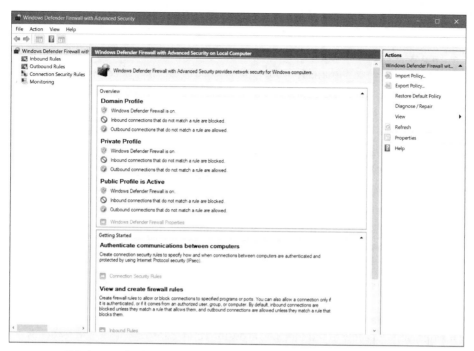

FIGURE 2-27 Windows Defender Firewall With Advanced Security

Here are the options and terms you need to be familiar with:

- In the left pane, your selection determines which items appear in the middle and right panes:

  - **Inbound Rules** Lists all configured inbound rules and enables you to double-click any item in the list and reconfigure it as desired. Some app rules are predefined and can't be modified, although they can be disabled. Explore the other nodes as time allows. You can also right-click Inbound Rules in the left pane and create your own custom rule. Rule types include Program, Port, Predefined, and Custom. They are detailed later in this section.

  - **Outbound Rules** Offers the same options as Inbound Rules, but these apply to outgoing data. You can also right-click Outbound Rules in the left pane and create your own custom rule.

- **Connection Security Rules** Connection security rules establish how computers must authenticate before any data can be sent. IP Security (IPsec) standards define how data is secured while it is in transit over a TCP/IP network, and you can require a connection to use this type of authentication before computers can send data. You'll learn more about connection security rules in the next section.

  - **Monitoring** Offers information about the active firewall status, state, and general settings for both the private and public profile types.

- In the right pane, you'll see the options that correspond to your selection in the left pane.

    - **Import/Export/Restore/Diagnose/Repair Policies**   Enables you to manage the settings you've configured for your firewall. Policies use the .wfw extension.

    - **New Rules**   Enables you to start the applicable Rule Wizard to create a new rule. You can also do this from the Action menu.

    - **Filter By**   Enables you to filter rules by Domain Profile, Private Profile, or Public Profile. You can also filter by state: Enabled or Disabled. Use this to narrow the rules listed to only those you want to view.

    - **View**   Enables you to customize how and what you view in the middle pane of the Windows Defender Firewall With Advanced Security window.

When you opt to create your own inbound or outbound rule, you can choose from four rule types. A wizard walks you through the process, and the process changes depending on the type of rule you want to create. The rules are as follows:

- **Program**   A program rule sets firewall behavior for a specific program you choose or for all programs that match the rule properties you set. You can't control apps, but you can configure traditional EXEs. Once you've selected the program for which to create the rule, you can allow the connection, allow the connection only if the connection is secure and has been authenticated using IPsec, or block the connection. You can also choose the profiles to which the rule will be applied (domain, private, or public) and name the rule.

- **Port**   A port rule sets firewall behavior for TCP and UDP port types and specifies which ports are allowed or blocked. You can apply the rule to all ports or only ports you specify. As with other rules, you can allow the connection, allow the connection only if the connection is secured with IPsec, or block the connection. You can also choose the profiles to which the rule will be applied (domain, private, public) and name the rule.

> **NOTE   CONNECTIVITY AND SECURITY**
>
> When you create inbound and outbound rules and when you opt to allow the connection only if the connection is secured by authenticating the connection with IPsec, the connection will be secured using the settings in the IPsec properties and applicable rules in the Connection Security Rules node. The next section covers how to create connection security rules.

- **Predefined**   This sets firewall behavior for a program or service that you select from a list of rules that are already defined by Windows.

- **Custom**   This is a rule you create from scratch, defining every aspect of the rule. Use this if the first three rule types don't offer the kind of rule you need.

You might encounter questions regarding how to create a rule on the exam. Therefore, you should spend a few minutes working through the wizard a few times, selecting different rule types each time, to become familiar with the process.

With Windows Defender Firewall With Advanced Security selected in the left pane and using the Overview section of the middle pane, select the Windows Defender Firewall Properties link to open the dialog box shown in Figure 2-28. Here, you can make changes to the firewall and the profiles, even if you aren't connected to the type of network you want to configure.

FIGURE 2-28 Viewing the Windows Defender Firewall properties

In Figure 2-28, the Domain Profile tab is selected. If you want, you can configure the firewall to be turned off when connected to a domain network. Additionally, you can strengthen the settings for the Public Profile and customize settings for the Private Profile. Finally, you can customize IPsec defaults, exemptions, and tunnel authorization on the IPsec Settings tab. Make sure to explore all areas of this dialog box and research any terms with which you are not familiar.

Configure connection security rules with IPsec

By default, Windows 10 does not always encrypt or authenticate communications between computers (there are exceptions). However, you can use Windows Defender Firewall With Advanced Security connection security rules to apply authentication and encryption to network traffic in your organization.

You can use IPsec network data encryption to ensure confidentiality, integrity, and authentication in data transport across channels that are not secure. Though its original purpose was to secure traffic across public networks, many organizations have chosen to implement IPsec to address perceived weaknesses in their own private networks that might be susceptible to exploitation.

If you implement IPsec properly, it provides a private channel for sending and exchanging potentially sensitive or vulnerable data, whether it is email, FTP traffic, news feeds, partner and supply-chain data, medical records, or any other type of TCP/IP-based data. IPsec provides the following functionality:

- Offers mutual authentication before and during communications
- Forces both parties to identify themselves during the communication process
- Enables confidentiality through IP traffic encryption and digital-packet authentication

Connection security rules are used to force authentication between two peer computers before they can establish a connection and transmit secure information. To secure traffic with IPsec using a connection security rule, you must allow the traffic through the firewall by creating a firewall rule. Connection security rules do not apply to programs and services. Instead, they apply only between the computers that are the two endpoints.

EXAM TIP

Connection security rules specify how and when authentication occurs, but they do not allow those connections. To allow a connection, you must create an inbound or outbound rule. During the inbound or outbound rule creation, you choose the required conditions for the connection, including requiring that the connections have been authenticated by using IPsec. When you do, connections will be secured using the settings in the IPsec properties and rules in the Connection Security Rule node.

Windows Defender Firewall with Advanced Security uses IPsec to enforce the following configurable rules:

- **Isolation**   An isolation rule isolates computers by restricting connections based on credentials, such as domain membership or health status. Isolation rules allow you to implement an isolation strategy for servers or domains.

- **Authentication Exemption**   You can use an authentication exemption to designate connections that do not require authentication. You can designate computers by a specific IP address, an IP address range, a subnet, or a predefined group, such as a gateway.

- **Server-To-Server**   This type of rule usually protects connections between servers. When you create the rule, you specify the network endpoints between which communications are protected. You then designate requirements and the authentication that you want to use.

- **Tunnel**   This rule enables you to protect connections between gateway computers. It is typically used when you are connecting across the internet between two security gateways.

- **Custom**   There might be situations in which you cannot configure the authentication rules that you need by using the rules available in the New Connection Security Rule Wizard. However, you can use a custom rule to authenticate connections between two endpoints.

> **NEED MORE REVIEW?**   **LAYERING SECURITY USING WINDOWS DEFENDER FIREWALL WITH ADVANCED SECURITY**
>
> To find out more about using and configuring Windows Defender Firewall with Advanced Security refer to the Microsoft website at *https://docs.microsoft.com/windows/security/ threat-protection/windows-firewall/windows-firewall-with-advanced-security*.

Create firewall rules

To create a rule, from within the Windows Defender Firewall With Advanced Security management console, first select the appropriate node and then select New Rule from the Actions pane. You can then complete the wizard to create your rule. As an example, to create a new inbound rule to enable network traffic for a program, perform the following procedure:

1. Select **Inbound Rules** and then select **New Rule** in the **Actions** pane.
2. On the **Rule Type** page, select **Program** and then select **Next**.
3. On the **Program** page, select **This program path**, browse and select the program executable, and then select **Next**.
4. On the **Action** page, choose **Allow the connection** and select **Next**.
5. On the **Profile** page, select which network location profiles are affected by the rule and select **Next**.
6. Provide a name and description for your rule and select **Finish**.

EXAM TIP

To configure port-based or custom rules properly, you might need to know about the TCP and UDP ports that common networking apps use. For further information, visit *https:// www.iana.org/assignments/service-names-port-numbers/service-names-port-numbers. xhtml*.

In addition to using the Windows Defender Firewall With Advanced Security management console, you can use the following Windows PowerShell cmdlets to configure and manage firewall settings and rules.

- `Get-NetFirewallRule`   Displays a list of available firewall rules
- `Enable-NetFirewallRule`   Enables an existing firewall rule
- `Disable-NetFirewallRule`   Disables an existing firewall rule
- `New-NetFirewallRule`   Creates a new firewall rule
- `Set-NetFirewallRule`   Configures the properties of an existing firewall rule

Implement encryption

Two encryption technologies are available for Windows 10 devices: Encrypting File System (EFS) and BitLocker. Both tools are available for use on all Windows 10 editions except for Windows 10 Home. Although both technologies offer robust methods of encryption, you need to understand how to implement each method as well as the use case for each so that you can decide the more appropriate tool to use in a given scenario. Just because BitLocker is more modern, you should not assume it is better or worse than EFS. Both provide Windows 10 users with strong encryption.

Implement Encrypting File System

The built-in Encrypting File System (EFS) is a powerful method of restricting access to files within an NTFS environment. Although EFS has been available since Windows 2000, very few organizations routinely implement file- and folder-level encryption. Most organizations requiring encryption will choose to use BitLocker Drive Encryption, which encrypts complete drives.

Where EFS is utilized, most issues reported to the help desk relating to EFS often result from an overly enthusiastic member of staff encrypting some of their own files. By default, they have permission to encrypt their own files because they have the Creator Owner special identity.

The best way to ensure that EFS is not inadvertently used, potentially causing problems later, is to implement some or all of the following measures:

- Stand-alone computers that are not domain-joined should back up their encryption keys to ensure they can be used for recovery purposes later.

- Explain the (strict) usage criteria of EFS in the staff handbook/policy.

- Train IT staff on the use of EFS and the potential implications of unauthorized usage.

- Plan and document where EFS will be applied and who will apply it.

- Place sufficient restrictions across the domain to prevent unauthorized use of EFS.

- Implement an EFS Data Recovery Agent (DRA) so that if EFS is misused, then an administrator within the organization can recover any encrypted files.

- Implement employee-leaving procedures and scan for encrypted files to ensure all encrypted files are decrypted or ownership transferred.

- Disable, rather than delete, user accounts for a fixed time period in case the user account needs to be reactivated in order to remove EFS from corporate resources.

It's necessary to ensure that selected users and members of IT departments appreciate that EFS is an extremely secure method of protecting files and that often this level of protection is not necessary. Only the original file owner who applied the encryption can access the file and remove the encryption.

If an organization does not have a DRA in place, one needs to be created as soon as possible. Doing so will enable subsequent files encrypted with EFS to be decrypted by the DRA, if needed.

The process for creating a DRA certificate in Windows 10 for a device that is not domain-joined can be performed using this procedure:

1. Open a **PowerShell** window or a command prompt window. (This does not require administrative privilege.)

2. Navigate to the location where you want to store your DRA certificate.

3. Type **cipher /r: file name** and press **Enter**.

4. Provide a password to protect the DRA certificate. (This can be null.)

To install the DRA so that a user can use it, follow these steps:

1. Sign in with the user credentials of the user for whom you want to create access to the DRA.

2. In the search box, type **secpol.msc**.

3. In the left pane of **Local Security Policy**, double-click **Public Key Policies**, right-click **Encrypting File System**, and then select **Add Data Recovery Agent**.

4. In the **Add Recovery Agent Wizard**, select **Next**.

5. Browse to the location of the DRA recovery certificate. (It will have a .cer file extension.)

6. Select the certificate, and then select **Open**.

7. When you are asked if you want to install the certificate, select **Yes > Next > Finish**.

8. In the right pane of **Local Security Policy**, scroll across and note that **Intended Purposes** for the certificate is set to **File Recovery**.

9. Open a command prompt window, and enter **gpupdate** to update Group Policy.

Once the DRA has been created, all EFS encrypted files can be recovered by the DRA.

The encrypted files that are already encrypted are not automatically updated when a DRA is created. Existing encrypted files cannot be recovered by the DRA unless they are opened and closed by the resource owner, which causes the DRA to update the file. To update all encrypted files on a local drive, you can enter `cipher.exe /u` in an elevated command prompt on the system containing the encrypted files.

ENCRYPT FILES AND FOLDERS BY USING ENCRYPTING FILE SYSTEM

When used with a Data Recovery Agent (DRA), Encrypting File System (EFS) is a very secure method to protect sensitive data by encrypting files and folders. Because EFS was first introduced in Windows 2000, EFS often suffers from being dismissed as being old or obsolete. Many people pass over EFS in favor of BitLocker Drive Encryption or BitLocker To Go. Don't be fooled, though. EFS offers functionality that BitLocker does not, and despite EFS having been available for many years, it still offers an incredibly secure method of enterprise-grade encryption.

It is important to use EFS and a DRA together. Without a DRA available within your organization, you may never regain access to an EFS-encrypted resource. The DRA will help to recover data if the encryption key is deleted or if the machine has been lost or compromised.

EFS offers encryption at a file and a folder level, and it cannot be used to encrypt an entire hard disk. Instead, you would use BitLocker (covered later in this section) to encrypt an entire drive. Users can encrypt any file or folder they have created on an NTFS-formatted hard disk by right-clicking the resource and selecting Properties from the context menu that appears. In the Advanced Attributes dialog box (shown in Figure 2-29), select Encrypt Contents To Secure Data.

FIGURE 2-29 Enabling EFS encryption

Encryption should not be used without prior planning and establishing some safeguards to secure the encryption keys that are used. EFS protects data from unauthorized access, and it is especially effective as a last line of defense from attacks, such as physical theft.

EFS uses Windows Public Key Infrastructure (PKI) and a fast encryption algorithm to protect files. The public and private keys generated during encryption ensure that only the user account that encrypted the file can decrypt it. Encrypted data can be decrypted only if the user's personal encryption certificate is available, which is generated through the private key. Unless exported by the user, this key cannot be used by anyone else, and EFS prevents any access to the data. EFS will prevent attempts to copy or move encrypted data by anyone except users who have the proper credentials. If the user deletes their account or leaves the company, any encrypted resources will not be accessible, which could lead to data being lost. The only way to prevent data loss is to ensure that a DRA has previously been created so that an administrator can use the DRA to decrypt the resource.

Here are some key points you need to learn about EFS:

- The process of encryption and decryption happens behind the scenes and is not visible to users.
- Encryption occurs when you close files; decryption occurs when you open them.

- EFS is available only on NTFS volumes.

- EFS keys aren't assigned to a computer; they are assigned to a specific user.

- If a hacker gains access to the user's PC while the user is signed in, the hacker will be able to access and open EFS-protected files.

- The file owner can move or copy an EFS-protected file.

- You can't use EFS and compression together; it's one or the other.

- If the file owner moves an EFS-protected file to a volume that does not support EFS (such as FAT32), the file will be decrypted.

- Encrypted files and folders are no longer colored green in File Explorer; now they include a padlock icon on each file.

- EFS uses Advanced Encryption Standard (AES), which uses a 256-bit key algorithm, a credible industry standard of encryption.

- EFS is only available on Windows 10 Pro, Enterprise, and Education editions.

By default, any user can use EFS to encrypt any file for which they have ownership. Unless company policy requires EFS, you should consider disabling EFS with Group Policy until a DRA is created.

It is vital that a DRA be in place before EFS is enabled. Without a DRA, even an administrator is unable to recover EFS-protected files and folders. For the exam, you need to be able to configure a DRA using the command-line tool Cipher.exe.

Once you have created a DRA, you should update the encryption of each currently encrypted file to have the new DRA applied by using `cipher /u`. You can continue to encrypt your files and folders within File Explorer using the Encrypt Contents to Secure Data option shown previously in Figure 2-29.

> **NOTE   DRA AND EFS: THE SEQUENCE IS IMPORTANT**
>
> Only encrypted files that are created after the DRA has been created can be recovered using the DRA.

PERFORM BACKUP AND RECOVERY OF EFS-PROTECTED FILES

Built into Windows is a wizard for users who want to use EFS to create a file encryption certificate and key and back up these files. After you first encrypt files or folders, you will see the EFS pop-up notification in the notification area of the desktop asking you to back up your encryption key.

You can use the following steps to start the wizard and complete the process to configure an EFS certificate:

1. Open **Control Panel** and select **User Accounts**.

2. Select **Manage your file encryption certificates** to open the **Encrypting File System Wizard**.

3. Select **Next**. The wizard asks for your file encryption certificate; you can select your existing certificate, or you can create a new certificate.

4. Select **Create a New Certificate**, and then select **Next**.

5. On the **Create A Certificate** page, select **Make a new self-signed certificate and store it on my computer** and select **Next**.

6. Provide a backup location and password and select **Next**.

7. On the **Update your previously encrypted files** page, select **All Logical Drives** and select **Next**.

8. On the **Your encrypted files have been updated** page, select **Close**.

In addition to the Cipher.exe command-line tool, you can use the Certificates MMC (CertMgr.msc) to manage or back up your personal EFS certificate. You can also import your certificates to a new computer that doesn't already contain your certificate. In the event of your certificate being lost, perhaps due to a failed computer or corrupted profile, you can import the DRA certificate onto a new computer, which would allow recovery of the encrypted files.

To import your EFS certificate into your personal certificate store via the Certificate Import Wizard, you should follow these steps:

1. Open Certificates MMC by entering **CertMgr.msc** into the search box.

2. Select the **Personal** folder.

3. Select **Action > All Tasks > Import**.

4. Work through the **Certificate Import Wizard** to import the PFX certificate.

> **NEED MORE REVIEW?** **CIPHER.EXE**
>
> For more information about Cipher.exe, refer to *https://docs.microsoft.com/windows-server/ administration/windows-commands/cipher*.

Some common parameters used with the Cipher.exe command include:

- **/c** Displays information about an encrypted file
- **/d** Decrypts specified files and directories
- **/s:<directory>** Performs the specified operation on all subdirectories in the specified directory
- **/u** Updates all encrypted files on the local drives (useful if you need to update previously encrypted files with a new recovery certificate)
- **/u /n** Finds all encrypted files on a local drive
- **/?** Displays help
- **/x** Backs up the EFS certificate and keys to the specified file name

- **/r:<FileName>** Generates an EFS recovery agent key and certificate, based on the user account, and then writes them to a PFX file (Personal Information Exchange file, which contains a certificate and private key) and a CER file (Security Certificate file, which contains only the certificate)

After you have encrypted your first file or folder, Windows 10 will prompt you to make a backup of the EFS certificate and key, as shown in Figure 2-30. This reminder will appear in the notification area and it will reappear on a regular basis until you back up the EFS certificate and key or choose Never Back Up. You need to ensure you do take a backup and store it safely in a location separate from that of the files.

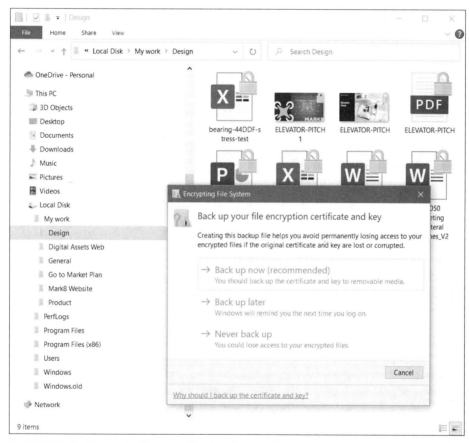

FIGURE 2-30 Backing up the file encryption certificate and key

TROUBLESHOOT ENCRYPTING FILE SYSTEM

When users report that they are unable to use EFS to encrypt files, you need to verify that all the four statements are correct:

- A recovery agent policy has been defined, which prevents the use of EFS unless a DRA has been created.

- The file volume is NTFS; EFS is only supported on NTFS.
- The file is not compressed. NTFS allows files to be encrypted or compressed, not both.
- You have Write access to the file. You need to be able to save the encrypted file.

Other examples of help desk EFS issues include the following scenarios and possible answers:

- **I can't open files I have encrypted.**   Only users with the correct EFS certificate and private key for the file can open EFS-protected files. Has the user account been deleted/re-created since the file was created? Use a DRA to recover the file and have the user encrypt the file again.

- **Will I get a warning that I will lose the EFS protection on my file when I copy my file a FAT32 USB drive?**   If the user has the necessary NTFS permissions to move or copy the file, then Windows will carry out the operation without error or warning. Encrypted data copied to a drive not formatted with NTFS will lose the EFS protection.

- **I saved a file that is protected using Windows Information Protection (WIP) to a FAT32 USB drive. The file looks like it is encrypted using EFS. Is this correct?**   WIP is supported in Windows 10 to protect files. Protected files look and behave like EFS files, but they do not use EFS. The file is an encrypted PFILE that stores the Enterprise Data Protection metadata, which can be stored on a FAT32 drive.

- **I can't open an EFS file after upgrading from a previous version of Windows.**   You can still recover the files by importing the EFS certificate and key from your old computer into your new computer.

- **My antivirus check program runs but I get "Access Denied" error messages.**   An antivirus check program can only read your encrypted files. If the device is a shared computer and other users have encrypted files on the hard disk, the antivirus tool will not be able to access these files. Other users need to perform a virus check for files by signing in on the device.

Configure BitLocker

BitLocker Drive Encryption enables you to encrypt an entire hard disk, which can be the Windows operating system drive or a data drive. Only the Windows 10 Pro, Enterprise, and Education editions support BitLocker in both x86 and x64-bit varieties. During the encryption process, BitLocker Drive Encryption will configure the drive that contains the operating system to have a system partition and an operating system partition.

EXAM TIP

Two partitions are required to run BitLocker because pre-startup authentication and system integrity confirmation must occur on a separate partition from the drive that is encrypted.

If these partitions are not present the process will automatically modify the partitions as required.

Many modern computers now ship with a Trusted Platform Module (TPM), which is a microchip that is used to securely store cryptographic information, such as the encryption keys that BitLocker uses. BitLocker supports versions 1.2 and 2.0 of the TPM specification, and information contained on the TPM is more secure from external software attacks and physical theft. If a device has been tampered with—for instance, a hard drive has been removed from the original computer—BitLocker will prevent the drive from being unlocked. BitLocker will seek remediation from the user by entering BitLocker recovery mode and requiring the user to enter a 48-digit recovery key. Although a TPM is the most secure option, BitLocker technology can also be used on devices without a TPM by configuring a GPO to require that BitLocker obtain the required cryptographic information from a USB flash drive. This information must be presented to unlock the volume.

NEED MORE REVIEW?   **OVERVIEW OF BITLOCKER DEVICE ENCRYPTION IN WINDOWS 10**

For more information about Windows BitLocker, visit *https://docs.microsoft.com/en-us/ windows/security/information-protection/bitlocker/bitlocker-device-encryption-overview-windows-10.*

When configuring BitLocker, you must consider the following:

- **The requirements for hardware and software**   These include TPM versions, BIOS configuration, firmware requirements, drive size, and so on.

- **How to tell if your computer has a TPM**   An administrator might opt to enter TPM.msc in Search. An end user might opt to access Control Panel, All Items, open BitLocker Drive Encryption, and see if they can turn on BitLocker. If a TPM isn't found, you'll have to configure the Group Policy setting called Require Additional Authentication At Startup, which is located in Computer Configuration\Administrative Templates\ Windows Components\BitLocker Drive Encryption\Operating System Drives. You need to enable this policy and then select the Allow BitLocker Without a Compatible TPM check box.

- **The credentials required to configure BitLocker**   Only administrators can manage fixed data drives, but standard users can manage removable data drives. (The latter can be disabled in Group Policy.) Standard users can also change the PIN or password on operating system drives to which they have access via BitLocker.

- **How to automate BitLocker deployment in an enterprise**   One way is to use the command-line tool Manage-bde.exe. Manage-bde command-line tools you might use in your own work are detailed later in this section. There are other ways to automate BitLocker deployment in an enterprise, including using Windows Management Instrumentation (WMI) and Windows PowerShell cmdlets.

- **The reasons BitLocker might start in recovery mode** Reasons include disabling the TPM, making changes to the TPM firmware, making changes to the master boot record, and faults on the drive, motherboard, or TPM.

- **How to manage recovery keys** Recovery keys let you access a computer in the event that BitLocker doesn't permit access. There are many ways to store these keys for fixed drives, including saving them to a folder or your Microsoft account online, printing them, and storing the keys on multiple USB drives.

> **NOTE USING BITLOCKER WITHOUT TPM**
>
> You can only enable BitLocker on an operating system drive without a compatible TPM if the BIOS or UEFI firmware can read from a USB flash drive in the boot environment. This is because BitLocker requires a startup key. If you do this, though, you won't be able to take advantage of the pre-startup system integrity verification or multifactor authentication.

Understand BitLocker key protectors

BitLocker offers users several protection options. Administrators can choose which type of protection users should adopt to unlock a BitLocker-encrypted drive. BitLocker supports multi-factor authentication for operating system drives, enabling you to require additional authentication, such as adding a smart card or a USB drive with a startup key on it or requiring a PIN on startup. These are called *key protectors*.

BitLocker offers multiple key protectors that can be used to unlock a protected system:

- **TPM + startup PIN + startup key** This is the most secure combination. The encryption key is stored on the TPM chip. The user might find this option cumbersome because it requires multiple authentication tasks.

- **TPM + startup key** The encryption key is stored on the TPM chip. The user needs to insert a USB flash drive that contains a startup key.

- **TPM + startup PIN** The encryption key is stored on the TPM chip. The user needs to enter a PIN to unlock the device.

- **Startup key only** The user needs to insert a USB flash drive with the startup key on it. The device doesn't need to have a TPM chip. The BIOS must support access to the USB flash drive before the operating system loads.

- **TPM only** The encryption key is stored on the TPM chip, and no user action is required.

With all the BitLocker authentication methods, the drive is encrypted until unlocked. When the BitLocker encrypted drive is in recovery mode, you can also unlock the drive by using either the recovery password or recovery key:

- **Recovery password** This is a 48-digit number typed on a regular keyboard or by using the function keys (F1–F10) to input the numbers.

- **Recovery key** This is an encryption key created when BitLocker is first employed and is used for recovering data encrypted on a BitLocker volume. Often, the encryption key is stored on removable media.

Because the TPM chip together with BitLocker protects the hard drive, administrators can also configure BitLocker to operate without additional unlock steps; provided the device (and TPM) recognize the drive, it will be unlocked.

With BitLocker enabled, the drive is no longer susceptible to data theft. On a system that is not encrypted, simply removing the drive from the PC and attaching it as a secondary drive in another PC allows the data to be read, which bypasses all NTFS security.

EXAM TIP

Administrators can fine-tune the settings within Group Policy for BitLocker, and you would do well to review the available GPOs in detail because they are likely to appear on the exam. Review the GPOs located in Computer Configuration\Policies\Administrative Templates\ Windows Components\BitLocker Drive Encryption.

Enable BitLocker without a TPM

By default, a modern Windows device such as a Surface Pro will contain a TPM, and BitLocker Drive Encryption will be already enabled when shipped. When the user signs on to the device for the first time with a Microsoft account, the recovery key is saved to their Microsoft account.

If a TPM isn't found, select Cancel on the BitLocker Drive Encryption and follow the displayed instructions to configure Require Additional Authentication At Startup GPO located in Computer Configuration\Administrative Templates\Windows Components\BitLocker Drive Encryption\Operating System Drives. Enable this GPO and select the Allow BitLocker Without A Compatible TPM check box, as shown in Figure 2-31.

FIGURE 2-31 Configuring BitLocker to work without a TPM

A new GPO is included with Windows 10 and can be found at Computer Configuration\Policies\Administrative Templates\Windows Components\BitLocker Drive Encryption\Operating System Drives\Configure Pre-boot Recovery Message And URL. This GPO enables administrators to configure a custom recovery message and to replace the existing URL that is displayed on the pre-boot recovery screen when the operating system drive is locked. This enables administrators to provide information to the user, such as help desk support contact information.

Configure BitLocker

If you want to use BitLocker to encrypt the operating system drive on a supported Windows 10 device, the drive must be formatted as NTFS. Perform these steps to encrypt the drive using BitLocker:

1. Launch **Control Panel,** select **System and Security**, and then select **BitLocker Drive Encryption**.

2. Select the operating system drive and select **Turn on BitLocker**. (If you receive an error that the device can use a TPM chip, either enable the TPM within the BIOS or Unified Extensible Firmware Interface (UEFI) settings or enable the **Require additional authentication at startup** Group Policy setting, which is referred to earlier in this section.)

3. On the **BitLocker drive encryption setup** page, select **Next**.

4. On the **Preparing your drive for BitLocker** page, if prompted, select **Next**. (If your system has a Windows Recovery Environment, this will need to be manually enabled and moved to the system drive after the drive is encrypted.)

5. If you are presented with a warning message regarding the Windows Recovery Environment, select **Next**.

6. Choose how to unlock your drive at startup. (**Enter A Password** is used in this example.)

7. Enter the password, reenter to confirm, and then select **Next**.

8. On the **How do you want to back up your recovery key?** page, select one of the options, then select **Next** and back up your key. (Optionally, you can choose to back up the key in a secondary location.)

9. On the **Choose how much of your drive to encrypt** page, select to encrypt either the used disk space or the entire drive and select **Next**.

10. On the **Choose which encryption mode to use** page, select either the newest encryption mode or the compatible mode and select **Next**.

11. On the **Are you ready to encrypt this drive?** page, choose to allow the option **BitLocker system check to take place (default)**, or deselect the option and then select **Continue**.

12. Restart the PC, enter the BitLocker password, and allow the drive to be encrypted in the background. In the taskbar notification area, there should be an icon indicating that BitLocker Drive Encryption is in progress.

> *NOTE* **BITLOCKER IS IMMEDIATELY ENFORCED**
>
> When BitLocker Drive Encryption starts to encrypt the device, the drive is protected, and it will require unlocking during startup, even if the encryption process has not fully completed encrypting every file.

From within the BitLocker Drive Encryption page in Control Panel, you can review the BitLocker status and perform additional tasks, including suspending protection, backing up your recovery key, changing the BitLocker password, removing the password, and turning off BitLocker.

> *NOTE* **USED DISK SPACE ONLY**
>
> An improvement to BitLocker enables administrators to choose whether to encrypt only the used disk space or to encrypt the entire drive during the initial deployment of Windows. Choosing the first option significantly reduces the time to deploy and requires less administrative effort, though purists will tell you this is slightly less secure.

Configure BitLocker using command-line tools

Administrators can also manage BitLocker Drive Encryption using the command-line tool Manage-bde.exe or by using the command prompt, PowerShell, and WMI. Managing recovery keys is discussed later.

Several parameters can be used with the **Manage-bde** command to manage BitLocker, as listed in Table 2-11.

TABLE 2-11 **Manage-bde** command parameters

Parameter	Description
Manage-bde -status	Provides information about all drives on the computer, whether or not they are BitLocker-protected.
Manage-bde on	This encrypts the drive and turns on BitLocker. Use the UsedSpaceOnly switch to set the encryption mode to Used Space Only encryption.
Manage-bde -off	This decrypts the drive and turns off BitLocker. All key protectors are removed when decryption is complete.

Parameter	Description
`Manage-bde -pause &` `Manage-bde -resume`	Use with a drive letter to pause or resume encryption or decryption.
`Manage-bde -lock &` `manage-bde -unlock`	Use with a drive letter to lock and unlock access to BitLocker-protected data.
`Manage-bde -autounlock`	Manages automatic unlocking of a data drive.
`Manage-bde -protectors`	Manages protection methods for the encryption key.
`Manage-bde -changepassword`	Modifies the password for a data drive.
`Manage-bde -changepin`	Modifies the PIN for an operating system drive.
`Manage-bde - forcerecovery`	Forces a BitLocker-protected drive into recovery mode on restart.
`Manage-bde -changekey`	Modifies the startup key for an operating system drive.
`Manage-bde WipeFreeSpace`	Wipes the free space on a drive.
`Manage-bde -help or -h`	Displays complete Help at the command prompt.

> **NEED MORE REVIEW?**   **MANAGE-BDE COMMAND-LINE TOOL**
>
> More information on using the manage-bde command-line tool is available in this article at *https://docs.microsoft.com/windows-server/administration/windows-commands/manage-bde*.

Windows 10 offers built-in support for BitLocker PowerShell cmdlets, as listed in Table 2-12. You can also use `Get-help <BitLocker cmdlet>`, such as `Get-Help Enable-BitLocker -examples`.

> **NOTE**   **POWERSHELL HELP**
>
> You may need to use the `update-help` cmdlet to allow PowerShell to display the most current help files and examples, which may assist your understanding.

TABLE 2-12 BitLocker PowerShell cmdlets

Cmdlet	Description
`Add-BitLockerKeyProtector`	Adds a key protector for a BitLocker volume
`Backup-BitLockerKeyProtector`	Saves a key protector for a BitLocker volume in Active Directory Domain Services (AD DS)
`Clear-BitLockerAutoUnlock`	Removes BitLocker automatic unlocking keys
`Disable-BitLocker`	Disables BitLocker encryption for a volume

Cmdlet	Description
`Disable-BitLockerAutoUnlock`	Disables automatic unlocking for a BitLocker volume
`Enable-BitLocker`	Enables encryption for a BitLocker volume
`Enable-BitLockerAutoUnlock`	Enables automatic unlocking for a BitLocker volume
`Get-BitLockerVolume`	Gets information about volumes that BitLocker can protect
`Lock-BitLocker`	Prevents access to encrypted data on a BitLocker volume
`Remove-BitLockerKeyProtector`	Removes a key protector for a BitLocker volume
`Resume-BitLocker`	Restores BitLocker encryption for the specified volume
`Suspend-BitLocker`	Suspends BitLocker encryption for the specified volume
`Unlock-BitLocker`	Restores access to data on a BitLocker volume

> **NEED MORE REVIEW:** **CONFIGURE BITLOCKER USING POWERSHELL CMDLETS**
>
> For more information about how to configure BitLocker using PowerShell cmdlets, visit this reference article at *https://docs.microsoft.com/powershell/module/bitlocker/?view=win10-ps*.

Using PowerShell, you can obtain very detailed information from systems, including status, key protectors used, encryption method, and type. If you run the `Get-BitLockerVolume | format-list` cmdlet to provide information about an encrypted drive without first unlocking the drive, the amount of information obtained will be restricted.

Upgrade a BitLocker-enabled computer

BitLocker is designed to protect your computer from preboot changes, such as updating the BIOS or UEFI. If you upgrade your computer, for example, with a BIOS firmware upgrade, this can cause the TPM to perceive it is under attack. In order to prevent Windows 10 from entering BitLocker recovery mode, you should take some precautions when upgrading a BitLocker-enabled computer. Before updating the BIOS, carry out the following steps:

1. Temporarily suspend BitLocker by opening the **BitLocker Drive Encryption** in **Control Panel** and selecting **Suspend Protection** on the operating system drive, which places it in disabled mode.

2. Upgrade the system or the BIOS.

3. BitLocker protection will be automatically turned back on following a reboot, but if this default behavior has been modified, you should turn BitLocker on again by opening **BitLocker Drive Encryption** in **Control Panel** and selecting **Resume Protection** on the operating system drive.

Forcing BitLocker into disabled mode keeps the data encrypted, with the volume master key encrypted with a clear key. The availability of this unencrypted key disables the data protection that BitLocker offers, but it ensures that the subsequent computer startup will succeed without further user input. After the BIOS upgrade, BitLocker is reenabled so that the unencrypted key is erased from the disk and BitLocker protection is functional again. The encryption key will be resealed with the new key that has been regenerated to incorporate new values of the measured components that may have changed during the system upgrade.

> **NOTE THROUGHOUT SUSPENSION, DATA IS ENCRYPTED**
>
> Although BitLocker is suspended, the drive remains encrypted and all new data written to the disk is still encrypted. Suspension prevents BitLocker from validating system integrity at startup and is a security risk; therefore, the protection status should be resumed at the earliest opportunity.

Move a BitLocker-encrypted drive to another computer

Moving a BitLocker-encrypted drive to another BitLocker-enabled computer requires that you turn off BitLocker temporarily (by using the Suspend Protection option). After the move is complete, you need to reenable BitLocker, which will then resume BitLocker protection.

The PowerShell command for suspending BitLocker encryption on the system drive is:

```
Suspend-BitLocker -MountPoint "C:"
```

Sometimes a system change can cause the BitLocker system integrity check on the operating system drive to fail. This prevents the TPM from releasing the BitLocker key to decrypt the protected operating system drive and requires the user to enter recovery mode. Examples of system changes that can result in a BitLocker system integrity check failure include:

- Moving the BitLocker-protected drive to a new computer
- Installing a new motherboard with a new TPM
- Turning off, disabling, or clearing the TPM
- Making changes to any boot configuration settings
- Making changes to the BIOS, UEFI firmware, master boot record, boot sector, boot manager, Optical ROM, or other early boot components or boot configuration data

When Windows 10 upgrades itself from one version to another, such as 1803 to 1809, there should be no issues with BitLocker because the system will automatically perform the suspend and resume actions during the process.

Configure startup key storage and recovery options

You know that without access to the encryption key contained in the TPM or stored in the startup key, you are unable to unlock a BitLocker-encrypted drive.

You should ensure that you're familiar with BitLocker-related terminology:

- **Recovery password and recovery key**   When you first configure BitLocker, it will create a recovery key and prompt you to store it safely. You'll need to provide this recovery key if the TPM is unable to validate that the drive hasn't been tampered with or if the startup key, password, or PIN have not been supplied during boot time.
- **Password**   A password or passphrase is created to protect fixed, removable, and operating system drives with or without a TPM. The password length can be set in Group Policy and can consist of eight to 255 characters.
- **PIN**   When you use a TPM, you can configure BitLocker with a PIN that the user must type during the initial startup of the device to allow Windows 10 to start. The PIN can consist of between 4 to 20 digits, and the length can be set in the Configure Minimum PIN Length For Startup Group Policy setting.
- **Enhanced PIN**   This enables administrators to force the use of a complex PIN, just like a password or passphrase (including spaces), by configuring the Allow Enhanced PINs For Startup GPO setting. This policy is applied when you turn on BitLocker and is configurable only for operating system drives.
- **Startup key**   This is stored on a USB flash drive and can be used with or without a TPM. To use this method of unlock, the USB flash drive must be inserted every time the computer starts. The USB flash drive can be formatted by using NTFS, FAT, or FAT32.
- **TPM Lockout**   By default, TPM 2.0 will lock the user out for two hours whenever the TPM is under attack. (TPM 1.2 lockout duration varied by manufacturer.)

Configure BitLocker To Go

A portable version of BitLocker, BitLocker To Go, is aimed at protecting removable USB devices and uses the same technology as BitLocker Drive Encryption, but it does not require use of a TPM. BitLocker To Go can protect flash drives, Secure Digital (SD) cards, and removable hard disks formatted with NTFS, FAT16, FAT32, or exFat file systems. BitLocker To Go is available for users with Windows 10 Pro, Windows 10 Enterprise, or Windows 10 Education.

To create a BitLocker To Go drive, follow these steps:

1. Insert a removable drive.
2. Open **Windows Explorer** (though it may open automatically).
3. Right-click the removable drive and select **Turn BitLocker on**.
4. After the **BitLocker Drive Encryption Wizard** opens, choose how to unlock the drive and select **Next**.

5. On the **How do you want to back up your recovery key?** page, choose an option, and then once the password is saved, select **Next**.

6. On the **Choose how much of your drive to encrypt** page, select to encrypt either the used disk space or the entire drive and select **Next**.

7. On the **Choose which encryption mode to use** page, select either the newest encryption mode or the compatible mode and select **Next**.

8. On the **Are you ready to encrypt this drive?** page, select **Start encrypting**.

9. The encryption process will commence. Once the process is complete, you can close the wizard.

If the option to encrypt the drive is not available, you need to check that you are using a supported version of Windows and that the feature has not been disabled by Group Policy.

Once a removable drive has been encrypted, each time you insert the removable drive into a device, you will need to unlock it with one of the following methods:

- A recovery password or passphrase. (This complexity can be set within Group Policy.)
- A smart card.
- Select the option Always Auto-Unlock This Device On This PC.

The last option is useful for users who frequently use removable drives because it reduces the likelihood of frustration of entering the password every time they use their removable drives. If the removable drive is used on other devices once the user unlocks the removable drive, it can also be configured to auto-unlock if required.

Standard users can turn on, turn off, or change configurations of BitLocker on removable data drives. They are also able to change their own password for encrypted drives via BitLocker Drive Encryption in Control Panel. However, if a user loses or forgets the password for the data or removable drive, you need to have access to the BitLocker recovery key to recover the data and unlock the drive.

EXAM TIP

It is important to remember that a TPM is *not* required for BitLocker To Go. The encryption keys are secured using a password or passphrase or smart card, and not by a TPM.

The following GPOs are available within the BitLocker To Go settings found at Computer Configuration\Policies\Administrative Templates\Windows Components\BitLocker Drive Encryption\Removable Data Drives:

- Control use of BitLocker on removable drives.
- Configure use of smart cards on removable data drives.
- Deny Write access to removable drives not protected by BitLocker.
- Configure use of hardware-based encryption for removable data drives.
- Enforce drive-encryption type on removable data drives.

- Allow access to BitLocker-protected removable data drives from earlier versions of Windows.

- Configure use of passwords for removable data drives.

- Choose how BitLocker-protected removable data drives can be recovered.

Users of Windows 10 Home cannot encrypt removable data drives, but they can access BitLocker To Go–enabled data drives and have read-only access to the data, if they provide the correct recovery password, passphrase, or smart card.

Understand BitLocker and BitLocker To Go data recovery

You need to support users who have devices that will not boot into Windows because of BitLocker-related issues during boot time. There are several situations in which BitLocker will enter into BitLocker recovery mode because of a perceived threat to the system, such as one of the following:

- Repeatedly failing to provide the startup password.

- Changing the startup boot order to boot another drive in advance of the hard drive.

- Changing the NTFS partition table, such as creating, deleting, or resizing a primary partition.

- Entering the PIN incorrectly too many times so that the anti-hammering logic of the TPM is activated.

- Turning off, disabling, deactivating, or clearing the TPM.

- Upgrading critical early startup components, such as a BIOS or UEFI firmware upgrade, causing the related boot measurements to change.

- Adding or removing hardware (for example, inserting a new motherboard or video card into the computer).

- You can also force a BitLocker-protected device into recovery mode by pressing the F8 or F10 key during the boot process.

> **NOTE   BITLOCKER RECOVERY GUIDE**
>
> The following article provides a useful list of examples of specific events that will cause BitLocker to enter recovery mode when attempting to start the operating system drive: *https://docs.microsoft.com/windows/device-security/bitlocker/bitlocker-recovery-guide-plan.*

When the device has entered the BitLocker recovery mode, you need to recover the drive by using one of these methods:

- Supply the 48-digit recovery password.

- Allow a domain administrator to obtain the recovery password from Active Directory.

- Allow an administrator to obtain the recovery password from Azure Active Directory.

- Run a script to reset the password, using PowerShell or VBScript, which uses the key package.

For stand-alone and small-business users, the BitLocker recovery key is stored in the user's Microsoft account at *https://onedrive.live.com/recoverykey*. You will need to use the keyboard number or function keys to enter the number to unlock the drive. Once the operating system has started, users can then re-create a new startup key; otherwise, the BitLocker recovery mode will remain in place.

For corporate users, there are several settings that can be configured in Group Policy that will define the recovery methods that require Windows to save BitLocker recovery information to Active Directory. The GPOs found in the subfolders of Computer Configuration\Administrative Templates\Windows Components\BitLocker Drive Encryption are as follows:

- Choose How Bitlocker-Protected Operating System Drives Can Be Recovered
- Choose How Bitlocker-Protected Fixed Drives Can Be Recovered
- Choose How Bitlocker-Protected Removable Drives Can Be Recovered

For each of these GPOs, you can also select the Do Not Enable BitLocker Until Recovery Information Is Stored In Active Directory check box to keep users from enabling BitLocker unless the device is connected to the domain and the backup of BitLocker recovery information to Active Directory has succeeded.

Once BitLocker recovery information has been saved in Active Directory, the recovery information can be used to restore access to a BitLocker-protected drive by using the Manage-bde command-line tool introduced earlier.

NOTE **BITLOCKER FAQ**

You need to take some time to review BitLocker. It is an important feature that protects against data loss. Read the BitLocker frequently asked questions (FAQ) resources at *https:// docs.microsoft.com/windows/device-security/bitlocker/bitlocker-frequently-asked-questions*.

In an Azure Active Directory environment, you can locate the BitLocker key within the Azure Active Directory Admin Center. Locate the device, and if the Windows 10 machine has been encrypted, you can use the BitLocker recovery key or provide it to the user to recover their device.

To view or copy the BitLocker keys within Azure Active Directory, you need to be the device owner or have one of the following roles assigned:

- Global Administrator
- Help Desk Administrator
- Security Administrator
- Security Reader
- Intune Service Administrator

Configure Windows Defender Antivirus

Microsoft Defender Antivirus is built into Windows 10 and helps protect your computer from spyware, malware, and viruses. Microsoft Defender Antivirus is compatible with Hyper-V and therefore it can detect malicious software within a virtual machine. Microsoft Defender Antivirus uses antivirus definition files to determine whether software it detects is malicious and will alert you to potential risks found. The definitions are automatically installed as they are released.

You can use Microsoft Defender to run several types of scan; Quick, Full, or Custom, as shown in Table 2-13. In addition to the automatic detection, if you suspect spyware has infected a specific area, you can run a targeted scan on a drive or a folder.

TABLE 2-13 Microsoft Defender Antivirus scan options

Scan Options	Description
Quick	Checks common areas that malicious software are likely to infect.
Full	Checks all files and all running apps on the device.
Custom	Allows targeted scanning of specific drives and folders.
Windows Defender Offline Scan	Allows users to find and remove difficult-to-remove malicious software. The system will need to reboot, and the scan can take about 15 minutes.

There are several options and settings available for users to fine-tune how Microsoft Defender Antivirus will operate. For example, you can configure the scan schedule, choose when Microsoft Defender Antivirus excludes processes, and configure the behavior when a scan identifies malicious software on your system.

Microsoft Defender Antivirus real-time protection is configured to detect and prevent spyware and other unwanted software from running on a device. Not all unwanted software seeks to destroy or corrupt your files. There are many types of malicious software that give unauthorized parties remote access to your device or stealthily collect and transmit information from your device to unauthorized third parties.

Here are some common types of malware:

- **Computer viruses**   Designed to replicate malicious code, often using email attachments or embedded within files.
- **Computer worms**   Designed to automatically replicate across networks and overload systems due to increased volume of traffic.
- **Trojan horses**   Files are hidden within other files or applications and, once activated, aim to provide unauthorized third parties with remote access to the infected device.
- **Ransomware**   Targets files and encrypts them. Users are then asked to pay a nominal ransom fee, often in Bitcoin or other hard-to-trace cryptocurrency, to recover the data. Often after paying the ransom, the files remain inaccessible.

- **Spyware** Tracking software, such as a keylogger, that reports to the third party how a device is used.

Email provides attackers with the most common attack vector for delivering malware. Increasingly, attacks from websites, pirated software, video, and music files are also becoming common.

You can help protect against infection by following these guidelines:

- Windows Defender is automatically enabled. Do not disable it.
- Antimalware definitions should be updated automatically.
- All software should be from a reputable source.
- All software and Window 10 updates should be applied automatically.
- Deter using or installing pirated or unsigned software.
- Be vigilant and suspicious of email attachments.
- Don't open links in spam or phishing emails.

Microsoft has improved the performance of Windows Defender Antivirus, and it provides an excellent antimalware solution that reduces the probability that malware will compromise your device.

In addition to the built-in protection that runs in real time on your device, if you believe your system has been infected you can run use the Microsoft Defender Offline scanning tool. This tool will run from a trusted environment, without starting the operating system. The scan can take up to 15 minutes, and you will need to reboot your system for the scan to complete.

To run a Microsoft Defender Offline Scan from Windows Defender Security Center, perform these steps:

1. Open **Windows Security**, and select **Virus & threat protection**.
2. Select **Scan options** under **Current threats**.
3. Select **Microsoft Defender Offline scan**, and select **Scan now**.
4. In the **Save your work** dialog box, select **Scan**.
5. If prompted by UAC, select **Yes**. The message that **You're about to be signed out** will appear and your device will restart to run the scan offline. When your PC restarts, you will see Microsoft Defender Offline tool initiating. Microsoft Defender Offline will then perform a quick scan of your device, as shown in Figure 2-32. When the offline scan has completed, your device will automatically restart.

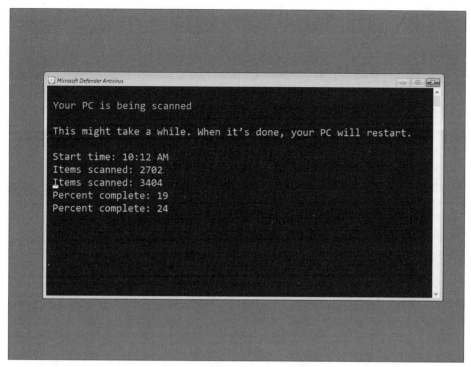

FIGURE 2-32 Microsoft Defender Offline scanning tool

For your device to be protected, you should ensure that Windows Defender Antivirus is correctly configured. To review the Windows Defender Antivirus configuration, follow these steps:

1. Open the **Settings** app and select **Update & Security**.

2. On the **Update & Security** page, select **Windows Security**.

3. On the **Windows Security** page, select **Open Windows Security**.

4. Verify that your device is being protected and that **Virus & threat protection** is active. (You'll see a tick mark on a green background.)

5. Select the **Protection history** and review all recent items. Here, you can view **Current**, **Quarantined**, and **Allowed threats**. Review the results of any **Quarantined** or **Allowed** items that were on your device.

6. To verify that the threat definitions are up to date, select **Virus & threat protection**.

7. On the **Virus & threat protection** page, view the **Last update** date under **Virus & threat protection updates**, as shown on Figure 2-33. This should be within 24 hours of the current time. You can also select the **Check for updates** option to force a sync to the update server.

8. Close the **Windows Security App**.

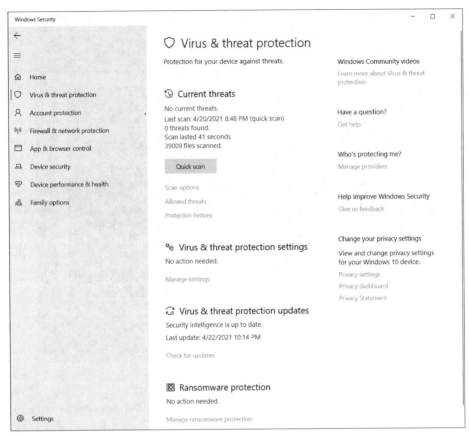

FIGURE 2-33 Viewing the Virus & Threat Protection settings

If you prefer to automate device antivirus actions using PowerShell, there are 12 cmdlets that you can use to perform tasks that protect your device, as shown in Table 2-14.

TABLE 2-14 Microsoft Defender Antivirus PowerShell cmdlets

Cmdlet	Function
Add-MpPreference	Modify Microsoft Defender Antivirus settings.
Get-MPComputerStatus	View the status of Microsoft Defender Antivirus software.
Get-MPPreference	View Microsoft Defender Antivirus scan and update preferences.
Get-MpThreat	View threat detection history.
Get-MpThreatCatalog	View list of known threats from the definitions catalog.
Get-MpThreatDetection	View active and previous detected malware threats.
Remove-MpPreference	Remove default actions or exclusions.

Cmdlet	Function
Remove-MpThreat	Remove an active threat.
Set-MpPreference	Configure Microsoft Defender Antivirus scan and update preferences.
Start-MpScan	Trigger a scan on the device.
Start-MpWDOScan	Trigger a Microsoft Defender Offline scan.
Update-MpSignature	Update a device's antimalware definitions.

If you prefer to use the command prompt, you can use Mpcmdrun.exe to trigger a Microsoft Defender Antivirus scan and other tasks. You need to run Mpcmdrun.exe from within the following location:

```
%ProgramFiles%\Windows Defender\MpCmdRun.exe
```

For example, to trigger a full scan, run the following command:

```
MpCmdRun.exe -Scan -ScanType 2
```

To discover all command-line options for this tool, use the following command:

```
mpcmdrun.exe /?
```

> **NOTE   CONFIGURE AND MANAGE MICROSOFT DEFENDER ANTIVIRUS WITH THE MPCMDRUN.EXE COMMAND-LINE TOOL**
>
> The following article provides a useful list of examples of specific tasks that you can perform using the Mpcmdrun.exe command-line tool: *https://docs.microsoft.com/en-us/microsoft-365/security/defender-endpoint/command-line-arguments-microsoft-defender-antivirus?view=o365-worldwide.*

Chapter summary

- Local accounts are local to the Windows 10 device, and the password is stored in the SAM database.
- Most settings are configured within the Settings app and not Control Panel.
- The administrator has full permissions and privileges on a Windows 10 device and can manage all the objects on the computer.
- The Creator Owner is a special identity that has special administrator-level permissions to the resources over which they have ownership.
- Azure Active Directory (Azure AD) is a cloud-based identity authentication and authorization service.
- Devices can be joined or registered to Azure AD.

- Azure AD supports registering of bring-your-own-device (BYOD) scenarios for multiple types of devices, including Windows 10, iOS, Android, and macOS.

- Only Windows 10 devices can be joined to Azure AD.

- Existing Windows 10 devices can be joined to Azure AD using the Accounts section of the Settings app.

- The Device Enrollment Manager (DEM) account in Microsoft Intune is a special account that allows you to enroll up to a maximum of 1,000 devices.

- Windows 10 supports NTFS as the default file system.

- The Quick Access area is new in Windows 10 and appears at the uppermost left area of the File Explorer navigation pane. It shows the frequently used files and folders.

- Effective Permissions is useful to determine the permissions a particular user would have through NTFS permissions.

- Windows 10 NTFS uses six Basic Permissions and 13 Advanced Permissions for securing files and folders.

- When you apply permissions to groups, an explicit Allow setting will override an implicit Deny permission.

- Use the ICACLS command-line tool to configure and view permissions on files and folders on a local computer and reset them to defaults.

- Inheritance of permissions can be useful when applying permissions to a large environment because the permissions will be automatically propagated based on the default inheritance setting.

- You can use the Effective Access feature to ensure that your NTFS permissions are as expected.

- If you have administrative privileges, you can take ownership of an object, such as a file, and allocate it to another user or group.

- You can reset the permissions of all the folders, files, and subfolders using the command `icacls <file name> /reset`.

- Only files stored on a NTFS-formatted hard drive have a Security tab in their File properties.

- Windows 10 uses a feature called Network Discovery, which uses a new layer 2 protocol called Link Layer Topology Discovery (LLTD) to identify other devices present on the local subnet.

- Share permissions can be Read, Change, or Full.

- The registry is a database, which is split into multiple separate files known as hives.

- You use the built-in Registry Editor (Regedit.exe) tool to view, search, and modify the registry's contents.

- Local Security Policy allows you to configure security policies, such as a password or audit policy, on a local computer.

- User Rights policies are used to determine what rights a user or group of users have on a device and relate to activities or tasks that the user can perform.

- User Rights assignments affect what users can do to a system, and Security Permissions affect which access permissions a user has.

- Use the Resultant Set of Policy (RSoP) tool to check and troubleshoot Group Policy settings.

- Use the GPResult command-line tool to verify what Group Policy Objects have been applied to a user or computer.

- The Windows Security app collects and displays the security status of your device and will trigger notifications through the Action Center.

- User Account Control (UAC) helps protect the operating system from unauthorized configuration changes and app installations.

- UAC elevation prompts can be prompts for consent or prompts for credentials.

- Whenever UAC prompts the user for consent, it uses a feature called Secure Desktop to focus the activity only on the UAC prompt and prevents malware from interacting with the UAC process.

- Windows 10 is protected by the Windows Defender Firewall, which acts as a network barrier.

- You can allow an app through the Windows Defender Firewall or create connection security rules using Windows Defender Firewall With Advanced Security.

- Windows 10 supports two encryption technologies: Encrypting File System (EFS) and BitLocker.

- Windows 10 Home does not support encryption.

- You should always create a Data Recovery Agent (DRA) whenever EFS is used within an enterprise so that encrypted files can be recovered.

- EFS can be managed through the GUI or by using the command-line tool Cipher.exe.

- BitLocker Drive Encryption enables you to encrypt an entire hard disk.

- Devices with a Trusted Platform Module (TPM) can securely store the encryption keys that BitLocker uses.

- BitLocker supports versions 1.2 and 2.0 of the TPM specification.

- BitLocker offers users several key-protection options, including storing the key protectors on a TPM, a smart card, or a USB drive with a startup key on it. BitLocker also allows you to require a PIN on startup.

- On a modern Windows device, BitLocker Drive Encryption will be already enabled when shipped. When the user signs in to the device for the first time with a Microsoft account, the recovery key is saved to their Microsoft account.

- For personal and small-business users, a BitLocker recovery key is stored in their Microsoft accounts at *https://onedrive.live.com/recoverykey*.

- On devices without a TPM, you can configure the Require Additional Authentication At Startup GPO setting to allow BitLocker to be used without a compatible TPM.

- Before upgrading your computer—for example, performing a BIOS firmware upgrade—you should suspend BitLocker Drive Encryption. By default, after a reboot, protection will be automatically resumed.

- If a device enters BitLocker recovery mode, you will need to recover the drive by supplying the 48-digit recovery password.

- The BitLocker recovery password can be stored in Active Directory or Azure Active Directory.

Thought experiment

In these thought experiments, demonstrate your skills and knowledge of the topics covered in this chapter. You can find the answers to these thought experiments in the next section.

Scenario 1

Adatum has 3,000 workstations currently running Windows 10. Most of the users belong to the Active Directory domain, but 50 research engineers in the R&D department do not. The research engineers need to access special 3D printing hardware that is located within their secure area. Adatum needs to ensure that only the research engineers can use the specialized printing devices.

As a consultant for Adatum, answer the following questions:

1. What type of group will you use for the research engineers?

2. How will you ensure that only the research engineers are able to print to the 3D printer?

3. You find that a user has been using the 3D printer for personal use outside of normal office hours. How would you investigate this matter?

4. What measures could you undertake to reduce the likelihood of users printing outside of normal office hours?

Scenario 2

Your organization, Contoso Electronics, has recently deployed Windows 10 laptop devices. All devices run Window 10 Pro. The company security policy requires that all company data stored on devices must be encrypted.

A remote worker had their laptop stolen and purchased a replacement device from the local computer store. The device is installed with Windows 10 Home edition and does not have a TPM.

You must ensure that the company data stored on devices is encrypted at all times.

Answer the following questions for your manager:

1. What encryption technology should be implemented at Contoso Electronics?

2. On devices without a TPM chip available, how can you configure encryption?

3. You create a provisioning package to enable encryption and send the PPKG file to the remote worker. The provisioning package failed to configure the AES-CBC 128-bit encryption method required by the security policy. What could prevent the encryption method from being configured?

Scenario 3

Your organization wants to use Group Policy to configure power settings on the sales department laptops. All laptops are identical. You add a new Group Policy to remove the sleep feature on the laptops. Some members of the sales department report that they can still put their laptops into sleep mode. You access one of the sales departmental laptops and confirm that the GPO has not been applied.

Answer the following questions for your manager:

1. What GUI tool could you use to verify whether the GPO is being delivered to the laptop?

2. Some members of the sales department work out of the office, often in rural locations. How could location affect the effectiveness of the GPO?

3. How could you ensure that all members of the sales department receive the GPO?

4. What command-line tool could you use to verify what GPOs have been delivered to the laptop?

Scenario 4

Adatum Corporation uses Microsoft 365 and has an IT security policy in place that requires company laptop devices to be encrypted at all times. Many of the remote workers operate from home, and the IT policy allows these users to choose a corporate-owned device from an authorized device list. Employees selected various devices, including the Surface laptop, which come preinstalled with Windows 10 Home.

All company data is stored in Microsoft 365 cloud-based storage, such as OneDrive for Business and SharePoint Online. The sales department often needs to leave customers with USB thumb drives that contain presentations, which include sensitive information.

Respond to the security manager, who has raised the following concerns:

1. The Surface laptops do not currently support EFS or BitLocker Drive Encryption. What should you do first?

2. You need to recommend an encryption solution for the company data stored on the sales department laptop devices so that they comply with the IT security policy. What should you recommend?

3. How will your encryption solution be deployed to the remote staff?

Thought experiment answers

This section provides the solutions for the tasks included in the Thought experiments section.

Scenario 1

1. Create a Research Engineers Local Group.

2. Add only the research engineers to the Research Engineers Local Group and grant print permissions for the 3D printer to the Research Engineers Local Group.

3. Investigate the logs within Event Viewer, and look for instances in which a print job has been sent to the 3D printer outside of normal office hours. You could enable logging within the Microsoft-Windows-PrintService Operational logs.

4. You should restrict the hours that the printer is available. Within the Print Servers section of the Printer Management console, select the correct printer and then open the Advanced tab of Printer Properties. Configure the Available From and Available To times for the printer.

Scenario 2

1. Contoso Electronics should implement BitLocker drive encryption technology on all Windows 10 devices.

2. On the new device purchased by the remote worker, you should configure and enable the Require Additional Authentication At Startup GPO.

3. The provisioning package should upgrade the edition of Windows 10 from the Home to the Pro edition on the new device purchased by the remote worker.

Scenario 3

1. Use the Resultant Set of Policy (RSoP) tool to diagnose and troubleshoot Group Policy settings.

2. The GPOs are only delivered once the user connects to and logs into the Active Directory Domain. If members are unable to connect their laptops to the organization, such as by using a VPN or via a wired or a Wi-Fi network, they might be using cached credentials, and therefore, they will not receive the new GPO.

3. Ask the members of the sales department to connect to the corporate network using a VPN or via the internal wired or Wi-Fi network. Once connected, they should then log on so that they can receive the new GPO.

4. Use the GPResult tool to display a report of the GPOs that have been applied to a system.

Scenario 4

1. You need to upgrade the device license on the Surface laptops to Windows 10 Pro or Windows 10 Enterprise before encryption can be used.

2. You could ensure that devices use BitLocker Drive Encryption. In this way, all data stored on the device will be encrypted.

3. The Surface laptops can be joined to Azure Active Directory by the user or by using Windows Autopilot. Once joined, they can be auto-enrolled into Microsoft Intune. Once managed by Intune, they will receive device policies to enforce encryption.

Configure storage and connectivity

Computing devices do not typically work in isolation. Usually, devices are connected to networks to enable users to access services and resources. It's therefore important that you know how to connect devices to networks and how to configure network settings.

Users need to access data stored on file servers, in network-attached storage, and on other computers. You'll need to know how to enable this access. You'll also need to know how to manage and protect data by using file- and folder-level data protection.

Cloud technologies continue to improve in terms of both speed and reliability, and more users will start to rely on Microsoft OneDrive and other cloud services for their file storage. During this transition to the cloud, you must understand how to configure and manage the storage hardware in Windows 10.

Skills covered in this chapter:

- Skill 3.1: Configure networking
- Skill 3.2: Configure data access and protection

Skill 3.1: Configure networking

The ability to connect devices running Windows 10 to both wired and wireless networks is important, whether this is a home network or your organization's network infrastructure. To configure networking settings correctly, you must understand fundamental IP settings and know how to configure name resolution.

It is also important to know how to configure virtual private networks (VPNs) to enable remote connectivity to your organization's network infrastructure. In addition, Exam MD-100: Windows 10 also covers network troubleshooting issues, and it is, therefore, important to know how to use Windows 10 networking tools to investigate and resolve network-related problems.

Configure client IP settings

Before you can configure any other network settings, such as name resolution or firewall settings, you must have a grasp of the underlying fundamentals of networking and how to configure both Internet Protocol version 4 (IPv4) and Internet Protocol version 6 (IPv6) network settings.

Overview of IPv4

IPv4 is a mature networking protocol and is widely used on most internet-connected client devices. Each client on an IPv4 network is assigned a unique IPv4 configuration that identifies that client device. This configuration is based on a number of elements:

- **An IPv4 address** IPv4 uses a 32-bit binary address, which is divided into four octets (or groups of eight digits), each of which is converted to a decimal number. Thus, 11000 0001010100000001000100000001 becomes 11000000.10101000.00010001.00000001 and converts to 192.168.17.1.

- **A subnet mask** A subnet mask is also a 32-bit binary string, entered as four decimal digits; it is used to indicate the client's unique identity, known as the host ID, and the subnet where the client resides, known as the *network ID*.

- **A default gateway address** To facilitate communications between network segments, or subnets, each client device is assigned the IPv4 address of a router in the local network that is used to forward network traffic destined for devices in other subnets.

- **A Domain Name System (DNS) server address** DNS enables the client computer to resolve names into IPv4 or IPv6 addresses.

> ***NEED MORE REVIEW?*** **IPV4 ADDRESSING**
>
> To review further details about IPv4 addressing fundamentals, refer to the Microsoft website at *https://docs.microsoft.com/en-us/previous-versions/windows/it-pro/windows-server-2008-R2-and-2008/dd379547(v=ws.10)*.

Subnets

A *subnet* is a network segment. One or more routers separate the subnet from other subnets. Each subnet on an internet has a unique ID, just as each host within a subnet has a unique ID. You must use the 32 bits of an IPv4 address to define both the host's ID and the subnet ID in which that host resides.

SIMPLE NETWORKS

Remember that each 32-bit IPv4 address is divided into four octets. In simple IPv4 subnetting, whole octets are reserved for defining the subnet portion of the IPv4 address, as shown in Figure 3-1; consequently, the remaining whole octets are available for defining the host portion of the address.

FIGURE 3-1 An IPv4 address using a simple Class C network addressing scheme

This simple subnetting is referred to as *classful addressing*, by which the address class, A, B, or C, defines the number of octets reserved for host and subnet IDs. Table 3-1 shows how this works.

TABLE 3-1 Characteristics of the default IPv4 address classes

Class	First Octet	Default Subnet Mask	Number of Networks	Number of Hosts per Network
A	1 to 127	255.0.0.0	126	16,777,214
B	128 to 191	255.255.0.0	16,384	65,534
C	192 to 223	255.255.255.0	2,097,152	254

> **NOTE OTHER ADDRESS CLASSES**
>
> There are also class D and class E addresses. Class D addresses are used for multicasting when a client device is part of a group. Class E addresses are reserved and are not used for hosts or subnets.

COMPLEX NETWORKS

For some situations, using a classful addressing scheme can be ideal. But for many situations, it might be important to have more flexibility over the number of bits allocated to the subnet address portion of an IPv4 address. For example, instead of using 8, 16, or 24 bits for the subnet, you can use 12 or 18.

Bear in mind that the more bits you allocate to subnetting, the fewer bits remain for the host portion of the IPv4 address. That is, you can have more subnets, each containing fewer hosts, or you can have few subnets, each containing many hosts. Figure 3-2 shows how changing the subnet mask changes the subnet ID without changing the octets that define the whole IPv4 address. This scheme is often referred to as classless addressing, or Classless Interdomain Routing (CIDR).

IP address	192	168	17	1

Subnet mask	255	255	240	0

Network ID	192	168	16	0

FIGURE 3-2 An IPv4 address using a classless network addressing scheme

In Figure 3-2, notice how changing the subnet mask from 255.255.255.0 to 255.255.240.0 shifts the device from subnet 192.168.17.0 to 192.168.16.0. In this case, by shifting the mask to the left, we have allocated more bits to describe hosts in each subnet, with correspondingly fewer subnets. You can see that to express a host's IPv4 configuration properly, not only must you state the IPv4 address, but you must also state the subnet mask. For example, in Figure 3-2 this host has an IPv4 configuration of 192.168.17.1/255.255.240.0.

EXAM TIP

You will often see devices with IPv4 configurations shown as 192.168.17.1/20. The number after the slash denotes the number of sequential binary 1s in the subnet mask (20 in this instance). If the mask were 255.255.248.0, that would be represented as /21.

NEED MORE REVIEW? **IPV4 ROUTING**

To review further details about IPv4 subnetting and routing, refer to the Microsoft website at https://docs.microsoft.com/en-us/previous-versions/windows/it-pro/windows-server-2008-R2-and-2008/dd379495(v=ws.10).

Public and private addressing

Devices that connect directly to the internet require a unique public IPv4 configuration. However, because of the limitation of the 32-bit addressing scheme of IPv4, there is a limit to the number of hosts that can be connected to the internet using a public configuration. To alleviate this potential but significant problem, many organizations use private IPv4 configurations for their network clients, only using public IPv4 configurations for internet-facing devices, such as routers.

The Internet Assigned Numbers Authority (IANA) has defined the address ranges shown in Table 3-2 as being available for private use. A technology such as network address translation (NAT) is used to enable devices using private IPv4 configurations to communicate with the internet.

TABLE 3-2 Private IPv4 address ranges

Class	Mask	Range
A	10.0.0.0/8	10.0.0.0–10.255.255.255
B	172.16.0.0/12	172.16.0.0–172.31.255.255
C	192.168.0.0/16	192.168.0.0–192.168.255.255

Configuring an IPv4 connection

Devices running Windows 10 are configured to obtain an IPv4 configuration automatically by default, as shown in Figure 3-3.

FIGURE 3-3 The Internet Protocol Version 4 (TCP/IPv4) Properties dialog box

Typically, Windows 10-based devices obtain their IPv4 configurations from a Dynamic Host Configuration Protocol (DHCP) service, perhaps running on a Windows Server 2019 server computer, or provided as a service on a device such as a router or wireless access point (wireless AP).

EXAM TIP

If a Windows 10–based device fails to obtain an IPv4 configuration from a DHCP server, it reverts to using an Automatic Private IP Address (APIPA). If your computer has an IPv4 address that starts with 169.254.*X.Y*, it is using an APIPA address. APIPA enables only local, subnet-based communications at best. You can override this behavior by selecting the Alternative Configuration tab in the Internet Protocol Version 4 (TCP/IPv4) Properties dialog box, shown in Figure 3-3, and choosing User Configured. Then specify the IPv4 configuration to use when DHCP is unavailable.

To view or configure the IPv4 settings on your computer, perform the following procedure:

1. Right-click the network icon in the system tray and then select **Open Network & Internet settings**.

2. Select **Change adapter options**.

3. Right-click the appropriate network adapter and then select **Properties**.

4. Double-click **Internet Protocol Version 4 (TCP/IPv4)**.

You can then configure the IPv4 settings. Select Use The Following IP Address and then specify the following: IP Address, Subnet Mask, Default Gateway, Preferred DNS Server, and Alternative DNS Server (Optional).

You can also configure a number of options from the Advanced TCP/IP Settings dialog box. In the Internet Protocol Version 4 (TCP/IPv4) Properties dialog box, select Advanced to open the Advanced TCP/IP Settings dialog box, shown in Figure 3-4.

Configure the options on the following tabs:

- **IP Settings** Enables you to configure additional IPv4 addresses and default gateways manually for this network interface.

- **DNS** You can define additional DNS server addresses for name resolution and additional DNS suffix processing options.

- **WINS** The Windows Internet Name Service (WINS) is an older name resolution service used by earlier versions of Windows and Windows Server. Generally, you do not need to configure anything here.

FIGURE 3-4 The IP Settings tab of the Advanced TCP/IP Settings dialog box

CONFIGURING IPV4 FROM THE COMMAND LINE AND BY USING WINDOWS POWERSHELL

In addition to configuring IPv4 settings from the user interface, you can use the Netsh.exe command-line tool and Windows PowerShell cmdlets. You can use the Netsh.exe command-line tool to reconfigure many network-related settings. For example, the following command reconfigures the IPv4 settings:

```
Netsh interface ipv4 set address name="Ethernet" source=static addr=192.168.17.1
mask=255.255.240.0 gateway=192.168.31.254
```

There are numerous Windows PowerShell cmdlets that you can use to view and configure network settings, some of which are described in Table 3-3.

TABLE 3-3 Windows PowerShell IPv4 networking-related cmdlets

Cmdlet	Purpose
Get-NetIPAddress	Displays information about the IP address configuration
Get-NetIPv4Protocol	Displays information about the IPv4 protocol configuration
Set-NetIPAddress	Changes the IP address configuration
Set-NetIPv4Protocol	Changes the IPv4 protocol configuration

For example, to change the IPv4 configuration for a network connection with Windows PowerShell, use the following cmdlet:

```
Set-NetIPAddress -InterfaceAlias Ethernet -IPAddress 192.168.17.1
```

Overview of IPv6

It's still the case that almost all computers and other devices connect to the internet by using an IPv4 configuration. However, more network services and devices now require an IPv6 configuration, so it's important to understand the IPv6 fundamentals, including how to configure IPv6. There are a number of reasons to consider IPv6. These include:

- **Services that require IPv6**   Services, such as DirectAccess, use IPv6 to facilitate remote connections.

- **Larger address space**   IPv6 uses a 128-bit address space, providing a vast increase in the availability of addresses for devices on the internet.

- **Hierarchical addressing**   IPv6 uses a structured address space, which is more efficient for routers, helping to optimize network communications.

- **Support for stateless and stateful autoconfiguration**   You can configure your IPv6 devices to use DHCPv6 to obtain a stateful configuration, or you can rely on router discovery to use a stateless configuration, simplifying the process of enabling IPv6 on your network devices.

IPv6 addressing

As mentioned, IPv6 uses a 128-bit addressing scheme. This is usually written in hexadecimal. The following is an example of an IPv6 address:

```
2001:CD8:1F2D::2BB:FF:EF82:1C3B
```

IPv6 uses the following three address types:

- **Unicast addresses** Packets are delivered to a single interface.
- **Multicast addresses** Packets are delivered to multiple interfaces.
- **Anycast addresses** Packets are delivered to multiple interfaces that are the closest in routing distance.

Unlike IPv4, IPv6 does not use broadcast messages. Instead, unicast and anycast addresses in IPv6 can have the following scopes:

- **Link-local** IPv6 hosts on the same subnet
- **Site-local** IPv6 hosts in the same organization, also known as private site addressing
- **Global** IPv6 internet addresses

EXAM TIP

Unicast site-local addresses are similar to IPv4 private addresses and have the FEC0::/64 prefix. Unicast link-local addresses are similar to IPv4 APIPA addresses and have the FE80::/64 prefix.

Configuring an IPv6 connection

Configuring IPv6 is almost identical to the process of configuring IPv4. By default, Windows 10 uses automatic IPv6 configuration. If a DHCPv6 server is available, it obtains its configuration from that service; otherwise, it will use stateless autoconfiguration.

As with IPv4, you can use the Windows user interface to configure IPv6, as shown in Figure 3-5, or you can use Netsh.exe or Windows PowerShell.

FIGURE 3-5 The Internet Protocol Version 6 (TCP/IPv6) Properties dialog box

To review or configure the IPv6 settings on your computer, perform the following procedure:

1. Right-click the network icon in the system tray and then select **Open Network & Internet Settings**.

2. Select **Change Adapter Options**.

3. Right-click the appropriate network adapter and then select **Properties**.

4. Double-click **Internet Protocol Version 6 (TCP/IPv6).**

Numerous Windows PowerShell cmdlets are available that you can use to review and configure IPv6 network settings, some of which are described in Table 3-4.

TABLE 3-4 Windows PowerShell IPv6 networking-related cmdlets

Cmdlet	Purpose
Get-NetIPAddress	Displays information about the IP address configuration
Get-NetIPv6Protocol	Displays information about the IPv6 protocol configuration
Set-NetIPAddress	Changes the IP address configuration
Set-NetIPv6Protocol	Changes the IPv6 protocol configuration

For example, to change the IPv6 configuration for a network connection with Windows PowerShell, use the following cmdlet:

```
Set-NetIPAddress -IPAddress 2001:CD8:1F2D::2BB:FF:EF82:1C3B -PrefixLength 64
```

Configure name resolution

Devices running Windows 10 communicate over networks by using names rather than IPv4 or IPv6 network addresses. A service on the Windows 10–based device, known as a client resolver, resolves names into IPv4 or IPv6 addresses. To configure Windows 10 networking, you must know how to configure name resolution.

Although IP addressing is not especially complex, it is generally easier for users to work with host names rather than with the IPv4 or IPv6 addresses of hosts, such as websites, to which they want to connect. When an application, such as Microsoft Edge, references a website name, the name is converted to the underlying IP address by using a process known as *name resolution*. Windows 10–based devices can use two types of names:

- **Host names** A host name, up to 255 characters in length, contains only alphanumeric characters, periods, and hyphens. A host name is an alias combined with a fully qualified domain name (FQDN). For example, the alias *computer1* is prefixed to the domain name contoso.com to create the host name, or FQDN, of *computer1*.contoso.com.

- **NetBIOS names** Less relevant today, NetBIOS names use a nonhierarchical structure based on a 16-character name. The sixteenth character identifies a particular service running on the computer named by the preceding 15 characters. Thus, LON-SVR1[20h] is the NetBIOS server service on the computer called LON-SVR1.

The way a client computer resolves names varies based on its configuration but is typically resolved as indicated in Figure 3-6.

FIGURE 3-6 Typical stages of name resolution in a Windows 10 client

The following process identifies the typical stages of name resolution for Windows 10–based devices.

1. Determine whether the queried host name is the same as the local host name.

2. Search the local DNS resolver cache for the queried host name. Windows 10 updates the cache when records are successfully resolved. In addition, Windows adds the contents of the local Hosts file to the resolver cache.

3. Petition a DNS server for the required host name.

EXAM TIP

Windows 10 devices also use Link-Local Multicast Name Resolution for networks that do not provide DNS. You can find out more on the Microsoft Press Store website at *https://www. microsoftpressstore.com/articles/article.aspx?p=2217263&seqNum=8.*

NEED MORE REVIEW? IPV4 NAME RESOLUTION

To review further details about IPv4 name resolution, refer to the Microsoft website at *https://docs.microsoft.com/en-us/previous-versions/windows/it-pro/windows-server-2008-R2-and-2008/dd379505(v=ws.10).*

CONFIGURE DNS SETTINGS

To configure DNS settings for either IPv4 or IPv6, perform the following procedure:

1. Right-click the network icon in the system tray and then select **Open Network & Internet settings**.

2. Select **Change adapter options**.

3. Right-click the appropriate network adapter and then select **Properties**.

4. Double-click either **Internet Protocol Version 4 (TCP/IPv4)** or **Internet Protocol Version 6 (TCP/IPv6)**.

5. Select **Use the following DNS server addresses** and then enter a valid IPv4 or IPv6 address for a DNS server that is accessible to the client.

You can also configure DNS settings by using Netsh.exe, as follows:

```
netsh interface ip set dns name="Ethernet" static 192.168.16.1
```

Alternatively, you can use Windows PowerShell to configure the DNS client settings:

```
Set-DNSClientServerAddress -interfaceIndex 12 -ServerAddresses ('192.168.16.1')
```

CONFIGURE ADVANCED DNS SETTINGS

In addition to configuring the basic DNS client settings, you can configure advanced DNS settings, as displayed in Figure 3-7. To configure these settings, from either the Internet Protocol Version 4 (TCP/IPv4) Properties dialog box or the Internet Protocol Version 6 (TCP/IPv6) Properties dialog box, select Advanced and then select the DNS tab.

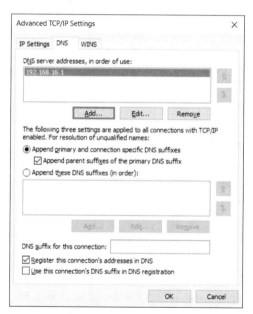

FIGURE 3-7 The DNS tab of the Advanced TCP/IP Settings dialog box

The advanced DNS settings are as follows:

- **Append primary and connection-specific DNS suffixes** This option controls how the DNS resolver on the local client appends the DNS suffixes during queries. For example, if you query **www** and your computer's primary suffix is **contoso.com**, the contoso.com suffix is appended to your query to make **www.contoso.com**.

- **Append parent suffixes of the primary DNS suffix** In this example, the parent suffix of **contoso.com** is **com**. This option determines whether, after attempting **www.contoso.com**, the DNS resolver tries **www.com**.

- **Append these DNS suffixes (in order)** This option enables you to define suffixes and order them for queries.

- **DNS suffix for this connection** You can define a DNS suffix for each network interface card installed in your device.

- **Register this connection's address in DNS** Windows-based devices can register their IPv4 addresses with DNS servers that support dynamic updates of host records, such as the DNS server role service in Windows Server.

- **Use this connection's DNS suffix in DNS registration** This option determines whether the IP addresses and the connection-specific domain name of this connection are registered with DNS.

Configure mobile networking

With users increasingly working from home and other locations, it's becoming ever more important to enable them to use their mobile devices for connectivity to their workplace resources. Windows 10 supports a number of mobile networking features to help make this possible.

Set up Windows 10 for a cellular data plan

Some devices with Windows 10 installed can support connectivity by using cellular networks. This is useful for users who cannot always connect to Wi-Fi networks but who still need access to corporate services and resources.

To enable and configure cellular remote access in Windows 10, you must obtain a cellular data plan from a telecom provider. Microsoft can provide this service.

> **NEED MORE REVIEW? GET ONLINE WITH PAID CELLULAR DATA**
>
> To find out more about getting online with Microsoft cellular data packages, refer to the Microsoft website at *https://support.microsoft.com/en-us/help/4027933/windows-10-get-online-with-paid-cellular-data*.

Typically, your telecom provider must provide you with a suitable SIM card for your Windows 10 device. The SIM size might vary depending on the vendor of the device you intend to use. For example, if you or your users are intending to connect using a Microsoft Surface Pro device, you must obtain a Nano SIM from your telecom provider. Note that you can use the SIM card from your cellphone for this, but it must be the right size. Some hardware vendors, including Microsoft, support a built-in SIM, or Embedded SIM (eSIM). This enables you to use cellular data without obtaining a separate, physical SIM from a telecom provider. You can also combine the use of an external SIM and an eSIM, effectively creating a device that has two data plans; perhaps one for business and one for personal use—much like some users use their cellphones with dual-SIM.

After you have installed the SIM into your Windows device, you must configure Windows 10 to connect using cellular data. If you use a Microsoft data plan, you can configure network access simply by running the Mobile Plans app. This app is built into Windows 10. The app detects your eSIM (or SIM) and then guides you through the setup process. To set up cellular network access, use the following procedure:

1. Connect to the internet using a wired or wireless connection.

2. Select the **Network** symbol on the taskbar, look for **Get Connected** beneath the name of your mobile operator, and then select **Connect with a data plan**. This will open the Mobile Plans app.

3. In **Mobile Plans**, do one of the following, depending on what your computer displays on the screen:

   - On the **Connect your device** page, enter your cellphone number, and then select **Find my mobile operator**. This enables you to determine if your telecom provider offers any plans.

      - If they do, select **Continue**. A webpage opens on your telecom provider's website. Sign in (using your existing mobile account details) or create a new account if needed, and then follow the steps to add your device to your account.

      - If your provider doesn't offer plans, select **Choose from a list of mobile operators**. Choose a new provider, and then select **Continue** to go to the telecom provider's website to set up a new account and plan.

   - On the **Select a mobile operator to get online now** page, select a telecom provider, select **Continue** to go to their site, sign in, and then choose a plan.

When you want to use your mobile data connection, use the following procedure to connect:

1. Select the **Network** icon in the system tray.

2. In the list of available networks, choose the mobile network.

If you experience any problems with your cellular connections, use the following steps to troubleshoot your connection:

1. Open the **Settings** app.

2. Select **Network & Internet**.

3. Assuming you have an eSIM or compatible SIM, you should see a Mobile tab on the left. Select the **Mobile** tab.

4. If you have multiple SIMs, then select whichever SIM you want to use for a given data plan, and select **Use this SIM for mobile data**.

5. Open the **Mobile Plans** app and choose a mobile operator from those listed.

6. Follow the previous instructions to set up a plan with your telecom provider.

Set up Windows 10 as a mobile hotspot

Windows 10 devices are becoming lighter and more mobile. Often, users have multiple connected devices, including laptops, tablets, and cellphones. Virtually ubiquitous internet connectivity enables users to adopt an "always on" lifestyle. When users face situations where traditional connections, such as corporate Wi-Fi or Ethernet, are not available, they will look for other forms of connectivity, such as Wi-Fi hotspots; they also might use their mobile devices to connect to the internet.

Broadband tethering, referred to as a Windows 10 mobile hotspot, enables users to share their own internet connections with others by enabling the device to function as a wireless "hotspot." Similarly, users can connect to other users' shared personal "hotspots," provided they have the necessary credentials.

To connect to a shared mobile hotspot connection, follow these steps:

1. In **Settings**, select **Network & Internet**.
2. As shown in Figure 3-8, select the **Mobile hotspot** tab.
3. In the **Share my internet connection from** list, choose the appropriate network connection.
4. Select **Edit** and enter a **Network name** and **Network password**. These are used by other users that connect to your device.
5. Finally, enable the **Share my Internet connection with other devices** option.

FIGURE 3-8 Enabling a mobile hotspot

Configure VPN client

In Windows 10, creating a VPN enables data to be transferred through a virtual private network using a secured connection (known as a tunnel) over a public network, such as the internet, as shown in Figure 3-9.

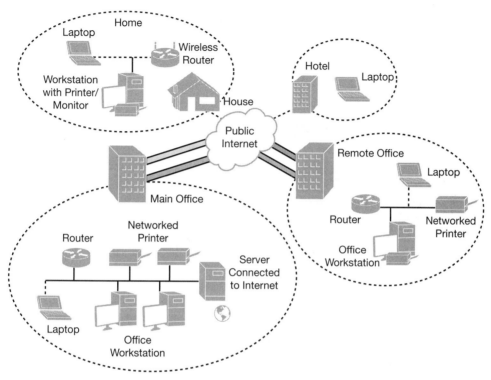

FIGURE 3-9 Using a VPN to connect locations securely over the internet

Except in a few specialized scenarios, nearly all dial-up remote connections have been replaced by broadband-enabled VPN communications. Windows 10 still supports Point-to-Point Protocol (PPP), which can be used with a dial-up connection. This is an old protocol, but because it creates a direct connection and maintains a dedicated link between the two points, it is used as the starting point for most dial-up and PPP connections.

VPN protocols

Windows 10 supports four commonly used VPN protocols. Each protocol offers different characteristics and age, as described next. Typically, the newest protocol will be the most secure.

- **Point-to-Point Tunneling Protocol (PPTP)** PPTP is the oldest and what is considered one of the least secure of all supported VPN protocols. However, it can be used successfully in low-security scenarios because it is very easy to set up and still offers more protection than using PPP over the internet. PPTP creates the tunnel and then can use several authentication methods, including the Microsoft Challenge Handshake Authentication Protocol versions 1 and 2 (MS-CHAP v1 and MS-CHAP v2), Extensible

Authentication Protocol (EAP), and Protected Extensible Authentication Protocol (PEAP). If EAP is used, certificates can be used with PPTP; otherwise, they are not necessary.

- **Layer 2 Tunneling Protocol (L2TP)**   This protocol uses the IP security extensions (IPsec) for encryption and encapsulation. L2TP encapsulates the messages with IPsec, and then encrypts the contents using the Data Encryption Standard (DES) or Triple DES (3DES) algorithm. The encryption keys are provided by IPsec using Internet Key Exchange (IKE). L2TP/IPsec can use preshared keys or certificates for authentication. Using a preshared key is useful during testing and evaluation but should be replaced with a certificate in a production environment.

- **Secure Socket Tunneling Protocol (SSTP)**   This is a recent protocol introduced with Windows Server 2008 and supported on Vista SP1 or later. It encapsulates PPP traffic using the Secure Sockets Layer (SSL) protocol, which is widely supported on the internet and passes through TCP port 443, which is the same as SSL. Using the Extensible Authentication Protocol-Transport Layer Security (EAP-TLS) authentication protocol together with certificates makes SSTP a versatile and widely used protocol.

- **Internet Key Exchange, Version 2 (IKEv2)**   IKEv2 is most useful for mobile users and is the default protocol for Windows 10 and Windows 8.1 when trying to connect to remote access servers. This protocol is partially supported on Windows 7 and later versions of Windows and provides support for IPv6 traffic and the IKEv2 Mobility and Multi-homing (MOBIKE) protocol through the Windows VPN Reconnect feature, which allows automatic reconnection if a VPN connection is lost. Authentication is offered using EAP, PEAP, EAP-MS-CHAPv2, and smart cards. IKEv2 will not support older authentication methods, such as Password Authentication Protocol (PAP) and Challenge-Handshake Authentication Protocol (CHAP), which offer little protection.

Authenticating remote users

Windows users authenticate using Kerberos when accessing the local network, but for remote authentication, this protocol is not suitable; a separate protocol, which protects against network intrusion, must be used. During the initial negotiation sequence (using PPP) when a client connects to the remote computer, each party must agree on a shared authentication protocol to use. By default, Windows 10 will use the strongest protocol that both parties have in common.

In the Add A VPN Connection Wizard, Windows 10 offers three sign-in options when configuring a VPN, such as:

- Username and password
- Smart card
- One-time password

In addition to these options, you can configure Windows 10 to use the common authentication protocols:

- **EAP-MS-CHAPv2**   This protocol uses Extensible Authentication Protocol (EAP), which offers the default and most flexible authentication option for Windows 10 clients. It provides the strongest password-based mechanism for the client side, with certificates used on the server side. Authentication can be negotiated based on certificates or smart cards, and EAP-MS-CHAPv2 is likely to be further extended and developed as technology advances. Windows 10 will aim to use this method for authentication connections where possible. IKEv2 connections must use EAP-MS-CHAPv2 or a certificate.

- **PAP**   This is the least secure protocol since it uses plaintext passwords. It should be used only when other authentication methods cannot be negotiated.
- **CHAP**   CHAP is used for down-level client compatibility and has been surpassed by MS-CHAP v2. This protocol uses a preshared key between the client and server to enable encryption to take place.
- **MS-CHAP v2**   This protocol is stronger than the CHAP protocol, with significantly improved security when partnered with EAP to enable encryption of the password.

Creating a VPN connection in Network And Sharing Center

To create a VPN in Windows 10, from the Network And Sharing Center, under Change your network settings, select Set up a new connection or network and then select Connect to a workplace.

To configure your VPN connection, in the Connect to a Workplace Wizard, provide the following information.

- **How do you want to connect?**   You can connect by using an existing internet connection or by dialing directly to your workplace.
- **Internet address**   This is the name or IP address of the computer that you connect to at your workplace, as shown in Figure 3-10. Typically, this is an FQDN, such as remote. adatum.com.
- **Destination name**   This is the name of your VPN connection.

FIGURE 3-10 The Connect To A Workplace Wizard

After you have created the VPN connection, from the Network And Sharing Center, select Change adapter settings, right-click your VPN connection, and select Properties. As shown in Figure 3-11, you can then configure additional options as required by your organization's network infrastructure.

FIGURE 3-11 The Security tab of a VPN connection

These settings must match the remote access device that your device connects to, and includes the following options:

- **Type of VPN** Point-to-Point Tunneling Protocol (PPTP), Layer Two Tunneling Protocol with IPsec (L2TP/IPsec), Secure Socket Tunneling Protocol (SSTP), or Internet Key Exchange version 2 (IKEv2)

- **Data encryption** None, Optional, Required, or Maximum Strength

In the Authentication section, you choose either Use Extensible Authentication Protocol (EAP) or Allow These Protocols. If you choose to use EAP, you then configure one of the following:

- Microsoft: EAP-AKA (Encryption Enabled)

- Microsoft: EAP-SIM (Encryption Enabled)

- Microsoft: EAP-TTLS (Encryption Enabled)

- Microsoft: Protected EAP (PEAP) (Encryption Enabled)

- Microsoft: Secured Password (EAP-MSCHAP v2) (Encryption Enabled)

- Microsoft: Smart Card Or Other Certificate (Encryption Enabled)

If you choose Allow These Protocols, you then configure the following options:

- Unencrypted Password (PAP)

- Challenge Handshake Authentication Protocol (CHAP)
- Microsoft CHAP Version 2 (MS-CHAP v2)
  - Automatically Use My Windows Log-on Name And Password (And Domain, If Any)

Using the Settings app to create and configure a VPN

You can also use the Settings app to create and configure VPN connections. Use the following procedure:

1. Select **Start** and then select **Settings**.
2. In **Settings**, select **Network & Internet**.
3. Select the **VPN** tab, and then, in the details pane, select **Add a VPN connection**.
4. On the **Add a VPN connection** page, enter the following information:
   - **VPN** provider: Windows (Built-In)
   - **Connection name**
   - **Server name or address**
   - **VPN type:** Automatic (Default). You can also choose PPTP, L2TP/IPsec with certificate, L2TP/IPsec with pre-shared key, SSTP, or IKEv2.
   - **Type of sign-in info:** Username and password, Smart card, One-off password, or Certificate.
   - **Username and password**, although these options are only configurable if you selected username or password as the Type of sign-in info.
5. Select **Save**.

After you have created the VPN, you can manage it from Network Connections in Control Panel. Alternatively, on the VPN page in the Network & Internet node in Settings, you can select the VPN and then choose Advanced Options. From there, you can reconfigure the VPN's settings.

VPN profiles

Although manually configuring VPN connections is relatively simple, completing the process on many computers, with the same or similar settings, is very time-consuming. In these circumstances, it makes sense to create a VPN profile and then distribute the profile to your users' computers.

When you use VPN profiles in Windows 10, you can take advantage of a number of advanced features:

- **Always On**   This feature enables Windows to automatically connect to a VPN. The Always On feature can be triggered by sign-in when the desktop is unlocked, and on network changes. When the Always On profile is configured, the VPN remains always connected unless the user disconnects manually or logs off the device. The profile is optimized for power and performance, and the profiles can be pushed and managed on devices using mobile device management (MDM) tools.

- **App-Triggered VPN** You can configure the VPN profile to respond to a specific set of apps; if a defined app loads, then the VPN initiates.
- **Traffic Filters** To protect the server from a remote attack, an administrator can configure policies on a Windows 10 device to inspect and, if necessary, filter VPN traffic before it is enabled to travel over the VPN. Two types of Traffic Filter rules are available:
  - **App-based rules** An app-based rule will only enable VPN traffic originating from applications that have been marked as being allowed to traverse the VPN interface.
  - **Traffic-based rules** Enterprise-level traffic-based rules enable fine-tuning of the type of traffic allowed. By using the industry-standard rules covered by five tuple policies (protocol, source IP address, destination IP address, source port, and destination port), administrators can be very specific on the type of network traffic that is allowed to travel over the VPN interface.

    An administrator can combine both app-based rules and traffic-based rules.
- **LockDown VPN** The LockDown VPN profile is used to enforce the use of the VPN interface. In this scenario, the device is secured to only allow network traffic over the VPN, which is automatically always on and can never be disconnected. If the VPN is unable to connect, then no network traffic will be allowed. The LockDown profile overrides all other VPN profiles and must be deleted before other profiles can be added, removed, or connected.

You can create and distribute Windows 10 VPN profiles with these advanced settings by using Microsoft Intune and/or Endpoint Configuration Manager.

> **NEED MORE REVIEW? VPN CONNECTIONS IN MICROSOFT INTUNE**
>
> To review further details about VPN connections in Microsoft Intune, refer to the Microsoft website at *https://docs.microsoft.com/intune/vpn-settings-configure*.

> **NEED MORE REVIEW? HOW TO CREATE VPN PROFILES IN CONFIGURATION MANAGER**
>
> To review further details about creating VPN profiles in Configuration Manager, refer to the Microsoft website at *https://docs.microsoft.com/en-us/sccm/mdm/deploy-use/create-vpn-profiles*.

Enable VPN Reconnect

VPN Reconnect uses the IKEv2 protocol with the MOBIKE extension to automatically reestablish a lost VPN connection without user intervention. For mobile users, the prevalence of dropped Wi-Fi or LTE connections can be frequent because of volatile signal strength. It is best to use and configure VPN Reconnect for your mobile users because doing so reduces the frustration of having to reconnect manually, and it will also increase productivity.

The network outage time can be configured from 5 minutes up to an interruption of 8 hours. To enable VPN Reconnect, follow these steps:

1. On the taskbar, in the search box, enter **VPN**.
2. Select **VPN settings** from the returned list.
3. In the **Settings** app, select **Change adapter options**.
4. Select the appropriate VPN adapter, and then select **Change settings of this connection**, as shown in Figure 3-12.
5. Select the **Security** tab in the **VPN Properties dialog box**, and select **Advanced settings**.
6. In the **Advanced Properties** dialog box, select the **Mobility** option on the **IKEv2** tab.
7. Modify the **Network outage time** as necessary.
8. Select **OK** twice.

FIGURE 3-12 Configuring the Network Outage Time for VPN Reconnect

Troubleshoot networking

Windows 10 is a reliable and robust operating system, and the networking technologies built into it are tried and tested. However, networking is an inherently complex area, and problems might occur on your network.

When you are facing a networking problem, use an appropriate procedure for troubleshooting the issue. This procedure might include the following steps:

1. Determine the scope of the problem. Knowing how many users are affected can help you determine possible causes.

2. Determine the IP configuration. Verify that the network configuration of affected devices is correct.

3. Determine the network's hardware configuration. Determine whether any problems exist with the networking hardware or device drivers for that hardware.

4. Test communications. Perform a series of tests that help you pinpoint the nature of the problem. Tests might include:

   ■ Verifying basic communications

   ■ Checking the routing and firewall configuration of your network

   ■ Testing name resolution

   ■ Testing connectivity to specific applications on servers

It's important that you know how to troubleshoot network-related problems that occur on your network to minimize disruption to your users.

Network troubleshooting tools

Windows 10 provides a number of tools that you can use to diagnose and resolve many network-related issues. These tools are described in Table 3-5.

TABLE 3-5 Windows 10 network troubleshooting tools

Tool	Purpose
Event Viewer	Windows collects information about system activity into event logs. For example, the System log stores information about IP conflicts and network-related service failures.
Windows Network Diagnostics	You can use Diagnose Connection Problems to help you diagnose and repair a network issue. Windows Network Diagnostics presents possible descriptions of the issue and suggests a potential solution. You can access this tool by clicking Troubleshoot Problems in Network And Sharing Center.
IPConfig	Use this command-line tool to display the current TCP/IP configuration of your Windows 10–based device. You can use the command with the following switches: **ipconfig /all** View detailed configuration information. **ipconfig /release** Release the leased configuration back to the DHCP server. **ipconfig /renew** Renew the leased configuration. **ipconfig /displaydns** View the DNS resolver cache entries. **ipconfig /flushdns** Purge the DNS resolver cache. **ipconfig /registerdns** Register or update the client's host name with the DNS server.
Ping	This command-line tool can be used to verify connectivity to a target computer system by sending a series of network packets to that target system. Consider that many firewalls block the ICMP packets Ping uses, so you might receive false negatives. Type **ping www.contoso.com**.
Tracert	Use this tool to determine the path that packets take to a designated target computer system, which helps you diagnose routing-related problems.
NSLookup	Use this tool to troubleshoot name resolution.

Tool	Purpose
Pathping	This traces a network route similar to how the Tracert tool works but provides more statistics on the hops through the network.
Windows PowerShell	In addition to the configuration cmdlets referred to earlier, a number of Windows PowerShell cmdlets are available that you can use to troubleshoot and test network connectivity. For example, the **test-connection** cmdlet behaves in a way similar to Ping.exe. Enter **test-connection www.contoso.com**.
Network Troubleshooter	You can use the Network Troubleshooter tool from within Network & Internet in the Settings app. On the Status tab, select Network Troubleshooter. A wizard starts that scans the network configuration for problems and, where possible, makes suggestions about fixes. This is very similar to the Windows Network Diagnostics tool mentioned earlier.
Network Reset	You can use the network reset tool from within Network & Internet in the Settings app. On the Status tab, select Network Reset. Note that you should use Network Reset as a last resort. This is because it removes and then reinstalls your network adapters and related settings. Network Reset can help restore your internet connection, but it might result in additional configuration work after the reset has been performed.

Troubleshoot name resolution

Many network failures can be caused by a failure in name resolution, such as when the wrong server IP address is returned or a service has not registered itself with a DNS server correctly (or at all). When troubleshooting name resolution issues, use a suitable procedure, which might consist of the following steps:

1. Clear the DNS resolver cache. Use the **Ipconfig /flushdns** command from an elevated command prompt. Clearing the cache ensures that all subsequent name resolution attempts are performed rather than being satisfied from DNS resolver cache. You can also use the **Clear-DnsClientCache** Windows PowerShell cmdlet to achieve the same thing.

2. Attempt to verify basic connectivity by using an IP address. Use the **Ping** command, or the **test-connection** Windows PowerShell cmdlet, to verify communications to an IP address; for example, type **test-connection 172.16.16.1**.

3. Attempt to verify connectivity to a host name. Using the same tools, check whether you can communicate with a host by using its name, for example, **test-connection LON-DC1**. If this is successful, it is likely that your problem is not related to name resolution.

4. If the test is not successful, edit the Hosts file. Add the correct IP address and name to your hosts file. For example, add the line **172.16.16.1 LON-DC1.adatum.com** to C:\Windows\System32\Drivers\Etc\Hosts. Repeat the procedure to verify connectivity to a host name. Name resolution should now be successful.

5. Display the resolver cache. Use the **Get-DnsClientCache** cmdlet (or use **IPConfig /displaydns**) to verify that the entry appears in a resolved cache. You have proven that the problem is likely a name resolution issue. Remove the entry from the Hosts file and clear the resolver cache.

6. Test the name server by performing a query against it by using the **Resolve-dnsname lon-DC1.adatum.com** cmdlet. Alternatively, use the **NSLookup .exe -d2 LON-cl1. adatum.com** command. You can review the partial output from the **Resolve-dnsname** cmdlet in Figure 3-13.

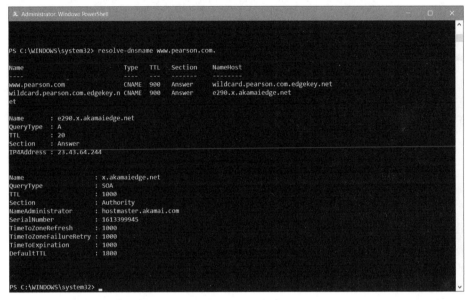

FIGURE 3-13 Using **Resolve-dnsname** to test name resolution

The information returned from the name server test shows IP addresses of the server you queried against. It also shows which name servers provided the response. It is important to know how to interpret this returned information to diagnose any failures or faults properly.

> **NEED MORE REVIEW? DIAGNOSING NAME RESOLUTION PROBLEMS**
>
> To find out more about troubleshooting name resolution, refer to the Microsoft website at *https://technet.microsoft.com/library/cc959340.aspx.*

Configure Wi-Fi profiles

You can configure wireless networks by using one of several modes to suit your requirements and using one of a number of standards to secure the network and achieve compatibility between your wireless devices.

Modes

Wireless networking can be configured in one of three modes:

- **Ad-hoc** This setting enables you to configure a wireless connection between devices in a peer-to-peer manner without requiring a wireless access point (AP).

- **Wi-Fi Direct**   This setting is a wireless networking standard that you can use to connect your wireless devices without a wireless AP. Similar to ad hoc wireless networking, it is typically used to connect to peripherals such as printers and media players.
- **Infrastructure**   Based on wireless APs, infrastructure networks consist of wireless local area networks to enable communications between wireless client devices.

Standards

To ensure compatibility between wireless networked devices, a number of standards have evolved. The 802.11x wireless standards are described in Table 3-6.

TABLE 3-6 802.11 wireless standards

Standard	Definition
802.11a	Provides up to 54 megabits per second (mbps) and uses the 5 gigahertz (GHz) range. Not compatible with 802.11b. Sometimes referred to as Wi-Fi 2.
802.11b	Provides 11 mbps and uses the 2.4 GHz range. Sometimes referred to as Wi-Fi 1.
802.11e	Defines Quality of Service and multimedia support.
802.11g	For use over short distances at speeds up to 54 Mbps. Backward compatible with 802.11b and uses the 2.4 GHz range. Often referred to as Wi-Fi 3.
802.11n	Increases data throughput at speeds up to 100 Mbps, and it uses both 2.4 GHz and 5 GHz ranges. Often referred to as Wi-Fi 4.
802.11ac	Builds on 802.11n to achieve data rates of 433 Mbps. 802.11ac uses the 5 GHz frequency range. Often referred to as Wi-Fi 5.
802.11ax	Improves on 802.11ac and designed to operate between 1 and 6 GHz at data rates of around 10 Gbps. Usually referred to as Wi-Fi 6.

Security

It is comparatively easy to gain access to a wireless network, so it is important to secure network traffic on your wireless network infrastructure. A number of wireless security standards exist that can help, as described in Table 3-7. When choosing a security method, ensure that your wireless devices and infrastructure support that method.

TABLE 3-7 Wireless security standards

Standard	Explanation
Wired Equivalent Privacy (WEP)	WEP is an old wireless security standard, and a number of documented security issues surround it. Use WEP only if there is no choice.
Wi-Fi Protected Access (WPA)	WPA has two variations: **WPA-Personal:** Easier to implement than WPA Enterprise and, therefore, ideal for smaller networks. Authentication is based on a password. The password and the network service set identifier (SSID) generate encryption keys for each wireless device. **WPA-Enterprise:** Designed for larger networks and requires the use of a Remote Authentication Dial-In User Service (RADIUS) server to provide for authentication.
WPA2	An improved version of WPA that is the de facto Wi-Fi security standard. It employs larger encryption key sizes than WPA.

Configure wireless settings

After you have selected the appropriate wireless infrastructure components and chosen your wireless security standard, you must set up and configure your wireless network in Windows 10.

CONNECT TO A WIRELESS NETWORK

To connect to a wireless network, in the system tray select the network icon to review a list of available wireless networks. Select the appropriate network and then select Connect. Enter the required security information as displayed in Figure 3-14 and select Next.

FIGURE 3-14 Connecting to a wireless network

CONFIGURE EXISTING WIRELESS NETWORKS

To review or edit your existing wireless networks, from Settings select Network & Internet. On the Wi-Fi tab, displayed in Figure 3-15, you can configure the following options:

- **Show available networks**   Enables you to review the currently available Wi-Fi networks within range of your device.

- **Hardware properties**   Enables you to review the properties of your Wi-Fi connection, including SSID, Protocol, Security type, Network band, Network channel, IPv4 and IPv6 configuration, and details about your Wi-Fi adapter.

- **Manage known networks**   Enables you to review, configure, or forget any Wi-Fi networks to which your device has connected. To forget a Wi-Fi connection, select it, and then select Forget. To configure a Wi-Fi network, select it, and then select Properties. You can then review or configure the following:

  - Connect Automatically When In Range

  - Network Profile: Public Or Private. This option is only available when you are connected to the specific Wi-Fi network.

  - Set As Metered Connection

- **Random hardware addresses**   Enables your computer to use a different hardware address for each network to which it connects. This can help secure your device by making it harder to track your device's location.
- **Hotspot 2.0 networks**   Under this heading, you can enable the following option:
  - Let Me Use Online Sign-Up To Get Connected

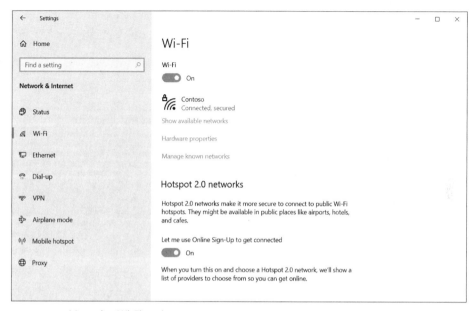

FIGURE 3-15 Managing Wi-Fi settings

HOTSPOT 2.0 NETWORKS

For connecting to public Wi-Fi networks, Windows 10 supports the Hotspot 2.0 wireless 802.11u Wi-Fi standard. This makes connecting to hotspots in public places, such as airports, or coffee shops, easier and more secure.

Your device will attempt to connect you to available public hotspots automatically, in a similar fashion to cellular-style "roaming."

There are several benefits to using Hotspot 2.0:

- Public hotspots become easier and more secure. Your device will detect which Wi-Fi network is authentic and connect automatically.
- Network providers can partner with other providers. This will allow great network coverage and allow cellular-style "roaming."
- Encryption is enforced and utilizes enterprise-grade WPA2 encryption.

When you attempt to join a Hotspot 2.0 network for the first time, Windows 10 presents an Online Sign-Up screen with a list of available network providers. After you have set up an account with one of the providers, your device will be able to connect to other Hotspot 2.0 networks automatically in the future.

ADVANCED SETTINGS

To configure advanced wireless settings, from the Network And Sharing Center, under View Your Active Networks, select the wireless network you want to configure, as shown in Figure 3-16. Then, in the Wi-Fi Status dialog box, click Wireless Properties. You can then view the security settings for your wireless network connection.

FIGURE 3-16 Managing advanced Wi-Fi settings

You can also manage wireless networks by using Netsh.exe. For example, to list the wireless network profiles on your computer, type:

```
Netsh wlan show profile
```

> **NEED MORE REVIEW?** **USING NETSH.EXE TO MANAGE WIRELESS NETWORKS**
>
> To find out more about managing Wi-Fi settings by using Netsh.exe, refer to the Microsoft website at *https://docs.microsoft.com/en-us/previous-versions/windows/it-pro/windows-server-2008-R2-and-2008/dd744890(v=ws.10)*.

CONFIGURING WI-FI DIRECT

Wi-Fi Direct is a standard developed with the Wi-Fi Alliance, is fully supported by Windows 10, and enables Wi-Fi Direct devices to connect seamlessly to one another. This can be achieved by using Miracast over Infrastructure (which uses Ethernet if a network access point or secure ad hoc Wi-Fi network is available) or over a private ad hoc wireless network as and when required.

Wi-Fi Direct enables you to interact with other hardware—for example, to print to a wireless printer or to send your PowerPoint presentation to an external display.

Devices that are utilizing Wi-Fi Direct include mobile phones, cameras, printers, TVs, PCs, and gaming devices, such as Xbox One.

Wi-Fi Direct is similar to Bluetooth, but 10 times faster. Wi-Fi Direct transfers data at up to 250 Mbps, whereas Bluetooth 4.0 transfers data at up to 25 Mbps.

As the technology continues to mature, Microsoft has upgraded and enhanced the application programming interface (API) support with Windows 10 for developers to use when writing their software. Original equipment manufacturer (OEM) vendors are gradually incorporating Wi-Fi Direct into their devices, such as printers utilizing Wi-Fi Direct. Unlike with Bluetooth, only one device needs to support Wi-Fi Direct, though they will still pair in much the same way as Bluetooth. For example, Miracast enables a Windows device to wirelessly display on to a projected screen, such as a TV or projector. Miracast is ideal for enabling screens that do not have built-in support for Wi-Fi Direct because it uses a High-Definition Multimedia Interface (HDMI) adapter, which plugs into the remote screen. Windows 10 can wirelessly connect to the Miracast adapter.

To use the Wi-Fi Direct technology, a user will turn on or enable the Wi-Fi Direct device, such as a Miracast adapter or printer, and Windows 10 will locate the device wirelessly and connect. Once the device is connected, application files that are required for the user interface, such as display or printer dialog screens, are received directly from the Wi-Fi Direct device.

Some characteristics of Wi-Fi Direct are as follows:

- **Distance between devices (ad hoc Wi-Fi)**   Compared with Bluetooth, which creates a personal area network of just a few feet, Wi-Fi Alliance states that Wi-Fi Direct devices can reach each other over a maximum distance of up to 656 feet.

- **Security**   Wi-Fi Direct uses either WPA2-PSK or WPA2-Enterprise security, which uses AES 256-bit encryption with a key-based encryption and authentication method.

- **Speed**   Wi-Fi Direct claims device-to-device transfer speeds of up to 250 Mbps.

- **Services**   Wi-Fi Direct Send, Wi-Fi Direct Print, Wi-Fi Direct for DLNA, Miracast, and Miracast over Infrastructure are the five services that currently utilize the Wi-Fi Direct standard.

To set up Wi-Fi Direct in Windows 10, you need a compatible network adapter. Type **ipconfig /all** at the command line and verify that one of the network adapters listed returns the Description value Microsoft Wi-Fi Direct Virtual Adapter, as shown in Figure 3-17.

```
Wireless LAN adapter Local Area Connection* 2:

   Media State . . . . . . . . . . . : Media disconnected
   Connection-specific DNS Suffix  . :
   Description . . . . . . . . . . . : Microsoft Wi-Fi Direct Virtual Adapter
   Physical Address. . . . . . . . . :
   DHCP Enabled. . . . . . . . . . . : Yes
   Autoconfiguration Enabled . . . . : Yes
```

FIGURE 3-17 Viewing available network adapters with `ipconfig`

After you have checked that your wireless network adapter supports Wi-Fi Direct, use the Netsh.exe command-line tool to set up your Wi-Fi Direct network. You can use the following command to start the process of enabling Wi-Fi Direct:

```
netsh wlan set hostednetwork mode=allow ssid=Wi-Fidirect key=passphrase
```

Use the following command to start Wi-Fi Direct:

```
netsh wlan start hostednetwork
```

To stop the Wi-Fi Direct network, use this:

```
netsh wlan stop hostednetwork
```

Skill 3.2: Configure data access and protection

Being able to access your data from anywhere is a key feature of Windows 10, whether in a small workgroup, in a large enterprise across a LAN, or when mobile using the internet. This skill discusses multiple methods of sharing configuration and setting access permissions on the share so that you are in control of who can see or edit the data. This skill also describes how you can configure online storage using Microsoft OneDrive and OneDrive for Business.

This skill covers how to:

- Configure file and folder permissions
- Configure shared permissions
- Configure, manage, and optimize local storage
- Configure OneDrive and OneDrive for Business

Configure file and folder permissions

Although permissions have been part of NTFS and earlier versions of Windows, for your exam preparation you must ensure that you are familiar with NTFS and the security features it offers.

Most users are familiar with using the File Explorer tool to view and manage files and folders. When administering shared files and folders over a network, File Explorer is still the primary tool to configure file- and folder-level permissions.

Select file systems

Windows 10 supports many file systems, including NTFS, ReFS, exFat, FAT32, and FAT, which are described in Table 3-8. The most commonly used file systems are NTFS and FAT32, with ReFS becoming popular for servers and storage applications.

TABLE 3-8 File formats commonly used with Windows 10

File System	Description
NTFS	Enterprise-class file system, used by Windows for over 30 years.
ReFS	Similar characteristics to NTFS. Not seen as a replacement for NTFS, but rather an improvement over NTFS for specific purposes. Designed for large volumes requiring additional resilience.
exFat	Designed by Microsoft for flash storage devices. Extended file allocation table. Supported on Windows since Vista SP1. Volume size limit of 256 terabytes (TB). File size up to 16 EB. Supports more than 1,000 files per directory.
FAT32	Supported by Windows 95 SP2 and later versions; extended FAT16 to allow larger number of files per partition. File size limit of 4 GB. Volume size limit of 32 GB.
FAT	Sometimes referred to as FAT16. Introduced in 1981 and supported by DOS, OS/2, Linux, Windows 3.x, and later versions. Volume size limit of 4 GB.

> *NOTE* **FAT FILE SYSTEM**
>
> FAT is a simple file system and offers no native file-level encryption, compression, or local security for FAT or FAT32. Anyone with access to the file can read, change, or delete any file stored on a FAT partition.

NTFS

NTFS is the native file system Windows 10 uses and is widely used across most Windows operating systems; it offers you the ability to protect and secure files. NTFS offers the following characteristics:

- File-level compression
- Per-user volume quotas
- Symbolic links and junction points
- Volume sizes up to 256 TB
- Up to $2^{32} - 1$ files per volume
- Maximum implemented file size is 256 TB minus 64 KB, or 281,474,976,645,120 bytes
- File names and total path size limited to 255 characters
- Enterprise-level file and folder encryption
- Metadata transactional logging to ensure that file structure can be repaired
- Limited self-healing capabilities

ReFS

Windows 10 includes support for the more recent Resilient File System (ReFS), which has been designed to respond to the increased scale, access speed, and distributed nature of storage currently available. ReFS is not intended to replace NTFS but offers benefits to users such as storage stability, flexibility, scalability, and availability.

> **NOTE ReFS**
>
> ReFS is only available on Windows 10 Enterprise and Windows 10 Pro for Workstation editions.

ReFS offers enhanced data integrity and self-healing capabilities with the intention that repairs can be made while the operating system remains online.

Storage Spaces uses ReFS and is covered later in this chapter. When Storage Spaces is configured to use ReFS, it can automatically repair corrupted data to ensure that data is always available and resilient during drive failures.

Some ReFS characteristics are:

- Maximum file size of 16 exabytes (EB)
- Maximum volume size of 1 yottabyte (YB)
- Compatibility with existing APIs and technologies
- Does not support NTFS compression or Encrypting File System (EFS)
- Cannot boot Windows 10 from an ReFS volume
- Built-in resilience:
    - Transactional write model—Offers protection against power failures
    - Proactive repairing/self-healing—Corruption detection, automatic repairs
    - Data integrity—Reduces disk corruption through checksums employed on metadata
- Improved availability—Repairs ReFS volumes while still online
- Scalability—Works with extremely large datasets, in excess of 1 petabyte (PB)

ReFS supports long file names and file paths, with the total path size limited to 32,768 characters.

Use File Explorer to manage files and folders

The most common tool used to manage files and folders is File Explorer, which is located on the taskbar and on the Start screen. Typical functions provided through File Explorer include:

- Creating new folders and files
- Viewing and accessing files and folders
- Searching for files and information contained in files
- Managing properties of files and folders
- Previewing contents or thumbnails of files and folders

The Quick Access area is new in Windows 10 and appears at the uppermost left area of the File Explorer navigation pane; it includes pinned shortcuts for frequently used files and folders such as the Desktop, Downloads, Documents, Pictures, and Music. As you browse and access files in other folders on your computer, folder shortcuts for these items appear in the right navigation pane under Frequent Folders or Recent Files. You can modify the behavior of Quick Access by right-clicking Quick Access and selecting Options to open the Folder Options dialog box displayed in Figure 3-18.

On a shared computer, you might want to clear the check boxes for Show Recently Used Files In Quick Access and Show Frequently Used Folders In Quick Access.

FIGURE 3-18 File Explorer Quick Access

Set file and folder permissions

Volumes formatted using either NTFS or the more recent ReFS enable you to configure file and folder permissions. File permissions are robust, reliable, and effective, and they enable you to configure granular permissions on both files and folders that determine how individual users and groups can use the objects.

The creator of the resource, such as a file or folder, is automatically assigned the special status of creator-owner, and the creator can grant or deny permissions to it. Administrators and anyone given the Full Control permission also can modify permissions for that file or folder.

To modify permissions to a file or folder, select the Security tab in the object's properties, as displayed in Figure 3-19.

FIGURE 3-19 Security permissions for a file

If a user leaves your organization or their account is deleted, an administrator can take ownership of the users' files and folders to modify permissions by changing the Owner principal found in the Advanced settings in Properties.

If you have the permission to modify the security settings in the access control list (ACL), you can add or remove users or groups and then grant or deny a specific permission level. In organizations, you assign permissions to groups rather than to multiple users because doing so minimizes administrative effort.

Review the abbreviations relating to objects that you might use when applying security permissions, as shown in Table 3-9.

TABLE 3-9 Security permission abbreviations

Name	Abbreviation	Description
Access control list	ACL	A list of trustees (users and groups) with permissions for the object.
Access control entry	ACE	Identifies specific permissions granted to a user or group. Each ACE identifies the trustee and specifies the access rights allowed, denied, or audited for that trustee.
Discretionary access control list	DACL	Specifies which trustees are allowed or denied access to an object.
System access control list	SACL	Specifies which users and groups will be audited when they perform actions, such as creating, modifying, or deleting objects.

When configuring permissions for files and folders, you can configure basic or advanced permissions. Unless you are seeking a very fine degree of control to a resource, you typically work with basic permissions and assign them to groups and users, as described in Table 3-10.

TABLE 3-10 Basic file and folder permissions for NTFS and ReFS

File permission	Description
Full Control	Complete authority and control of all file or folder permissions.
Modify	Ability to read a file, write changes to it, and modify permissions.
Read & Execute	Ability to see folder content, read files and attributes, and start programs.
Read	Ability to read a file but not make any changes to it.
Write	Ability to change folder or file content and create new files.
Special Permissions	Indication of whether additional advanced permissions have been configured for the file or folder.

> **NOTE   BASIC AND ADVANCED PERMISSIONS**
>
> If you are familiar with older versions of Windows, you might notice that Windows 10 uses the modern naming for permissions as follows: Standard Permissions has been changed to Basic Permissions, and Special Permissions has been changed to Advanced Permissions.

Basic permissions are easier to manage and document. Under the hood, a basic permission is made from a combination of individual advanced special permissions. Consider that permissions for folders can have a different effect on files, as described in Table 3-11.

TABLE 3-11 Basic NTFS file and folder permissions

Basic Permission	Description: When Applied to a Folder	Description: When Applied to a File
Full Control	Permits reading, writing, changing, and deletion of files and subfolders. Allows the modification of permissions on folders.	Permits reading, writing, changing, and deletion of the file. Allows modification of permissions on files.
Modify	Permits reading, writing, changing, and deletion of files and subfolders. Does not allow changes to permissions on folders.	Permits reading, writing, changing, and deletion of the file. Does not allow changes to the permissions on files.
Read & Execute	Allows the content of the folder to be accessed and executed.	Allows the file to be accessed and executed (run).
List Folder Contents	Allows the contents of the folder to be viewed.	Does not apply to files.

Basic Permission	Description: When Applied to a Folder	Description: When Applied to a File
Read	Allows content to be read.	Allows access to the contents. Does not allow files to be executed.
Write	Allows addition of files and subfolders to the folder.	Allows a user to modify but not delete a file.

Behind the basic permissions is a matrix of 13 advanced permissions that can also be applied to files and folders. Each basic permission is a collection of one or more advanced permissions, as described in Table 3-12.

TABLE 3-12 Basic and advanced permissions

Advanced Permission	Full Control	Modify	Read & Execute	List Folder Contents	Read	Write
Traverse Folder/ Execute File	X	X	X	X		
List Folder/Read Data	X	X	X	X	X	
Read Attributes	X	X	X	X	X	
Read Extended Attributes	X	X	X	X	X	
Create Files/Write Data	X	X				X
Create Folders/Append Data	X	X				X
Write Attributes	X	X				X
Write Extended Attributes	X	X				X
Delete Subfolders And Files	X					
Delete	X	X				
Read Permissions	X	X	X	X	X	X
Change Permissions	X					
Take Ownership	X					

We recommend that you use basic permissions unless there is a clear requirement for setting advanced permissions; otherwise, the permissions can become complex and difficult to troubleshoot. If you do use the advanced permissions, it is best practice to document any modifications so that you can review the configuration and, if necessary, reverse the settings.

Many inexperienced users who configure file permissions can complicate the settings on files by setting advanced permissions (frequently using deny permissions) and setting permissions for individual users instead of setting permissions for groups. There is a strict canonical order or hierarchy of how Deny and Allow permissions can interoperate, and the general rule is that a Deny setting prevents an Allow setting.

EXAM TIP

Remember the principle of least administration when applying NTFS or ReFS permissions. If you want to prevent a user or group from having any access to a resource, you could set no permissions. If neither Allow nor Deny permission is explicitly configured or inherited on a resource, users are prevented from accessing the file or folder.

Review Table 3-13 to understand the relationship between Deny and Allow settings and how the behavior changes, depending on how the setting is applied.

TABLE 3-13 Allow and Deny NTFS permissions

Permission Type	Description	Check Box Status
Explicit Deny	The user is denied the permission on the file or folder.	The check box is selected.
Explicit Allow	The user is allowed the permission on the file or folder.	The check box is selected.
Inherited Deny	Deny permission is applied to the file or sub-folder by permissions given to the parent folder.	The check box is dimmed but selected.
Not configured	When no permissions are assigned, the user has no permission to access the file or folder.	The check box is cleared.
Inherited Allow	Allow permission is applied to the file or subfolder by permissions given to the parent folder.	The check box is dimmed but selected.

> **NOTE   WHEN ALLOW OVERRIDES DENY**
>
> When applying permissions to groups and allowing inheritance, sometimes one group has an explicit Allow setting and another group has an inherited Deny setting. If a user is a member of both groups, the explicit Allow setting will override the implicit Deny.

Although most administrators will use File Explorer to set individual ACLs for files and folders, you can also use Windows PowerShell or the ICACLS command-line utility.

Windows PowerShell offers two cmdlets that you can use to manage file and folder permissions: **Get-Acl** and **Set-Acl**. For additional information and examples of how to use these cmdlets, type **Get-Help Get-Acl** or **Get-Help Set-Acl**.

ICACLS enables you to configure and view permissions on files and folders on a local computer. Some of the most common ICACLS parameters and permission masks are described in Table 3-14.

TABLE 3-14 Common ICACLS parameters and permission masks

Parameter/ Permission Mask	Description
/grant	Grants specific user access rights. Permissions replace previously granted explicit permissions.
/deny	Explicitly denies specified user access rights. An explicit Deny ACE is added for the stated permissions, and the same permissions in any explicit grant are removed.
/reset	Replaces ACLs with default inherited ACLs for all matching files.
F	Full access.
M	Modify access.
RX	Read and execute access.
R	Read-only access.
W	Write-only access.
(OI)	Object inherit.
(NP)	Do not propagate inherit.

To grant a permission, use the /grant switch, as the following example on an existing file called My New Files in C:\Working Folder shows:

1. Open File Explorer.
2. Navigate to the folder on which you want to set permissions.
3. Select **File** and then select **Open Windows PowerShell as administrator**.
4. Run the following command:

```
Icacls 'My new files.rtf' /grant 'Demo:(OI)(M)'
```

5. Enter **Icacls 'My new files.rtf'** to review the permissions.

> **NEED MORE REVIEW? ICACLS**
>
> This Microsoft resource provides additional information for you to review relating to ICACLS. Visit *https://docs.microsoft.com/windows-server/administration/windows-commands/icacls*.

Understand permissions inheritance

Setting file permissions on hundreds of files and folders would take a long time, especially if each setting were configured manually. Fortunately, you don't need to because, by default, NTFS and ReFS security permissions are inherited from their parent folder. In this way, permissions "flow" from top to bottom and follow the folder hierarchy. By default, inheritance is enabled because this facilitates more efficient administration. NTFS enables you to disable inheritance from flowing from a parent folder to the child.

You can review the inheritance status of a file or folder in File Explorer by following these steps:

1. Open **File Explorer**.

2. Navigate to the folder whose inheritance settings you want to review.

3. Right-click the file or folder, and select **Properties** and then select **Advanced**.

4. On the **Permissions** tab, review the permission entries and notice the **Inherited from** column, as shown in Figure 3-20.

FIGURE 3-20 NTFS inheritance

Figure 3-20 shows a Disable Inheritance button. If you select this button, you are presented with two choices, as shown in Figure 3-21.

FIGURE 3-21 Blocking inheritance

In the Block Inheritance dialog box, there are two options:

- **Convert inherited permissions into explicit permissions on this object**   Prevents inherited permissions from being able to "flow" from top folders to the subfolders. Current inherited permissions are changed by the system from implicit permissions to explicit permissions. This can result in hundreds or thousands of inherited permissions being changed into explicit permissions.

- **Remove all inherited permissions from this object**   Removes all permissions and gives you a folder structure with no permissions set. Care needs to be taken with this option because it is very easy to remove all access—even system access—to the file structure.

The option to convert inherited permissions to explicit permissions stops inheritance from flowing from the parent folders and changes the permissions on all child items from implicit permissions to explicit permissions. You can then modify the permissions.

If you choose the second option, Remove All Inherited Permissions From This Object, you completely remove all permissions. This provides you with a folder structure with no permissions at all.

Both options are powerful and can have far-reaching effects. Best practice recommends employing inheritance wherever possible to ease administration. You should also document and test your outline folder structure before it becomes too large. A big change on a small structure is simple to put in place, whereas modifying a large, established file structure could be cumbersome.

Understanding move, copy, and permissions inheritance

When you have to move or copy a folder from one location to another, you should understand how NTFS will perform the task with respect to how permissions on the resource are modified. Table 3-15 describes the behavior that NTFS adopts when copying files from one folder to another folder, and between partitions.

TABLE 3-15 Effect of moving or copying NTFS files

Action	Effect
Copy or move a file or folder to a different volume	Inherits the permissions from the destination (new location) folder.
Copy or move a file or folder within the same NTFS volume	Inherits the permissions from the new parent folder, and explicitly assigned permissions are retained and merged with the inherited permissions.
Copy a file or folder to a non-NTFS volume	The copy of the folder or file loses all permissions.

> **NOTE WHAT HAPPENS WHEN YOU MOVE AN NTFS-PROTECTED FILE TO A FAT VOLUME?**
>
> If you're moving a file or folder from NTFS to a non-NTFS partition, such as a FAT32 volume, all NTFS file and folder permissions will be lost because FAT32 does not support file and folder permissions. Only Creator Owners and users with the Modify permission (and administrators) can perform this task because they have permission to move files and folders. When moving files to a FAT32 volume, the process involves saving the object onto the new file system, losing the original file permissions in the process, and then deleting the original object.

When you copy a file or folder within the same volume or between volumes, the user must have Read permission for the source folder and Write permission for the destination folder.

When you move a file or folder within the same volume or between volumes, you need to have both Write permission for the destination folder as well as Modify permission for the source file or folder. This is because Windows 10 will move the resources (Write) and then delete (Modify) the resources from the source folder once it has completed the copy to the destination folder.

View Effective Access

You might be required to determine the access that a user has to a resource. Within the Advanced options of an object's Security settings, you will find the Effective Access tab (previously called Effective Permissions), as displayed in Figure 3-22. When setting permissions in a corporate environment, you should verify that NTFS permissions are applied correctly and use the Effective Access feature to ensure that the results are as expected.

FIGURE 3-22 Determining effective access

For example, for a resource, if you assign a user the Read permission and assign the Modify permission to a group that the same user is a member of, the effective access permissions are a combination of the Read permission and the Modify permission, which is the Modify permission.

When you combine permissions that include Deny permissions, NTFS will evaluate the Deny permissions before the Allow permissions that are set on the same resource, with explicit Deny taking precedence over all Allow permissions.

If Deny and Allow permissions are set at different levels within a folder structure, or nested within each other, that can create unexpected results. For example, if Deny is set at the top-level folder and an Allow permission is set at its subfolder, Allow can take precedence and override Deny because the Allow permission is explicit and not implicit.

When assigning permissions to several groups, remember that the security settings have a cumulative effect; you should review the effective permissions obtained for the user by following these steps:

1. Open Windows Explorer.

2. Navigate to the file or folder whose effective permissions you want to view.

3. Right-click the file or folder, select **Properties**, and select the **Security** tab.

4. Select **Advanced** and then select the **Effective Access** tab.

5. Next to User/Group, select **Select a user**.

6. In the **Select User or Group** dialog box, click in the **Enter the object name to select (examples)** box, enter the name of a user or group, and then select **OK**.

7. Select **View effective access**.

You should now be able to review the detailed effective permissions of the user or group for that file or folder.

Be careful when using the Effective Access tool and reviewing permissions on folders that you own since the permissions given to the Creator Owner of the object are not taken into account.

Take ownership of resources

It is possible to remove access to a particular user or group on an object, such as a folder. Sometimes, this happens accidentally when configuring permissions, but typically, it will happen when the user who originally created the resource leaves the organization and the resource is then said to be "orphaned."

In the Advanced Security Settings dialog box for an object, you will find the Effective Access tab, and at the top of this screen, as shown in Figure 3-22, is an option to change the object owner. As long as you have administrative privileges, you can take ownership of the object and allocate it to another user or group. You can reset the permissions of all the folders, files and subfolders using the command **icacls <file name> /reset**, using an elevated command prompt.

Resolve file permission issues

The type of security that can be configured on Windows 10 is determined by the file system in place. NTFS, the default underlying file system, offers several security options, but you may also encounter removable drives or legacy systems that use FAT, FAT32, or exFAT, none of which offers file security.

It has been many years since NTFS was established as the default file system of choice for all recent Windows client and server operating systems. NTFS file permissions offer administrators a powerful tool for granting, controlling, auditing, and denying access to resources. Unlike share-level permissions, NTFS operates at the file level, which means NTFS permissions are applicable to resources shared over a network or accessed locally.

When troubleshooting resource access issues, you must determine the following:

1. Is the file system in NTFS?

2. Are the files and folders being accessed locally or over the network?

It is easy to test if the file system is using NTFS by checking to see if there is a Security tab on the volume on which the resource resides, as shown in Figure 3-23. The Security tab relates to NTFS permissions.

FIGURE 3-23 An NTFS-formatted volume displaying a Security tab

File and folder permissions can be complex and sometimes difficult to manage, especially for an inexperienced administrator. Often the most challenging environment is one in which a newly hired administrator must adopt an existing organization, which has an existing problematic NTFS permission infrastructure in place that has very little documentation. Required small changes can sometimes have unintended consequences, which pose security risks.

The role of the system administrator is to optimize data security and to make sure that data is accessible to the right users. If users are denied access to files to which they have rights or are given access to privileged files, it is a major problem that needs immediate remediation.

> **NOTE NEW VERSUS LEGACY FOLDER STRUCTURE**
>
> Sometimes when adopting an existing NTFS permission infrastructure, it is better to design and re-create the file and folder permission structure rather than adopt a legacy environment.

File and folder permissions are cumulative, which means a user may have been given various group memberships as well as explicit permissions to resources that they are able to access. If a user has not been given any implicit or explicit permissions, they will not have access. If a combination of permissions for a resource has been set, you'll need to calculate the cumulative effect of all permissions.

Faced with an issue resulting from lack of access or over privilege, you need to start troubleshooting the problem by determining the effective permissions for the files or folders in question. Establish the scope. For example, who does this problem affect, and is it confined to a single user or a group of users? Establishing the effective permissions will allow you to quickly determine permissions that apply and provide you with a starting point.

User-effective permissions are based on the total of all permissions that they have been granted or denied. Take special care to look for any Deny permissions because these are infrequently set. However, when Deny permissions are set, they are powerful because any explicit Deny permission will have precedence over Allow entries.

REAL WORLD   **DOCUMENT ALL CHANGES**

The best practice when configuring file and folder permissions is to document a plan for how the permissions will be applied to the predefined users, groups, and folders. Ensure that all new users, groups, and folders are created according to the plan, and then apply permissions to this structure. After the file permissions plan has been created, repeat for the Share permissions. Once permissions have been configured, continue to the testing phase where you perform tests for selected users to establish whether their effective access to resources matches the intended objectives of the plan. Over time, your NTFS change log will prove extremely useful when troubleshooting file permission access issues.

Configure shared permissions

Data is often shared in an organization, perhaps within a team for project work or between you and your boss. You must know how this can be achieved in Windows 10 within a networked environment, whether that is at home or in a larger workplace network. You must be able to manage shared files and printers.

File and printer sharing is disabled by default, and it is automatically turned on when you share the first folder on a Windows 10 device. If you want to configure this setting manually, you can do so in the advanced sharing settings in the Network And Sharing Center in Control Panel.

Another consideration is that when sharing is enabled, the Windows Defender Firewall is automatically configured to allow users to access shares on a computer in the network. This is a potential security risk. Although the firewall settings are configured automatically when you first share a folder, they are not returned to their default status even if you remove all shared folders.

Configure folder shares

When you share a folder, other users can connect to the shared folder and its contents across the network. Shared folders available on the network are no different from normal folders, and they can contain applications, corporate data, or private data.

When creating a network share, be careful that you do not accidentally provide access to a user or group of users who should not have access. By default, everyone on the network is given read access to the share, although you can change this setting.

Normally, a shared folder is located on a file server, but in a small network environment, the sharing can be located on a Windows 10–based computer or network-attached storage (NAS) device. When you're choosing the device or server, keep in mind that the resources should be available whenever the users need them and that, often, this means the server is always on.

By providing a central location for shared folders to reside on, you enable the following features:

- Simplification of management
- User familiarity
- Ease in backing up data
- Consistent location and availability

When a user tries to use resources accessed on a shared folder, the access permissions are determined by taking into consideration both the share permission and the NTFS security permissions. The most restrictive set of permissions prevail.

Ensure that you do not create shared folders where the share permissions (SMB) become the primary access security mechanism. They are more restrictive than the NTFS permissions because users gaining access to the resource locally or by logging on through Remote Desktop would completely bypass SMB permissions. It is therefore essential for NTFS permissions to be configured independently to protect the resource.

To allow access to a locally stored folder across a network, first share the folder. Files contained in folders are also shared, but files cannot be specifically shared independently, except from within a user profile.

SERVER MESSAGE BLOCK

Shares are provided by the Server Message Block (SMB) application-layer network protocol and not by NTFS. You can see what version of SMB your Windows 10 operating system is using by following these steps:

1. Sign in to your computer by using an administrative user account.
2. Open **File Explorer** and navigate to a shared or mapped folder on the network so that the shared files are visible in the right navigation pane.
3. On the File Explorer menu, select **File** and then select **Open Windows PowerShell As Administrator**.
4. Accept UAC if prompted.
5. Enter the Windows PowerShell cmdlet **Get-SmbConnection**.

   Windows PowerShell should report the SMB version (dialect) in use, as shown in Figure 3-24.

```
Administrator: Windows PowerShell                                    –  □  ×
PS Z:\> Get-SmbConnection

ServerName      ShareName UserName         Credential                           Dialect NumOpens
---------       --------- --------         ----------                           ------- --------
192.168.1.92    4tb       DESKTOP\andrew   MicrosoftAccount\▇▇▇▇▇▇▇▇▇▇ 1.5      9
81RTM           down      DESKTOP\andrew   MicrosoftAccount\▇▇▇▇▇▇▇▇▇▇ 3.0.2    9


PS Z:\>
```

FIGURE 3-24 Windows 10 SMB version

> **NEED MORE REVIEW?** SMB 3.0 OVERVIEW
>
> This Microsoft resource, although focused on Windows Server and SMB 3.0, offers useful information about the benefits of using the latest version of SMB compared to previous versions. Visit *https://docs.microsoft.com/windows-server/storage/file-server/file-server-smb-overview*.

CONFIGURE NETWORK DISCOVERY

The network discovery feature was introduced in Windows Vista and uses a new layer 2-level protocol called Link Layer Topology Discovery (LLTD). It allows Windows to identify other devices present on the local subnet and, when possible, establish the quality of service (QoS) bandwidth capabilities of the network.

Knowing what is on the network increases the communication between devices. One downside of this increased awareness capability is that the firewall security settings are slightly relaxed. This means that not only does your computer see other network computers and devices, it also becomes discoverable on the network by other Windows clients.

> **EXAM TIP**
>
> Administrators working in a domain environment can manage the settings of the two network discovery settings, LLTD Mapper (LLTDIO) and Responder (RSPNDR), in Group Policy settings. The Group Policy settings can be found here: Computer Configuration\Policies\Administrative Templates\Network\Link Layer Topology Discovery.

Network discovery is tightly linked to network location profiles and to Windows Defender Firewall configuration. As you have seen, by default, network discovery is enabled for devices connecting to networks that are assigned the Domain or Private network location profile, but network discovery is disabled on public networks.

To change network discovery settings, from the Network And Sharing Center, select Change Advanced Sharing Settings. As shown in Figure 3-25, you can then configure network discovery for each network location profile.

FIGURE 3-25 Advanced Sharing Settings

CREATE A SHARE BY USING THE SHARED FOLDERS SNAP-IN

You can create and manage file shares centrally on your computer by using the Shared Folders snap-in, which can be loaded into an empty Microsoft Management Console (MMC). You can also use the snap-in found in Computer Management.

When you create a new share in the Shared Folders snap-in, the Create A Shared Folder Wizard appears and guides you through specifying the folder path, share name, description, and other settings, as shown in Figure 3-26.

By default, the share name will be the same as the folder name, and permissions for the share are set at read-only access for the Everyone group, but you can choose other options or full customization by completing the underlying Share Permissions DACL page.

The Shared Folders snap-in enables you to view existing shares and modify their properties, including settings such as offline file status, share permissions, and even the NTFS security permissions.

FIGURE 3-26 The Computer Management Create A Shared Folder Wizard

EXAM TIP

To launch the Create A Shared Folder Wizard directly from a command prompt, use Shrpubw.exe.

SHARE FOLDERS BY USING FILE EXPLORER

There are multiple methods of sharing a folder using File Explorer:

- Use the **Share with** option, found on the **Share** tab on the ribbon bar (also called Network File And Folder Sharing).
- Select **Advanced security** from the **Share** tab on the ribbon bar.
- Use the **Sharing** tab in the **Properties** dialog box.
- Use the **Give access to** context menu by right-clicking a folder to be shared.

All the methods present you with slightly different GUIs and wizards from which to choose the sharing options. Although they all result in sharing folders that can be accessed across the network, the main difference between each method is the speed and simplicity that some offer the novice.

In practice, most home users and small businesses prefer to use the sharing wizards found on the ribbon bar, but more experienced users seek the advanced level of control that can be gained through the Sharing tab in the Properties dialog box.

Review the options for configuring shares and pay attention to the limitations of the wizard-based methods. The wizards configure the file system permissions automatically, based on the limited choices they present.

The Share tab in File Explorer enables you to launch the File Sharing Wizard and provides the same functionality as the Share With shortcut menu. Next to this is Advanced Security, which enables you to fine-tune the sharing beyond the limitations of the File Sharing Wizard.

When you configure basic sharing permissions, you have one of two simplified options:

- **Read** Users and groups can open but cannot modify or delete files.
- **Read/Write** Users and groups can open, modify, or delete a file and modify permissions.

After you create a share, all users see the share name over the network. Only users who have at least the Read permission can view its content.

NOTE ADMINISTRATORS CAN SHARE FILES AND FOLDERS

To share a file or folder across the network in Windows 10, you must be a member of the Administrators group or provide UAC credentials for an administrator.

SHARE FOLDERS FROM THE COMMAND PROMPT

The command prompt enables you to share a folder by using the net share command. To create a simple share, you would use the following example:

```
net share MyShareName=c:\Temp\Data /remark:"Temp Work Area"
```

This command shares the C:\Temp\Data folder with the share name MyShareName and includes a description of Temp Work Area. You must have administrative privileges to create a shared folder by using net share.

Review the additional command-line options that you can use with net share, as shown in Table 3-16.

TABLE 3-16 net share command-line options

Option	Description
/Grant:user permission	Enables you to specify Read, Change, or Full Share permissions for the specified user
/Users:number	Enables you to limit the number of users who can connect to the share concurrently (default and maximum for Windows 10 is 20 users)
/Remark:"text"	Enables you to add a description to the share
/Cache:option	Enables you to specify the offline files caching options for the share
sharename /Delete	Enables you to remove an existing share

SHARE FOLDERS BY USING WINDOWS POWERSHELL

If you need to script the creation of shares, Windows PowerShell is the most appropriate choice and provides several cmdlets that enable you to manage shares in Windows 10. PowerShell offers more in both scope and functionality than `net share` and will continue to expand in the future.

Here is an example command for creating a share:

```
New-SmbShare -Name MyShareName -Path c:\Temp\Data
```

Other PowerShell cmdlets used in the administration of shares are described in Table 3-17.

TABLE 3-17 Windows PowerShell Share cmdlets

Cmdlet	Description
Get-SmbShare	Lists the existing shares on the computer
Get-SmbShareAccess	Lists the access control list of the SMB share
New-SmbShare	Creates a new SMB share
Set-SmbShare	Modifies the properties for an existing share
Remove-SmbShare	Deletes an existing share
Grant-SmbShareAccess	Sets the share permissions on an existing share
Get-SmbShareAccess	Lists the current share permissions for a share

SHARE FILES BY USING FILE EXPLORER

Files typically cannot be shared without first sharing the parent folder. In Windows 10, files that reside in the user profile, such as Documents, Downloads, and Pictures folders, can be shared. To do this, follow these steps:

1. Sign in to your computer using an administrative user account.

2. Open **File Explorer** and navigate to the user profile.

3. Right-click a folder, such as Pictures, in the user's profile.

4. Select **Give access to** and then select **Specific people**, as shown in Figure 3-27.

FIGURE 3-27 Share, using the sharing wizard

5. In the **Choose people to share with** dialog box, enter a user or group and select **Add**.

6. Set **Permission Level** to **Read** or **Read/Write** and select **Share**.

7. Note that you are sharing. The File Sharing Wizard completes, and the files are shared.

8. Optionally, you can use the links in the File Sharing Wizard to send someone the links to the shares.

9. Select **Done**.

You can also share a file using the Share icon on the Share ribbon bar. Select the file or multiple files and then click Share on the ribbon bar, as shown in Figure 3-28.

FIGURE 3-28 Sharing files from Windows Explorer

The Share option is also available within other apps, including Microsoft Edge. The set of targets, including contacts and other apps, will depend on which apps are installed on your device and offers a simplified method of sharing files quickly and with minimum effort.

Configure shared folders permissions

Permissions that are set on the share determine the level of access a user has to the files in the share. They can be set on FAT or later file systems. When you use NTFS, be careful not to restrict access at the share level, because doing so might affect the effective permissions. You can configure the permissions when you share a folder and set a level that the user or group will have when they connect to the folder through the share across the network.

Sharing permissions have three options:

- **Read** Users and groups can view the files, but they cannot modify or delete them.
- **Change** Users and groups can open, modify, delete, and create content, but they cannot modify file or folder permissions; the Change permission incorporates all Read permissions.
- **Full** Users and groups can perform all actions, including modifying the permissions; the Full permission incorporates all Change permissions.

Unlike in earlier versions of Windows, there is no longer a visual icon or indicator in File Explorer to distinguish whether a folder is shared. All shared folders on your device appear in the Shared Folders node of the Computer Management console. You can also view the shared folders that exist on your device by using the `Get-SmbShare` Windows PowerShell cmdlet or by typing **net view \\localhost /all** at the command prompt.

After a user has found the share in File Explorer, they can access the files directly. Another common way that users can connect to a shared folder over the network is by using the shares Universal Naming Convention (UNC) address. UNC addresses contain two backward slashes (\\) followed by the name of the computer that is sharing the folder and the shared folder name; for example, the UNC name for the Marketing shared folder on the LON-DC1 computer in the Fabrikam.com domain would be:

`\\LON-CL1.Fabrikam.com\Marketing`

TROUBLESHOOT SHARE PERMISSION ISSUES

Share permissions can cause you many problems when you're troubleshooting access to files and folders. You need to remember that Share permissions work together with file and folder permissions and that the most restrictive permission will apply. Another common cause of confusion is that Share permissions only affect shared resources over the network.

If your file system is configured with FAT or FAT32, there is no option to configure NTFS or ReFS permissions. If no Security tab is available in the resource's Properties dialog box, you know that it cannot be formatted with NTFS and the file system is likely to be FAT/FAT32, as shown in Figure 3-29.

FIGURE 3-29 A FAT32-formatted volume's Properties dialog box, with no Security tab

If you need to confirm the file system in use, you can view the properties of the drive by following these steps:

1. Open **File Explorer** and right-click the drive that is under review.
2. Select **Properties**.
3. On the **General** tab, review **File System**.
4. Select **OK** to close the dialog box.

COMBINE NTFS AND SHARE PERMISSIONS

Within a corporate environment, administrators share files over the network using Share permissions. If the volume is formatted with NTFS, there are likely to be NTFS permissions configured on the shared file as well. To fully understand the effects of these two sets of permissions, you will need to combine them.

When you're combining Share and NTFS permissions, restricting access to resources across the network can be easy. By accepting the default share permissions, you provide standard users with read-only access even if NTFS permissions are less restrictive.

Unfortunately, there is no wizard to diagnose which restrictions are in effect, but you can use the Effective Permissions feature in NTFS to determine the permissions being applied to a specific user or group (Principal).

NTFS is all about rules, and they are applied thoroughly by the file system. Wrongly applied settings, often combined with default inheritance, can instantly spread an incorrectly configured setting across hundreds of files. Unlike most computer operations, there is no undo option.

When troubleshooting access, always look for the most restrictive permission that has been set and evaluate whether it is being applied. If necessary, you can view the effective permissions. If the most restrictive permission is not being applied when the resource is being accessed, you must identify the problem. Some other permission must be overlapping and affecting the resource; perhaps the user is a member of the Administrators group or another group that has Full Control permissions? You can also test what permissions are effective both at the local access level as well as when accessing the resource over the network share.

Often, the cause of many permission-based issues when troubleshooting file and folder access is that the Share permissions being applied on the share are too restrictive. It is preferable to use the more powerful NTFS permissions because these will always be effective, regardless of how they are accessed (over the network share or locally).

RESET SHARE AND NTFS PERMISSIONS

If you simply cannot decipher which NTFS settings are creating the problems, or if the problems are too complex or widespread, you can try to reset the file and folder permissions by using the ICACLS command-line utility.

This is especially useful if you get locked out of files and folders because of incorrect or deleted NTFS permissions.

To reset permissions using ICACLS, follow these steps:

1. Sign in to your computer using an administrator user account.

2. Open **File Explorer** and navigate to the folder that is giving you the problems.

3. On the File Explorer menu, select **File** and then select **Open Windows PowerShell ss administrator**.

4. Accept the UAC prompt, if prompted.

5. Run the following command: **icacls * /RESET /T /C /Q**.

The process of resetting files and folders to their default settings is very quick. After the original operating system defaults have been applied, you can configure the desired settings.

Configure, manage, and optimize local storage

Most devices installed with Windows 10 are supplied with a single physical disk. This disk is usually partitioned as described here and shown in Figure 3-30:

- **EFI System partition**   This small partition is used to start the computer and contains the Windows 10 startup files.

- **Operating system boot partition**   This NTFS partition contains the Windows folder and is usually the only file system volume.

- **Recovery partition**   This small partition is used when Windows 10 enters the Windows Recovery Environment (Windows RE).

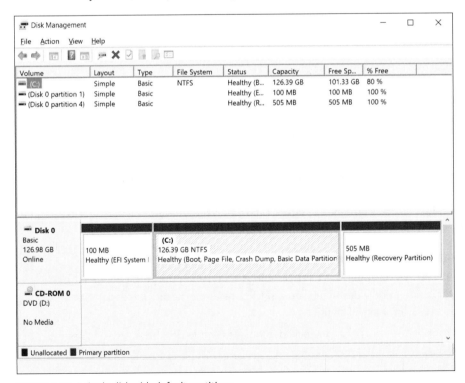

FIGURE 3-30 A single disk with default partitions

These days, the hard drive will probably be a solid-state drive (SSD). For tablets, the smaller mSATA form factor drive type might be used. These provide very high disk read/write performance and are often fixed directly to the motherboard.

You can use various tools and methods to manage Windows 10 disks and create volumes or partitions on them, including:

- Disk Management
- Windows PowerShell
- DiskPart

Disk Management

This is the traditional GUI tool used for performing most configuration and management tasks relating to disks and volumes. The GUI uses the familiar Microsoft Management Console (MMC) that most administrative tools use. You can connect to the disks on a local or remote computer and perform tasks on both basic and dynamic disks and virtual hard disks.

Examples of the types of disk management tasks that you can perform using the GUI include the following:

- Partition creation, including creating a basic, spanned, or striped partition.
- Disk conversion between basic disks to dynamic disks. (To convert a dynamic disk to a basic disk, you must first delete all present volumes.)
- Extending and shrinking partitions.
- Viewing information relating to disk and volumes, such as volume name, layout, type, file system, status, capacity, free space, and percentage of disk free for each volume.

To open Disk Management, follow these steps:

1. Right-click **Start** and select **Disk Management** or enter **diskmgmt.msc** in the search box and then select **diskmgmt**.
2. Wait for Disk Management MMC to open and load the disk configuration information, as shown in Figure 3-31.

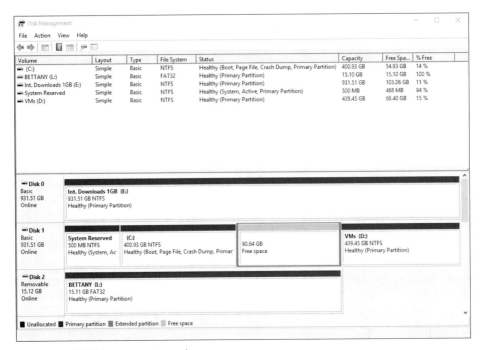

FIGURE 3-31 Disk Management console

You can use the Disk Management console to convert a basic disk to a dynamic disk by right-clicking the disk you want to convert and then selecting Convert To Dynamic Disk.

Windows PowerShell

Windows PowerShell offers many disk-related tasks from the command line; it can be used locally or remotely and can be scripted. Windows PowerShell now natively enables you to manage disks, volumes, and partitions and perform a range of tasks that cannot be performed using DiskPart or Disk Management.

Table 3-18 details some of the most common Windows PowerShell cmdlets that you should become familiar with.

TABLE 3-18 Common disk-related Windows PowerShell cmdlets

Command	Description	Additional Parameters
Get-Disk	Return one or more disks visible to the operating system.	-FriendlyName -Number
Clear-Disk	Cleans a disk by removing all partition information and placing it in an un-initialized state. Erases all data on the disk.	-Number -RemoveData -FriendlyName
Initialize-Disk	Initializes a RAW disk for first time use, enabling the disk to be formatted and used to store data.	-FriendlyName -PartitionStyle -VirtualDisk

Command	Description	Additional Parameters
Set-Disk	Updates the physical disk on the system with attributes.	-PartitionStyle -IsOffline -IsReadonly
Get-Volume	Gets the specified volume object or all volume objects if no filter is provided.	-DriveLetter -DiskImage -FileSystemLabel -Partition
Format-Volume	Formats one or more existing volumes or a new volume on an existing partition. Acceptable file formats include NTFS, ReFS, exFat, FAT32, and FAT.	-DriveLetter -FileSystem -FileSystemLabel
Get-Partition	Returns a list of all partition objects visible on all disks or, optionally, a filtered list using specified parameters.	-Disk -DriveLetter -PartitionNumber -Volume

> **NEED MORE REVIEW?** WINDOWS STORAGE MANAGEMENT–SPECIFIC POWERSHELL CMDLETS
>
> You can review all storage cmdlets for Windows PowerShell and syntax explanations and examples at *https://docs.microsoft.com/en-us/powershell/module/storage/?view=win10-ps.*

To shrink a partition in Windows PowerShell, run the following command:

```
Resize-Partition -DiskNumber 0 -PartitionNumber 2 -Size (50GB)
```

To create simple volumes in Windows PowerShell, run the following commands:

```
Get-Disk -Number 0 New-Partition -UseMaximumSize -DiskNumber 0 |

Format-Volume -Confirm:$false -FileSystem NTFS -NewFileSystemLabel Simple2 Get-
Partition -DiskNumber 0
```

Make a note of the partition number you just created to use in the next step:

```
Set-Partition -DiskNumber 0 -PartitionNumber <partition number> -NewDriveLetter G
```

Windows PowerShell is the preferred command-line method for disk operations. The Windows PowerShell storage cmdlets do not recognize dynamic disks, so we recommend that you use Storage Spaces rather than dynamic disks.

DiskPart

DiskPart is a built-in command-line tool that offers you all the functionality of Disk Management plus some advanced features that can also be scripted into BAT files to automate disk-related tasks. One limitation of DiskPart is that it only runs locally.

To open DiskPart, follow these steps:

1.   Open an elevated command prompt.

2.   Enter **DiskPart**.

     DiskPart launches in the command line.

3.   For a list of all DiskPart commands, enter **help** or **commands**, or enter **?**.

4.   When you have finished using DiskPart, you can leave the interface by entering **Exit** and pressing Enter.

The following list shows several DiskPart commands whose functions you should understand:

- **Active**   Marks the selected partition as the active partition
- **Add**   Enables you to add a mirror to a simple volume
- **Assign**   Enables you to assign a drive letter to a selected volume
- **Convert**   Converts between basic and dynamic disks
- **Create**   Enables you to create a volume, partition, or virtual disk
- **Extend**   Extends the size of a volume
- **Shrink**   Reduces the size of a volume
- **Format**   Used to format the volume or partition (for example, FORMAT FS=NTFS LABEL="New Volume" QUICK COMPRESS)

If you want to create a USB bootable drive manually that contains the Windows installation files, you can use DiskPart commands to create, partition, and mark the USB drive as active.

Work with VHDs

A VHD can be thought of as a container object that holds files, folders, and volumes. The container, or VHD, is a single file with the .vhd or .vhdx file extension. You can think of a VHD file being similar in concept to a ZIP file. Analogous container types could include ISO, RAR, and WIM; they are all objects that contain files and folders inside them.

Because a VHD is just a file, it is portable and can be saved and transported on a USB drive or copied over a network. Be aware, however, that VHDs can grow very large, and the original open file format of VHD, which had a maximum size of 2,048 GB, was soon changed to the VHDX format, which allowed up to a 64 TB file size. A VHD can contain data, but you can also install and boot to an operating system using the VHD.

Wherever possible because of the disk-intensive nature of VHD, consider using an SSD to host the VHDs. This is especially applicable if you use a single drive on your Windows 10–based computer and use virtual machines and VHDs as the disk I/O; performance is likely to degrade quickly because of the increased disk read/write times and disk activity.

You can continue to use either the VHD or VHDX specification for your hard drives, but you should know the main differences between the two formats. VHD offers users ease of use and backward compatibility, whereas the VHDX format offers improvements in both scale and functionality. You can compare the two choices in Table 3-19.

TABLE 3-19 Virtual hard disk format

Type	Features
VHD	Original format.
	Up to 2,048 GB (about 2 TB) in size.
	Compatible with virtualization technologies, including Virtual PC and Virtual Server.
	Useful when you are working with older operating systems and require backward compatibility.
	Can convert VHDX files to VHD by using Windows PowerShell.
VHDX	Introduced with Windows 8 and Windows Server 2012. Up to 64 TB in file size.
	Not compatible with operating systems older than Windows Server 2012 or Windows 8.
	Uses a 4 KB logical sector size to improve performance compared with VHD files.
	Offers protection against data corruption related to power failures by continuously keeping track of file updates in the metadata.
	Larger block sizes for dynamic and differencing disks.
	Can convert VHD files to VHDX by using Windows PowerShell or in the Hyper-V Manager.
	VHDX file format supports the shared virtual hard disk feature first available with Windows Server 2012 R2 and subsequent releases of Windows Server.
	Newer generation-2 virtual machines that are hypervisor-aware require VHDX file format.
	Shared VHDX allows guest clustering within Windows Server 2012 R2 and subsequent releases of Windows Server.
	VHDX format is not supported in Microsoft Azure.
VHD Set (VHDS)	Introduced with Windows 10 and Windows Server 2016.
	Same technical features as the VHDX format.
	Used as a shared virtual hard disk.
	Allows online resize.
	Supports host-based backup.
	Not supported in operating systems earlier than Windows 10.

There are multiple ways to create a virtual hard disk:

- Client Hyper-V Manager
- Disk Management
- Windows PowerShell

You can also use the DiskPart command-line tool, but this is becoming deprecated in favor of Windows PowerShell, which offers more extensive functionality and support.

Create VHDs with Hyper-V Manager

You can add the client Hyper-V feature to Windows 10 if the computer is running the Windows 10 Pro or Enterprise edition and has hardware that supports virtualization.

To create a virtual hard disk within Hyper-V Manager, complete the following steps:

1. Launch **Hyper-V Manager**.
2. In the **Action** pane, select **New** and then select **Hard Disk**.
3. Select the format for the disk as **VHD, VHDX, or VHD Set**, and then select **Next**.
4. Select the Disk Type (**Fixed, Dynamically expanding**, or **Differencing**) and select **Next**.
5. Provide the virtual disk with a name and storage location and select **Next**.
6. Configure the disk; the default settings are normally used and will create a new blank VHD with 127 GB. Select **Next** and then select **Finish**.

Use Disk Management to create VHDs

The Disk Management MMC includes a wizard that enables you to create a VHD that you can then mount and use. Not all of the VHD options are available in the Disk Management console, such as the ability to create VHD Sets or differencing disks; you should use Windows Power-Shell or Hyper-V Manager if these tasks are required.

To create a simple VHD file, follow these steps:

1. Right-click the **Start** button and select **Disk Management**.
2. Select **Action** on the menu bar and then select **Create VHD**.
3. Select the location where you want to store your VHD.
4. Configure the VHD format and VHD type and select **OK**.

   The new disk will appear in the lower pane of the screen and display the following characteristics:

   - Unknown Status
   - Not Initialized
   - Disk icon is cyan blue with down-pointing red arrow

5. To use the disk, initialize it by right-clicking the down-pointing red arrow on the disk icon and selecting **Initialize Disk**.
6. In the **Initialize Disk** dialog box, ensure that the disk you want to initialize is selected and choose **MBR (Default)** or **GPT partition style** and select **OK**.

   The disk is marked with the status of Basic, and you can now create a partition, allocate a drive letter, and format the drive with a file system just like a normal disk.

Apart from the icon color in Disk Management, there is no other visual indicator in File Explorer or Disk Management to indicate that the disk is virtual. After you have finished using the VHD, you can detach the disk by right-clicking the disk icon in the lower pane of Disk Management and selecting Detach VHD. After you have detached the VHD, the VHD file is no longer locked to Windows 10 and becomes a portable hard drive.

Create VHDs by using Windows PowerShell

Disk Management offers the ability to create basic VHDs in a GUI environment, but if you need to create more complicated VHDs, such as differencing disks, or if you need to create 20 VHDs for a team of developers to work with, it would be easier and quicker to build Windows Power-Shell scripts to do so. This section focuses on virtual hard disks.

You can manage every aspect of virtual disks with Windows PowerShell in both production and lab environments. Windows PowerShell enables you to configure, provision, and subsequently maintain all of your virtual estate rapidly. Windows PowerShell can be used to build a full virtual environment, including virtual disks, virtual machines, and virtual networks and switches.

More than 50 cmdlets are available in Windows PowerShell in Windows 10 that enable you to manage virtual and physical disks. This number will expand as new functionality is added. Table 3-20 outlines some of the common Windows PowerShell cmdlets that let you manage disks natively. After a VHD disk has been created, it is managed in the same way as a physical disk.

TABLE 3-20 Common native Windows PowerShell VHD and disk cmdlets

Command	Description	Additional Parameters
New-VHD	Creates one or more new virtual hard disks.	**-SizeBytes** sets the size, such as 10 GB. Set the VHD type by using the following parameters: **-Fixed** **-Differencing** **-Dynamic**
Get-Disk	Provides information on all disks.	**-FriendlyName** provides information about disks that have the specified friendly name. **-Number** provides information about a specific disk.
Convert-VHD	Converts the format, version type, and block size of a virtual hard disk file.	Specify the name of the new VHD as .vhdx or .vhd, and the cmdlet will use this format. **-VHDType** *<VHDType>* allows the specification of the VHD type such as **-Differencing** or **-Fixed**.
Clear-Disk	Cleans a disk by removing all partition information.	**-ZeroOutEntireDisk** writes zeroes to all sectors of a disk, effectively wiping it clear.
Initialize-Disk	Prepares a disk for use by the operating system. Default is to create a GPT partition.	**-PartitionStyle**<*PartitionStyle*> specifies the type of partition, either MBR or GPT.
Optimize-VHD	Optimizes the allocation of space in a non-fixed VHD/X. Used with the compact operation to optimize the files. Reclaims unused space and rearranges blocks, normally reducing the size of a virtual hard disk file.	**-Mode Full** (Default for VHD) Scans for zero blocks and reclaims unused blocks. **-Mode Retrim** Retrims the drive without scanning for zero blocks or reclaiming unused blocks. **-Mode Quick** (Default for VHDX) Reclaims unused blocks but does not scan for zero blocks.

Command	Description	Additional Parameters
Set-Disk	Updates a disk with the specified attributes.	**-PartitionStyle<*PartitionStyle*>** specifies the type of partition, either MBR or GPT. You can use this cmdlet to convert a disk to another type of partition style.
Get-Volume	Returns information on all volumes.	**-DriveLetter<*Char*>** gets information about the volume with the specified drive letter. **-FileSystemLabel<*String*>** returns information on NTFS file systems or Resilient File System (ReFS) volumes.

Two new cmdlets relate to the new VHD Set files, which can be used with Windows Server and Windows 10. These cmdlets are:

- **Get-VHDSet**   Obtains information about a VHD Set file such as a list of all checkpoints that the set contains.

- **Optimize-VHDSet**   Optimizes the allocation of space that VHD Set files use when used with the compact operation to optimize the files. Reclaims unused space and rearranges blocks, normally reducing the size of a VHD file.

To create a VHD, you use the New-VHD cmdlet. You must specify the path to the VHD, the name for the newly created VHD, the VHD type, the size of the disk, and the format type, as shown here:

```
New-VHD -Path D:\VHD\MyDynamicDisk.vhdx -SizeBytes 100GB -Dynamic
```

The New-VHD cmdlet executes and creates the VHD. As with Disk Management, the newly created VHD will not be mounted, initiated, or formatted without further action.

Windows PowerShell enables you to string instructions together and then execute them as a single action. The following example creates a new, dynamically expanding, 127 GB virtual hard disk with the .vhdx extension, mounts it, initializes it, and then formats the drive, using NTFS so that it is ready to use:

1. Select **Start**, enter **powershell**, right-click **Windows PowerShell**, and then select **Run as administrator**. Select **Yes** in the **UAC** dialog box.

2. Run the following PowerShell command:

```
New-VHD -Path "D:\VHDs\Test.vhdx" -Dynamic -SizeBytes 127GB | Mount-VHD -Passthru
|Initialize-Disk -Passthru |New-Partition -AssignDriveLetter -UseMaximumSize
|Format-Volume -FileSystem NTFS -Confirm:$false -Force
```

> ***NOTE*** New-VHD **CMDLET**
>
> The New-VHD cmdlet is only available when the Hyper-V feature is enabled.

Use Storage Spaces and storage pools

Storage Spaces is a technology that is useful for desktop or server devices that have multiple hard disks that can be combined to provide storage redundancy by pooling separate disks and allowing Storage Spaces to manage their administration effectively.

Storage Spaces uses NTFS and the ReFS file format to configure volumes, which provides greater file resilience through ReFS self-healing capabilities. The redundancy aspects are derived by distributing data across several disk drives and using virtual disk arrays in a RAID configuration or as mirror sets. The operating system maintains the logical disks and presents the virtualized disk as a logical unit number (LUN), which the system can then access. You might have seen the LUN terminology before; it is a term used with Storage Area Network protocols such as Fibre Channel or iSCSI.

The requirements for creating a virtual disk with Storage Spaces are described in Table 3-21.

TABLE 3-21 Creating virtual disks with Storage Spaces

Requirement	Description
Physical disk	Any size physical disks, such as Serial ATA (SATA), Serially Attached SCSI (SAS), or USB connected disks, can be used.
	You need a minimum of one physical disk to create a storage pool and more if you require mirrored disks.
	Disks must not be initialized or formatted.
Storage pool	A collection of one or more physical disks that you use to create virtual disks. All unformatted physical disks can be added to a storage pool.
Storage space	A logical disk created from one or more physical disks. It allows thin provisioning or just-in-time (JIT) disk allocations and can offer resiliency to physical disk failures through built-in functionality such as mirroring.
Disk drive	The drive letter allocated to the logical virtual disk and accessed through File Explorer.

A storage space is created from a storage pool. As you add additional disks, you can create redundant storage spaces. Four types of storage layouts are available to you with Storage Spaces, as described in Table 3-22.

TABLE 3-22 Storage Space storage layouts

Storage Option	Description	Redundancy
Simple	A simple space has data written across all disks in a logically sequential way that offers increased performance. With multiple disks, automatic data striping enables read/write operations to multiple segments of data concurrently.	Simple spaces provide no failover capabilities. If a disk that is storing the data fails, the data will be lost.

Storage Option	Description	Redundancy
Two-way or three-way mirrors	Mirrored spaces maintain multiple copies of the data by way of data duplication to ensure that all data is redundant. Two-way mirrors maintain two data copies, and three data copies are maintained for three-way mirrors. Data is also striped across the multiple physical drives, which offers the speed enhancements (greater data throughput and lower access latency) of striped disks without the data-loss risk of a simple space.	Data is mirrored so that if a single disk is lost, the data is available on another of the mirrored disks in the space. A resilient, two-way mirror requires a minimum of two physical disks and can tolerate a single drive failure. This requires a minimum of at least five physical disks for three-way mirroring and can tolerate two drive failures. The ReFS file format automatically maintains data integrity and can only be selected when using mirrored drives.
Parity	Parity is similar to RAID 5, which stores data, along with parity information across multiple physical drives. The parity writes are rotated across the available disks, which ensures an even distribution and drive optimization. A minimum of three physical drives is required for parity spaces.	Parity spaces have increased resiliency through disk read/write journaling so that if a drive is lost or corrupted, the missing data can be retrieved from the journal. The journal is stored across the remaining multiple disks.

A further feature that is available with Storage Spaces is how you provision the virtual disk spaces for use. Storage Spaces offers you two schemes:

- **Thin provisioning**   Enables you to allocate an intended storage that has greater capacity than is physically present at the time of creation. If you over-specify the amount of capacity compared to the data you currently have, the storage space engine disregards the extra storage capacity until datasets grow to require the storage. At this point, the extra storage is allocated. At any point, you increase the maximum size of an existing storage space and add drives as they are required at a later date. Thin provisioning is more economical and efficient because it allows organizations to deploy physical storage only when needed, thereby saving on operating costs, such as datacenter rack space costs associated with storing unused drives in situ.

- **Fixed provisioning**   Similar to traditional fixed storage allocation methods, by which you specify that the spaces will not increase beyond the initial storage capacity allocated at the same time as storage space creation. With fixed provisioning, you specify the hard limit for the size of the storage pool.

Configure Storage Spaces

When you have connected your physical drives to your computer, you can configure Storage Spaces by using the following steps:

1. Select **Start**, enter **Storage Spaces**, and then select **Manage Storage Spaces**.

2. Select **Create a new pool and storage space**.

3. If prompted, accept the UAC prompt.

4. Select the drives you want to add, as shown in Figure 3-32.

FIGURE 3-32 Selecting the drives to create a storage pool

All drives that are offline are automatically selected. Storage Spaces automatically identifies available drives to create the storage pool.

5. Select **Create pool**.

6. When the create pool operation completes, on the **Enter a name**, **resiliency type**, **and size for the storage space** page, shown in Figure 3-33, provide a name for the storage space and select the drive letter you want to use.

7. Select either the NTFS or ReFS file system. (Only if you choose a mirrored resiliency type can you format the storage space by using either the NTFS or the ReFS file system.)

8. Select the type of resiliency you require. This will depend on how many drives you have added to the storage space. But options include **Two-Way Mirror**, **Three-Way Mirror**, and **Parity**.

9. Set the **Size (maximum)** of the storage space. The size can be larger than the current capacity of the storage pool.

10. Select **Create storage space** to create your storage pool in the storage space.

FIGURE 3-33 Creating the storage space

After the storage pool has been created, the Manage Storage Spaces console manages and maintains it within Control Panel, where you can add, rename, or delete drives. If a physical disk is removed permanently from the pool, it must be reformatted before it can be used in another PC. Just like with mirrored or RAID disk sets, if you need to move the pooled disks to another computer, always move them as a unit so that their integrity is maintained.

As part of your exam preparation, create a storage space, provision a storage pool, and simulate a drive failure. In Figure 3-34, one of the physical drives used to create the storage space has been disconnected from the computer. Even with only one drive, the E drive continues to be available within File Explorer, and applications and users will be unaware of the failure until they review any notification in the Action Center.

If the removed physical drive is replaced, the storage pool checks the integrity of the pool and makes the necessary repairs. When it's repaired and full operational resiliency is restored, the icon changes from a warning symbol to the check mark indicating that everything is OK, as was originally shown before the disruption.

Storage Spaces can use ReFS for mirrored resilient spaces, offering built-in automatic file repair. This helps prevent data loss and can be carried out while the disks are online and do not require a system reboot to check and repair errors. ReFS and Storage Spaces therefore provide enhanced resiliency in the event of storage device failure.

EXAM TIP

Be aware of the self-healing capabilities ReFS offers, which are used for mirrored storage spaces. Remember that ReFS cannot be used for simple or parity resiliency types.

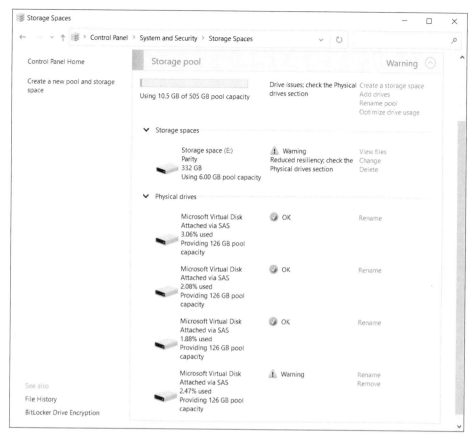

FIGURE 3-34 Reduced storage pool resiliency

Manage Storage Spaces by using Windows PowerShell

You can script the creation, repair, and administration of Storage Spaces by using Windows PowerShell. There are many more storage management–specific cmdlets that relate to storage operations. Some of the Storage Spaces–specific cmdlets that can be used are described in Table 3-23.

TABLE 3-23 Storage cmdlets in Windows PowerShell

Storage Cmdlets	Description
New-StoragePool	Creates a new storage pool, using a group of physical disks
Add-PhysicalDisk	Adds a physical disk to a storage pool for the creation of one or more VirtualDisk objects
Get-StoragePool	Gets a specific storage pool or a set of storage pool objects that are available
Set-StoragePool	Modifies the properties of the specified storage pool
Set-PhysicalDisk	Sets the attributes on a specific physical disk

Storage Cmdlets	Description
Get-VirtualDisk	Returns a list of VirtualDisk objects that are available
New-VirtualDisk	Creates a new virtual disk in the specified storage pool
Repair-VirtualDisk	Deletes an existing virtual disk and reclaims the space for use by other virtual disks in the same storage pool
Optimize-StoragePool	Rebalances a storage space configured as simple or mirrored, optimizing files based on disk space, disk size, and file size
Update-StoragePool	Upgrades the storage pool metadata to enable new features and functionality on pre–Windows 10 storage pools
RemovePhysicalDisk	Removes a physical disk from a specified storage pool
Remove-StoragePool	Deletes a storage pool and associated virtual disk objects

To list all the cmdlets that are available, use the `Get-Command -Module Storage` cmdlet.

NEED MORE REVIEW? **STORAGE CMDLETS IN WINDOWS POWERSHELL**

You can review the documentation relating to Storage Spaces Windows PowerShell cmdlets on MSDN at *docs.microsoft.com/en-us/powershell/module/storage/?view=win10-ps.*

Work with removable storage

Removable devices such as USB flash drives and Secure Digital High-Capacity (SDHC) memory cards are common and can offer portability benefits but also pose a potential threat to data security and loss. In this section, you learn how to work with removable devices.

FORMAT REMOVABLE DEVICES

You can format removable devices in the same way as you can configure hard drives. All drives without a file format, or that have one that Windows 10 doesn't understand, are considered *RAW*. To use the drive, first format the drive. If you insert an unformatted drive in your USB port, Windows prompts you to format the drive.

Depending on the size of your drive, you can format the drive using the FAT, FAT32 (default), NTFS, or exFat file format, using the format wizard. Be mindful when formatting a USB drive because, when you perform a quick format, the drive is not checked for errors. Although this is quicker, the system won't mark bad sectors on the drive, and this can lead to data integrity problems later on.

For drives larger than 32 GB, exFat is a good general-purpose format; it handles files larger than 4 GB and optimizes the drive space well. For smaller drives, FAT32 is best because it is compatible with virtually all operating systems and is fast.

You should format using NTFS if you are seeking advanced functionality such as file permissions on individual files and folders.

Secure removable devices

Data stored on USB flash drives is inherently insecure and should be protected. This can be achieved by using NTFS permissions, encrypted using EFS, or by using BitLocker encryption.

The most appropriate of these methods in an enterprise scenario is likely to be using BitLocker To Go because users understand it easily, and you can manage and configure the feature by using Group Policy.

BitLocker To Go is not designed to replace EFS or NTFS permissions; it adds an additional layer of security and protection on removable drives, including SDHC cards, USB flash drives, and external hard disk drives. BitLocker To Go is available in the Pro, Enterprise, and Education editions of Windows 10 only.

When encrypting removable media with BitLocker To Go, you have two options:

- **Encrypt used disk space only**   Encrypts only the part of the drive that currently has data stored on it. This is quicker and appropriate in most cases.

- **Encrypt entire drive**   Encrypts the full volume, including areas that contain no data, which takes longer to complete.

> **NOTE   BITLOCKER TO GO REQUIREMENTS**
>
> To encrypt a removable drive by using BitLocker To Go, the drive must be formatted with NTFS, FAT, FAT32, or exFat file system and have at least 64 MB of available space. Because removable drives are portable and typically not tied to one device, BitLocker To Go does not require use of a Trusted Platform Module (TPM) chip. The full volume encryption key and the volume master key are stored on the encrypted drive.

To enable BitLocker Drive Encryption on a removable drive, perform the following steps:

1. Insert a USB drive into your computer.
2. Open **File Explorer** and right-click the USB drive in the left pane.
3. Select **Turn on BitLocker** from the context menu.
4. The **Starting BitLocker Wizard** appears and initializes the drive.
5. On the **Choose how you want to unlock this drive** page, choose **Use a password to unlock the drive**.
6. In the **Enter your password** and **Reenter your password** boxes, enter a password and select **Next**.
7. On the **How do you want to back up your recovery key?** page, select **Save to a file**.
8. In the **Save BitLocker recovery key as** dialog box, select **This PC\Documents**.
9. In the **Save BitLocker recovery key as** dialog box, select **Save** and then select **Next**.
10. On the **Choose how much of your drive to encrypt** page, select **Encrypt used disk space only (faster and best for new PCs and drives)** and then select **Next**.
11. On the **Choose which encryption mode to use** page, select **Compatible mode (best for drives that can be moved from this device)** and select **Next**.
12. In the **Are you ready to encrypt this drive?** page, select **Start encrypting**.

When the encryption has completed, BitLocker is fully enabled on the removable drive. If you eject the USB drive and then insert the drive back into your PC or another computer, Windows 10 prompts you to enter the password to unlock the drive.

Configure OneDrive and OneDrive for Business

OneDrive is a cloud-based service designed for storing files and synchronizing settings aimed at the consumer market. Microsoft gives each user 5 GB of free cloud storage for personal use. To access the service, the user must use a Microsoft account, and the service can be accessed natively from a computer or smartphone.

Consumers can upgrade their personal OneDrive account to a Microsoft 365 Family or Microsoft 365 Personal subscription (which offers additional software benefits and 1 terabyte of OneDrive storage space).

A business-oriented service called OneDrive For Business is based on Microsoft SharePoint technologies; it stores data in a specialized library in the cloud. OneDrive For Business plans are available that allow business usage and can be purchased as a standalone plan or as part of a Microsoft 365 Business or Enterprise subscription. You can add multiple OneDrive for Business accounts to your device, but only one personal account can be added.

OneDrive desktop app

OneDrive is integrated with Windows 10, using the OneDrive app, and when you sign in to Windows with a Microsoft account, a OneDrive folder is created in File Explorer at C:\Users\ Username\OneDrive.

To protect against data loss, you should use OneDrive as your preferred location for all your data. When you add, modify, or delete files stored in the OneDrive favorite, your changes are replicated to OneDrive as long as you are online.

If you are using an operating system other than Windows 10, you might still be able to use the OneDrive desktop app; it is available to download from *www.microsoft.com/microsoft-365/ onedrive/download* or the Microsoft Store, and is supported on the following operating systems:

- Windows 7 or newer
- Windows Server 2008 R2 or newer
- macOS Sierra 10.12 or newer
- iPhone, iPad, or iPod touch with iOS 9.0
- Android
- Windows Phone 7.5 or later
- Xbox

The OneDrive app, located in the taskbar notification area, lets you modify synchronization settings. You can choose to synchronize all or selected files and folders from your cloud storage account to your device.

The OneDrive desktop app and sync client is preinstalled on Windows 10 devices and allows you to access your files stored in your online OneDrive if you use a Microsoft account to sign in to the app.

Once the app is configured, you can open File Explorer and locate a OneDrive icon. This icon represents a folder that is where the files you want to be kept in sync will be stored on your PC locally. By default nothing is stored—you must select files and folders and then they will be available.

If you add a new folder in the OneDrive folder within File Explorer, it will be available immediately in the cloud version of OneDrive and will be synchronized.

To configure OneDrive to synchronize folders from your OneDrive to your device, use these steps:

1. Right-click the **OneDrive** icon in the notification tray and select **Settings**.
2. On the **Account** tab, select **Choose Folders**.
3. On the **Sync your OneDrive files to this PC** screen select the check boxes for the folders and files that you want to sync.
4. Select **OK**.
5. On the **Account** tab, select **OK**.

The files will begin downloading immediately and the OneDrive app will monitor changes to local files as well as your cloud-based files, and it will maintain the synchronization.

On the notification area, the OneDrive for Business desktop app is colored blue whereas the consumer version is white. When displayed in File Explorer, both icons are blue, and the name of the account is listed after the business version to help differentiate.

OneDrive Files On Demand

OneDrive Files On Demand is a new feature available within OneDrive. This feature allows all your files and folders stored in OneDrive to be viewable within File Explorer on your PC without them actually being downloaded to your hard drive. You will be able to change each file and folder status to configure whether the resource should be stored locally.

You can turn on the Files On Demand feature by using these steps:

1. Sign in to **OneDrive** using your Microsoft account.
2. Right-click the white or blue OneDrive cloud icon in the notification area.
3. Select **Settings**.
4. On the **Settings** tab, select the **Save space and download files as you use them** box in the **Files On-Demand** section.

Once that setting is enabled, placeholders for all of your OneDrive content will be displayed in File Explorer. If you want to hide any folders from appearing in the OneDrive location in File Explorer, such as for privacy reasons, you can hide them by using these steps:

1. Sign in to OneDrive using your Microsoft account.
2. Right-click the white or blue OneDrive cloud icon in the notification area.

3. Select **Settings**.

4. On the **Account** tab, select **Choose Folders** in the **Choose Folders** area.

5. Clear the check box next to the folder you want to hide on this device.

After the OneDrive desktop app has retrieved a list of all files and folders from your One-Drive cloud account, you can browse to your OneDrive folder and see new cloud icons next to each item indicating the status of the file or folder availability as follows:

- **Online-only files**   Online-only files are placeholders only and don't use space on your computer. If you open the file and your device is connected to the internet, it is down-loaded and opened.

- **Locally available files**   After you have downloaded and opened any of your OneDrive files, they become locally available. You can open a locally available file at any time, even without internet access. To remove the local copy of the file, you can right-click the file and select Free Up Space.

- **Always available files**   If you choose the "Always keep on this device" option, files have the green circle with the white check mark. These files will be downloaded to your device and will be always available even when your device is not connected to the internet.

OneDrive web portal

Although integration is tight between the Windows 10 OneDrive app and the online version of OneDrive, the online version currently has slightly more functionality, although it can be slower to manipulate your files, depending on available bandwidth.

In the portal, users can:

- Manage all their files stored on OneDrive.

- Access previous versions of files.

- Access the OneDrive Recycle Bin.

- Buy more storage (Microsoft 365 subscription-based).

- Configure advanced sharing options for files and folders.

- Create Microsoft Excel surveys.

Users of mobile phones can also allow the automatic upload of all photos to their private OneDrive photos folder. With photos consuming some of your free 5 GB cloud storage each time you take a picture, you may be surprised at how quickly the quota is used up, but adding additional storage is relatively inexpensive. If you subscribe to Microsoft 365, OneDrive comes with 1 TB of storage and the ability to install Office applications locally on your PC, Mac, or iPad.

In OneDrive, you can access Microsoft Office Online, which enables you to create Word, Excel, Microsoft PowerPoint, and Microsoft OneNote files. After you create an Office online file, you can share the documents online, collaborate with other users, and edit documents at the same time. In addition, you can create text documents and Excel surveys. The surveys are simple; others can fill them out just by opening the link to the survey. You then see everyone's response compiled in the online spreadsheet.

Privacy is a significant concern for many users, especially when discussing personal data. Although OneDrive is aimed at consumers and is therefore not suitable (or licensed) for use with enterprise data, Microsoft has upgraded the level of security and encryption to protect data held on the OneDrive service. Data is now protected with Perfect Forward Secrecy (PFS) encryption when you access OneDrive through the web portal, *onedrive.live.com*, mobile OneDrive application, and OneDrive sync clients.

Chapter summary

- Each device on a network requires a unique IPv4 and, optionally, IPv6 configuration.
- Windows 10–based network devices use name resolution to change names in IP addresses for network communications.
- Windows 10 supports four commonly used VPN protocols. These are Point-to-Point Tunneling Protocol (PPTP), Layer 2 Tunneling Protocol (L2TP), Secure Socket Tunneling Protocol (SSTP), and Internet Key Exchange, Version 2 (IKEv2).
- Windows 10 uses common authentication protocols, including EAP-MS-CHAPv2, PAP, CHAP and MS-CHAP v2.
- VPN Reconnect is a feature supported when using IKEv2, which enables VPN connections to be automatically reestablished if they are broken. VPN Reconnect uses the IKEv2 tunneling protocol with the MOBIKE extension.
- Always On, App-Triggered VPN, and LockDown VPN profiles are new VPN features in Windows 10 that enable administrators to implement enterprise-grade VPN requirements.
- Wi-Fi Direct enables Windows 10 devices to interact with other hardware, such as printers, TVs, PCs, and gaming devices.
- Windows 10 provides a number of tools that you can use to help troubleshoot networking issues.
- Windows 10 supports NTFS as the default file system.
- The Quick Access area appears at the uppermost left area of the File Explorer navigation pane. It shows the frequently used files and folders.
- Effective Permissions is useful to determine the permissions a particular user would have through NTFS permissions.
- Windows 10 NTFS uses 6 Basic Permissions and 13 Advanced Permissions for securing files and folders.
- When you're applying permissions to groups, remember that an explicit Allow setting will override an implicit Deny permission.
- Use the ICACLS command-line tool to configure and view permissions on files and folders on a local computer and reset them to defaults.

- Inheritance of permissions can be useful when applying permissions to a large environment because the permissions will be automatically propagated based on the default inheritance setting.

- You can use the Effective Access feature to ensure that your NTFS permissions are as expected.

- If you have administrative privileges, you can take ownership of an object, such as a file, and allocate it to another user or group.

- You can reset the permissions of all the folders, files, and subfolders using the command `icacls <file name> /reset`.

- Share permissions can be Read, Change, or Full.

- Storage Spaces lets you utilize unused storage disk drives, including SATA, SAS, and USB drives, and combine the drive capacity to create a virtual disk for storing data. It's used on Windows 10 clients and servers, and enables users to benefit from an "easy to expand storage" facility and optional data redundancy with fault tolerance without the typical high cost of ownership that a traditional SAN facility would incur.

- Storage Spaces can be forcibly optimized using the `Optimize-StoragePool` PowerShell cmdlet, which is useful after disks have been added or removed.

- OneDrive is a free, cloud-based, consumer-oriented file storage service that is built into Windows 10 and used by many other operating systems through the OneDrive app.

- OneDrive On Demand Files shows placeholders for all files not hidden. In addition, files can be configured to always be stored locally.

- OneDrive Fetch Files On Your PC enables you to access locally stored files from the OneDrive web portal.

Thought experiment

In these thought experiments, demonstrate your skills and knowledge of the topics covered in this chapter. You can find the answers to these thought experiments in the next section.

Scenario 1

You have been hired to deploy Windows 10 at a new office for Adatum Corporation. The office was a greenfield site with no computer infrastructure, and it only has the network cabling and wireless infrastructure (which was installed by a contractor). You must help plan and implement networking services at the new location and verify that all equipment is working on the network.

As a consultant for Adatum, answer the following questions about networking:

1. You connected a number of devices to the wireless APs in the new building. They seem to be connected, but you want to verify that they can communicate with each other. Is it true that the **Test-Connection** Windows PowerShell cmdlet is the equivalent of the **Ping** command-line tool?

2. You want to be able to view the current network configuration of the installed laptops in the new building. Which of the following commands enable you to do this?

   A. `Ping`

   B. `Tracert`

   C. `NSlookup`

   D. `IPconfig`

   E. `Get-NetIPAddress`

   F. `Netsh`

3. You are troubleshooting name resolution to the LON-DC1 domain controller. You suspect a problem might reside with the configured DNS server that was just installed at the site. If you create an entry for LON-DC1 in the local Hosts file of a test computer running Windows 10, which is used first, the DNS server or the local resolver cache?

4. You have been asked to set up a VPN solution for some users who want to work from home. Which VPN tunneling protocols can you use with Windows 10?

5. You notice that one of your computers has an IPv4 address that starts 169.254. What could this mean?

Scenario 2

You have recently implemented a new network-shared storage facility for your organization. This storage is formatted using NTFS and has been shared to groups containing users within Active Directory. Users of the design department will use the local storage to store CAD drawings in two folders: Current Projects and New Projects. The files within the New Projects folder are confidential. You notice that users who are not part of the design department are able to access the CAD files.

You must ensure that the network-shared storage facility is accessed by the design department personnel only.

Answer the following questions for your manager:

1. How will you ensure that only design department personnel can access the storage?

2. What share-level permissions should you grant on the storage?

3. You need to confirm to your manager that members of the organization who are not in the design department do not have access to the files contained in the storage. How will you reassure your manager?

4. You need to provide an audit trail of the access to the New Projects folder. How will you proceed?

Scenario 3

You want to reuse some hard drives that you have and create a Storage Space with them. You have four disks; each disk is 500 GB in capacity, but two of them have 200 GB of data that you want to keep. You want to configure them to offer fault tolerance so that if any one disk fails, you do not lose any data. You do not need to use all of the available disks as part of the Storage Spaces solution. Answer the following questions about how you should set up Storage Spaces:

1. Which types of resiliency could you choose: simple, mirrored, three-way mirror, or parity?

2. How many of the four disks would you use?

3. How will you ensure that the data on the two drives will not be lost?

Scenario 4

You are helping a small consulting business configure its file and folder strategy. Eleven employees work from a single office, which also acts as a technology center, home to a show-case demonstration area and meeting rooms. The company is still in the startup growth phase, and financial resources are restricted. It currently does not use a domain environment, but its location has excellent internet access and uses the cloud extensively for email, Dropbox, and OneDrive. All devices use Windows 10 Pro with Microsoft accounts, and no dedicated IT support is available.

You need to ensure that the company can share files and folders in a cost-effective way.

Answer the following questions on behalf of the company:

1. The staff members have personal experience using OneDrive. Could they use OneDrive for file storage and sharing in the small company?

2. Employees need to have access to their data resources when not connected to the internet. How would OneDrive help them?

3. In the demonstration area of the business, a Windows tablet is used as a media playback device. It is configured to play a slideshow of all media files within a specified directory on the local drive. How would you ensure that this device has the latest media content available at all times?

4. The owner has concerns about using OneDrive for Business for storing business resources and the long-term viability of using OneDrive for Business. Should the owner be concerned?

Thought experiment answers

This section provides the solutions for the tasks included in the thought experiment.

Scenario 1

1. Yes, the **Test-Connection** Windows PowerShell cmdlet is the equivalent of the Ping command-line tool.

2. The **IPconfig**, **Get-NetIPAddress**, and **Netsh** commands enable you to view the network configuration of computers running Windows 10.

3. The DNS resolver cache is checked before a DNS server is petitioned.

4. You can use the following VPN tunneling protocols: Point-to-Point Tunneling Protocol (PPTP), Layer Two Tunneling Protocol with IPsec (L2TP/IPsec), Secure Socket Tunneling Protocol (SSTP), or Internet Key Exchange version 2 (IKEv2).

5. It means that the device is configured to obtain an IPv4 address automatically and has been unable to obtain an IPv4 configuration from a DHCP server. This might be because the DHCP server is offline or because an insufficient number of addresses are available on the server.

Scenario 2

1. Create a design department security group, add all the design department personnel to the group, and give the design department group NTFS access to the storage.

2. You should give full-access, share-level permissions for the design department group.

3. You should use the Effective Access feature to verify the NTFS permissions in place. In the Advanced Security settings for the shared folders, evaluate the effective access permissions for a user or group that is not a member of the design department group.

4. Enable Auditing for success and failure in Group Policy, and then enable auditing on the New Projects folder to track both successful access to the folder and failed attempts.

Scenario 3

1. You could create a storage pool and choose to use either a two-way mirror or a parity storage pool with the four drives.

2. Answers may vary, but you can add additional drives to increase the size of a storage pool; therefore, you can utilize all four drives.

3. You should label the disks carefully to ensure that you do not accidentally use the incorrect disk because all drives that are added to the storage pool will be formatted, and the data will be deleted. You should use the two blank disks to create a new storage pool and provision a new storage disk, which is a two-way mirror with the two blank disk drives, and then back up the 200 GB data onto this new storage pool. You can add the remaining drives to the storage pool after the data transfer has completed.

Scenario 4

1. Each employee could continue to use OneDrive for personal use. For business use, the company should purchase either a standalone OneDrive for Business plan or an Office 365 subscription that includes OneDrive for Business. They can then create folders to contain their work files, which could then be shared among the employees as required. Alternatively, the owner/manager could create folders in the company OneDrive for Business and then share the folders (with edit permissions) with the staff to create, store, and synchronize resources.

2. The employees could configure the OneDrive app settings to synchronize their local devices with the files and folders they use. They could then work on these files; the files would then synchronize automatically when the users are connected to the internet.

3. Answers may vary. You could use OneDrive. Create a shared folder stored on OneDrive for Business to contain the media. Employees can then add new content to this media folder in OneDrive for Business. Configure the media playback device to synchronize with this folder and maintain the device connection to the internet.

4. Answers may vary. OneDrive is aimed at the consumer audience, whereas OneDrive for Business is an enterprise solution. The data stored in both OneDrive and OneDrive for Business is encrypted and therefore secure from unauthorized access. Employees should be granted access to only the shared resources they require. The default amount of space per OneDrive for Business is 1 TB, but the amount can be unlimited depending on the OneDrive for Business plan that the company purchases.

Maintain Windows

After you have deployed computers in your organization, you must maintain those computers. If users experience problems with their computers, you may be required to perform system recovery. If users have lost files, you may be called on to recover those missing files.

Computers typically do not remain in the same state throughout their use. In most organizations, computers are updated periodically. With the new Windows as a service model for feature updates, you must be aware of how and when Windows Updates are applied. You may also need to know how to manage updates and, in certain circumstances, troubleshoot the application of updates. Even in normal circumstances, it is necessary to monitor your users' computers to help ensure the ongoing reliable use of those computers.

Finally, to save having to visit users' computers to maintain and manage them, you should know how to remotely manage Windows 10 computers. This chapter covers those aspects of the MD-100 Windows 10 exam that relate to Windows 10 monitoring and maintenance.

Skills covered in this chapter:

- Skill 4.1: Configure system and data recovery
- Skill 4.2: Manage updates
- Skill 4.3: Monitor and manage Windows
- Skill 4.4: Configure remote connectivity

Skill 4.1: Configure system and data recovery

In this skill, you review how to configure system and data recovery options for Windows 10. If you have experience with an earlier version of Windows, you may be familiar with many of the options because some are included in Windows 10. To prepare for the exam, we recommend that you work through all the wizards and tools to ensure that you're comfortable with each process, paying particular attention to the newer features, tools, and options.

> **This skill covers how to:**
> - Perform file recovery
> - Recover Windows 10
> - Create and manage system restore points
> - Troubleshoot the startup process

Perform file recovery

Windows 10 provides a number of tools that you or your users can use to recover files. These tools include:

- Windows Backup and Restore (Windows 7)
- WBAdmin
- File History
- Previous Versions

Use Windows Backup And Restore

Windows 10 includes the Backup And Restore (Windows 7) tool, which allows the creation of backups of your data. In addition to restoring files and folders, you can use this tool to create backups of files contained in folders, libraries, and whole disk volumes.

You cannot save your backups to the disk on which Windows 10 is installed, so you must provide another location, such as an external USB drive, network drive, or non-system local disk. To open the Backup And Restore (Windows 7) tool in the GUI, open the System And Security section of Control Panel or use the Backup And Restore (Windows 7) item listed in the Settings app.

To create a backup of your files and folders and a system image, follow these steps:

1. Open the **Settings** app, and then select **Update & Security**.
2. In the navigation pane, select **Backup**, and in the details pane, select **Go to Backup and Restore (Windows 7)**.
3. In the **Backup and Restore (Windows 7)** window, select **Set up backup**.
4. On the **Select where you want to save your backup** page, choose the location and select **Next**.
5. On the **What do you want to back up?** page, select **Let Windows choose (recommended)** and select **Next**.
6. On the **Review your backup settings** page, select **Change schedule**.
7. On the **How often do you want to back up?** page, leave the **Run backup on a schedule (recommended)** check box selected and, if necessary, modify the backup schedule.
8. Select **OK**.
9. On the **Review your backup settings** page, select **Save settings and run backup**.

The backup begins, and you review the progress as displayed in Figure 4-1. The first backup takes the longest time because it is a full backup. Subsequent backups are incremental and can take only a few minutes to complete.

When the backup is complete, use the links on the Backup And Restore (Windows 7) page to see the size of the backup on disk, edit the schedule, and manage the disk space the Backup And Restore (Windows 7) tool uses.

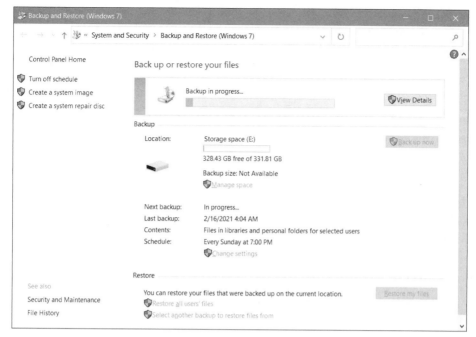

FIGURE 4-1 Backup And Restore (Windows 7)

When backing up your system, you can opt for the recommended settings, which create a backup of all files and folders in your user profile (including libraries) as well as a system image. The system image files are large, likely to be approximately 10 GB in size. You can specify the frequency and time when Windows 10 performs backups or retain the default backup schedule of Sunday at 7 PM every week.

If you require more specific scheduling, you can modify the triggers in the AutomaticBackup job in Task Scheduler after you have enabled scheduled backups. Available options to trigger a scheduled backup include:

- On A Schedule
- At Logon
- At Startup
- On Idle
- On An Event
- At Task Creation/Modification
- On Connection/Disconnect To A User Session
- On Workstation Lock/Unlock

If you want to choose specific libraries and folders for the backup manually, select Let Me Choose on the What Do You Want To Back Up? page when initially setting up the backup. Although you cannot select individual files for backup, you can clear the check box to include a system image of the drive.

The Backup And Restore (Windows 7) tool uses the Volume Shadow Copy Service (VSS) to create the backups. The initial backup creates a block-level backup of the files to the backup file and uses the virtual hard disk (VHD) file format. VSS greatly enhances the performance of the backup operation because subsequent backups copy only the data that has changed since the previous backup, which is typically a smaller amount of data, thus making the incremental backup much faster.

Each time you run a backup, the Backup And Restore (Windows 7) tool creates a new restore point, which the Previous Versions feature in File Explorer can use (and is covered later in this chapter).

> **NOTE BACK UP NTFS ONLY**
>
> The Backup And Restore (Windows 7) tool can only be used to back up data that is stored on file system volumes formatted as NTFS.

To restore libraries, folders, or files from a backup, you can use the Restore My Files link in the lower right of the Backup And Restore (Windows 7) screen. You can select which backup set to use and restore items to their original locations or to different locations. To restore data from a backup, use these steps:

1. On the **Backup and Restore (Windows 7)** page, select **Restore my files**.

2. The **Restore files** dialog box presents you with access to the latest backup. If you want to choose an alternative backup, select **Choose a different date**, select the correct backup, and select **OK**.

3. Locate the files or folders you intend to restore by using one of these three options:

   - **Search**   Type part of the name of the file you intend to restore. Select the file or select **Select All** to restore all the found files. Select **OK**. (The search speed is very fast.)

   - **Browse for files**   Select the backup name with the correct date and timestamp and browse to the folder that contains the items you want. Select the items and select **Add Files**.

   - **Browse for folders**   Select the backup name with the correct date and timestamp and browse to the folder that you want. Select the folder and select **Add Folder**.

   You can choose multiple files and folders and use any of the three options or combinations of the options to locate the items you want.

4. Select **Next**.

5. On the **Where do you want to restore your files?** page, choose to restore to the original location or browse and select a different location.

6. If you restore an item to a location that contains the same item name, you are prompted to choose one of the following:

   - **Copy and replace**   The item restored from the backup overwrites the item in the destination location.

- **Don't copy** Nothing changes, and no item is restored.
- **Copy, but keep both files** The original item remains as is, and the file name of the restored item is modified to show it is a version of the same item.
- **Do this for all conflicts** If you're restoring multiple items, you can apply the same choice to each conflict.

7. When the restoration is complete, the **Your files have been restored** page appears, and you can select the **View restored files** link.

8. Select **Finish**.

Perform a backup and restore with WBAdmin

In addition to the Backup And Restore (Windows 7) tool, Windows 10 includes another backup tool, the Windows Backup tool, which you can use from a command line. This tool is also found in Windows Server and is useful if you need to automate or create a backup job on several computers.

Use the WBAdmin.exe command-line utility to create, configure, and restore backup jobs. In this section, you review some of the commonly used applications for WBAdmin.

BACKING UP USING WBADMIN

The Windows 10 version of WBAdmin is a simplified version of the utility that is available with the Microsoft Server operating systems and offers some low-level features such as the generation of index listings of all files and folders within an image data file.

To perform a recovery using WBAdmin, you must be a member of the Backup Operators group or the Administrators group, or you must have been delegated the appropriate permissions. You must also run wbadmin from an elevated Command Prompt. A number of the subcommands are not supported in Windows 10, and you must boot to Windows Recovery Environment (RE) to perform a restore operation of data that was created using the wbadmin start backup subcommand.

Table 4-1 lists the command-line syntax of WBAdmin.

TABLE 4-1 WBAdmin command-line syntax

Command	Description
wbadmin get versions	Lists the details of backups available from the local computer or from a specified computer.
wbadmin enable backup	Configures and enables a regularly scheduled backup.
wbadmin start backup	Runs a one-time backup; if used with no parameters, it uses the settings from the daily backup schedule.
wbadmin get items	Lists the items included in a backup.
wbadmin start recovery	Runs a recovery of the volumes, applications, files, or folders specified. Supported only in a Windows Recovery Environment (RE).

For example, if you connect a removable hard drive to your computer that uses the drive letter E, the following examples guide you through the process of performing a backup and restore using the WBAdmin command-line tool.

To back up the entire contents of the C drive to a backup drive located on E, follow these steps:

1. Open an elevated Command Prompt.

2. Run the following command:

   ```
   WBAdmin start backup -BackupTarget:E: -Include:C:
   ```

3. Enter **Y** to begin the backup operation.

   The tool creates a shadow copy of the volume and then creates a block copy of the volume, as displayed in Figure 4-2. A simple log file relating to the operation is created, and this is stored in C:\Windows\Logs\WindowsBackup\.

The WBAdmin utility saves the image backup in a WindowsImageBackup folder on the target drive.

After you have created a backup, you can list backup images created on the system by running this command:

```
WBAdmin get versions -backupTarget:E:
```

RESTORING DATA USING WBADMIN

To recover from a backup that you have previously created with WBAdmin, start Windows RE, and then open the Windows RE Command Prompt. Enter **WBAdmin get versions backuptarget:d:** to provide the version information of the available backups. (You may have to change the drive letter to correspond to your system).

For example, to recover a backup of volume E from May 31, 2021, at 17:12, enter the following command at a Command Prompt:

```
WBAdmin start recovery -version:05/31/2021-17:12 -itemType:Volume -items:\\?\
Volume{a6f2e427-0000-0000-0000-501f00000000}\ -BackupTarget:D: -RecoveryTarget:E:
```

FIGURE 4-2 WBAdmin command-line tool

Configure File History

File History is a file recovery method that provides users with an easy and user-friendly method of retrieving files after they have been accidentally deleted or modified. Once enabled, File History will automatically create a backup of all user files that have been modified on an hourly schedule. As long as the backup destination location does not become full, File History can continue to store changes indefinitely.

To turn on File History, follow these steps:

1. Open **Settings**, select **Update & Security**, and select **Backup**.

2. Select the plus (**+**) icon labeled **Add a drive**. File History will search for drives.

3. In the **Select a drive** dialog box, select the external hard drive that you want to use for File History.

4. On the **Back up using File History** page, verify that the **Automatically back up my files** toggle is **On**.

Once enabled, File History will save copies of your files for the first time. This will happen as a background operation, and you can continue to work normally.

File History saves your files from your user profile and all the folders located in your libraries, including OneDrive, that are synced to your device if OneDrive is used. You can manually include or exclude folders on the Backup Options page. To manually include additional folders to be monitored by File History, perform the following steps:

1. Open **Settings**, select **Update & Security**, and select **Backup**.

2. Select the **More options** link.

3. On the **Backup options** page, select **Add a folder**.

4. Select the folder that you want to back up and select **Choose this folder**, as displayed in Figure 4-3.

5. Ensure that the folder is listed in the list of folders under **Back up these folders**.

6. Close the **Backup Options** page.

There are two other methods for adding a folder to the File History list of folders:

- **Add folders to one of the existing libraries already backed up by File History**   File History will protect these folders.

- **Use File Explorer**   Select the folder, select History in the Home ribbon, and then select the Include It In Future Backups link.

You can configure many of the File History settings multiple ways, and you need to be familiar with each of them:

- File History in Control Panel

- Backup in the Settings app

- History item on the File Explorer ribbon

Within the advanced settings screen of File History, accessed from the See Advanced Settings link on the Backup Options page, you can configure the following:

- Modify the frequency of the File History backup from every 10 minutes to daily.

- Open File History event logs to view recent events or errors.

- Define the length of time to keep saved versions of your files.

- Manually clean up older versions of files and folders contained in the backup to recover space on the backup drive. You could also use the command-line tool FhManagew.exe to delete file versions based on their age stored on the File History target device.

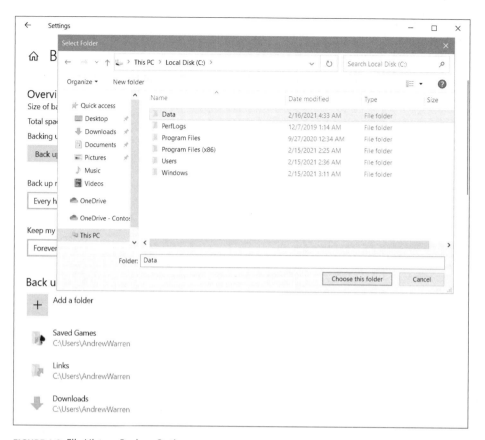

FIGURE 4-3 File History Backup Options

> **NOTE FILE HISTORY RESTORE POINTS**
>
> Previous Versions is a feature that uses the File History restore points and allows you to select one of the file version histories; it is accessed within File Explorer. Previous Versions is covered later in this chapter.

FILE HISTORY FILE RECOVERY

You can open File History file recovery, as displayed in Figure 4-4, in several ways:

- **History icon**   Open File Explorer and navigate to the folder that contains a modified or deleted file, and then select History on the Home ribbon. The File History page will open, and you can view the recoverable files.

- **Restore personal files**   Open File History in Control Panel and select the Restore Personal Files link on the left side.

- **Restore files from a current backup** The Restore Files From A Current Backup link is at the bottom of the page in the following location: Settings\Update & Security\Backup\More Options\Backup Options.

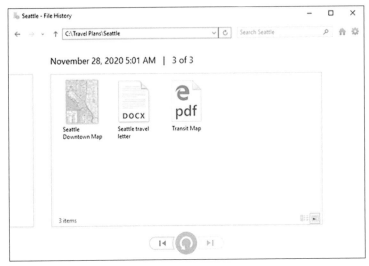

FIGURE 4-4 Restoring your personal files using File History

On the File History page, you can navigate through each restore point by using the left and right arrow buttons. Each restore point has a date and time to help you decide which version of the file or files to restore. You can select one or more files to revert and then select which version of the file by navigating through the backups that have been made by File History. If you right-click the file or folder, you can preview the file to view the contents. If you want to proceed to recover the file, select the green button on the File History screen. The file or files selected will be restored, and File Explorer will open with the restored files displayed.

FILE HISTORY SUPPORT FOR ENCRYPTION

Protecting files and folders using Encrypting File System (EFS) is supported on NTFS when using Windows 10 Pro and Windows 10 Enterprise versions. File History supports backing up files that are encrypted using the EFS as long as the drive selected for the backup is formatted as an NTFS volume. Without NTFS, data cannot be encrypted using EFS. Therefore, if the destination drive does not use NTFS, File History will not back up encrypted files.

If you use BitLocker Drive Encryption to protect your data on your PC and use File History to back up this data to a removable drive, the data will no longer be protected. You should consider enabling BitLocker To Go on the removable drive to protect the contents. The File History is designed to back up on a per-user basis and is performed using the local user account, which means only files and folders that you have access to will be backed up.

Restore previous versions of files and folders

Previous Versions, which has been reintroduced in Windows 10, is a file and folder feature that lets users view, revert, or recover files that have been modified or deleted by mistake. Previous Versions uses the File History feature or restore points created during backups in Backup And Restore (Windows 7). One of these features must be configured to use the Previous Versions feature.

After you have enabled File History or created a Backup And Restore (Windows 7) backup, browse in File Explorer to the location where the modified or deleted files are stored. If one of these methods has "protected" the file or folders being browsed, the Previous Versions tab shown in File Explorer will list the available restore points for your data. Until one of these tasks has been performed, the Previous Versions tab will be empty.

VSS is used by Previous Versions to monitor and preserve copies of modified files on an automatic schedule. Earlier in the chapter, you saw that the Backup And Restore (Windows 7) tool also creates a restore point each time you create a backup. After the initial File History restore point has been created, subsequent restore points may take only a few minutes to complete.

If you configure File History and also use the Backup And Restore (Windows 7) tool, multiple restore points will be available on the Previous Versions tab. The Previous Versions feature is available on all file systems if File History is used. The Backup And Restore (Windows 7) tool can be used only to back up data using NTFS volumes.

To revert files to a previous version, use these steps:

1. Ensure that **File History** is turned on.

2. Create a folder on your computer—for example, **C:\Travel Plans\York**—and then create or save a text file called **Things to do** in the folder.

3. In File History, select **Run Now**.

4. Open Things to do, modify the contents, save the file, and exit.

5. In File History, select **Run Now**.

6. Right-click **Things to do** and select **Restore Previous Versions**.

7. On the **Previous Versions** tab, note that the Things to do.txt file has two previous versions listed, one of which is the original file. Modify the file again. There will not be another Previous Version listed until the next restore point is created by File History.

8. To manually create a new restore point, return to **File History** and select **Run Now**. Select the Things to do.txt file and notice that it now has three file versions listed, as displayed in Figure 4-5.

FIGURE 4-5 Restoring previous versions of files and folders in File Explorer

9. Delete the Things to do.txt file.

10. To recover the last version of the file that was saved by File History, right-click the C:\Travel Plans\York folder and select **Restore Previous Versions**.

11. On the **Previous Versions** tab, select the Travel Plans folder, select the drop-down Open menu, and select **Open in File History**.

12. **File History** opens. Double-click the folder that contained the deleted file.

13. Select the deleted file, and select the green restore button.

14. Verify that the Things to do.txt file has been restored to the C:\Travel Plans\York folder.

Recover files from OneDrive

OneDrive allows you to store your files online. You can sync files between your PC and One-Drive. You can access files from OneDrive.com from just about any device that is connected to the internet. You can use the OneDrive Recycle Bin to recover files that you accidentally delete from your OneDrive account.

The OneDrive Recycle Bin can retain deleted items for between 3 and 30 days, if you are signing in using your Microsoft account. If you sign in with your Microsoft 365 account, deleted items are retained for up to 93 days. The actual retention period is dependent on the size of the Recycle Bin, which is set to 10 percent of the total storage limit by default. If the Recycle Bin is full, old items will be deleted to make room for new items as they are added to the Recycle Bin, and this may have an impact on the default retention period.

To recover deleted files from your OneDrive.com, follow these steps:

1. Browse to your **OneDrive.com**, or right-click the cloud icon in the notification area and select **View Online**.

2. On the left side of the page, select the **Recycle Bin**.

3. If the Recycle Bin is not visible, select the three horizontal lines in the top-left corner of the screen and select **Recycle Bin**.

4. Select the items that you want to recover.

5. Select **Restore** on the menu.

OneDrive will restore the items and they will be removed from the Recycle Bin.

At present, you are not able to modify the retention settings or increase the size of the Recycle Bin for OneDrive.com. If you use the Recycle Bin often and you are concerned about whether your deleted files will be protected by the Recycle Bin, you could consider increasing the space provided to the Recycle Bin by upgrading to a paid OneDrive storage plan such as Microsoft 365 Personal. If space is limited, you could also review the items currently in the Recycle Bin and select items for permanent deletion to free up space, as displayed in Figure 4-6.

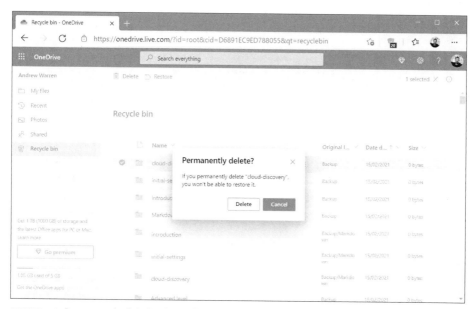

FIGURE 4-6 Permanently deleting items from the OneDrive Recycle Bin

When you delete files using the OneDrive.com interface or from your OneDrive folders within File Explorer, the deleted files will be automatically synchronized to the OneDrive.com Recycle Bin and the File Explorer Recycle Bin (or Trash if you are using OneDrive on a Mac). If you use the Restore All or Empty Recycle Bin option, you need to be aware that these tasks are irreversible.

The Search feature within OneDrive.com is a powerful method of locating files stored in your OneDrive. Search results do not include items in the OneDrive Recycle Bin or the File Explorer Recycle Bin.

ONEDRIVE DOCUMENT VERSION HISTORY

For Office documents, such as Microsoft Word and Microsoft Excel files, OneDrive.com maintains previous versions of these documents where available. To view the available versions stored in OneDrive, navigate to the Office file, right-click it, and choose Version History. OneDrive will open the file in a new browser tab. You can then see the list of available versions in the left pane, and you can review the contents of each file, as displayed in Figure 4-7.

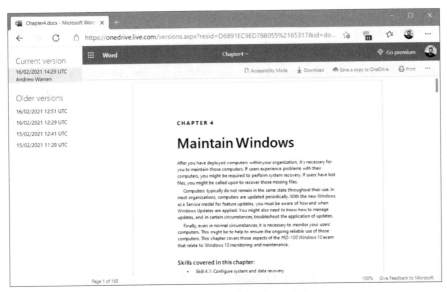

FIGURE 4-7 Microsoft Office previous versions available in OneDrive

The older versions are listed together with the date and time when the file was last saved. If you select an older version of the document from the list of older versions in the left pane, OneDrive will open the older file in the tab, and it will display the name of the modifier. You can choose to download or restore this older version from the link displayed in the left pane.

Recover Windows 10

Windows 10 is a reliable operating system. However, occasionally you will encounter problems with your users' devices that require you to perform some sort of operating system recovery. The severity of the problem will determine your particular course of action, and because of this, Microsoft has provided a number of recovery tools in Windows 10.

Some of these are relatively benign and enable you to investigate and resolve the underlying problem with little effect on the operating system. Others are more intrusive and can result in resetting the operating system to an earlier point in time or even to its initial state. These recovery tools include:

- Recovery Drive
- System Restore
- Windows RE
- Reset This PC
- Fresh Start
- System Image Restore
- System Repair Disk

Configure a recovery drive

Windows 10 computers have a recovery partition, which contains a full image of the system. If your computer does not start properly, you can use the recovery partition to start up.

You can also copy the contents of the recovery partition to a removable storage device so that if your recovery partition becomes inaccessible or corrupted, you will still be able to recover your system.

Disk drive space on many small form-factor devices and tablets might be smaller than available on a laptop or PC. This can limit the availability for an original equipment manufacturer (OEM) to include a recovery partition on devices shipped with Windows 10. If there is no recovery partition, you can still create a bootable Universal Serial Bus (USB) flash drive–based recovery drive; you can use this drive to boot into the Windows Recovery Environment (Windows RE). You will then need to access a system image that you have created or that is provided by the OEM.

To create a recovery drive, follow these steps:

1. Search for **Recovery Drive** and select **Create A Recovery Drive**.

2. Accept the **User Account Control (UAC)** prompt, providing the necessary credentials, if required.

3. Select the **Back up system files to the recovery drive** option, and select **Next**. Windows 10 will prepare the recovery image.

4. If you have not already connected a backup device to the system, on the **Connect a USB flash drive** page, connect a drive that has at least 16 GB capacity.

5. On the **Select the USB flash drive** page, select the drive for the recovery drive, as displayed in Figure 4-8, and select **Next**.

6. On the **Create the recovery drive** page, read the warning that the USB drive contents will be deleted, and select **Create**. The **Creating the recovery drive** page appears with a progress bar, which will indicate which phase of the process is being performed. The

process can take up to 30 minutes, depending on the performance of the PC and the media. The tool performs the following actions:

- Prepares the drive
- Formats the drive
- Copies Recovery Drive utilities
- Backs up system files

7. On the last page, select **Finish**.

When the recovery drive has been provisioned on the removable media, if your device has a recovery partition, you will see a link to delete the recovery partition from your PC. This relates to the Windows 10 device recovery partition and not the newly created recovery drive. If you want to free up the space on your device, you need to select this option. It is important to store the recovery drive in a safe place because you will not be able to recover your device if you have lost the recovery drive and you have deleted the recovery partition.

FIGURE 4-8 Creating a recovery drive

NOTE **SDHC MEMORY CARDS**

Some devices support the use of Secure Digital High-Capacity (SDHC) memory cards. The Recovery Drive Wizard can use an SDHC card as an alternative to using a USB flash drive.

You should carefully label your Recovery Drive media after they have been created. Note that a 64-bit (x64) recovery drive can only be used to reinstall a device with 64-bit architecture. The Windows 10 Recovery Drive cannot be used to repair earlier versions of Windows.

Configure System Restore

You can use System Restore to restore a computer that has become unstable. System Restore offers a reliable method of recovering systems by restoring the operating system to a restore point created during a period of stability.

Once enabled, System Restore will automatically create restore points at the following opportunities:

- **Whenever apps are installed**   If the installer is System Restore compliant.
- **With updates**   Whenever Windows 10 installs Windows updates.
- **Based on a schedule**   Windows 10 includes scheduled tasks, which can trigger restore point creation.
- **Manually**   You can create a System Restore from the System Protection screen.
- **Automatically**   When you use System Restore to restore to a previous restore point, Windows 10 will create a new restore point before it restores the system using the selected restore point.

To turn on System Restore and manually create a system restore point, follow these steps:

1. Open Control Panel and select **System and Security**.
2. Select **System**. The **Settings** app opens. Scroll down and select the **System protection** link.
3. The **System Properties** dialog box appears with the System Protection tab open.
4. To turn on the System Restore feature, select the **Local Disk (C:) (System)** drive, and then select **Configure**.
5. In the **System Protection for Local Disk (C:)** dialog box, select **Turn on system protection**.
6. Under **Disk Space Usage**, move the slider for the **Max Usage** to allow room on the restore points to be saved (5 percent is a reasonable amount), as displayed in Figure 4-9.
7. Select **OK** twice.

FIGURE 4-9 Configuring System Restore properties

You can also use PowerShell to configure System Restore. Some of the available commands that you need to review are as follows:

- **Enable-ComputerRestore**   Enables the System Restore feature on the specified file system drive
- **Disable-ComputerRestore**   Disables the System Restore feature on the specified file system drive
- **Get-ComputerRestorePoint**   Gets the restore points on the local computer
- **Checkpoint-Computer**   Creates a system restore point

The following command enables System Restore on the C drive of the local computer:

```
PS C:\> enable-computerrestore -drive "C:\"
```

> **NOTE**   **SYSTEM RESTORE REQUIRES NTFS AND USES VOLUME SHADOW COPY SERVICE**
>
> System Restore uses the Volume Shadow Copy Service (VSS) and is only available on drives that are formatted with NTFS.

If the amount of space allocated for the restore points is used up, System Restore automatically deletes the oldest restore points. If you require more restore points to be available, you must allocate a larger proportion of the hard disk to the feature.

After the system has created restore points, you are protected, and the system should be recoverable.

To recover your system, you can open the System Restore Wizard one of two ways:

- **System Protection**   If your system allows you to sign in to Windows, you can open System Restore from the Windows 10 GUI.
- **Windows Recovery Environment (Windows RE)**   If the system doesn't allow you to sign in, you can start your computer with Windows RE and open the System Restore Wizard from the Advanced options.

> **NOTE**   **WINDOWS RE**
>
> Windows RE is built on Windows Preinstallation Environment (Windows PE), which is a cut-down version of Windows that offers only limited functionality.

IDENTIFYING AFFECTED APPS AND FILES

When you're using System Restore to restore a computer to an earlier state, the wizard will allow you to scan the restore point and advise you which apps and files will be affected by performing the operation. To restore your computer's configuration to an earlier state, use the following procedure:

1. Open **System Protection**.
2. Select **System Restore**.

3. On the **Restore System Files And Settings** page, select **Next**.

4. On the **Restore your computer to the state it was in before the selected event**
page, choose the restore point that you want to be restored, as displayed in Figure 4-10.

FIGURE 4-10 Applying a system restore point to your system

5. Optionally, select **Scan For Affected Programs**, or select **Next**.

6. On the **Confirm Your Restore Point** page, select **Finish**.

7. On the warning screen, select **Yes**.

8. System Restore will now prepare your computer and restart. The process can take some
time to complete.

9. When the process is complete, the system will restart, and you can sign in to Windows.

10. You will be presented with a summary of the system restore status, and a confirmation
that your documents have not been affected.

11. Select **Close**.

> **NOTE   SYSTEM RESTORE IN WINDOWS RE**
>
> When using System Restore in Windows RE—as a protection against unauthorized access to
> the system—you need to select a user account and provide the user's password before you
> can use the System Restore feature.

MODIFYING THE TASK SCHEDULE

After you have enabled the System Restore feature, you can modify the default task schedule for
when you want automatic restore points to occur by modifying the SR scheduled task as follows:

1. Search for a Task and select the **Task Scheduler** item.

2. In the **Task Scheduler Microsoft Management Console (MMC)**, expand the node on the left to locate Task Scheduler Library\Microsoft\Windows\SystemRestore.

3. Double-click the **SR task** in the middle pane.

4. In the **SR Properties (Local Computer)** dialog box, select the **Triggers** tab.

5. On the **Triggers** tab, select **New**.

6. In the **New Trigger** dialog box, configure the schedule that you require. For example, you can configure Windows to create a daily system restore point at noon.

7. Ensure that the **Enabled** check box is selected and select **OK**.

8. On the **Triggers** tab, select **OK**. In the **Task Scheduler MMC**, the trigger is now displayed and enabled.

9. Close the **Task Scheduler MMC**.

Opening Windows RE

To open Windows RE and use safe mode or other advanced troubleshooting tools, you can attempt to start Windows 10 in advanced troubleshooting mode by using one of the following options:

- Open Settings, and select Update & Security. Select the Recovery tab, and if available, select Restart Now under Advanced Startup.

- Restart the device using the Recovery Drive.

- Boot the device using Windows 10 installation media and select the Repair Your Computer option.

- Press the Shift key and select the Restart option on the Start menu.

In addition to these methods, Windows will automatically start in Windows RE after detecting the following issues:

- Two consecutive failed attempts to open Windows

- Two consecutive unexpected shutdowns that occur within 2 minutes of boot completion

- A Secure Boot error

- A BitLocker error on touch-only devices

After Windows 10 boots to the advanced troubleshooting mode, you must select Troubleshoot; then on the Advanced Options screen, you can access some or all the following options, as displayed in Figure 4-11:

- **Startup Repair** Fix problems that are preventing Windows from starting.

- **Startup Settings** Change Windows startup behavior.

- **Command Prompt** Used for advanced troubleshooting.

- **Uninstall Updates** Remove quality or feature updates.

- **UEFI Firmware Settings** Used to modify UEFI settings.

- **System Restore** Use a system restore point to restore Windows.

- **System Image Recovery** Recover Windows using a system image file.

FIGURE 4-11 Windows 10 advanced troubleshooting mode

NOTE **WINDOWS 10 DOES NOT SUPPORT F8 AT STARTUP**

Unlike versions prior to Windows 10, you can't access the advanced troubleshooting mode by pressing F8 during the startup process. However, you can reenable the F8 support by modifying the boot configuration data (BCD).

The advanced troubleshooting mode shown in Figure 4-11 allows you to select the Startup Settings, which restarts Windows in a special troubleshooting mode that might be familiar to users of other versions of the Windows operating system. Selecting the Startup Settings troubleshooting mode presents you with the following options:

- **Enable debugging** Start Windows 10 in troubleshooting mode, monitoring the behavior of device drivers to help determine if a specific device driver is causing Windows 10 to behave unexpectedly.

- **Enable boot logging** Windows 10 creates and writes to a file named Ntbtlog.txt to record the device drivers installed and loaded during startup.

- **Enable low-resolution video** Start Windows 10 in a low-resolution graphics mode.

- **Enable Safe Mode** Windows 10 starts with a minimal set of drivers, services, and applications to allow you to troubleshoot the system using the GUI. Safe mode does not include network connectivity.

- **Enable Safe Mode with Networking** Safe mode with networking enables network connectivity.

- **Enable Safe Mode with Command Prompt** Safe mode using a Command Prompt window rather than the Windows GUI.

- **Disable driver signature enforcement**   Allows you to load device drivers that do not have a digital signature.

- **Disable early launch anti-malware protection**   Start Windows 10 without the early launch antimalware functionality running. This mode is useful for identifying whether early launch antimalware is affecting a driver or app from being loaded.

- **Disable automatic restart after failure**   Stops Windows 10 from automatically restarting after a system failure occurs.

You can cancel and reboot your system normally by pressing Enter. To select an option that you require, you need to press the number key or function key F1–F9 that corresponds to the list of items as displayed in Figure 4-12.

If you press F10, you are taken to another screen with the option to open the recovery environment. This option reboots the system and returns you to the Advanced Options screen, as shown previously in Figure 4-11.

Startup Settings

Press a number to choose from the options below:

Use number keys or functions keys F1-F9.

1) Enable debugging
2) Enable boot logging
3) Enable low-resolution video
4) Enable Safe Mode
5) Enable Safe Mode with Networking
6) Enable Safe Mode with Command Prompt
7) Disable driver signature enforcement
8) Disable early launch anti-malware protection
9) Disable automatic restart after failure

Press F10 for more options
Press Enter to return to your operating system

FIGURE 4-12 Windows 10 Startup Settings

> **NOTE   LAST KNOWN GOOD CONFIGURATION**
> Windows 10 does not support the Last Known Good Configuration startup option that was present in Windows 7 and earlier versions of Windows.

Reset This PC

If other methods of recovering your system fail or your problems reoccur, you can revert your system to the state similar to how it was when you purchased it or when you first installed Windows 10. Typical issues that prevent the use of other tools mentioned in this chapter include a damaged hard drive or a malware attack that encrypts the drive.

Windows 8 first introduced the option to refresh or recycle your computer; Windows 10 has improved the performance and reliability of this feature. You will see the words *recycle* and *reset* used interchangeably by Microsoft to mean the same thing, although the Windows interface options typically use the term *reset*. The Reset This PC option consolidates the two options (Refresh Your PC and Reset Your PC) that were available in Windows 8 and Windows 8.1.

For enterprise users who suffer from an unstable or corrupted system, often the quickest remedy is to deploy a fresh system image from the deployment server to the device. Home users and small organizations can use a similar solution, but rather than use a deployment server on the network such as Windows Deployment Services (Windows DS), Windows 10 is able to re-image the device itself. Selecting the Reset This PC option effectively reinstalls the Windows 10 operating system and allows you to either keep your files or remove everything.

To start the recovery process, follow these steps:

1. Open the **Settings** app.
2. Select **Update & Security**.
3. Select **Recovery**.
4. On the **Reset this PC** page, select **Get started**.

   The screen will be dimmed, and you will be presented with the options displayed in Figure 4-13:

   - **Keep my files**   Removes apps and settings but keeps your personal files
   - **Remove everything**   Removes all your personal files, apps, and settings

5. Select **Keep my files**.
6. On the **How would you like to reinstall Windows?** page, you are prompted to choose between:

   - **Cloud download**   Choose this option to download and reinstall Windows from a cloud source. You are likely to download a more up-to-date version of Windows 10.
   - **Local reinstall**   Choose this option to reinstall Windows from a local source. You can accelerate the recovery process by chosing this option.

7. On the **Additional Settings** page, you can review your choices. Select **Change Settings**, or if you're happy, select **Next**. A summary screen displays and describes the actions that will be performed. You can select the **View apps that will be removed** link to review which apps will be removed during the reset procedure.

8. Select **Reset**. The reset process begins.

FIGURE 4-13 Reset This PC options

After the reset process has completed and you've signed in, you will have a list of removed apps on the desktop. This file, called Removed Apps, is discussed more in the next section.

> **NOTE   RECYCLE THE DEVICE**
>
> If you want to recycle a device, you can use the Reset This PC option to make the device available for use by someone else. If you choose Remove Everything, the device reverts to the out-of-box experience (OOBE) state. You can then use a deployment process, such as Windows Autopilot, to configure the device for reuse in your organization—with minimal user intervention.

If you selected Remove Everything, then you can also choose to clean your drive. Cleaning the drive helps ensure that your content is not recoverable by the new owner of the device. This option is ideal if you are seeking to recycle your PC and want to make it difficult for someone to recover your removed files. When the system reset is complete, you are offered the OOBE. You must configure the device, install any apps, and modify any settings that you would like.

To clean your drive, follow these steps:

1. Select **Reset this PC**, and select **Remove everything**.

2. On the **How would you like to reinstall Windows?** page, choose either **Cloud download** or **Local reinstall**.

3. On the **Additional Settings** page, select **Change Settings**.

4. On the **Choose settings** page, displayed in Figure 4-14, select **Clean data?**. If you have multiple hard disks and you want to clean them all, also select **Delete files from all drives?**. Select **Confirm**.

5. Review your chosen options, and then select **Next**.

6. Finally, when prompted, select **Reset**.

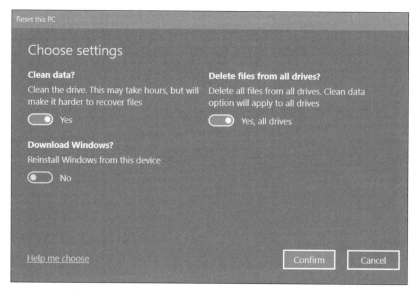

FIGURE 4-14 Choose settings options for Remove Everything operations

Perform a Fresh Start

Versions of Windows 10 1909 and earlier provided another way to reset the system called Fresh Start. Fresh Start performs three actions:

- Reinstalls Windows 10 while retaining your data
- Removes all installed apps and bloatware
- Installs the latest security updates

Fresh Start has been consolidated in Reset This PC in Windows 10 2004 and newer.

Creating a system image backup

As mentioned earlier, included with Windows 10 is the Backup And Restore (Windows 7) tool, which you can use to back up and restore selected files and folders. You can also use this tool to create a system image of your computer.

To create a system image backup, follow these steps:

1. In **Settings**, select **Update & Security** and then select the **Backup** tab.

2. In the **Details** pane, select **Go to Backup and Restore (Windows 7)**.

3. In **Backup and Restore (Windows 7)**, select **Set up backup**.

4. On the **Select where you want to save your backup** page, choose the location and select **Next**.

5. On the **What do you want to back up?** page, select **Let me choose** and then select **Next**.

6. Select any folders that you want to back up, but make sure you select the **Include a system image of drives** check box, as displayed in Figure 4-15.

7. On the **Review your backup settings** page, select the **Change schedule** link.

8. On the **How often do you want to back up?** page, leave the **Run backup on a schedule (recommended)** check box selected, and choose when you want the backup to be performed.

9. Select **OK**.

10. On the **Review your backup settings** page, select **Save settings and run backup**.

11. The backup will begin.

FIGURE 4-15 Performing a system image backup

> *NOTE* **ADVANCED BACKUP SCHEDULING**
>
> Backup And Restore (Windows 7) allows you to create a simple backup schedule. If you modify the Automatic Backup task in Task Scheduler, you can specify a more complex backup schedule—for example, to back up multiple times per day or to back up when your workstation is in the locked state.

USING SYSTEM IMAGE RECOVERY

When you use the System Image Recovery process in Windows RE, Windows 10 replaces your computer's current operating system state with the system image that has been created by the Backup And Restore (Windows 7) tool.

You should only use System Image Recovery if other recovery methods are unsuccessful because it will overwrite data on your computer. During the restore process, you can't choose individual items to restore. All the apps, system settings, and files are replaced. Any data files stored locally on your computer that you have created or modified since the system image was created will not be available after you use System Image Recovery unless you have saved them to another location, such as OneDrive.

To recover a device with a system image, follow these steps:

1. Open **Settings**, and then select **Update & Security**.

2. Select **Recovery**, and then, under **Advanced Startup**, select **Restart Now**.

3. In Windows RE, on the **Choose An Option** page, select **Troubleshoot**.

4. On the **Troubleshoot** page, select **Advanced options**.

5. On the **Advanced options** page, select **System image recovery**. Allow the system to reboot, and Windows will prepare for System Image Recovery.

6. On the **System image recovery** page, select your user account.

7. Enter your password and select **Continue**.

8. On the **Re-image your computer** page, verify the system image is correctly selected, as displayed in Figure 4-16, and select **Next**.

FIGURE 4-16 Using the System Image Recovery Wizard

9. On the **Choose additional restore options** page, select **Next** and then select **Finish** to start the restoration process.

10. In the **Re-image your computer** dialog box, read the warning, and then select **Yes**. The **Re-image your computer** process will now proceed.

11. Once completed, Windows will need to restart. Click **Restart now**, or you can wait and allow Windows to automatically restart. When Windows restarts, you will be presented with the sign-in screen.

Creating a system repair disk

In addition to a system image, you can use the Backup And Restore (Windows 7) tool to create a system repair disk. You can use a system repair disk to recover Windows 10 in the event of a drive or other catastrophic failure.

A system image can be incorporated into any backup when using the Backup And Restore (Windows 7) tool. However, creating a system repair disk requires that you manually create a repair disk, as follows:

1. Open **Backup And Restore (Windows 7)** in **Control Panel**.

2. Insert a blank writable CD or DVD into your device.

3. On the **Backup And Restore (Windows 7)** screen, select the **Create a system repair disc** link.

4. In the **Create a system repair disc** dialog box, select **Create disc**, as displayed in Figure 4-17.

FIGURE 4-17 Creating a system repair disc

The system repair disc is useful if Windows 10 will not automatically boot in the advanced startup options. In this situation, insert the system repair disc and your computer will boot from the recovery media automatically. If it doesn't, you might need to change the boot order.

Troubleshoot the startup process

Windows 10 has an efficient and reliable startup architecture. It is rare that you will need to get involved in resolving startup problems. However, when startup problems do occur, they can be difficult to resolve unless you understand the underlying process.

Components of the startup architecture

The startup architecture consists of four main components:

- **Windows Secure Boot**   All computers are potentially vulnerable to malicious software, such as computer viruses. This is especially true during the early startup phases when the operating system's protective components may not yet be available. To mitigate this issue, Windows 10 implements Secure Boot. If your computer supports the Unified Extensible Firmware Interface (UEFI), you can enable Secure Boot in your computer's UEFI settings. Once Secure Boot is enabled, when the computer starts and before control is transferred to the operating system, each piece of software is checked for a valid digital signature. Only software deemed safe is loaded, including all low-level operating system drivers and files.

- **Windows Boot Manager**   This consists of a single file, BOOTMGR, which resides in the root directory of the active disk partition. This partition is not assigned a drive letter. The Windows Boot Manager, BOOTMGR, reads the Boot Configuration Data (BCD) from the boot store. BOOTMGR replaces the NTLDR program from Windows XP and earlier. The BCD identifies the location and state of any operating systems installed on the local computer. The BCD is a database. Windows XP used a simple text file called Boot.ini.

- **Windows OS Loader**   Winload.exe is located in the \Windows\System32 folder on the operating system partition, which is typically assigned the drive letter C. Winload.exe initializes memory and then transfers control to the Windows kernel; this is a file called Ntoskrnl.exe located in C:\Windows\System32.

- **Windows Resume Loader**   Winresume.exe is also located in the \Windows\System32 folder on the operating system partition. If the boot store identifies that there is a hibernation image (hiberfil.sys) on the local computer, then BOOTMGR has passed control to Winresume.exe rather than Winload.exe. Winresume.exe then returns the computer to its pre-hibernation state.

NOTE **PARTITIONING**

Your computer typically has three partitions on its installed hard disk. All of these will be primary partitions. The first partition will be marked as active and will contain the files necessary to perform the initial startup of the operating system; this partition, or drive, is often referred to as the System partition (although it contains the boot store and low-level boot files). The second partition automatically is assigned the drive letter C and contains the operating system; it is often referred to as the Boot partition. The third partition is the recovery partition containing Windows RE. You might also have a vendor-specific recovery partition.

NOTE **FAST STARTUP**

By default, Windows 10 is configured to use Fast Startup. When you shut down your computer, part of the operating system's state is stored in Hiberfil.sys. However, this is not true hibernation; instead, it is a hybrid state. We recommend using Fast Startup because it enables your computer to start up far more quickly. You can configure Fast Startup in Power Options in Control Panel.

The Windows 10 startup process

When you start a computer installed with Windows 10, as displayed in Figure 4-18, the following process occurs:

1. **Power-on self-test**   When you power up your computer, the UEFI or, on older computers, the Basic Input/Output System (BIOS), performs a number of fundamental checks. This is referred to as the power-on self-test (POST).

    The critical check that the POST performs is to verify the presence and accessibility of a configured boot device, such as a hard disk. The hard disk must contain a valid master boot record (MBR). The MBR enables the computer to identify and access partition information on the attached disk. The computer accesses the primary active partition (which contains the Windows 10 boot sector) and loads BOOTMGR.

2. **Read the boot configuration data**   BOOTMGR accesses the BCD from the system partition. This enables BOOTMGR to determine the location of any installed operating systems and, where necessary, to display a startup menu on computers configured with multiple operating systems (referred to as dual-boot or multiboot systems). BOOTMGR also determines whether the computer has a hibernation file.

3. **Winload.exe or Winresume.exe**   If a Hiberfil.sys file exists, BOOTMGR passes control to Winresume.exe to restore the operating system from the pre-hibernation state. If no Hiberfil.sys file exists, BOOTMGR passes control to Winload.exe.

    Winload.exe initializes memory and scans the computer's registry to locate device drivers configured with a Start value of 0. These include low-level hardware components, such as hard disk controllers and peripheral bus components. Winload.exe then scans the registry for device drivers assigned a Start value of 1.

Finally, control is passed to the operating system Kernel, Ntoskrnl.exe, and all drivers in memory; the Kernel is then initialized.

4. **Load drivers** After the kernel initializes, any remaining required drivers are loaded and initialized.

5. **Session Manager** The kernel loads the Windows Session Manager (Smss.exe), which among other things, initializes the Windows subsystem (Csrss.exe). The display will now switch from character mode to graphical mode.

6. **Sign in** After the Windows subsystem loads, the Winlogon service starts. This displays the sign-in page, and the local user can sign in to the computer.

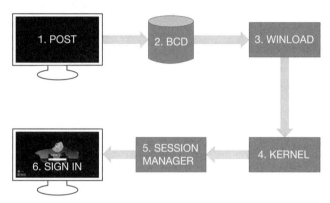

FIGURE 4-18 The Windows 10 startup process

Available options for startup recovery

If your computer does not start properly, or at all, you can choose from a number of repair and recovery tools, depending on the particular situation:

- **Windows RE** If your computer won't start, then start from the product DVD and select Repair Your Computer In Setup. You can then access the full set of recovery tools in Windows RE, including System Restore, System Image Recovery, Startup Repair, Command Prompt, and Startup Settings. Generally, if the problem is related to low-level startup files, such as the boot sector, BOOTMGR, and the BCD, choosing the Startup Repair option is generally successful in fixing startup problems.

- **Advanced Startup Settings** If the startup problem lies elsewhere than with the startup files, you should be able to successfully start your computer in Safe Mode. Start from the product DVD, and in Setup, select Repair Your Computer. From the Advanced options menu, select Startup Settings, and then choose Safe Mode. Advanced Startup Settings include:
  - Enable Debugging
  - Enable Boot Logging

- Enable Low-Resolution Video

- Enable Safe Mode

- Enable Safe Mode With Networking

- Enable Safe Mode With Command Prompt

- Disable Driver Signature Enforcement

- Disable Early Launch Antimalware Protection

- Disable Automatic Restart After Failure

- **System Configuration tool**   If your computer starts but with errors, you can access Safe Mode by running the System Configuration tool (Msconfig.exe). On the Boot tab, shown in Figure 4-19, select the appropriate Safe Boot option. Note that the computer remains in Safe Mode until you return to System Configuration to revert to Normal startup on the General tab.

FIGURE 4-19 System Configuration tool

- **Automatic Failover**   If your computer experiences startup problems, assuming that your computer still has the (default) recovery partition, Windows will fail over to Windows RE from this recovery partition.

The boot store

The boot store contains information that enables the low-level startup components of Windows 10 to locate any installed operating systems on the attached hard disk(s). Generally, it is not necessary to make changes to the BCD. However, it is important that you know how to make changes in case you must troubleshoot the startup environment.

Typically, you make changes to the BCD by reconfiguring Windows. For example, you might use the System Configuration tool to force Safe Mode. You might decide to make changes to the Startup And Recovery settings to choose the default operating system (assuming several are installed). Both these changes are made in the user interface but are reflected in the BCD.

However, you can also work directly with the BCD using a number of command-line tools. For example, Figure 4-20 shows the output from the `bcdedit.exe /enum` command; this command enumerates and displays all boot store entries.

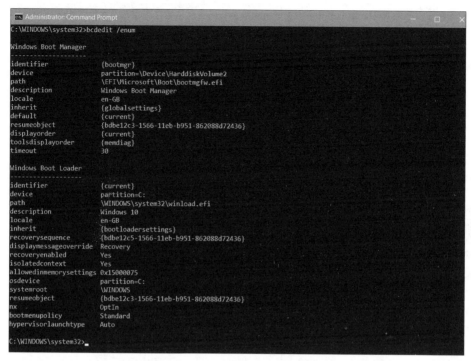

```
Administrator: Command Prompt                                          —   □   ×

C:\WINDOWS\system32>bcdedit /enum

Windows Boot Manager
--------------------
identifier              {bootmgr}
device                  partition=\Device\HarddiskVolume2
path                    \EFI\Microsoft\Boot\bootmgfw.efi
description             Windows Boot Manager
locale                  en-GB
inherit                 {globalsettings}
default                 {current}
resumeobject            {bdbe12c3-1566-11eb-b951-862088d72436}
displayorder            {current}
toolsdisplayorder       {memdiag}
timeout                 30

Windows Boot Loader
--------------------
identifier              {current}
device                  partition=C:
path                    \WINDOWS\system32\winload.efi
description             Windows 10
locale                  en-GB
inherit                 {bootloadersettings}
recoverysequence        {bdbe12c5-1566-11eb-b951-862088d72436}
displaymessageoverride  Recovery
recoveryenabled         Yes
isolatedcontext         Yes
allowedinmemorysettings 0x15000075
osdevice                partition=C:
systemroot              \WINDOWS
resumeobject            {bdbe12c3-1566-11eb-b951-862088d72436}
nx                      OptIn
bootmenupolicy          Standard
hypervisorlaunchtype    Auto

C:\WINDOWS\system32>
```

FIGURE 4-20 Output from BCDEdit.exe

MODIFYING THE BOOT STORE

There are a number of tools with which you can directly edit the BCD:

- **BCDEdit.exe** You can use BCDEdit.exe from an elevated Command Prompt. It enables you to
  - Add BCD store entries
  - Modify BCD store entries
  - Delete entries
  - Export the BCD
  - Import into the BCD
  - List entries
  - Query entries
  - Make global changes
  - Change the default time-out

- **Bootrec.exe**   You can use Bootrec.exe to manually rebuild the BCD based on a scan that the program performs. You must run Bootrec.exe in Windows RE in the Command Prompt tool. There are a number of parameters that you can use:
    - **/FixMbr**   Resolves MBR corruption issues
    - **/FixBoot**   Corrects boot sector corruptions
    - **/ScanOS**   Scans the hard disk(s) for Windows installations and displays any not listed in the BCD
    - **/RebuildBcd**   Scans the hard disk(s) for Windows installations and prompts you to add any discovered to the BCD

Managing devices and device drivers

For hardware to function properly, it requires special software designed for Windows 10 to communicate with it. This software is referred to as a *device driver*. When Windows 10 detects new hardware, the system automatically attempts to install one of the built-in drivers included as part of the operating system. These drivers are located in the Windows 10 Driver Store, or you can download them through Windows Update. A common reason for a computer to fail to start, or to start with errors, is because a device driver is faulty or corrupted.

INSTALL DEVICES

New and updated hardware device drivers are regularly submitted to Microsoft by the equipment vendor for testing and cataloging. If the Windows Update feature is enabled, Windows 10 automatically detects the presence of new device drivers, downloads them, and installs them.

New hardware is typically installed automatically when it's added to Windows 10; the operating system detects and identifies the new hardware through the Plug and Play feature. Windows 10 supports new hardware connected through a variety of connection methods, including USB (1.0 through 3.1), Wi-Fi, and Bluetooth. In addition to backward compatibility for existing and earlier hardware, emerging technologies, such as near-field communication (NFC) and Miracast for wireless displays, also have built-in support in Windows 10.

Device Manager is intended for advanced users or for managing or troubleshooting a hardware device issue. Device Manager provides information about each device, such as the device type, device status, manufacturer, device-specific properties, and device driver information.

There are multiple ways to load the Device Manager, including:

- Right-clicking the Start button and selecting Device Manager
- Typing **Device Manager** into Search
- Opening Control Panel, selecting Hardware And Sound, and then selecting Device Manager

The Device Manager default view (devices by type) is shown in Figure 4-21.

You can expand and explore each node in Device Manager and then select a device. All devices have properties, and you can view them by right-clicking the desired device and selecting Properties.

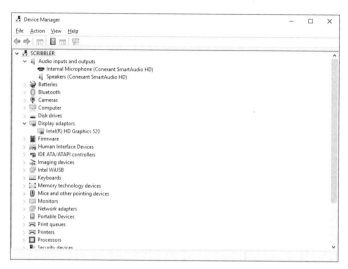

FIGURE 4-21 Device Manager showing the devices by type view

The Properties dialog box for a device is shown in Figure 4-22.

If you added a new peripheral and Windows 10 does not immediately recognize it, first check that the device is connected properly and that no cables are damaged. You should ensure that the external device is powered on and not in sleep or standby mode. You can also open Device Manager and start the Scan For Hardware Changes Wizard from the Action menu, which will locate previously undetected hardware and then configure it for you.

FIGURE 4-22 Device Properties

UPDATE DEVICE DRIVERS

Most computers that you'll work with have different hardware components, such as motherboards, disk controllers, graphics cards, and network adapters. Fortunately, Windows 10 is designed to work with an extensive list of hardware devices, and it benefits from Plug and Play, which tries to detect new devices automatically and then installs the correct driver software. If Windows has a problem with a device, you must troubleshoot the cause. Troubleshooting can involve locating the correct or updated device drivers and installing them.

Windows 10 automatically attempts to install a device driver, and if one is not available locally, it attempts to locate one through Windows Update. For most systems, devices and their associated drivers remain constant and require no further administrative effort. In the following instances, you might need to update, disable, or reinstate a previous driver:

- Windows 10 detects that a newer driver is available through Windows Update.
- You want to install a newer device driver manually, typically obtained from the manufacturer's website.
- The device is not performing or functioning correctly with the current driver.
- A new or beta version of a driver is causing stability issues.

To update a specific driver, select the device in Device Manager and select Update Driver Software from the context menu.

Windows 10 offers you two choices for updating the driver:

- Search Automatically For Updated Driver Software
- Browse My Computer For Driver Software

Typically, most users allow Windows to locate, download, and install an updated device driver automatically if one is available through Windows Update. This method is the default.

If you have the installation media that came with the hardware, you can use the browse feature to locate the correct driver. The Windows 10 Update Driver Software Wizard can automatically search through the subfolders in the media and locate all the relevant drivers for the device.

If you have already downloaded a specific device driver from the manufacturer—for example, a video driver from NVIDIA or AMD/ATI—you might need to run the driver installation wizard included in the download files, which contains additional software besides the device driver.

If Windows determines that the current driver is the most up-to-date or best driver available, you can confirm the version number of the driver by viewing the properties of the driver in Device Manager. If you have a more recent driver that you want to use, you must manually uninstall the current driver and then manually install the more recent driver.

DISABLE INDIVIDUAL DRIVER UPDATES OR WINDOWS UPDATES

Sometimes it is important to remove a device driver completely from the system. It might be corrupted or incompatible with your system. If Windows determines that the driver is valid and up-to-date, it is impossible to use another device driver while the current driver is present. To uninstall an unwanted device driver, use the following steps:

1. Open **Device Manager**.
2. Locate the device with the problem driver, right-click it, and choose **Uninstall device**.
3. In the **Uninstall device** dialog box, select **Uninstall**.

If the item relates to an unwanted Windows Update, use the following steps.

1. Open **Settings**, select **Update & Security**, and on the **Windows Update** tab, select **View update history**.
2. Select **Uninstall updates**. In **Control Panel**, on the **Installed Updates** page, locate and uninstall the unwanted update by selecting it from the list and then selecting **Uninstall**.

If you have difficulty uninstalling the driver, try restarting the computer and attempting the procedure again. Only as a last resort should you try to delete the software manually. You can use the PnPUtil.exe command-line tool and remove the INF files that are associated with the device:

```
PnPUtil.exe -a -d <path to the driver> \<drivername>.inf
```

We discuss using the PnPUtil.exe command-line tool later in this chapter.

NOTE   DRIVER INSTALLATION AND REMOVAL ARE ADMINISTRATIVE FUNCTIONS

You must use administrative privileges to install or uninstall a device or driver package by using Device Manager.

Because different hardware types have different functions and features, review the tabs in the properties screen. Not all devices have the same tabs, and some devices do not offer the ability to view or modify the device driver.

TURN ON OR OFF AUTOMATIC DEVICE DRIVER INSTALLATION IN DEVICE INSTALLATION SETTINGS

Sometimes installing an updated driver can cause your computer to lose functionality, and you may decide to uninstall the driver. Windows 10 automatically attempts to reinstall the driver, which is not desirable. In this situation, you might need to turn off the automatic device driver installation setting by following these steps:

1. Open **Control Panel**, and under **Hardware and sound**, select **Devices and printers**.
2. Under **Devices**, right-click the icon that represents your computer (it should have your computer name), and select **Device installation settings**, as displayed in Figure 4-23.

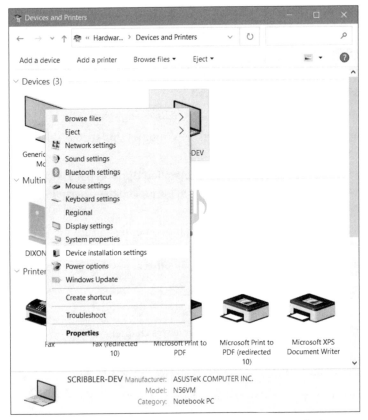

FIGURE 4-23 Disabling the automatic device driver software installation

3. In the **Device installation settings** dialog box, choose **No (your device might not work as expected)**. (Yes is the default setting.)

4. Select **Save changes**.

PERFORM A DRIVER ROLLBACK

Sometimes a driver problem can cause the system to become unstable. In Device Manager, you can roll back an updated driver to its previous version. If the system allows you to start normally, you can perform this task by following these steps:

1. Open **Device Manager**.

2. Right-click the device that you want to roll back and then select **Properties**.

3. In the **Properties** dialog box, select the **Drivers** tab and then select **Roll back driver**.

4. In the **Driver package rollback** dialog box, select **Yes**.

The Driver Package Rollback feature can only be used to revert to a previously updated driver. If you have not installed a later driver, the option in Device Manager will be unavailable.

If your system is unstable or won't start up properly because of a faulty driver, such as a video driver, you may need to restart the computer in Safe Mode to access Device Manager and perform the driver rollback. Windows 10 automatically detects startup failures and should boot into the advanced startup menu. To access Safe Mode, use the following procedure:

1. Open **Settings**, select **Update & Security**, and then select the **Recovery** tab.

2. Under the **Advanced startup** heading, select **Restart now**.

3. When your PC restarts, select **Troubleshoot** from the **Choose an Option** menu.

4. Select **Advanced options**.

5. Select **Startup Settings** and select **Restart**. You see the **Startup Settings** screen, as displayed in Figure 4-24.

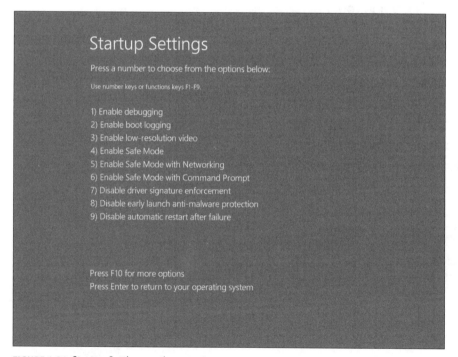

FIGURE 4-24 Startup Settings options

6. Select **Safe Mode** by pressing the 4 key.

7. Sign in to the system and roll back the driver as described earlier.

The rollback feature remembers only the last driver that was installed and doesn't keep copies of multiple drivers for the same device.

Resolve driver issues

One of the most common issues with device drivers relates to users attempting to install a driver designed for an earlier operating system or a different architecture. In some cases, on previous versions of Windows, it might have been possible to install a Windows 7 driver on a Windows 8–based computer, but this is not a supported operation for Windows 10 and should be avoided in a production environment. As is the case with other software installations, you can't use a 32-bit driver for a 64-bit resource. You can't use a 64-bit driver to communicate with a 32-bit resource, either.

> **NOTE** **DEVICE MANAGER ERROR TROUBLESHOOTING**
>
> Device Manager marks a device that is not operating normally with a yellow exclamation point. When troubleshooting a device, you can check the error that Device Manager reports. For a detailed list of errors that Device Manager reports, see the article at *https://docs. microsoft.com/en-us/windows-hardware/drivers/install/device-manager-error-messages*.

USE DRIVER VERIFICATION TOOLS

If you encounter issues with drivers that seem to relate to malware or missing drivers, you can use a command-line tool called sigverif.exe, which checks whether any drivers have been installed on the computer that have not been signed. The check can take several minutes to complete. To run this tool, perform the following steps:

1. Open a Command Prompt.
2. Enter **sigverif.exe**. The **File Signature Verification** tool appears.
3. Review the **Advanced options**.
4. Select **Start** and view the results, as displayed in Figure 4-25.

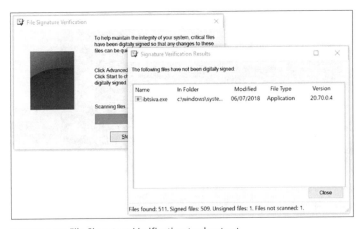

FIGURE 4-25 File Signature Verification tool output

The sigverif.exe tool is useful if you need to locate an unsigned driver. However, there is a more powerful driver verification tool, Driver Verifier, which is built into Windows 10.

With the enhanced kernel mode operation and reliance on signed drivers, Windows 10 should be less prone to frequent Stop errors. Although less likely, even signed drivers can cause problems, especially if you have an exotic combination of hardware inside your computer. If you do encounter instability, use the built-in Driver Verifier to discover whether a faulty driver is causing the problem.

The Driver Verifier Manager Wizard can help you troubleshoot, identify, and resolve common device driver problems, and you can then remove, reinstall, or roll back the offending driver with Device Manager.

To run the series of driver tests, follow these steps:

1. Open an elevated Command Prompt.

2. Enter **verifier.exe**. The **Driver Verifier** tool appears.

3. Review the settings in the tool. Depending on which option you choose, you might need to restart your computer for the tool to recognize all loaded drivers.

4. After you have selected drivers to be tested, restart the computer, restart the application, and then select **Display information about the currently verified drivers**.

Driver Verifier Manager tests each specified driver at startup and then enables you to perform a live test of each loaded driver by running a range of tests, as displayed in Figure 4-26. If it detects a problem, the tool can identify the driver, and then you can disable it.

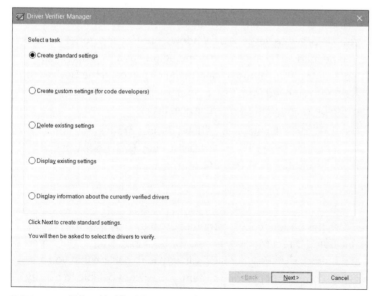

FIGURE 4-26 Driver Verifier Manager tool

VIEW DEVICE SETTINGS

Device drivers provide Windows 10 with the information required to populate the device details that you find in Device Manager. If only a few details are available to view, the device might have been installed using the built-in driver. You may be able to install a driver from the manufacturer's website, which will give additional information through Device Manager.

The default Device Manager screen enables users to work directly in the Properties dialog box of a device and provides information about the device that the hardware and device driver provide. The following is a review of Device Manager features that you can use to explore the available information so that you can configure the driver settings.

In Device Manager, explore these four menu options:

- **File**   This menu enables you to exit the console and optionally delete the record of the console customizations you make to the console settings.

- **Action**   This menu enables you to access the action-specific tasks relating to the highlighted hardware, including Update Driver Software, Disable, Uninstall, Scan For Hardware Changes, Add Legacy Hardware, Properties, and Help.

- **View**   This menu enables you to change how the console view displays advanced information relating to the devices listed in Device Manager. Some hardware is also hidden from normal view, and this option can be set to show hidden devices. The Customize option enables you to show or hide items within the console. You can view devices by:

  - Device type or connection

  - Resources by type or connection

- **Help**   This menu offers access to help topics relating to Device Manager and the console.

There are several advanced views in Device Manager that standard users do not normally use. These include the connection type and hidden device views, as follows:

- **Show Hidden Devices**   In previous versions of Windows, printers and non–Plug and Play (PnP) devices could be marked by the device manufacturer as a NoDisplayClass type of device, which prevents it from automatically being displayed in the Device Manager. Devices that have been removed from the computer—but whose registry entries are still present—can also be found in the hidden devices list.

- **Devices By Type**   This is the default view, and it shows devices grouped by familiar device name, such as Network Adapters, Ports, and Disk Drives. Each node can be expanded by selecting the > symbol to the left of the node name.

- **Devices By Connection**   You can view devices based on the hardware connection, such as physical or virtual.

- **Resources By Type**   Use this option to view resources organized by how they connect to system resources, including Direct Memory Access (DMA), Input/Output (IO), Interrupt Request (IRQ), and Memory. Unless your BIOS allows you to declare that you are not using a Plug and Play–compliant operating system, you will not be able to modify these settings.

- **Resources By Connection**   This view is for advanced users only and is not particularly useful on a modern system. Viewing the device hardware resources by DMA, IO, IRQ, and Memory were useful for earlier versions of Windows prior to the introduction of Plug and Play, which allowed the operating system to manage automatically the resources required by devices.

SUPPORT FOR OLDER HARDWARE

Some of the advanced settings in Device Manager are seldom used but have been retained for backward compatibility with older devices that do not support Plug and Play. Modern hardware peripherals must support Plug and Play, which allows Windows 10 to assign hardware resources automatically to new devices. If you look on the Resources tab of a device's Properties dialog box in Device Manager, you see that a check box is selected indicating that Windows 10 is using automatic settings, as displayed in Figure 4-27. The setting is unavailable and cannot be modified unless you disable the BIOS/UEFI setting, which declares that the operating system is Plug and Play–compliant.

FIGURE 4-27 Automatic resource allocation

The Plug and Play standard for connecting devices to Windows is nearly two decades old. Some hardware still exists that requires the administrator to install it manually. In Device Manager, the Add Hardware Wizard enables you to install hardware that does not support Plug and Play (PnP). To install such hardware, perform the following steps:

1. Open **Device Manager**.
2. On the **Action** tab, select **Add legacy hardware**.
3. On the **Welcome to the add hardware wizard** page, select **Next**.

4. Select one of these options:

   ■ Search for and install the hardware automatically (recommended)

   ■ Install the hardware that I manually select from a list

5. Follow the wizard prompts to finish the configuration of the hardware and provide the driver when requested.

> **NOTE** **NON-PNP (OLDER) DEVICES ARE NOT SHOWN IN WINDOWS 10**
>
> Since Windows 8 and Windows Server 2012, non-PnP devices have not been represented in Device Manager as viewable nodes.

DRIVER SIGNING

One of the reasons Windows 10 is more secure than earlier versions of Windows is that kernel mode drivers must now be submitted to and digitally signed by the Windows Hardware Developer Center Dashboard portal. Windows 10 will not load kernel mode drivers that the portal has not signed. To ensure backward compatibility, drivers that are properly signed by a valid cross-signing certificate will continue to pass signing checks on Windows 10.

Windows 10 also introduces the Universal Windows driver, which is designed to work on all OneCoreUAP-based editions of Windows, such as Windows 10 for desktop editions (Home, Pro, Enterprise, and Education), Windows 10 Mobile, and Windows 10 Internet of Things Core (IoT Core).

A Universal Windows driver has access to the trusted kernel and has a limited range of the interfaces that are available to a Windows driver. OEMs can supplement the driver functionality by including additional software, but this software will be external to the driver. Windows 10 security is more robust by locking down the kernel to signed drivers and encouraging developers to use the Universal Windows driver model.

If you have a specific need to install an unsigned driver—for example, if you are a developer and work with drivers, and you want to test the driver functionality without having to sign the driver digitally each time—you can invoke a special boot-time configuration setting that bypasses the security the Windows 10 driver enforcement model provides. To load an unsigned driver (not recommended), you can follow these steps:

1. Sign out of Windows 10.

2. On the sign-in screen, select the **Power** button, hold down the Shift key, and select **Restart**.

3. On the **Choose An Option** screen, choose **Troubleshoot**.

4. Choose **Advanced Options**.

5. On the **Advanced Options** screen, select **Startup Settings** and select **Restart**. **Advanced Boot Options** appears.

6. Choose **Disable driver signature enforcement**, as displayed in Figure 4-28.

7. Install the unsigned driver and then restart the computer.

```
Startup Settings

Press a number to choose from the options below:

Use number keys or functions keys F1-F9.

1) Enable debugging
2) Enable boot logging
3) Enable low-resolution video
4) Enable Safe Mode
5) Enable Safe Mode with Networking
6) Enable Safe Mode with Command Prompt
7) Disable driver signature enforcement
8) Disable early launch anti-malware protection
9) Disable automatic restart after failure




Press F10 for more options
Press Enter to return to your operating system
```

FIGURE 4-28 Disable Driver Signature Enforcement

Manage driver packages

When device drivers are created by an OEM, they are deployed with the hardware in a driver package that includes all the files and information required for Windows 10 to communicate with the hardware. Let's see how driver packages are managed and how to install, provision, and import driver packages on Windows 10 devices.

USE THE DRIVER STORE

You learned earlier that the driver package can include an information file (INF file), any files that the INF file references, and a CAT file that contains the digital signature for the device driver. Windows 10 uses the Driver Store to hold device drivers that have been installed or prestaged.

All Windows 10 kernel mode drivers must be digitally signed by the Windows Hardware Developer Center Dashboard portal. Windows 10 will prevent the loading of new kernel mode drivers that are not signed by the portal. This is an important change from previous versions of Windows and will make the operating system more secure. Previously, it was possible for a hacker to gain unauthorized access to a system by using a flaw in an unsigned device driver. Ensuring that all drivers are digitally signed removes the ability for a malicious hacker to add or modify device driver contents.

If you are creating a custom installation image, or if you build and deploy many computers, you can speed up the driver installation process by preloading the Windows 10 Driver Store with the specific drivers for the peripheral devices that your devices will be using. When Windows 10 finds the drivers it needs in the Driver Store (located in %SystemRoot%\System32\DriverStore), it uses these local drivers and does not download them from Windows Update.

Preinstalling a driver is a two-stage process, and the first stage must be carried out with administrator credentials. You need to add the driver package to the Driver Store and then ensure that the hardware is attached; Windows 10 then automatically locates and installs the local driver.

There are a few ways to deploy drivers to the Driver Store, and the most appropriate method will depend on your physical network infrastructure, network connectivity, and level of administrative privileges on devices, among other things.

> **NOTE** **AVOID DELETING FILES FROM THE DRIVER STORE**
> Take care not to delete driver packages manually from the Driver Store. Doing so can cause an inconsistency among the INF file, the Driver Store catalog, and the driver in the Driver Store. For more information, go to *https://docs.microsoft.com/windows-hardware/drivers/install/how-devices-and-driver-packages-are-uninstalled*.

USE PNPUTIL.EXE TO MANAGE DRIVER PACKAGES

To prestage the installation of a specific hardware device, you can install a driver manually before connecting the device by using the PnPUtil.exe command-line tool. This tool can be useful when you are distributing a laptop to a remote user who you know has a local printer or scanner. Standard users cannot normally install device drivers, but if the driver package is already in the Driver Store, this is possible.

Run the PnPUtil.exe tool by using administrative privileges. You can use it to manage the Driver Store; you can add, delete, and list driver packages. You saw earlier that a driver package consists of all the information Windows 10 requires to install and trust the driver, including the following:

- **Driver files** Dynamic link library (DLL) files with the .sys file extension.
- **Installation files** Text files containing all the information needed to install a driver. These INF files include information, such as driver name and location, driver version information, and registry information. These files are copied to the %SystemRoot%\Inf directory during installation. Every installed device must have an INF file.
- **Driver Catalog file** Contains a cryptographic hash of each file in the driver package. These hashes are used to verify that the package was not altered after it was published (created). Digitally signing the catalog file proves the file has not been altered because only the digital signature owner can sign the file.

- **Additional files**   These are files such as a device installation application, device icon, device property pages, and additional files.

For enhanced security, Windows 10 uses a single kernel model across all editions of Windows 10, and Windows 10 encourages the use of a new universal driver model. This universal INF file is required when deploying device drivers to an offline system image, such as when building a Windows 10 Mobile system (which does not support Plug and Play).

The syntax for the PnPUtil.exe command-line tool is as follows:

```
PnPUtil.exe a <path to the driver> \<drivername>.inf
```

The full list of parameters is shown in Table 4-2.

TABLE 4-2 PnPUtil.exe parameters

Parameter	Description
-a	Adds a driver package to the Driver Store.
-d	Removes a driver package from the Driver Store.
-e	Lists the driver packages that are currently in the Driver Store.
-f	Forces the deletion of the specified driver package from the Driver Store; cannot be used with the −i parameter.
-i	Installs the driver package on matching devices that are connected to the system. Cannot be used with the −f parameter.
/?	Displays help.

An example command to add the INF file specified by MyDevice.inf to the Driver Store (located at %SystemRoot%\System32\DriverStore) is:

```
PnPUtil.exe -a C:\Temp\MyDevice.inf
```

EXAM TIP

After a driver has been added to the Driver Store, the driver is referenced in the store through its published name, which might be different from the driver package (INF) name. You can review the published name by viewing the contents of the INF file.

In addition to the PnPUtil.exe tool, you can use the following Windows PowerShell cmdlets:

- **Get-PnpDevice**   Displays information about PnP devices
- **Get-PnpDeviceProperty**   Displays detailed properties for a PnP device
- **Enable-PnpDevice**   Enables a PnP device
- **Disable-PnpDevice**   Disables a PnP device

An example Windows PowerShell command to enable the device with an instance ID of 'USB\VID_5986&;PID_0266&;MI_00\7&;1E5D3568&;0&;0000' is as follows:

```
PS C:\> Enable-PnpDevice -InstanceId 'USB\VID_5986&;PID_0266&;MI_00\7&;
1E5D3568&;0&;0000'
```

For more information about, or for the syntax of, any of the Windows PowerShell cmdlets, you can use the **Get-Help *<cmdlet name>*** cmdlet, such as the following:

```
Get-Help <cmdlet name> -Examples
```

DOWNLOAD DRIVER PACKAGES

Drivers are packaged together; each driver package consists of all the software components needed for your device to work with Windows.

Most drivers are obtained directly by using built-in tools such as Windows Update. However, if you are provisioning systems, you might want to deploy the PC with the required drivers already imported and configured.

Device drivers can be accessed to perform a malicious attack on your systems. Therefore, you should ensure that driver packages are sourced only from reputable locations, such as the manufacturer's own website. You should avoid third-party driver repository websites because some sites repackage drivers and include spyware or freeware products in the installation files.

The built-in Windows 10 driver packages are often just the core drivers created by your device manufacturer and provided by Microsoft through the Windows Hardware Quality Labs (WHQL), which tests and digitally signs the drivers. Video drivers often include additional software support and hardware functionality. For example, drivers sourced directly from NVIDIA or AMD for their graphics cards include the NVIDIA Control Panel or the AMD Catalyst control panel, respectively.

If you are seeking the most up-to-date or even a beta version of a device driver, you must download it directly from your device manufacturer. In most cases, you will not need to upgrade your device driver after Windows 10 is installed. If everything is working properly, you probably won't have to install extra hardware drivers.

If you are a gamer, it can be beneficial to ensure that your graphics card drivers are using the latest versions so that they support the latest PC games.

You should consider downloading new driver packages in the following scenarios:

- **If you play PC games** Install the latest graphics drivers directly from your graphics card manufacturer because they are often required to play the latest games. Newer versions can also improve graphics performance.

- **When you need a hardware utility** Install the latest version if the manufacturer-provided driver package includes a hardware utility, such as a network configuration tool or ink monitor for your printer.

- **To resolve a bug** Bugs can be found in released drivers and will often be fixed in the most up-to-date version.

- **To install hardware manually** If Windows Plug and Play does not automatically detect and install the hardware, you may have to download the driver package from the manufacturer and install the device driver.

ADD PACKAGES USING DISM

The Deployment Image Servicing and Management (DISM) tool is included as part of the Windows 10 operating system. This tool is useful for offline image servicing. DISM is a command-line tool that you can use to maintain images and apply them with Windows Updates. It is also used to add and remove Windows features, including language packs, and to manage device drivers.

If you have a custom Windows 10 image, you can use DISM to modify it, and the changes will be visible when you next deploy the image. This can be useful when you know that a driver has been updated since you built the deployment image. Using DISM to inject the new driver saves you from having to rebuild the whole image. Using DISM is similar to using a file compression tool, such as WinRAR, whereby you add or remove new files and then WinRAR reseals the WIM, VHD, or VHDX file so that it is ready for deployment.

When you use DISM to install a device driver to an offline image, the device driver is added to the Driver Store. When the image is booted, PnP runs, looks for drivers in the store, and associates them with the corresponding devices on the computer on which they're being installed.

To add drivers to an offline image by using DISM, use these steps:

1. Open an elevated Command Prompt.

2. Establish the name or index number for the image that you are servicing by running:

   ```
   Dism /Get-ImageInfo /ImageFile:C:\test\images\install.wim
   ```

3. Mount the offline Windows image by running the following:

   ```
   Dism /Mount-Image /ImageFile:C:\test\images\install.wim /Name:"Windows Offline
   Image" /MountDir:C:\test\offline
   ```

4. You can now add the driver, located in the C:\Drivers folder, to the image by running:

   ```
   Dism /Image:C:\test\offline /Add-Driver /Driver:C:\drivers\New_driver.inf
   ```

5. If you have additional drivers in a folder, you can use the **/Recurse** option, which installs all the drivers from a folder and all its subfolders. To do this, run:

   ```
   Dism /Image:C:\test\offline /Add-Driver /Driver:c:\drivers /Recurse
   ```

6. You can review the drivers in the Windows image by running:

   ```
   Dism /Image:C:\test\offline /Get-Drivers
   ```

   In the list of drivers, notice that the added drivers have been renamed Oem*.inf. This ensures that all driver files in the Driver Store have unique names. For example, the New_Driver1.inf and New_Driver2.inf files are renamed Oem0.inf and Oem1.inf.

7. To complete the operation, commit the changes and unmount the image by running:

   ```
   Dism /Unmount-Image /MountDir:C:\test\offline /Commit
   ```

MANAGE DRIVER PACKAGES WITH DISM

During the life of a Windows 10 installation, the system downloads and installs multiple versions of device driver packages over time. For devices with small hard drive capacity, be aware of how to locate and delete outdated driver packages that the system retains.

You can use the built-in Disk Cleanup tool to remove device driver packages that have been kept after newer drivers are installed.

To clean up old device drivers by using the Disk Cleanup tool, perform these steps:

1. Select **Start**, enter **Disk Cleanup**, and then select the **Disk Cleanup** app.

2. In the **Drive Selection** dialog box, select **(C:)** and select **OK**.

3. On the **Disk Cleanup** results screen, select **Clean up system files**.

4. In the **Drive selection** dialog box, select **(C:)** and select **OK**.

5. On the **Disk Cleanup** results screen, select **Device driver packages** and select **OK**.

6. On the **Are you sure you want to permanently delete these files?** page, select **Delete Files**.

All driver packages that were installed during the Windows 10 setup process are stored in a directory called WinSxS, the side-by-side component store. This folder contains driver packages and operating system components so that you can add devices later without having to supply device drivers. If disk space is limited, you can purge the WinSxS directory contents; doing so can be helpful because it could occupy a significant amount of disk space.

To analyze the Windows Component Store for driver packages and other files that can be deleted, you can use the DISM tool by using the following steps:

1. In an elevated Command Prompt, run the following:

    ```
    DISM /Online /Cleanup-Image /AnalyzeComponentStore
    ```

    The tool analyzes your system. Typical results are shown in Figure 4-29.

2. When the analysis is complete, you can initiate a cleanup of the Windows Component Store by running the following command:

    ```
    DISM /Online /Cleanup-Image /StartComponentCleanup /ResetBase
    ```

FIGURE 4-29 Analyzing the Component Store (WinSxS) with DISM

Managing Services

Another possible cause of startup problems in Windows 10 is services; these are software components that function with the operating system and usually require no user intervention. Usually, services start before a user signs in to a Windows computer.

If your computer experiences problems when starting, you can use the following tools to help to identify whether the issue relates to operating system services:

- **Event Viewer**   If services have problems, then generally errors are written to the Windows log files. You use the Event Viewer tool to access these log files. Event Viewer is discussed in more detail later in this chapter.

- **Log files**   Outside of the built-in capabilities of the Windows logs, you can also enable additional logging within specific Windows components or within a particular app. For instance, you can enable more detailed logging of the startup process by selecting Boot Logging in the Advanced Startup Options menu.

- **Stop codes**   Windows 10 is very robust and system crashes are rare. However, when they occur, you can use the stop codes generated to help to identity the cause. These stop codes might suggest that a service is the root cause of a system crash.

- **Notifications**   Within the Action Center, you can view notifications from Windows about system events, including possible problems.

If your computer does not start as a result of an issue with services, you can attempt to resolve the problem in a number of ways. These include:

- **Safe Mode**   Start your computer in Safe Mode; doing so reduces the number of services running and might enable you to start your computer successfully. Once started, you can then investigate the possible causes using the tools just listed.

- **Windows RE** Start your computer into Windows RE and then select the Command Prompt tool. Using commands such as **Net.exe** and **Sc.exe** enables you to manually control service behavior.

- **MSConfig.exe** The System Configuration tool has a Services tab that you can use to control service startup. You can choose to disable specific services from this console. You can also focus only on those services that are not built in to Windows, as displayed in Figure 4-30.

FIGURE 4-30 Viewing the non-Microsoft services in System Configuration

Skill 4.2: Manage updates

Keeping computers safe and protected from external threats such as malware and malicious hackers is a big challenge. In earlier versions of Windows, you could decide whether the operating system was automatically updated with the latest features, security updates, and fixes through the Windows Update feature. Some users chose to disable automatic updates, and these computers are vulnerable to attack. With over a billion Windows devices worldwide, even if this number is a small percentage of the total, it might mean millions of devices are unprotected.

Windows 10 changes the game with regard to updates and security because it will continually and automatically benefit from new updates rolled out through Windows Update. To enhance the security protection delivered in Windows 10, the consumer can no longer turn off security updates. Enterprise users will have some leeway on the timing of updates and upgrades, and they can still choose to test updates and deliver them internally, using Windows Server Update Service (WSUS) or other management tools to keep their devices updated. For organizations that require deployment of a static installation of Windows 10 that will not have upgrades, Microsoft ships a special build of Windows 10, which is discussed later in this skill.

Plan for Windows Updates

In order to keep your Windows computers running efficiently and securely, it is important to install updates from Microsoft when they become available. In the past, these updates were designed primarily to fix identified problems or security vulnerabilities. However, with Windows 10, Microsoft has introduced a new update model: Windows as a service.

With Windows as a service, updates are designed not only to resolve perceived defects in software, but also to add new features to the operating system. Instead of releasing new versions of Windows every few years, Microsoft now provides continual updates that provide new features to Windows 10.

As an IT professional supporting Windows 10 users, it's important that you know how to manage updates within your organization. A significant part of this goal is based on a good understanding of the new Windows as a service model.

Windows as a service

Windows as a service is more about Windows deployment than it is updating; in other words, the update mechanism is used to deliver, or deploy, new builds of Windows instead of relying on more traditional deployment methods.

As an organization, this means that instead of planning and performing operating system upgrades, such as from Windows 7 to Windows 10, you use Windows Update to continually introduce new Windows 10 features as the operating system evolves. This means that the update process becomes a continual process, based on small incremental updates rather than significant upgrades every few years.

Two types of update are delivered in this way:

- **Feature updates** These add significant functionality to the Windows 10 operating system, and to date, these updates have been deployed twice a year, typically in spring and fall. Until recently, these updates have been identified by their year and month. But this has now changed. Updates are currently identified by the year and the half of the year when they are due for public release. For example, this book and its companion exam are based on Windows 10 20H2, which shipped in the second half of 2020. Other, earlier, feature updates include Windows 10 1909 and Windows 10 2004.

- **Quality updates**   These provide reliability and security updates and fixes. Microsoft deploys these updates monthly on the second Tuesday of the month. They are cumulative, meaning that even if you miss an update, by applying a subsequent update you receive all previous updates.

DEFERRALS

Business users of Windows 10 can determine when these updates apply. Broadly, you can configure deferral periods for both Feature and Quality updates. These deferrals define a number of days that you defer the application of released updates.

When an update is imminent, Microsoft makes it available to early adopters. When the update is finalized, the update is distributed to Windows devices around the world.

As part of the planning process for updates, you should consider participating in the early release scheme for updates for some of your users' computers. This will enable you to test the effect of the updates on your organization's Windows 10 computers. You can also use the deferrals to determine precisely when, after an update has been released, you will apply it to the majority of your computers.

The illustration in Figure 4-31 gives an example of how this might work. When an update is released to early adopters, you can begin the planning process for the deployment of that update. When it's released, you can make it available to a small subset of your computers. Finally, you can distribute the update more widely.

You can continue to use a Windows 10 version for 18 months after it has been made widely available. You must then start the process over again. It's quite likely that many organizations will choose to perform continual, rolling updates. Consequently, it's possible that some of your users' computers will be using one version of Windows 10 while other users are using earlier or later versions.

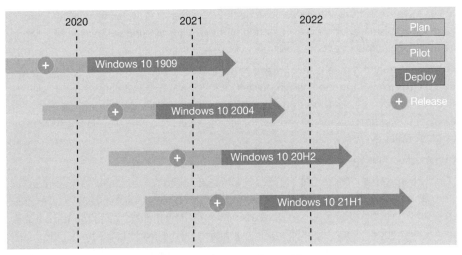

FIGURE 4-31 Windows as a service feature updates over the past few years

Select the appropriate servicing channel

In order to implement updates within your organization, you must decide on which computers will receive updates, and how quickly they will receive them after Microsoft releases them. Part of this decision is about selecting a servicing channel. You must also consider deferral periods for these updates.

Users of Windows 10 Home editions have no control over how their computers receive these updates. However, users in business and educational organizations who are using Windows 10 Pro, Windows 10 Enterprise, or Windows 10 Education editions can control their update experience using servicing channels.

- **Servicing channels** Microsoft provides several servicing channels. These channels determine when updates are applied to a computer. These channels are as follows:
  - **Windows Insider Program** For early adopters. There are three channels available to insiders: Fast, Slow, and Release Preview. Those on the Fast channel receive early and frequent updates, those on Slow receive less frequent updates, and those on Release Preview receive what you may think of as being a pre-release beta of the finalized updates. Note that these channels are also referred to as Dev Channel, Beta Channel, and Release Preview Channel, respectively.
  - **Semi-Annual Channel** The default channel. Users receive updates fairly quickly after Microsoft releases them.
  - **Long-Term Servicing Channel** A specialized version of Windows 10 Enterprise that doesn't receive feature updates. This is not a channel you configure, but rather a version of Windows 10 Enterprise that you license (Windows 10 Enterprise LTSC).
- **Deployment rings** You can define deployment rings by using Group Policy Objects (GPOs) or Microsoft Intune. These deployment rings use a selected servicing channel and additional Windows settings to determine when updates apply. By configuring groups of computers with matching settings, you can control updates to that group.

Select the servicing channel

You cannot select a servicing channel directly through the user interface in Windows 10. Instead, you must use either GPO settings or Microsoft Intune to control this setting. However, you can subscribe to the Windows Insider Program through the user interface.

As mentioned, the Windows Insider Program enables Windows 10 users to gain insight into feature updates before they're released. They can also provide feedback to Microsoft during their evaluation of those feature updates. To opt in to the Windows Insider Program channel, follow these steps:

1. Open the **Settings** app.
2. Select **Update & Security** and then select the **Windows Insider Program** tab.
3. As displayed in Figure 4-32, on the **Windows Insider Program tab** and under the **Windows Insider Program** heading, select **Get started**.

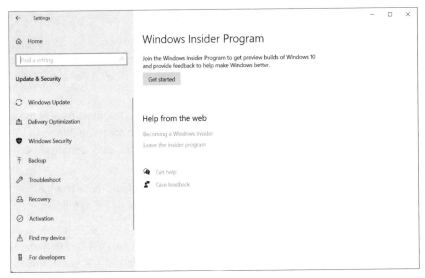

FIGURE 4-32 Windows Insider Program

Using deployment rings

By selecting an appropriate servicing channel, and then configuring feature update and quality update deferral values, you can create deployment rings. You may decide that you require a test group of computers that get updates early. You may also decide to create a group of computers that receive updates reasonably quickly after release. After testing, you may then want to enable the bulk of your remaining computers to receive the updates. You could achieve this by using the deployment rings described in Table 4-3.

TABLE 4-3 Suggested deployment rings

Ring	Channel	Feature deferral	Quality deferral	Explanation
Test	Windows Insider Program	0 days	0 days	Enables you to evaluate and test prerelease updates before they are deployed to your other devices. During this phase, you can begin to identify any potential issues with the updates.
Early	Semi-Annual Channel	0 days	0 days	Enables you to evaluate released updates on a small subset of your devices. This enables you to identify any possible problems before you deploy updates to the rest of your computers.
Standard	Semi-Annual Channel	60 days	30 days	For most of your users, the deferment values ensure that you have had adequate time to test updates and to identify possible problems.
Slow	Semi-Annual Channel	180 days	30 days	This ring might be used to ensure that updates are applied as long as possible after their release. Devices configured into this ring might be running critical apps or services.

To configure deployment rings for Active Directory Domain Services (AD DS) domain-joined devices, use GPO settings. These settings are discussed in the next section.

To configure deployment rings for non-domain-joined devices, use Microsoft Intune. You can configure the deployment rings using the Microsoft Endpoint Manager admin center, as displayed in Figure 4-33. Details about this process are beyond the scope for this book, since they are not covered in the MD-100 Windows 10 exam. Note that in the Microsoft Endpoint Manager admin center, deployment rings are referred to as *update rings*.

FIGURE 4-33 Microsoft Intune update rings

Configure Windows Update options

After you have planned your deployment rings, you must configure the Windows Update settings. With the exception of the servicing channel and deferrals, you can do this on a per-computer basis by using the Settings app. However, most organizations will use GPOs to configure AD DS domain-joined computers and use Intune Windows 10 update rings to configure cloud-based Windows 10 devices.

Configuring settings on an individual computer

To configure the Windows Update settings on an individual computer, open the Settings app and select Update & Security. You can then configure the following settings.

WINDOWS UPDATE

Select the Windows Update tab, as displayed in Figure 4-34.

You can then configure active hours, view update history, and configure the following advanced options (discussed earlier):

- **Pause updates for 7 days** This setting enables you to temporarily stop the application of updates for a week. This is useful when troubleshooting updates.
- **Change Active Hours** This setting allows the user to identify the period of time when they expect the device to be in use. Automatic restarts after an update will occur outside of the active hours. The default is 8 AM to 5 PM.
- **View Update History** Provides access to the links to uninstall updates and to access recovery options. You can also see a list of recent updates, as displayed in Figure 4-35. To uninstall updates, select the link and select the update you want to remove.

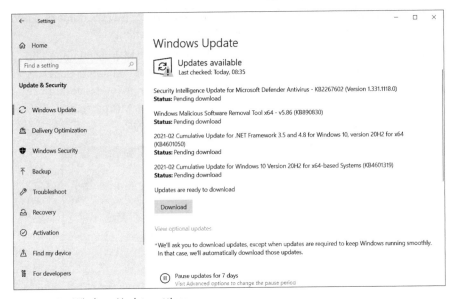

FIGURE 4-34 Windows Update settings

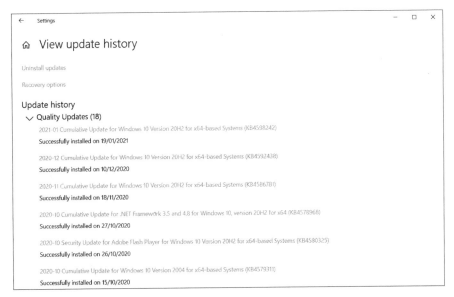

FIGURE 4-35 Viewing update history

- **Advanced options** On the Advanced options page, shown in Figure 4-36, you can configure the following properties:
  - **Receive updates for other Microsoft products when you update Windows** Users can choose to include updates for other Microsoft products in addition to Windows, and use the users' sign-in info to automatically sign back in to the device to complete the installation following an update.

- **Download updates over metered connections**   Enables users to ensure they receive updates, even when connected using cellular data.

- **Update notifications**   Allows Windows to display a notification when a restart is required following updates.

- **Pause updates**   Enables the user to turn off updating for a period of up to 35 days.

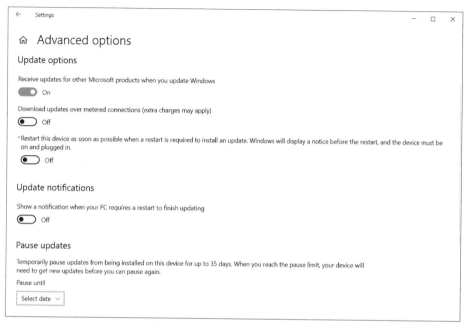

FIGURE 4-36 Changing advanced Windows Update options

DELIVERY OPTIMIZATION

In Windows 10, you have several options regarding how Windows updates and Microsoft Store apps are delivered to the computer. By default, Windows obtains updates from the Microsoft Update servers, computers on the local network, and on the internet. Windows Update Delivery Optimization allows the application of updates more quickly than previous versions of Windows. Once one PC on your local network has installed an update, other devices on the network can obtain the same updates without downloading directly from Microsoft.

This process is similar to popular peer-to-peer file sharing apps. Only partial file fragments of the update files are downloaded from any source, which speeds up the delivery and increases the security of the process. If you allow delivery optimization to take place, you then can choose from the following options how your PC will obtain updates and apps from other PCs:

- **PCs on my local network**   Windows will attempt to download from other PCs on your local network that have already downloaded the update or app.

- **PCs on my local network, and PCs on the internet**   Windows will attempt to download from the PCs on your local network, and Windows also looks for PCs on the internet that are configured to share parts of updates and apps.

If Delivery Optimization is enabled, your computer can also send parts of apps or updates that have been downloaded using Delivery Optimization to other PCs locally or on the internet. To enable Delivery Optimization, from Settings, in Update & Security, select the Delivery Optimization tab, as displayed in Figure 4-37.

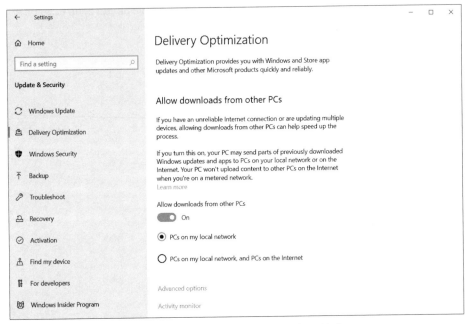

FIGURE 4-37 Editing the Delivery Optimization settings for Windows Update

Note that there are additional delivery optimization settings that you can configure by using GPO settings. These settings are discussed in the next section.

Configuring settings using GPOs

Although you can configure all your computers running Windows 10 manually, it is far easier and quicker to use Group Policy to configure your domain-joined computers. You can configure the following Windows Update settings using GPOs:

- Computer Configuration\Administrative Templates\Windows Components\Windows Update, as described in Table 4-4

- Computer Configuration\Administrative Templates\Windows Components\Delivery Optimization, as described in Table 4-5

- Computer Configuration\Administrative Templates\Windows Components\Windows Update\Windows Update for Business, as displayed in Table 4-6

To set a GPO to configure Windows Update, complete these steps:

1. On a domain controller, open **Group Policy Management**.

2. Right-click a GPO and then select **Edit**.

3. In the **Group Policy Management Editor**, shown in Figure 4-38, navigate to the appropriate node and edit the appropriate setting(s) as per the following tables.

4. Close the editor when you are finished. The GPOs will refresh to domain-joined computers.

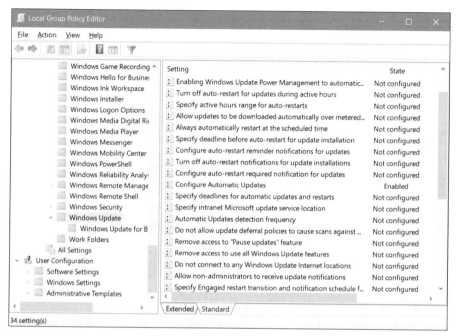

FIGURE 4-38 Editing the Windows Update GPO settings

TABLE 4-4 Windows 10 GPO settings in the Windows Update node

GPO Setting	Description
Turn Off Auto-Restart For Updates During Active Hours	Allows you to specify the active hours during which the PC won't restart.
Specify Active Hours Range For Auto-Restarts	Allows you to specify the maximum number of hours that active hours can be set. This time can be set between 8 and 18 hours.
Specify Deadline Before Auto-Restart For Update Installation	Allows you to enforce a restart 2–14 days after a restart is scheduled.
Configure Auto-Restart Reminder Notification For Updates	Allows you to specify when auto-restart reminders are displayed.
Turn Off Auto-Restart Notifications For Update Installations	Allows you to turn off all auto-restart notifications.
Configure Auto-Restart Required Notifications For Updates	Allows you to specify how the restart notifications are dismissed. By default, this is automatic after 25 seconds.

GPO Setting	Description
Configure Automatic Updates	Configure whether Windows Update can enable automatic updates on your computer. If this setting is enabled, you must select one of the five options in the Group Policy setting (also note there is no option 6): ■ 2 = Notify for download and auto install ■ 3 = Auto download and notify for install ■ 4 = Auto download and schedule the install ■ 5 = Allow local admin to choose setting ■ 7 = Auto Download, Notify to Install, Notify to Restart If you select option 4, you can also modify a recurring schedule; otherwise all installations will be attempted every day at 03:00.
Specify Intranet Microsoft Update Service Location	Configure whether Windows Update will use a server on your network to function as an internal update service.
Do Not Allow Update Deferral Policies To Cause Scans Against Windows Update	Allows you to prevent update deferral policies to cause scans against Windows Update.
Remove Access To Use All Windows Update Features	Enabling this policy removes user access to Windows Update scan, download, and install features.
Specify Engaged Restart Transition And Notification Schedule For Updates	Enabling this policy allows you to configure settings related to PC restart following a period of time when auto-restart settings have been configured.
Do Not Include Drivers With Windows Updates	If you enable this policy setting, Windows Update will not include drivers with Windows quality updates.
Configure Auto-Restart Warning Notifications Schedule For Updates	Controls when users receive notification reminders and warnings to restart their devices following an update installation.
Update Power Policy For Cart Restarts	For EDU devices that remain on charging carts overnight to receive updates to reboot during the scheduled install time frame.
Defer Windows Updates\Select When Feature Updates Are Received	Controls the type of feature updates to receive and when based on branch readiness level.
Defer Windows Updates\Select When Quality Updates Are Received	Controls the type of quality updates to receive and when to receive them based on branch readiness level.

The second table of GPO settings allows you to modify the Delivery Optimization settings in Windows 10 so that you can fine-tune and regulate the peer caching of updates.

TABLE 4-5 GPO settings in the Delivery Optimization node

GPO Settings	Description
Absolute Max Cache Size (In GB)	Allows you to limit the maximum size in GB for the Delivery Optimization cache. The default size is 10 GB.
Enable Peer Caching While The Device Connects Via VPN	Can allow the device to participate in Peer Caching while connected via VPN to the domain network to download from or upload to other domain network devices, while either on the VPN or via the corporate network.

GPO Settings	Description
Download Mode	Configures the use of Windows Update Delivery Optimization for downloads of Windows apps and updates as follows: ■ 0=HTTP only: No peering ■ 1=LAN: HTTP blended with peering behind the same NAT ■ 2=Group: HTTP blended with peering across a private group ■ 3=Internet: HTTP blended with Internet Peering ■ 99=Simple: Download mode with no peering ■ 100=Bypass mode: Do not use Delivery Optimization and use BITS instead
Group ID	Used to create a group ID to which the device belongs. Used to limit or to group devices.
Max Cache Age (In Seconds)	Specifies the maximum time in seconds that each file is held in the Delivery Optimization cache after downloading successfully. Default setting is 3 days.
Max Cache Size (Percentage)	Specifies the maximum cache size that Delivery Optimization uses as a percentage of available disk size. Default is 20%.
Maximum Download Bandwidth (In KB/s)	Specifies the maximum download bandwidth that the device can use across all concurrent download activities using Delivery Optimization.
Max Upload Bandwidth (In KB/s)	Defines the maximum upload bandwidth that a device will utilize for Delivery Optimization.
Minimum Background QoS (In KB/s)	Specifies the minimum download QoS (Quality of Service or Speed) for background downloads. Default is 500 KB/s.
Allow Uploads While The Device Is On Battery While Under Set Battery Level (Percentage)	Specify the value between 1 and 100 to allow the device to upload data to LAN and Group peers while on battery power. The device can download from peers while on battery regardless of this policy.
Minimum Disk Size Allowed To Use Peer Caching (In GB)	Specifies the required minimum disk size for the device to use Peer Caching. Default is 32 GB.
Minimum Peer Caching Content File Size (In MB)	Specifies the minimum content file size in MB enabled to use Peer Caching. Default value is 100 MB.
Minimum RAM Capacity (Inclusive) Required To Enable Use Of Peer Caching (In GB)	Specifies the minimum RAM size in GB required to use Peer Caching. Default value is 4 GB.
Modify Cache Drive	Specifies the drive Delivery Optimization will use for its cache.
Monthly Upload Data Cap (In GB)	Specifies the maximum total bytes in GB that Delivery Optimization is allowed to upload to internet peers in each calendar month. Default value is 20 GB.
Maximum Download Bandwidth (Percentage)	Specifies the maximum download bandwidth that Delivery Optimization uses. The default value is 0.

Windows Update for Business settings in GPO enable you to control which deployment ring your users' computers are configured for. By using these settings, you control which servicing channel your users' devices use, and deferment values for both feature and quality updates.

TABLE 4-6 GPO settings in the Windows Update for Business node

GPO Settings	Description
Select When Preview Builds And Feature Updates Are Received	This value enables you to select the servicing channel. You can choose between: ■ Preview Build – Fast ■ Preview Build – Slow ■ Release Preview ■ Semi-Annual Channel You can then also select a deferment value.
Select When Quality Updates Are Received	If you enable this value, you can then define a deferment value (in days) for quality updates.
Disable Safeguards For Feature Updates	Enable this setting when Feature Updates should be deployed to devices without blocking on any safeguard holds.
Manage Preview Builds	You can control whether your users' computers can be configured into the Insider Build servicing channel. Enable this value, and then choose whether the devices are enabled for preview builds, disabled for previews, or disabled after the next release becomes public.
Select The Target Feature Update Version	Enable this policy to specify a Feature Update version to be requested in subsequent scans.

Check for updates

It is not usually necessary to check for updates manually. However, you can easily do so by opening the Settings app. In Update & Security, on the Windows Update tab shown in Figure 4-39, select Check For Updates. Windows connects to Windows Update and retrieves a list of any pending updates. It's currently not visible as updates are already displayed as available.

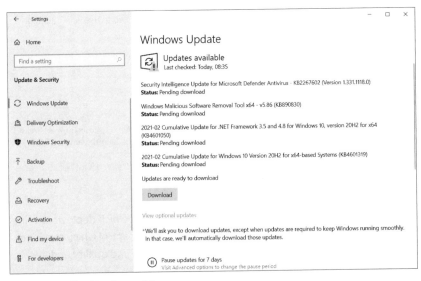

FIGURE 4-39 Checking for updates

Validate and test updates

It is important that you know how Windows updates might affect your users' devices. Consequently, you should take the time to validate and test updates before making them available across your organization.

We have already discussed how a servicing channel together with deferment values can be used to create the notion of deployment rings. Using deployment rings gives you an opportunity to obtain and test forthcoming updates before ongoing deployment.

In addition, you can consider using additional services to deploy Windows updates rather than relying solely on the Windows Update servers. Table 4-7 describes the additional options.

TABLE 4-7 Options for deployment of updates

GPO Settings	Description
WSUS	This is a Windows Server 2019 server role. WSUS downloads updates from the Windows Update server(s). You can then configure how these updates are propagated to your client computers. This gives you time to test and validate updates.
Windows Update For Business	Essentially, you can consider this to be similar to WSUS. However, it is maintained in the cloud by Microsoft and is available for devices running Windows 10 Pro, Windows 10 Education, or Windows 10 Enterprise. By configuring Intune deployment rings, or by configuring Windows Update for Business GPO values, you are using Windows Update for Business.
Endpoint Configuration Manager (formerly SCCM)	If you already have ECM for managing deployment, you can also use it to manage updates. ECM gives you great control and flexibility in managing updates.
Microsoft Intune	Intune is a cloud-based device and app management tool. It's especially useful for managing non-domain-joined devices. With Intune, you can approve updates, deploy updates, and remove updates.

When testing updates, it's important that you make sure that all devices, peripherals, and apps will work with the new updates. This is particularly relevant when considering the deployment of feature updates.

Troubleshoot updates

If a machine is not receiving updates and you have checked the Settings app and Group Policy settings to ensure that updates are not deferred or paused, you should verify that the two services in Windows relating to Windows Update are running.

The first is the Windows Update service, which checks which updates have been installed locally and what is available on the update servers. The Windows Update service also handles the download, installation, and reporting of the state of updates.

Background Intelligent Transfer Service (BITS) is a supplemental service that handles the transfer of update files in the most efficient manner. Both services need to be running for Windows Update to function correctly.

You can also use the Windows Update troubleshooter. This is located on the Additional Troubleshooters page, accessible on the Troubleshoot tab in Update & Security in the Settings app, as displayed in Figure 4-40.

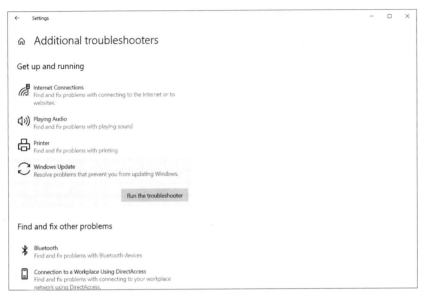

FIGURE 4-40 Running the Windows Update troubleshooter

Click Run The Troubleshooter. Windows attempts to check the required services and attempts to connect to the Windows Update server. If Windows identifies problems, as displayed in Figure 4-41, it might make recommendations on how best to resolve the issue(s).

FIGURE 4-41 Recommended fixes for Windows Update problems

Roll back updates

With the rhythm of regular updates becoming the method of keeping devices secure and up-to-date, there might be instances when an update causes problems and you need to consider removing the update completely by rolling it back. You may have experience with driver rollbacks; the same concept is used for rolling back Windows updates.

Sometimes you need to remove a single Windows update. You can perform this task in a number of ways—through Control Panel, the Settings app, or the Command Prompt.

UNINSTALL A WINDOWS UPDATE BY USING CONTROL PANEL

If you prefer to use Control Panel, you can see an Installed Updates list in Control Panel by following these steps:

1. Click the **Start** button and enter **Control Panel**, and select **Control Panel**.
2. Open **Programs** > **Programs And Features**.
3. Select **View Installed Updates**.
4. Select an update that you want to uninstall, as displayed in Figure 4-42.
5. If Windows allows you to uninstall it, **Uninstall** appears on the toolbar.
6. In the **Uninstall An Update** dialog box, select **Yes** to confirm.
7. Accept the UAC if prompted. A restart might be needed to complete the removal of the update.

FIGURE 4-42 Removing an update in Control Panel

UNINSTALL A WINDOWS UPDATE IN SETTINGS

The Settings app ultimately opens the same Installed Updates list in Control Panel. Perform these steps if you prefer to use the Settings app:

1. Open the **Settings** app and select **Update & Security**.

2. Select **Windows Update** and then select **View update history**. A list of your installed Windows Updates appears.

3. Select **Uninstall Updates** at the top of the screen. The link opens the **Control Panel > Programs > Programs and Features > View installed updates** page.

4. Select an update that you want to uninstall. If Windows allows you to uninstall it, **Uninstall** appears on the toolbar.

5. In the **Uninstall an update** dialog box, select **Yes** to confirm.

6. Accept the UAC if prompted. A restart might be needed to complete the removal of the update.

UNINSTALL A WINDOWS UPDATE BY USING THE COMMAND PROMPT

Sometimes you will want to remove the same update from multiple devices. After you have tested the command-line tool on your test device, you can use the Command Prompt or Windows PowerShell to script the command and distribute it to multiple devices by using Group Policy or Windows PowerShell.

You can use the Windows Management Instrumentation (WMI) command-line utility to generate a list of installed Windows Update packages on a Windows 10–based device, as displayed in Figure 4-43.

FIGURE 4-43 Command Prompt running the `wmic qfe list` command

To generate the list of installed Windows Update packages on your device, open a Command Prompt (or Windows PowerShell) and run the following command:

```
wmic qfe list brief /format:table
```

When you have identified an update that you want to remove, you can use the Windows Update Stand-Alone Installer (Wusa.exe) command-line tool to uninstall updates by providing the package number (from the Microsoft Knowledge Base) of the update to be uninstalled. The syntax for the tool is as follows:

```
wusa.exe /uninstall /kb:<KB Number>
```

Replace *<KB Number>* in the command with the actual KB number of the update you want to uninstall. The WMIC and WUSA commands work in either the Command Prompt or Windows PowerShell.

Skill 4.3: Monitor and manage Windows

After your computers are installed with Windows 10, it will be necessary to monitor and manage them. Windows 10 provides many tools with which to monitor your computers, including the Event Viewer, and a number of performance-monitoring tools, including Resource Monitor and Performance Monitor.

In addition to monitoring your computers, you must be familiar with how to manage important elements of the operating system, including printers and printing, indexing, and services.

This skill covers how to:

- Configure and analyze event logs
- Manage performance
- Manage the Windows 10 environment
- Configure local registry
- Schedule tasks

Configure and analyze event logs

A key built-in security tool in all Windows operating systems are event logs, which are accessed in the Windows Event Viewer and provide information regarding system events that occur. Event logs are generated as a background activity by the Event Log service and can include information, warning, and error messages about Windows components and installed applications and actions carried out on the system.

Understand event logs

You can start Event Viewer, as displayed in Figure 4-44, by entering **eventvwr.msc**.

Upon opening, the console retrieves the events that have occurred on your computer and displays them. You can configure the Event Viewer to work with event logs from remote computers; you must enable remote management in your firewall.

There are two types of log files:

- **Windows logs**   Includes Application, Security, Setup, System, and Forwarded Events
- **Applications and services logs**   Includes other logs from applications and services to record application-specific or service-specific events

FIGURE 4-44 Event Viewer with System log selected

Because logs are created as part of the operating system, they can provide forensic-level metadata that can help you understand problems that are difficult to diagnose, using real-time analysis of the system.

The Windows logs are described in more detail in Table 4-8.

TABLE 4-8 Built-in Windows logs

Log	Description	Log File Location	Default Log Size
Application	Events logged by installed applications.	%SystemRoot%\System32\Winevt \Logs\Application.Evtx	20,480 KB
Setup	Records events logged by Windows during setup and installation.	%SystemRoot%\System32\Winevt\ Logs\Setup.Evtx	1,028 KB
Security	Contains auditable events such as logon, logoff, privileged use, and shutdown.	%SystemRoot%\System32\Winevt\ Logs\Security.Evtx	20,480 KB
System	Contains events logged by Windows 10. This is the main system log.	%SystemRoot%\System32\Winevt\ Logs\System.Evtx	20,480 KB
Forwarded Events	Used when event forwarding is operational. This log records forwarded events from other computers.	%SystemRoot%\System32\Config \ ForwardedEvents.Evtx	20,480 KB

The default Windows 10 event log maximum file size is 20 MB. If your system reaches this maximum size, new events will overwrite old events.

Open Event Viewer and take some time to familiarize yourself by reviewing some logs. There are several levels of events, with descriptions as follows:

- **Information**   These logs provide information about changes related to a component or system process, usually a successful outcome.

- **Warning**   These events are not critical, although they could lead to more serious problems and should be investigated.

- **Error**   Events warn you that a problem has occurred.

- **Critical**   These events are the most severe and could lead to failure or loss of function. They are highly significant and indicate that a problem is occurring or has occurred.

- **Audit Success/Failure**   If you have enabled auditing, these log entries appear in the security log.

In Event Viewer, select each of the Windows logs and look at the types of events that have been generated. The Actions pane on the right side provides tools and wizards to help you work with logs, including saving a log, clearing/deleting entries in a log, opening a previously saved log, and attaching a task to an event.

Create a custom view

When you explore Event Viewer, you may find so many entries that it is hard to locate specific issues. You'll want to remove entries, but you should not clear a log on a production machine without first saving the log. A better method of removing log entries, such as informational or warning log entries, is to create a custom view that shows only specific events. This acts like a saved filter that you can invoke.

To create a custom view in Event Viewer that displays only Critical events in the System log, follow these steps:

1. Open **Event Viewer**.

2. On the **Action** menu, select **Create Custom View**.

3. On the **Filter** tab, select the **Critical** check box for **Event Level**.

4. In **By Log**, use the down arrow and expand **Windows Logs**; select only the **System** check box and then select **OK**.

5. Enter a name, such as **System-Critical**, for the log name, and select **OK**. The custom view immediately refreshes and displays log entries that match the criteria.

6. Check that your custom view filter—in this case, named System-Critical—is located in the left pane under the **Custom Views** node.

7. Close **Event Viewer**.

With all events, you can double-click the event log entry to reveal its Properties dialog box. The Event Properties dialog box provides you with additional detailed information together with a Copy button so that you can copy the event data to the Clipboard and then work with the data or seek help. Event descriptions have become easier to understand than in previous versions of Windows. The experience of reading event log entries will also help build your understanding.

Configure event subscriptions

You can configure Event Viewer to gather other computers' event logs. Manually connecting to other computers on a regular basis can be cumbersome. You can automate the collection of event logs from other computers by creating event subscriptions.

All computers participating in a subscription must be configured to allow remote administration. This is achieved by enabling the Windows Remote Management service on the source computer. On the collector computer, start the Windows Event Collector service, which enables the computer to collect events from remote devices. To configure the computers to collect and send events, perform the following two short procedures.

VIEW SUBSCRIPTIONS

To enable the collector computer to view subscriptions:

1. Open an elevated Command Prompt.
2. Enter **wecutil qc**.
3. Enter **Y** to start the **Windows Event Collector** service. The Windows Event Collector service announces that it was configured successfully.
4. Close the Command Prompt window.

To enable remote collection of events on the source computer, follow these steps:

1. Open an elevated Command Prompt.
2. Enter **winrm quickconfig**.
3. Enter **Y**; repeat when prompted. The WinRM firewall exception is now enabled.
4. Close the Command Prompt window.

You can create two kinds of subscriptions: collector-initiated and source computer–initiated. Table 4-9 describes these subscriptions, along with some of the key terms related to event subscriptions.

TABLE 4-9 Event subscription terms

Term	Description
Subscription	A group of events you configure based on specific criteria you create is called a subscription. Subscriptions enable you to receive events from other computers, called sources.
Source	The event source computer is the computer that provides you with events on your network. The source computer can be a PC or a server.
Collector	The event collector computer is the computer on which you view the collected events. The collector computer can be a PC or a server.

Term	Description
Collector-initiated subscription	In a collector-initiated subscription, the subscription must contain a list of all the event sources that need to be added one at a time. This is used on small networks because each must be configured manually.
Source computer–initiated subscription	The source computer transmits local events to the collector computer. This is a push type of arrangement, often configured using Group Policy.

CREATE A SUBSCRIPTION

To create a collector-initiated subscription, follow these steps:

1. Open **Event Viewer**.

2. Select the **Subscriptions** node.

3. If the option to start the **Windows Event Collection Service** dialog box appears, select **Yes**.

4. In the **Action** pane, select **Create Subscription**.

5. Enter a name and a description for the subscription, as displayed in Figure 4-45.

FIGURE 4-45 Creating an event subscription

6. Under **Subscription type and source computers**, select **Collector initiated** and then select **Select Computers**.

7. In the **Computers** dialog box, select **Add Domain Computers**, select the computer to be polled for subscriptions, and select **OK**.

8. Under **Events To Collect**, select **Select Events** and define the event criteria—such as event levels, log type, and event source—that will be used to match and collect events. Select **OK**.

9. Select **OK** to save and make the subscription active.

The new subscription is listed in the main pane of the Subscriptions node.

If you want to view events on other computers on your network, you can do so without creating a subscription. This approach is useful for ad hoc monitoring, for example, to see whether a particular event has occurred.

Access event logs remotely

When you want to quickly view event logs on a remote computer, you don't have to create a subscription. Instead, you can view the event logs directly. To view event logs on a remote system, follow these steps:

1. Open **Event Viewer**.

2. Right-click **Event Viewer (Local)** in the left pane and choose **Connect to Another Computer**.

3. When the **Select Computer** dialog box opens, select **Another Computer** and enter the name, the domain name, or the IP address of the computer, or select **Browse** to search for the computer on your network.

4. If you need to specify logon credentials, select the **Connect as another User** check box. Select **Set User** and enter the logon credentials for a local administrator or user on the remote device and then select **OK**.

> **NOTE VIEW EVENTS ON REMOTE COMPUTERS**
> You must have administrator privileges to view events on a remote computer. You must also configure Windows Firewall on all participants to allow traffic on TCP port 80 for HTTP or on TCP port 443 for HTTPS.

Manage performance

Windows 10 offers a number of tools that you can use to view and manage performance. Some of these provide a snapshot view of system performance. Others provide a means to collect and analyze performance data over a period of time.

You can use the following tools to manage performance in Windows 10:

- Task Manager
- Resource Monitor
- Performance Monitor

Monitor performance using Task Manager

If you have used an earlier version of Windows, you probably have used Task Manager. It is one of the most useful tools available in Windows for gaining an immediate insight into how a system is performing.

ACCESS TASK MANAGER

The Task Manager built into Windows 10 shows you which processes (tasks) are running on your system and, most important, shows the system resource usage that directly relates to performance. If a particular task or process is not responding or continues to run after you have closed the application, you can use Task Manager to view this behavior and force the offending process to end.

When troubleshooting, you may find that some users are comfortable using Task Manager to review the system status and end problematic tasks.

If you are moving to Windows 10 from Windows 7 or earlier, notice that Task Manager has been redesigned extensively and is now much more user-friendly, informative, colorful, and slightly less technical.

To open Task Manager, right-click the Start button and then select Task Manager. There are other ways to open Task Manager:

- Pressing Ctrl+Shift+Esc
- Right-clicking the taskbar, Cortana, or the Task View button and then selecting Task Manager

By default, Task Manager opens to show only the running applications, as you can see in Figure 4-46. While using this view, you can highlight any of the listed applications and select End Task to stop a running app.

FIGURE 4-46 Task Manager

If you select More Details, Task Manager reopens and displays seven tabs, which enable you to review specific areas of your computer activity. The tabs are described in Table 4-10.

TABLE 4-10 Task Manager tabs

Task Manager Tab	Description
Processes	Shows all running apps and background processes
Performance	Shows real-time statistics for CPU, memory, disk, Ethernet, Bluetooth, and Wi-Fi usage
App History	Shows historical data for universal and modern apps usage for the previous month
Startup	Lists the apps that start when the computer boots
Users	Lists all the users currently logged on to the computer locally and remotely
Details	Shows detailed statistics on all running and suspended processes
Services	Displays all running and stopped system services

Each tab offers you a different view of the system. Most users might be interested only in the simple view, whereas most IT professionals will only use the detailed version of Task Manager.

USING THE PERFORMANCE TAB

The Performance tab provides a graphical, real-time, statistical view for CPU, Memory, Disk, and Ethernet. If you have multiple Ethernet devices, such as Wi-Fi, these are listed. Figure 4-47 shows the Performance tab with Disk 0 selected. In the lower pane, below the graphics, you see additional information, such as read/write speed, capacity, and average response time. If you are connected to Wi-Fi and select Ethernet, you see the adapter name, Service Set Identifier (SSID), Domain Name Service (DNS) name, connection type, IPv4 and IPv6 addresses, and signal strength.

At the bottom of the Performance tab is an Open Resource Monitor link to the management console.

Monitor performance using Resource Monitor

Resource Monitor displays more information and activity statistics relating to your system resources in real time. It is similar to Task Manager, but it also enables you to dive deeper into the actual processes and see how they affect the performance of your CPU, disk, network, and memory subcomponents.

Open Resource Monitor by using the link on the Performance tab of Task Manager or search for **Resource** using the Start button. The executable for Resource Monitor is Resmon.exe, which you can run from a Run dialog box or a Command Prompt.

FIGURE 4-47 The Performance tab in Task Manager

When you open Resource Monitor, you see an overview of your system, with graphs for each area of the system subcomponent. Four further tabs are available: CPU, Disk, Network, and Memory. The statistics tracked on the Overview tab include the following:

- % CPU Usage
- CPU Maximum Frequency
- Disk I/O Bytes Per Second
- Disk % Highest Active Time
- Network I/O Bytes Per Second
- % Network Utilization
- Memory Hard Faults Per Second
- % Physical Memory Used

Review each tab; each subcomponent offers additional components, as displayed in Table 4-11.

TABLE 4-11 Resource Monitor components

System Component	Additional subcomponents
CPU	Processes Services Associated Handles Associated Modules
Memory	Processes Physical Memory
Disk	Processes With Disk Activity Disk Activity Storage
Network	Processes With Network Activity Network Activity TCP Connections Listening Ports

In each data collector, you can sort the output by selecting the column title. If you select one or more processes in the topmost section, selecting the check box on the left side creates a filter for the items across all four tabs. The selected item is highlighted in orange so that you can see how the item compares to the overall output, as displayed in Figure 4-48.

Resource Monitor is useful for troubleshooting performance issues that relate to high resource usage and you need to establish which process is using a more than normal amount of resources such as memory.

For more advanced analysis, you can right-click any column and choose additional columns by choosing Select Columns. Each tab has associated columns; the CPU panel offers the following additional columns:

- **Average Cycle**   Average percentage of CPU cycle time for the process (over a 60-second interval).
- **Cycle**   Current percentage of CPU cycle time the process is using.
- **Elevated**   The elevation status of the process. (If this is Yes, it is an elevated process.)
- **Operating System Context**   The operating system context in which the process is running.
- **Platform**   The platform architecture that the process is running.
- **User Name**   The name of the user or service that is running the process.

If you want to freeze the screen so that you can analyze the display or capture an image, you can select Monitor and then select Stop Monitoring.

FIGURE 4-48 Resource Monitor CPU view

Monitor performance using Performance Monitor and Data Collector Sets

You can use the Performance Monitor Microsoft Management Console (MMC) snap-in to monitor and track your device for the default set of performance parameters or a custom set you select for display. These performance parameters are referred to as *counters*. Performance Monitor graphically displays statistics and offers real-time monitoring and recording capabilities. By default, the update interval for the capture is set to one second, but this is configurable.

You can use Performance Monitor to record performance information in a log file so that it can be played back and used as part of your overall benchmarking process on a system being tested, or when collecting information to help you troubleshoot an issue. You can also create alerts that notify you when a specific performance criterion, such as a threshold or limit, has been met or exceeded.

The easiest way to learn how to use Performance Monitor is to run one of the two built-in collector sets and review the results:

- **System Diagnostics** Data Collector Set collects the status of local hardware resources and configuration data, together with data from the System Information tool.

- **System Performance** Data Collector Set reports the status of local hardware resources, system response times, and processes.

RUN THE PERFORMANCE MONITOR DATA COLLECTOR

To run the System Performance data collector and view the report, follow these steps:

1. Select **Start**, enter **Performance**, and then select **Performance Monitor** in **Control Panel**.

2. In the navigation pane, select **Data Collector Sets\System** and select **System Performance**.

3. On the toolbar, select the **Run** icon (green triangle). The collector runs for 60 seconds and then stops.

4. After the collector has stopped, in the navigation pane, select **Reports** and expand **System**.

5. Select the chevron arrow next to **System Performance** and then select the **Report** icon related to the collector you just ran. The latest report should be listed at the bottom. The **System Performance Report** appears in the results pane.

6. Review the **System Performance Report** and then close **Performance Monitor**.

When you review the report, as displayed in Figure 4-49, you can see how extensive and detailed the monitoring is. The report is saved and can be printed and refreshed to provide an up-to-date report, which you can compare to other reports.

The diagnostic or performance-monitoring data collector sets are useful when identifying the cause of performance deterioration, which might be a warning sign of potentially malfunction or failing hardware.

You can manually configure Performance Monitor to report on one or many parameters you select for display. You choose the counters that relate to the hardware and software installed on your system. If you add new hardware, such as a new network card, Performance Monitor updates the set of performance counters for the new resource.

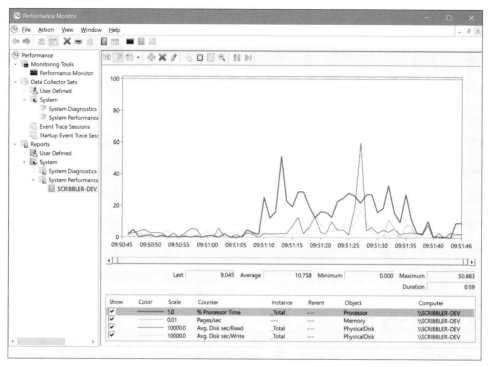

FIGURE 4-49 Viewing a report in Performance Monitor's reporting node

USE PERFORMANCE MONITOR

To use Performance Monitor, you start with a blank canvas and add items that you want to monitor. There are three components that you can add as follows:

- **Performance objects**   These relate to any system component that enables monitoring, such as

    - **Physical**   The memory, the processor, or the paging file

    - **Logical component**   For example, a logical disk or print queue

    - **Software**   For example, a process or a thread

- **Performance object instances**   These represent single occurrences of performance objects. You can choose individual instances, or you can track all instances of an object.

- **Performance counters**   These are the measurable properties of performance objects, such as the % Processor Time for the processor, as displayed in Figure 4-50.

After you have selected some counters, a moving graphical display shows the activity relating to the counters you selected. You can locate the color of the line from the key at the base of the graph and hide/show any counter by clearing the check box at the left of the counter.

FIGURE 4-50 Adding objects and counters to Performance Monitor

A selection of the most common performance objects that you may want to monitor are summarized in Table 4-12.

TABLE 4-12 Commonly tracked performance objects

Performance Object	Description
Memory	Monitors memory performance for system cache, physical memory, and virtual memory
IPv4	Monitors IPv4 communications
LogicalDisk	Monitors the logical volumes on a computer
Network Interface	Monitors the network adapters on the computer
PhysicalDisk	Monitors hard disk read/write activity and data transfers, hard faults, and soft faults
Print Queue	Monitors print jobs, spooling, and print queue activity
Processor	Monitors processor idle time, idle states, usage, deferred procedure calls, and interrupts

Because the monitoring is performed in real time, the effect of monitoring many counters can have an impact on the host system performance, which could distort the usefulness of the performance information. Therefore, you should test the number of counters and the frequency of data collection and witness the impact. To add new values to the Performance Monitor chart, follow these steps:

1. Select **Start**, and enter **perfmon. Performance Monitor** opens.

2. Select the **Performance Monitor** node in the left pane. The default counter for **% Processor Time** appears.

3. On the toolbar, select the plus (**+**) symbol to add an additional counter.

4. In the **Available Counters** area, expand **PhysicalDisk**, and select **% Idle Time**.

5. In the **Instances Of Selected Object** box, select **0 C:**, select **Add**, and select **OK**.

6. Right-click **% Idle Time** and then select **Properties**.

7. In the **Color** box, select blue, and then select **OK**. Leave **Performance Monitor** open.

To create a new data collector set based on a template, in Performance Monitor follow these steps:

1. In the left pane, expand **Data Collector Sets** and then select **User Defined**.

2. Right-click **User Defined**, select **New**, and then select **Data Collector Set**.

3. On the **Create new Data Collector Set** page, enter **Disk Activity** in the **Name** box, and then select **Next**.

4. In the **Template Data Collector Set** box, select **Basic** and select **Next**.

5. Select **Next** to accept the default storage location.

6. Select **Open properties for this data cllector set** and select **Finish**. The **Disk Activity Properties** dialog box appears; it has six tabs.

7. Review the General, Directory, Security, Schedule, Stop Condition, and Task tabs and select **OK**.

8. In the right pane, double-click **Disk Activity**. Three types of logs are displayed:

   - **Performance Counter** Collects data that is viewable in Performance Monitor
   - **Configuration** Records changes to registry keys
   - **Kernel Trace** Collects detailed information about system events and activities

9. Double-click **Performance Counter**.

10. Select the **Processor Counter** and select **Remove**.

11. Select **Add** and then select **PhysicalDisk** in **Available counters**.

12. Select **Add** and then select **OK**.

13. In the navigation pane, right-click **Disk Activity** and then select **Start**.

14. On the **Disk Activity** node, a small play icon appears for 60 seconds.

15. When **Data Collector Set** has stopped recording, right-click **Disk Activity** and then select **Latest Report**.

16. Review the report, which shows the data that the data collector set collected.

17. Close **Performance Monitor**.

Monitor system resources

Every computer system has a performance threshold that, if pushed beyond this level, will cause the system to struggle to perform optimally. If you overload the system, it eventually slows down as it attempts to service each demand with the available resources. Most systems include a capable processor and sufficient amount of RAM for everyday or general needs. Memory is automatically reclaimed from apps that are closed. However, when apps or web browser tabs are left open, and more apps are then opened, the overall ability for the system to perform is degraded.

UNDERSTAND BASELINE PERFORMANCE VS. REAL-TIME MONITORING

You have learned that with tools such as Performance Monitor, Resource Monitor, and Task Manager you can monitor your system activity and understand how demands on processor, RAM, networking, and disks affect your computer system. Real-time monitoring information is useful for instant diagnosis. Also, creating a baseline for your computer's performance can generate a system-specific report that can show what your performance statistics look like during normal or heavy use.

If you intend to deliver a device to a user who will use the device extensively for system-intensive tasks, such as video editing or computer-aided design, it might be useful to create a performance baseline for the device so that you can establish how the system performs normally and when under heavy load. This information will be useful to confirm that the device specification is suitable for the user. Also, it will be helpful if the user reports performance issues because you can run another performance baseline and compare the two baselines to evaluate whether the system environment has changed. For example, perhaps the user now regularly multitasks with new apps on the system that use additional memory.

In this scenario, when an issue or symptom occurs, you can compare your baseline statistics to your real-time statistics and identify differences between the two instances. When you can diagnose the issue, you can recommend a solution, such as to add memory.

The most appropriate tool to record a baseline in Windows 10 is Performance Monitor; it will help you review and report on the following areas in your system:

- Evaluate your system workload
- Monitor system resources
- Notice changes and trends in resource use
- Help diagnose problems

CREATE A PERFORMANCE BASELINE

To create a performance baseline that monitors key system components you can use to measure against a future performance baseline, follow these steps:

1. Select **Start**, then enter **perfmon. Performance Monitor** opens.
2. Select the **Data Collector Sets** node in the navigation pane.
3. Select **User Defined**, right-click **User Defined**, select **New**, and then select **Data Collector Set**.

4. In the **Create new Data Collector Set Wizard**, on the **How would you like to create this new data collector set?** page, in the **Name** box, enter **Initial PC Baseline**.

5. Select **Create manually (Advanced)** and then select **Next**.

6. On the **What type of data do you want to include?** page, select the **Performance counter** check box and then select **Next**.

7. On the **Which performance counters would you like to log?** page, in the **Sample interval** box, enter **1** and then select **Add**.

8. Include the following counters:
   - Memory > Pages/Sec
   - Network Interface > Packets/Sec
   - PhysicalDisk > % Disk Time
   - PhysicalDisk > Avg. Disk Queue Length
   - Processor > % Processor Time
   - System > Processor Queue Length

9. Select **OK** and then select **Finish**.

10. Right-click **Initial PC Baseline** and then select **Start**.

11. Simulate load on the system by starting several programs, including Microsoft Edge, Word 2019, Microsoft Excel 2019, and Microsoft PowerPoint 2019.

12. Close all Microsoft Office apps, close Microsoft Edge, and stop the Initial PC Baseline data collector set.

13. To view the baseline report, in **Performance Monitor**, expand the **Reports\User Defined node\Initial PC Baseline** and select the report to open it.

14. Print the report or view the report and record the values for the following counters:
   - Memory > Pages/sec
   - Network Interface > Packets/Sec
   - PhysicalDisk > % Disk Time
   - PhysicalDisk > Avg. Disk Queue Length
   - Processor > % Processor Time
   - System > Processor Queue Length

Troubleshoot performance issues

In normal operating conditions, the majority of users rarely experience performance issues with their devices after they have been configured with the necessary security, antimalware, productivity, and specialist software. Out of the box, Windows 10 is optimized for general user environments.

Over time, the device might gradually seem to become slower. If the user notices this decreased system performance, they might request help from the help desk.

You can avoid some performance degradation by performing regular maintenance, such as using the Disk Cleanup utility to remove temporary or unwanted files. Windows 10 does a good job at self-healing and maintaining the system and schedules many maintenance tasks to run automatically for you.

If poor performance occurs, investigate and troubleshoot the reason to establish whether there is a bottleneck—perhaps a memory-hungry app, multiple startup programs, or even malware. Another gradual but common occurrence is when a system runs out of disk space, especially because the majority of devices are now using solid-state drives (SSDs) that are typically smaller-capacity drives.

When looking at the factors that might influence your PC, consider some of the following:

- Windows 10 architecture: x86 or x64
- Processor speed, processor quantity, onboard cache memory, and cores
- Physical hard disks input/output speed, buffer size, and defragmentation state
- Memory: capacity, speed, and type
- Graphics card: throughput, memory, onboard processing speed, quantity, and drivers
- Network interface throughput, onboard processing capability, quantity, and drivers
- Application number, type, available optimizations, and architecture
- System, peripheral, and application drivers

Understand how system bottlenecks can occur, how to diagnose a system that is suffering from a performance bottleneck, and how to respond and recover from the problem. Some common performance bottlenecks that are useful to know about when troubleshooting are shown in Table 4-13.

TABLE 4-13 Performance bottlenecks

Performance Counter	Bottleneck
LogicalDisk\% Free Space	If this is less than 15 percent, you risk running out of free space for Windows 10 to use to store critical files.
PhysicalDisk\% Idle Time	If this is less than 20 percent, the disk system is overloaded. Consider replacing with a faster disk.
PhysicalDisk\Avg. Disk Sec/Read	If the number is larger than 25 milliseconds (ms), the disk system is experiencing read latency; suspect drive failure (or a very slow and/or old disk).
PhysicalDisk\Avg. Disk Sec/Write	If the number is larger than 25 milliseconds (ms), the disk system is experiencing write latency; suspect drive failure (or a very slow and/or old disk).
PhysicalDisk\Avg. Disk Queue Length	If the value is larger than two times the number of drive spindles, the disk might be the bottleneck.
Memory\% Committed Bytes in Use	If the value is greater than 80 percent, it indicates insufficient memory.
Memory\Available Mbytes	If this value is less than 5 percent of the total physical RAM, there is insufficient memory, which can increase paging activity.

Performance Counter	Bottleneck
Processor\% Processor Time	If the percentage is greater than 85 percent, the processor is overwhelmed, and the PC might require a faster processor.
System\Processor Queue Length	If the value is more than twice the number of CPUs for an extended period, you should consider a more powerful processor.
Network Interface\Output Queue Length	There is network saturation if the value is more than 2. Consider a faster or additional network interface.

Manage Windows 10 environment

In this section, you will learn how to manage printers, control and configure indexing, evaluate system stability, and configure and manage services.

Monitor and manage printers

Windows 10 provides additional options for you to manage your printing compared to previous versions of Windows. A new Print Management desktop app and the new Printers & Scanners options in the Settings app provide basic printer management such as Add, Remove, and Set As Default Printer.

You still have previous printer tools in the Devices And Printers section of Control Panel or from the link at the bottom of the Printers & Scanners options in the Settings app. The Devices And Printers Control Panel item is the same interface as in previous versions of Windows.

MANAGE PRINTERS BY USING PRINT MANAGEMENT

A new Print Management console is available for you to manage your device printers from a single management console. Print devices connected to your PC can be shared, and you can manage the properties of the device. The Print Management MMC, as displayed in Figure 4-51, is included in the Administrative Tools of Windows 10 Pro and Enterprise editions, and it lists all printers, drivers, and other print servers that you are connected to.

FIGURE 4-51 Managing printers

You can also access the Print Management console by selecting Start and entering **Printmanagement.msc**.

The Print Management console offers you a single location to perform the following printer-related management tasks:

- Add and delete print devices
- View printers and print servers
- Add and remove print servers
- Add and manage print drivers
- Deploy printers using Group Policy
- Open and manage printer queues
- View and modify status of printers
- Use the filter feature to view printers based on filters

If you right-click a printer, you are presented with a list of action items that can be performed on the selected printer. These can include the following tasks:

- Open Printer Queue
- Pause Printing
- List In Directory
- Deploy With Group Policy
- Set Printing Defaults
- Manage Sharing
- Print Test Page
- Enable Branch Office Direct Printing
- Properties
- Delete
- Rename
- Help

> *NOTE* **REMOTE PRINTERS**
> You can use the Print Management console to manage both local and remote printers. Devices And Printers in Control Panel can only manage locally connected printers.

MANAGE PRINTERS BY USING WINDOWS POWERSHELL

You can use more than 20 Windows PowerShell cmdlets to manage printers. Some of the most common cmdlets are shown in Table 4-14.

TABLE 4-14 Windows PowerShell printer cmdlets

Cmdlet	Description
Add-Printer	Adds a printer to the specified computer
Add-PrinterDriver	Installs a printer driver on the specified computer
Add-PrinterPort	Installs a printer port on the specified computer
Get-PrintConfiguration	Gets the configuration information of a printer
Get-Printer	Retrieves a list of printers installed on a computer
Get-PrinterDriver	Retrieves the list of printer drivers installed on the specified computer
Get-PrinterPort	Retrieves a list of printer ports installed on the specified computer
Get-PrinterProperty	Retrieves printer properties for the specified printer
Remove-Printer	Removes a printer from the specified computer
Remove-PrinterDriver	Deletes printer drivers from the specified computer
Remove-PrintJob	Removes a print job on the specified printer
Rename-Printer	Renames the specified printer
Restart-PrintJob	Restarts a print job on the specified printer
Resume-PrintJob	Resumes a suspended print job
Set-PrintConfiguration	Sets the configuration information for the specified printer
Set-Printer	Updates the configuration of an existing printer
Set-PrinterProperty	Modifies the printer properties for the specified printer

To list all the available cmdlets, run the following command in a Windows PowerShell window:

```
Get-Command -Module PrintManagement
```

Configure indexing options

To maintain the performance of Windows 10 search, the system automatically indexes data on your computer in the background. This data includes user-generated files, folders, and documents. Most users will never modify the default indexing settings, but you can add new areas to be indexed and exclude others. Common locations include your user profile areas and app data that you access frequently, such as Office apps.

If you store a lot of data in a storage space or a removable drive, you can add this location to Indexing Options to significantly speed up the performance of future searches in this location.

To view your existing indexing locations, select Start and enter **Index** and then select Indexing Options in Control Panel to open the Indexing Options dialog box shown in Figure 4-52.

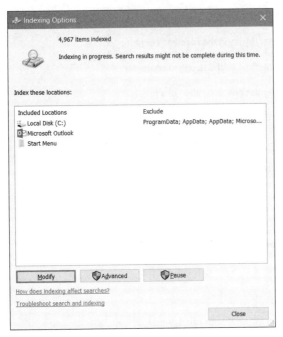

FIGURE 4-52 Indexing Options

You can use the Modify button to add or remove locations. In the Indexed Locations dialog box, you see the summary of locations. If you select Show All Locations, Windows 10 displays all the hidden locations, and this enables you to fine-tune the indexing to specific subfolders, if necessary. To select the Downloads and Documents folders in your profile, select the arrow next to the Users folder and then locate and select Downloads and Documents in your user profile.

After you apply changes to indexing, the indexing process doesn't happen immediately; rather, it runs as a background task whenever your machine is running but not being used. While the indexing process is incomplete, the message in the dialog box indicates that Indexing Speed Is Reduced Due To User Activity. When the process has finished, the message states Indexing Complete.

Be careful not to index everything on your disk. A large index can affect the search performance negatively.

In the Indexing Options dialog box, the Advanced button enables you to configure Index Settings and specify File Types to be excluded. You can include or exclude encrypted files, treat similar words as different words, delete and rebuild the index (useful if you suspect search is not working), and change the index location from the default C:\ProgramData\Microsoft.

On the File Types tab, you can exclude file types from the index and configure whether the index searches in the file contents or just in the file properties. You can also manually add new file types that have not been automatically included to index.

Evaluate system stability by using Reliability Monitor

Members of the desktop support team often report that it is difficult to ascertain the precise nature of calls that relate to poor performance or system instability. Reliability Monitor is an excellent tool for these situations because it enables you to review a computer's reliability and problem history and offers both the help desk and you the ability to explore the detailed reports and recommendations that can help you identify and resolve reliability issues. Changes to the system such as software and driver installations are recorded, and changes in system stability are then linked to changes in the system configuration.

To open Reliability Monitor, select Start and enter **reliability**. Then, select View Reliability History in Control Panel, or enter **perfmon /rel** at a Command Prompt. The tool displays a summary of the reliability history for your system, as displayed in Figure 4-53.

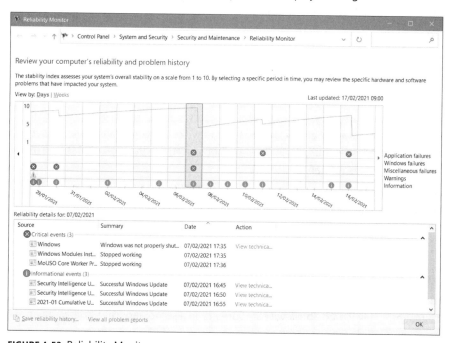

FIGURE 4-53 Reliability Monitor

The top half of the Reliability Monitor screen shows a line graph with a scale of 1 to 10 and a date timeline along the bottom axis. You can toggle the view from weeks to days. The graph rises and sinks over time, and at the low points are colored markers in red, blue, or yellow. Below the graph are the details that relate to system configuration changes, such as software and driver installations. When system changes result in a negative system stability, such as an app crashing or a service stopping, there might be a relationship between the two, and these relationships can be further explored. The graph gradually reaches the maximum level of 10 if the system does not experience negative system stability over a prolonged period.

Reliability Monitor is enabled by default in Windows 10. Reliability Monitor requires the Microsoft Reliability Analysis task, RacTask, to process system reliability data, which is a background process that collects reliability data. RacTask can be found in the Task Scheduler library under the Microsoft\Windows\RAC node.

The Reliability Monitor main features include:

- **System stability chart**   Provides a summary of annual system stability in daily/weekly increments. The chart indicates three levels of stability data: information, warning messages, and critical errors.

- **Records key events in a timeline**   Tracks events about the system configuration, such as the installation of new apps, operating system patches, and drivers.

- **Installation and failure reports**   Provides information about each event shown in the chart, including:

  - Software Installs/Software Uninstalls

  - App Failures

  - Hardware & Driver Failures

  - Windows Operating System Failures

  - Miscellaneous Failures

Because the tool offers a rolling view of reliability history, you can retain a copy of a point-in-time report. Select the Save Reliability History link to save complete details at periodic time points, such as annually. System builders and repair shops often use the report to demonstrate computer stability for future reference.

At the bottom of the Reliability Monitor screen are two additional links that list all computer problems and attempt to locate problem solutions from the internet. The Problem Reports And Solutions tool helps you track problems that are reported and checks for all available solution information to problems.

Configure and manage services

A service can best be described as a software component that interacts at one level with device drivers and, at another level, with app-level components. In a sense, services sit between apps and hardware devices and are considered a core part of the operating system, controlling user requests, through apps, to hardware resources.

These operating system services provide discrete functions in Windows 10 and require no user interaction. You can manage services in a number of ways, including from the Command Prompt, by using Windows PowerShell, and by using the management console.

USING THE SERVICES MANAGEMENT CONSOLE SNAP-IN

The most straightforward way to manage services is to use the Services management console snap-in, as displayed in Figure 4-54.

FIGURE 4-54 Managing services

You can use this console to review and manage services in the operating system. For example, to manage the status of a service (assuming it is not running), right-click the service and then select Start. If you want to stop or restart a running service, right-click the running service and then select either Stop or Restart.

You can also manage the settings of a service by double-clicking the desired service. In the Properties dialog box for the named service, as displayed in Figure 4-55, you can then configure the properties shown in Table 4-15.

FIGURE 4-55 Managing a specific service

TABLE 4-15 Configurable options for a Windows 10 service

Tab	Options and explanation
General	■ Service name. You cannot change this value, but it is useful to know what name Windows assigns to the service so that you can reference it when using a command-line tool or Windows PowerShell. ■ Startup type: Disabled, Manual, Automatic, Automatic (Delayed Start). This option enables you to determine the startup behavior of the service. ■ Start parameters. You can add properties to configure the service behavior when it starts.
Log On	Log on as Local System Account or This Account. Some services run in the context of the Local System Account. Others must be configured to use a specific, named account (for example, when communicating across the network with another service). You can create special local user accounts for the purpose of running services. When you define a specific user account and change the user password, you must update the password information on the Log On tab for the services that use that account.
Recovery	You can configure what happens when a service fails to start or crashes. Specifically, you can configure Windows 10 to attempt a restart of a service if it fails to start on the first attempt. On second attempts, you can choose another option, such as Restart The Computer. Available options for failures are Take No Action, Restart The Service, Run A Program, and Restart The Computer. If you select Run A Program, you can configure additional options for the path and name of the program, plus any runtime switches you want to apply.
Dependencies	Some services depend on other services, or groups of services, to run. In this way, Windows 10 can start efficiently by making sure only the required services are in memory. You cannot make changes on this tab, but it is informative to know whether a service has dependencies, especially when a service is failing to start properly.

USING COMMAND-LINE TOOLS

You can also use the command line to investigate and troubleshoot service startup. Table 4-16 describes some of the more common command-line tools you can use to work with services. To use these commands, open an elevated Command Prompt.

TABLE 4-16 Managing services from the command line

Command	Explanation
Net start	When used without arguments, lists the running services. When used with the name of a service, the service, if not running, is started. For example, **net start workstation** starts the Windows workstation service.
Net stop	Must be used with the name of a running service. For example, **net stop workstation** will stop the Windows workstation service.
Sc query	Displays a list of services.
Sc stop	Enables you to stop a named service. For example, to stop the spooler service, run: **Sc stop spooler**
Sc start	Enables you to start a named service. For example, to start the spooler service, run: **Sc start spooler**

You can also use Windows PowerShell to manage services. This is particularly useful because you can use Windows PowerShell to administer other computers remotely, including their services. In addition, you can script Windows PowerShell cmdlets, enabling you to store common administrative tasks for future use. Table 4-17 describes the cmdlets you can use to manage services in Windows 10. Open an elevated Windows PowerShell window to use these cmdlets.

TABLE 4-17 Managing services with Windows PowerShell

Cmdlet	Explanation
Get-service	Lists available services. To get a list of running services, use the following cmdlet: **Get-Service | Where-Object {$_.status -eq "running"}**
Stop-service	Enables you to stop the named service(s). For example: **Stop-service - name spooler**
Start-service	Enables you to start the named service(s). For example: **Start-service - name spooler**
Restart-service	Enables you to stop and start the named service(s). For example: **Restart-service - name spooler**
Set-service	Enables you to reconfigure the startup and other properties of the named service. For example, to change the display name of the Workstation service, use the following cmdlet: **set-service -name lanmanworkstation -DisplayName "LanMan Workstation"**

USE THE SYSTEM CONFIGURATION TOOL

If you are experiencing problems with starting your Windows 10 device and you suspect a service might be the cause of the problem, you can control which services start when you start your computer by using Safe Mode. This reduces the set of services that start to the minimum required to run Windows.

You can force your computer into Safe Mode during startup or use the System Configuration tool, **Msconfig.exe**. To access the System Configuration tool, run msconfig.exe. You can then configure your computer's startup behavior. Configurable options are described in Table 4-18.

TABLE 4-18 System configuration options

Tab	Options and Explanation
General	■ Select Normal Startup to configure normal operations on your computer. ■ Choose Diagnostic Startup to load a minimal set of devices and services. ■ Choose Selective Startup to be more selective about what is initialized during startup.

Tab	Options and Explanation
Boot	■ You can enable Safe Mode by selecting Safe Boot. Then you can choose additional options: Minimal, Alternate Shell, and Network. You can also start without the GUI, enable a boot log, and configure startup to use a base video driver and configuration. ■ The Advanced Options button enables you to restrict Windows to using fewer logical processors and a reduced amount of memory. These options are useful for re-creating a computer configuration in which a specific problem was experienced. ■ If multiple operating systems are installed on your computer, they are listed on this tab, enabling you to select between the available operating systems. ■ You can choose to make your boot selections permanent, but you should exercise caution with this option in case the settings you have selected are inappropriate.
Services	The Services tab displays the available operating system services and enables you to configure their startup behavior. For example, you can disable any services that you suspect might be causing issues with your computer. To disable a service, clear the check box next to its name.
Startup	The Startup tab enables you to access the Startup tab in Task Manager to control the startup behavior of apps.
Tools	The Tools tab provides a consolidated list of available system tools, including: Change UAC Settings, System Properties, Computer Management, Device Manager, and the Registry Editor.

Configure local registry

All settings within Windows 10 are ultimately stored in the Windows Registry. This is a database that contains details of all Windows settings, installed software, device drivers, and much more. Without the registry, Windows would not work.

Every reference to working the registry always stipulates that you should take great care when working with or editing the registry. An incorrect registry change can prevent your system from booting and can result in you having to completely reinstall the operating system. You should always take care and create a system backup before editing the registry.

Understanding the registry structure

The registry is a database that is split into multiple separate files known as hives, together with associated log and other support files.

You can find the registry files in %systemroot%\System32\Config\, though you will need to be an administrator to access this folder. Within this system folder, you should find several binary format "files" that the registry uses:

■ SAM (Security Accounts Manager used to store local passwords)

■ SECURITY

■ SOFTWARE

■ SYSTEM

■ DEFAULT

■ USERDIFF (used only for Windows upgrades)

In addition to the system files, the user-specific settings are stored within the user profile and are loaded into system memory when a user signs in. These registry files are located in the following locations:

- %userprofile%\ntuser.dat
- %userprofile%\AppData\Local\Microsoft\Windows\UsrClass.dat

Other notable registry files include the Boot Configuration Data (BCD) store, which stores its own file on the boot drive. The local services are located in %SystemRoot%\ ServiceProfiles\ LocalService and network services are stored in %SystemRoot%\ServiceProfiles\NetworkService.

The vast majority of changes to the hive files are made automatically by Windows whenever you install an application or change a setting or configuration by using the Settings app or Control Panel.

The main hives, or subtrees, which store settings for Windows 10 are shown in Table 4-19.

TABLE 4-19 Registry hives

Hive	Description
HKEY_CLASSES_ROOT	This hive relates to file association information relating to applications installed in the device. For example, it defines that the application for DOCX files is Microsoft Word. This hive contains application information derived from the settings that are stored in the HKEY_LOCAL_MACHINE\Software\Classes and HKEY_CURRENT_USER\Software\Classes hives.
HKEY_CURRENT_USER	This hive contains information for the signed-in user. Personalized settings such as background image, Windows color scheme, and font settings are stored in this hive.
HKEY_LOCAL_MACHINE	This hive stores computer-related configuration settings.
HKEY_USERS	This hive contains user-related configuration settings for all users who have signed in locally to the computer, including the currently signed-in user. The HKEY_CURRENT_USER hive is a subkey of HKEY_USERS. Edits to this hive will affect the user settings for the currently signed-in user.
HKEY_CURRENT_CONFIG	This hive contains current hardware profile information for the local computer.

Should you need to make a manual change, create a new entry, or modify an existing registry entry, these changes will typically take place in the following two hives:

- HKEY_LOCAL_MACHINE
- HKEY_CURRENT_USER

The primary tool for managing and editing the registry is the built-in registry editor.

Within the hives, settings containing values are stored in subtrees, keys, and subkeys. The hierarchical nature of the registry makes it easy to locate a registry value. An example of a key, subkeys, and value would be

```
Computer\HKEY_CURRENT_USER\Control Panel\Mouse
```

This key holds many subkeys, which Windows uses to store settings for the mouse.

The mouse settings can be modified in the registry, as displayed in Figure 4-56, or by using the Mouse item in Control Panel. If you enable mouse pointer trails in Control Panel, the registry subkey for MouseTrails is modified to have a value of 7.

FIGURE 4-56 Registry keys

Values are stored within each key and subkey that are used to configure the operating system. There are several value types that are used to store information such as numerical data, text, and variables like file paths. Often a value is empty or not defined, as displayed in the (Default) subkey in Figure 4-56. Table 4-20 lists common types of registry values.

TABLE 4-20 Registry value types

Value Type	Data Type	Description
REG_BINARY	Binary	Raw binary data. Values are normally displayed in hexadecimal format. Hardware information is often stored in these values.
REG_DWORD	DWORD	4-byte numbers (a 32-bit integer). Device-driver and service-related values are stored in these values.
REG_SZ	String	A fixed-length text string. Most of the values listed in the \HKEY_CURRENT_USER\Control Panel\Mouse keys are REG_SZ values.
REG_EXPAND_SZ	Expandable string	A variable length text string. Windows uses REG_EXPAND_SZ values to contain variables, such as file system paths.
REG_MULTI_SZ	Multiple strings	Multiple string values. These values are typically used when multiple values are required.

Understanding the Registry Editor

The built-in Registry Editor (Regedit.exe) allows you to view, search, and modify the registry's contents. Some common tasks that administrators can perform using the Registry Editor tool are as follows:

- Search the registry for a value, value name, subkey, or key
- Create, delete, and modify keys, subkeys, and values

- Import entries into the registry from an external (REG) file
- Export entries from the registry into an external (REG) file
- Back up the entire registry
- Manage the HKEY_LOCAL_MACHINE and HKEY_USERS registry hives on a remote computer

You can also import registry keys and values directly into the registry by using a text file with the .reg extension.

All REG files will use the following syntax for Registry Editor to understand them:

```
Windows Registry Editor Version 5.00
[<Hive name>\<Key name>\<Subkey name>]
"Value name"=<Value type>:<Value data>
```

Because REG files are associated with the registry, executing a REG file will merge it with— or import it to—the local Windows Registry. The contents of the REG file will add, delete, or modify one or more keys or values in the registry. Depending on the changes contained within the REG file, you may need to restart your computer after the changes have been made.

You can also use the import option on the File menu in the Registry Editor to import the settings, or you can use the command line with a script similar to the following example:

```
regedit /s C:\\Registry\\regsetting.reg \> nul
```

Using PowerShell to manage registry settings

The registry can be accessed directly using Windows PowerShell. The registry provider within PowerShell presents the registry like a file system, displaying the keys and subkeys as subfolders within a registry hive.

Windows PowerShell uses the abbreviated form of the hive nomenclature, where the HKEY_LOCAL_MACHINE hive becomes HKLM and HKEY_LOCAL_USER becomes HKLU.

To view the registry using Windows PowerShell, open an elevated Windows PowerShell Command Prompt and then enter the following, pressing Enter after each line:

```
Get-ChildItem -Path hklm:
Dir
```

You can also obtain a richer output by running this PowerShell command:

```
Get-Childitem -ErrorAction SilentlyContinue | Format-Table Name, SubKeyCount,
ValueCount -AutoSize
```

To create a new registry key, you can first use the Set-Location cmdlet to change to the appropriate registry subtree and key as shown here:

```
Set-Location "HKCU:\Software"
```

Alternatively, you can use the full path to the registry key in the cmdlet as follows:

```
New-Item -Path HKCU:\Software -Name "Demonstration" -Force
```

Use the following cmdlet to assign the new registry key a value of "demo":

```
Set-Item -Path HKCU:\Software\Demonstration -Value "demo"
```

To validate that the key value has been stored correctly, view the key in the registry, or enter:

```
Get-Item -Path HKCU:\Software\Demonstration
```

Schedule tasks

You have already learned that you can use Task Scheduler, displayed in Figure 4-57, in Windows to manage backup operations as well as to control the schedule for the automatic creation of system restore points. Let's examine Task Scheduler in more detail.

You can locate Task Scheduler by selecting Start, and then scrolling to Windows Adminstrative Tools. Then select Task Scheduler.

FIGURE 4-57 The Windows 10 Task Scheduler

To review an existing scheduled task, use the following procedure:

1. In **Task Scheduler**, in the navigation pane, expand **Task Scheduler Library**, expand **Microsoft**, and expand **Windows**. Most operating system tasks can be scheduled here.

2. Navigate to the appropriate service. For example, to review the System Restore task schedule, navigate to \SystemRestore.

3. Double-click the SR task in the middle pane.

4. In the **SR Properties (Local Computer)** dialog box, select the **Triggers** tab.

5. On the **Triggers** tab, select **New**.

6. In the **New Trigger** dialog box, configure the schedule that you require. For example, you can configure Windows to create a daily System Restore point at noon, as displayed in Figure 4-58.

FIGURE 4-58 Configuring a trigger for a task

7. Ensure that the **Enabled** check box is selected and select **OK**.
8. On the **Triggers** tab, select **OK**. In the Task Scheduler MMC, the trigger is now displayed and enabled.

Skill 4.4: Configure remote connectivity

When you have a large number of computers to manage, or a workforce that uses their devices in a number of locations, you must know how to manage those computers by using remote management tools.

This skill covers how to:

- Manage Windows remotely by using Windows Remote Management
- Configure remote assistance tools including Remote Assistance and Quick Assist
- Configure remote desktop access
- Manage Windows remotely by using PS remoting
- Manage Windows 10 remotely by using Windows Admin Center

Manage Windows remotely by using Windows Remote Management

Windows 10 provides a number of tools that you can use to manage your organization's computers remotely. These include Remote Assistance, Remote Desktop, Windows PowerShell remoting, and many management console snap-ins. Knowing which tools support a given situation helps you address your users' needs more quickly.

Remote management tools in Windows 10

You can use a variety of tools to manage Windows 10 devices remotely. Table 4-21 shows the available remote management tools in Windows 10.

TABLE 4-21 Windows 10 remote management tools

Tool	Purpose
Remote Assistance	A built-in tool that provides for interaction with the remote user. By using Remote Assistance, you can view or take remote control of the user's computer and perform remote management. You can also use a text-based chat facility to interact with the user.
Quick Assist	A built-in Microsoft Store app that enables you to offer or receive assistance quickly. As with Remote Assistance, you can view or take remote control of the user's computer and perform remote management. To initiate a session, participants exchange a six-digit security code.
Remote Desktop	A built-in tool that you can use to access a computer remotely over the Remote Desktop Protocol (RDP). In the past, users often accessed their computers from other locations by using Remote Desktop. Security concerns and the adoption of mobile devices have made this a less common use of this tool. However, you can also use Remote Desktop to manage a remote computer. It does not provide for user interaction and requires the computer's user to sign out before you can access the computer remotely.
Windows PowerShell	Windows PowerShell is a powerful command-line management tool and scripting environment. You can use it to perform virtually any management function in Windows 10. You can also use Windows PowerShell to manage remote computers. This is known as Windows PowerShell remoting.
Microsoft Management Console	Microsoft Management Console (MMC) is an extensible interface for management applications in both Windows clients and Windows Server. To perform management by using MMC, a specific tool for the management task, known as a snap-in, is loaded into the console. For example, to perform management of disks and attached storage, you add the Disk Management snap-in to MMC. You can use MMC snap-ins to manage Windows 10 devices remotely by targeting the remote computer from the MMC interface.

Selecting the appropriate remote management tool

Given that a variety of tools are available, it is important to know which one to use in a given situation. When considering the appropriate tool, use the guidance in Table 4-22 to help you make your choice.

TABLE 4-22 Selecting the appropriate Windows 10 remote management tool

Scenario	Tool
User requires help and guidance. For example, you must help the user perform a specific task in an application such as printing, using the appropriate settings.	Remote Assistance or Quick Assist
You must perform a single remote management task on a single computer and require no user interaction.	Remote Desktop or MMC
You must perform the same management task on several or many remote computers.	Windows PowerShell
You must perform a remote management task that you have performed many times in the past and expect to perform again in the future.	Windows PowerShell
You are unsure of the nature of a problem a user is experiencing on their computer and wish to investigate computer settings.	Remote Desktop
You want to be able to perform the same management task, using the same management tool on any computer.	MMC

As you can see from Table 4-22, you can sometimes use several methods to address a specific remote management scenario. It is therefore a question of choosing the most appropriate method. Generally, if you know you will be required to perform the same management task again, on the same or a different computer, it is worth considering Windows PowerShell remoting. If you need to provide user interaction, choose Remote Assistance or Quick Assist. After that, it's probably a personal preference of whether you use an MMC snap-in remotely or Remote Desktop.

Enabling remote management settings

Depending on the remote management tool you have decided to use, it is almost certain that you must configure the target computer (the one you wish to manage) and possibly the local management computer (the one you are using) to enable the selected remote management tool. For example, it is common to have to enable the appropriate feature through Windows Defender Firewall to allow for management of a remote Windows 10–based device.

CONFIGURING WINDOWS DEFENDER FIREWALL TO ENABLE REMOTE MANAGEMENT

To enable remote management through Windows Defender Firewall on a target computer, open Control Panel and complete the following procedure:

1. Right-click the network symbol on the taskbar, and then select **Open Network & Internet Settings**.
2. In **Settings**, select **Windows Firewall**.
3. In the **Windows Security** app, select **Allow an app through the firewall**.
4. In **Allowed apps** dialog box, select **Change settings**.
5. In the **Allowed apps and features** list, scroll down and select the appropriate management feature.

For example, as displayed in Figure 4-59, we selected Remote Assistance. This enables the selected management feature on the private network location profile. If you also wish to allow the remote management feature on public networks, select the Public check box.

FIGURE 4-59 Allowing Remote Assistance through Windows Defender Firewall

6. Select **OK**. The available remote management features are:

- Remote Assistance
- Remote Desktop
- Remote Event Log Management
- Remote Event Monitor
- Remote Scheduled Tasks Management
- Remote Service Management
- Remote Shutdown
- Remote Volume Management
- Virtual Machine Monitoring
- Windows Defender Firewall Remote Management
- Windows Management Instrumentation (WMI)
- Windows Remote Management
- Windows Remote Management (Compatibility)

It is not always feasible, or especially desirable, to reconfigure these settings manually on each computer to enable the appropriate remote management feature. Instead, in an Active

Directory Domain Services (AD DS) environment, you can use Group Policy Objects (GPOs) to configure the desired firewall settings.

ENABLING REMOTE MANAGEMENT THROUGH SYSTEM PROPERTIES

Both Remote Assistance and Remote Desktop can be enabled through the System Properties dialog box, as displayed in Figure 4-60. To access these settings, open the Settings app and follow these steps:

1. Select **System** and then select **About**.

2. In the details pane, under **Related Settings**, select **Advanced System Settings**.

3. Select the **Remote** tab.

FIGURE 4-60 Configuring Remote settings through System Properties

ENABLING REMOTE ASSISTANCE

To enable Remote Assistance, on the Remote tab of the System Properties dialog box, select the Allow Remote Assistance Connections To This Computer check box. Then, optionally, select Advanced. As displayed in Figure 4-61, you can then configure the following additional settings.

- **Allow this computer to be controlled remotely**   This setting enables you to determine whether the person providing remote support can take remote control of the computer or only view the computer desktop. This setting is enabled by default when Remote Assistance is enabled.

- **Set the maximum amount of time invitations can remain open**   One way of initiating a Remote Assistance session is for the user to invite the support person to connect. This setting defines the validity period of the invitations. The default is 6 hours.

- **Create invitations that can only be used from computers running Windows Vista or later** Windows Vista and later versions of Windows use a superior method of encrypting Remote Assistance network traffic. You should select this option if you are using Windows Vista and later on all support computers.

FIGURE 4-61 Configuring Remote Assistance advanced settings

ENABLING REMOTE DESKTOP

To enable Remote Desktop, on the Remote tab of the System Properties dialog box, select the Allow Remote Connections To This Computer check box. Then, optionally, select Allow Connections Only From Computers Running Remote Desktop With Network Level Authentication (Recommended), shown in Figure 4-60. This setting improves the security of the Remote Desktop network traffic between the management computer and the target computer.

Click Select Users. As displayed in Figure 4-62, you can then add the users or groups that you want to have remote access to this computer by using Remote Desktop. You can also enable Remote Desktop by opening the Settings app, selecting System, and then selecting the Remote Desktop tab.

FIGURE 4-62 Configuring Remote Desktop users

Using Microsoft Management Console (MMC) to manage remote computers

With both Remote Desktop and Remote Assistance, you use RDP to connect to a remote
computer. After you establish a connection, you can perform any management task interactively just as if you were sitting at the remote computer. This is not the case with either MMC or
Windows PowerShell remoting.

With MMC, you must enable the desired remote management feature by modifying the
Windows Defender Firewall configuration. Then you can use the appropriate management
console snap-in and target the desired remote machine.

Using MMC snap-ins to manage remote computers is easy. Some management snap-ins
enable you to specify additional computers to connect to from the console. As displayed in
Figure 4-63, you can right-click the uppermost node in the navigation pane and then select
Connect To Another Computer.

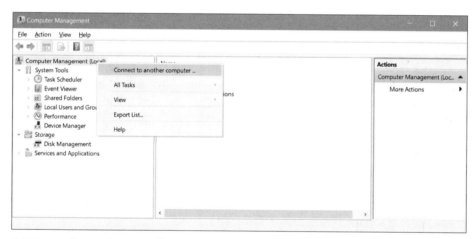

FIGURE 4-63 Connecting to another computer with MMC

If the management snap-in you want to use does not enable you to connect to additional
computers, you can create a new management console by running mmc.exe and adding the
appropriate snap-in to the empty console. When prompted, specify Another Computer.

It is important to realize that the remote computer must recognize you. This means that you must authenticate your connection by using a username and password that have the necessary management rights on the target computer. This step is simple in an AD DS domain environment because you can use domain admin credentials. However, in workgroup environments, this step is trickier. Generally, you must be able to provide credentials of a member of the target computer's local Administrators group.

In addition to authentication, the necessary Windows Defender Firewall feature must be enabled. After you have enabled the required remote management feature in Windows Defender Firewall and modified your MMC to connect to a remote computer using appropriate credentials, performing remote management is no different from performing local management.

Configure remote assistance tools including Remote Assistance and Quick Assist

As already mentioned, Remote Assistance is a built-in tool that provides for interaction with the remote user during a support session. You can view or take remote control of a remote user's computer and perform remote management of it.

Quick Assist is similar. It's a built-in Microsoft Store app that enables you to offer or receive assistance quickly. Using Quick Assist, you can view or take remote control of the user's computer and perform remote management of it.

Configure Remote Assistance

After you have enabled Remote Assistance, you can configure and use this tool to help your users administer and manage their computers remotely. There are two fundamental ways of initiating a Remote Assistance session: one is for the user to request assistance, and the other is for the support person to offer it.

REQUESTING HELP USING REMOTE ASSISTANCE

If a user is experiencing problems with their computer, they can request assistance from support personnel by using the Request Assistance feature of Remote Assistance. This is known as *solicited remote assistance*. To request assistance, the user must open Control Panel, select System And Security, and then select Launch Remote Assistance.

As displayed in Figure 4-64, you can then choose between:

- **Invite someone you trust to help you**   Choose this option if you require assistance.
- **Help someone who has invited you**   Choose this option if you can provide assistance.

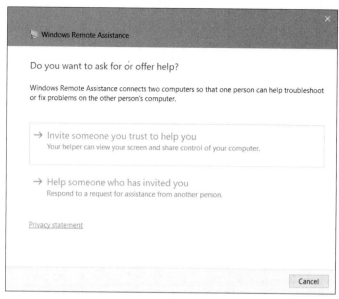

FIGURE 4-64 Requesting Windows Remote Assistance

To request help, select Invite Someone You Trust To Help You. You can then choose from among three options:

- **Save This Invitation As A File** Choose this option to create an RA Invitations file. These have a .msrclIncident file extension. You are prompted to save the request file. Store this file in a location that is accessible to the user from whom you are requesting help. Typically, this location will be a file server shared folder. After you have defined a save location, a dialog box appears with the password for the remote assistance session. Share this password with your helper. When your helper double-clicks the file you saved, they are asked for the password, and then the Remote Assistance session begins.

- **Use Email To Send An Invitation** If you choose this option, your default email program is opened by Remote Assistance, and the invitation file is automatically attached to an email message. You must enter the email address of the person you want to invite. When you send the message, the same dialog box appears containing the session password. Again, share this password with your helper. When your helper double-clicks the attached file in the email you sent, they are asked for the password, and then the Remote Assistance session begins.

- **Use Easy Connect** Easy Connect enables you to establish a Remote Assistance session without the need to use an invitation file. After you have established an Easy Connect session, you can save the name of the helper for future use, enabling you to receive remote assistance without the need to exchange a password.

EXAM TIP

Easy Connect only works if both computers are running Windows 7 or later and if both computers have access to the global peer-to-peer network. This network can sometimes be inaccessible to users of computers that are placed behind network routers that do not support the Peer Name Resolution Protocol. This protocol is used to transfer Remote Assistance invitations over the internet.

EXAM TIP

You can open the Windows Remote Assistance tool by running **Msra.exe** from the command line or the Windows Run dialog box.

OFFERING HELP WITH REMOTE ASSISTANCE

A user might not be in a position to request assistance. In these circumstances, an administrator can offer assistance. This is known as *unsolicited remote assistance*. To offer remote assistance, run Msra.exe and choose Help Someone Who Has Invited You. Then, on the Choose A Way To Connect To The Other Person's Computer page, select Advanced Connection Option For Help Desk, as displayed in Figure 4-65.

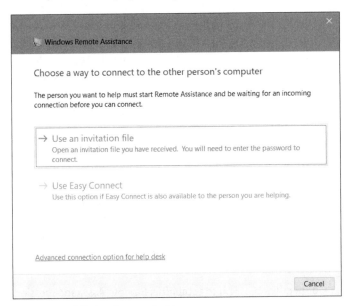

FIGURE 4-65 Offering Remote Assistance

On the Who Do You Want To Help page, in the Type A Computer Name Or IP Address box, enter the relevant computer name or IP address of the computer that you want to send the offer of help to and then select Next.

The user on the target computer must accept your offer, and then the remote assistance session is initiated. This is often a useful way to start a remote assistance session, especially when you are attempting to support novice users.

CONFIGURING REMOTE ASSISTANCE WITH GPOs

Although you can configure the necessary settings for Remote Assistance manually on each computer, in an AD DS domain environment it is easier to use GPOs to distribute the required settings. Table 4-23 shows the settings you can configure for Remote Assistance by using GPOs. To configure these settings, open Group Policy Management and locate the appropriate GPO. Open the GPO for editing and navigate to Computer Configuration > Policies > Administrative Templates > System > Remote Assistance.

TABLE 4-23 Configuring Remote Assistance with GPOs

Policy Setting	Explanation
Allow Only Windows Vista Or Newer Connections	Enables Remote Assistance to generate invitations with more secure encryption. This setting does not affect Remote Assistance connections initiated by unsolicited offers or Remote Assistance.
Turn On Session Logging	Enables session logging. Logs are stored in the user's Documents folder in the Remote Assistance folder.
Turn On Bandwidth Optimization	Provides performance improvements in low-bandwidth situations. Adjust from No Optimization through Full Optimization.
Customize warning messages	Enables you to customize warning messages.
Configure Solicited Remote Assistance	Enables solicited Remote Assistance on a computer. If you disable this setting, it prevents users from asking for Remote Assistance. You also can use this setting to configure invitation time limits and whether to allow remote control.
Configure Offer Remote Assistance	Enables unsolicited Remote Assistance on this computer.

USING REMOTE ASSISTANCE TO MANAGE A COMPUTER REMOTELY

After you have configured the desired settings and established a Remote Assistance session, you can perform the following tasks:

- **Request Control** Enables you to ask the remote user for permission to take remote control of their computer. The remote user must allow you to do this. Remember also that the ability to gain remote control is a configurable option.

- **Chat** Enables you to open a chat window to communicate with the remote user. You can use chat to explain what you are doing, or the remote user can use it to discuss the details of their computer problem.

Configure Quick Assist

There are no special setup requirements for Quick Assist. However, users must be able to authenticate with one another, and to initiate a session, participants must exchange a six-digit security code.

To use Quick Assist, select Start and then enter **Quick Assist**. Select the Quick Assist link. As displayed in Figure 4-66, you can then select the link to assist another person or enter a code from your assistant, depending on your situation.

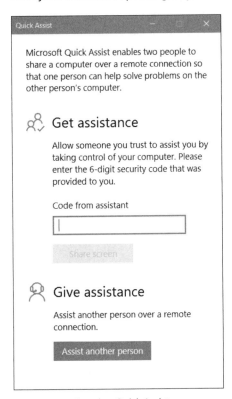

FIGURE 4-66 Opening Quick Assist

OFFERING HELP WITH QUICK ASSIST

To create a Quick Assist session, after opening Quick Assist at both ends of the session, the IT support person selects the Assist Another Person button, as displayed in Figure 4-66. Then use the following procedure to create a session:

1. A sign-in dialog box displays. Enter your **Microsoft Account** name and select **Next**.

2. Enter your password, select **Next**, and then record the secutity code, as displayed in Figure 4-67.

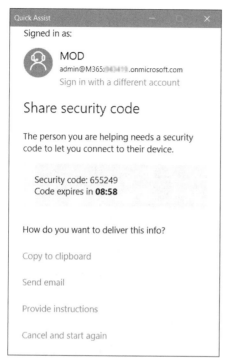

FIGURE 4-67 Reviewing the security code

3. Share the code with the person you want to help. Choose between copying the code to the clipboard, using an email message, or providing instructions.

4. At the remote end, the user being helped enters the provided code, and then selects **Share Screen**.

5. You now choose between **Take Full Control** or **View Screen**. Then select **Continue**.

6. The remote user now confirms the permissions you requested by selecting **Allow**.

7. The session opens, as displayed in Figure 4-68.

After you have opened a remote session, you can use the toolbar across the top of the display to perform the following actions:

- **Select Monitor** Enables you to select a remote a screen to review or interact with.
- **Annotate** Provides you with the ability to write.
- **Actual Size** Enables you to resize the screen output to actual size.
- **Toggle Instruction Channel** Turns on (or off) the chat window in which you can provide instructions to the remote user.
- **Restart** Enables you to initiate a restart of the remote computer.

- **Task Manager**   Enables Task Manager at the remote computer.
- **Reconnect**   Reconnects your session.
- **Pause**   Pauses the session without ending it.
- **End**   Terminates the session.

The remote session will time out after a period of inactivity, or you can end it as needed once you have finished helping the remote user.

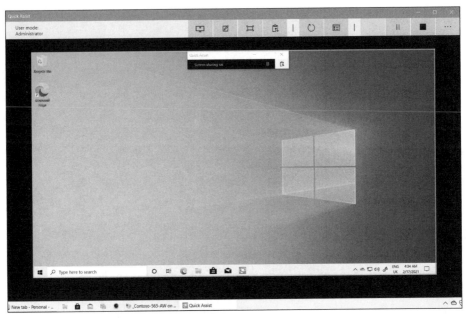

FIGURE 4-68 An active remote session using Quick Assist

Configure Remote Desktop access

After Remote Desktop is enabled on a computer, you can use the Remote Desktop Connection program to connect to the computer. When connected, you can use the computer as if locally signed in and perform all management tasks that your user account has the rights to perform. This makes using Remote Desktop particularly useful.

Creating and editing Remote Desktop connections

To create a Remote Desktop connection, from Start, select All Apps, select Windows Accessories, and then select Remote Desktop Connection. As displayed in Figure 4-69, you must then specify the computer that you want to connect to. Use either a computer name or an IP address. You can configure additional connection properties by using the options discussed in Table 4-24.

TABLE 4-24 Configurable Remote Desktop Connection options

Tab	Settings
General	<ul><li>Logon Settings:<ul><li>Computer</li><li>User Name</li><li>Allow Me To Save Credentials</li><li>Connection Settings:</li><li>Save</li><li>Save As</li><li>Open</li></ul></li></ul>
Display	<ul><li>Display Configuration:<ul><li>Small > Large</li><li>Use All My Monitors For The Remote Session</li></ul></li><li>Colors:<ul><li>Choose The Color Depth Of The Remote Session</li><li>Display The Connection Bar When I Use Full Screen</li></ul></li></ul>
Local Resources	<ul><li>Remote Audio:</li><li>Remote Audio Playback:<ul><li>Play On This Computer</li><li>Do Not Play</li><li>Play On Remote Computer</li></ul></li><li>Remote Audio Recording:<ul><li>Record From This Computer</li><li>Do Not Record</li></ul></li><li>Keyboard, Apply Windows Key Combinations:<ul><li>Only When Using The Full Screen</li><li>On This Computer</li><li>On The Remote Computer</li></ul></li><li>Local Devices And Resources:<ul><li>Printers</li><li>Clipboard</li></ul></li></ul>
	<ul><li>Smart Cards</li><li>Ports</li><li>Drives</li><li>Other Supported Plug And Play (Pnp) Devices</li></ul>
Experience	<ul><li>Performance:<ul><li>Modem (56 kbps)</li><li>Low-Speed Broadband (256 Kbps–2 Mbps)</li><li>Satellite (2 Mbps–16 Mbps With High Latency)</li><li>High-Speed Broadband (2Mbps–10 Mbps)</li><li>WAN (10 Mpbs Or Higher)</li><li>Detect Connection Quality Automatically</li><li>Persistent Bitmap Caching</li><li>Reconnect If The Connection Is Dropped</li></ul></li></ul>

Tab	Settings
Advanced	■ Server Authentication, If Server Authentication Fails: 　■ Connect And Don't Warn Me 　■ Warn Me 　■ Do Not Connect ■ Connect From Anywhere: ■ Connection Settings: 　■ Automatically Detect RD Gateway Server Settings 　■ Use These RD Gateway Server Settings 　■ Do Not Use An RD Gateway Server ■ Log-on Settings: 　■ Username 　■ Use My RD Gateway Credentials For The Remote Computer

FIGURE 4-69 Creating a Remote Desktop connection

When you have finished configuring the connection, on the General tab select Connect. You can also choose to save your configuration to an RDP file for subsequent use.

Customizing Remote Desktop settings from the command line

You can open the Remote Desktop Connection app by running Mstsc.exe from the command line or the Windows Run dialog box. The Mstsc.exe command also enables administrators to open the tool, with several parameters configured.

The default firewall port that Remote Desktop uses is 3389, and this firewall port must allow RDP traffic through for Remote Desktop to work. If an administrator changes the firewall port for RDP traffic, the revised port number must be specified in the command-line tool Mstsc.exe when opening the application.

The syntax for **mstsc** is

```
mstsc [<connection file>] [/v:<server[:port]>] [/admin] [/f[ullscreen]] [/w:<width>]
[/h:<height>] [/public] | [/span] [/multimon] [/edit "connection file"]
[/restrictedAdmin] [/remoteGuard] [/prompt] [/shadow:sessionID> [/control]
[/noConsentPrompt]] [/?]
```

The list of command-line parameters for Remote Desktop Connection are shown in Table 4-25.

TABLE 4-25 Command-line parameters for Remote Desktop Connection

Parameter	Description
<connection file>	Specifies the name of an RDP file for the connection.
/v:<Server[:<Port>]	Specifies the remote computer to which you want to connect.
/admin	This parameter is used to connect you to a session for the administration of a Remote Desktop Session Host server (the RD Session Host role service must be installed on the remote server).
/edit <"connection file">	Opens the specified RDP file for editing.
/f	Starts Remote Desktop Connection in full-screen mode.
/w:<Width>	Specifies the width of the Remote Desktop window.
/h:<Height>	Specifies the height of the Remote Desktop window.
/public	Runs the Remote Desktop in public mode, where passwords and bitmaps are not cached.
/span	This enables the Remote Desktop width and height to be matched with the local virtual desktop, spanning across multiple monitors if necessary.
/multimon	Configures the Remote Desktop session monitor layout to render it identical to the client configuration.
/restrictedAdmin	Connects to the remote PC or server in Restricted Administration mode, which prevents login credentials from being sent to the remote PC or server. Functionality and or compatibility may be impacted as the connection is made as local administrator.
/remoteGuard	Utilizes Remote Guard to protect the connection. No credentials are sent to the remote device; however, full access is provided.
/shadow:sessionID	Allows you to specify the SessionID to which you wish to connect.
/control	Allows control of the remote session.
/noConsentPrompt	Allows the connection to continue without user consent.
/?	Lists the available parameters.

Configuring Remote Desktop with GPOs

Just as with Remote Assistance, although you can configure Remote Desktop settings manually on each computer, in an AD DS domain environment it makes sense to configure these settings with GPOs. Table 4-26 describes the configurable GPO settings for Remote Desktop. To configure these settings, open Group Policy Management and locate the appropriate GPO. Open the GPO for editing and navigate to Computer Configuration\Policies\Administrative Templates\Windows Components\Remote Desktop Services.

TABLE 4-26 Configuring Remote Desktop with GPOs

Policy Setting	Explanation
Remote Desktop Connection Client\Do Not Allow Passwords To Be Saved	Determines whether users can save passwords on this computer from Remote Desktop Services clients.
Remote Desktop Connection Client\ Prompt For Credentials On Client Computer	If enabled, a user is prompted to provide credentials for a remote connection to a Remote Desktop server on their client computer rather than on the Remote Desktop server.
Remote Desktop Session Host\Connections\Allow Users To Connect Remotely By Using Remote Desktop Services	If enabled, users that belong to the Remote Desktop Users group on the target computer can connect remotely to the target computer, using Remote Desktop Services.
Remote Desktop Session Host\Device And Resource Redirection	You use these settings to specify whether to allow or prevent data redirection from local devices (such as audio and clipboard) to the remote client in a Remote Desktop Services session.
Remote Desktop Session Host\Security\ Set Client Connection Encryption Level	If enabled, all communications between clients and Remote Desktop servers is encrypted, using the encryption method specified. By default, the encryption level is set to High.
Remote Desktop Session Host\Session Time Limits	These policies control session time limits for disconnected, idle, and active sessions and whether to terminate sessions when specified limits are reached.

Troubleshooting Remote Desktop Connections

Remote Desktop is a powerful tool for administrators that enables them to manage PCs and servers within the enterprise. Some common problems encountered when trying to connect to a remote PC using Remote Desktop, and their resolution, are listed in Table 4-27.

TABLE 4-27 Troubleshooting Remote Desktop Connections

Problem	Possible resolution
The remote PC can't be found.	▪ Make sure you have the correct PC name. ▪ Try using the IP address of the remote PC.
There's a problem with the network.	▪ Ensure that the router is turned on (home networks only). ▪ Make sure that the Ethernet cable is plugged into your network adapter (wired networks only). ▪ See that the wireless switch on the PC is turned on (devices using wireless networks only). ▪ Make sure your network adapter is functional.

Problem	Possible resolution
The Remote Desktop port might be blocked by a firewall.	■ Contact your system administrator to check that Remote Desktop is not blocked. ■ Allow the Remote Desktop application through Windows Firewall. ■ Make sure the port for Remote Desktop (usually 3389) is open.
Remote connections might not be set up on the remote PC.	■ In the System Properties dialog box, under Remote Desktop, select the Allow Remote Connections To This Computer button.
The remote PC might only enable PCs that have Network Level Authentication set up to connect.	■ Upgrade to Windows 7, Windows 8 or Windows 8.1, or Windows 10, which support Network Level Authentication.
The remote PC might be turned off.	■ You can't connect to a PC that's turned off, asleep, or hibernating. ■ Turn on the remote PC.

Manage Windows remotely by using PS remoting

Although using Windows PowerShell cmdlets can sometimes seem daunting, they do offer a convenient and quick way of configuring many machines more quickly than by using a graphical tool. In addition, through the use of scripting, you can use Windows PowerShell to complete frequently performed management tasks.

Using Windows PowerShell to manage remote computers is referred to as *Windows PowerShell remoting*, but before you can use Windows PowerShell remoting, you must know how to enable and configure it.

Windows PowerShell is ubiquitous across the Windows platform, appearing in both Windows 10 and Windows Server. Therefore, using Windows PowerShell to perform management tasks on both local and remote computers makes sense because you can transfer those skills to other management and administration situations.

Many cmdlets in Windows PowerShell can be used with a **-ComputerName** parameter, making the use of the command remotely no more complex than specifying the name of the computer you want to run the command against. For example, to determine the IP configuration of a computer, you can run the following command:

```
Get-NetIPConfiguration -computername LON-CL1
```

However, not all cmdlets accept the **-ComputerName** parameter, and for these, you must enable and configure Windows PowerShell remoting. The function of Windows PowerShell remoting is to enable you to connect to one or several remote computers and execute one or more cmdlets or scripts on those remote computers and return the results to your local computer.

Although Windows PowerShell remoting is enabled by default on Windows Server, you must manually enable it on Windows 10. To do this, complete one of the following procedures:

■ If necessary, start the Windows Remote Management service. You must also enable Windows Remote Management through the Windows Defender Firewall. As displayed in Figure 4-70, you can do this by running the **winrm quickconfig** command at an elevated Command Prompt. When prompted, press Y and Enter twice.

FIGURE 4-70 Enabling Windows Remote Management

NOTE WINRM QUICKCONFIG AND THE PUBLIC NETWORK LOCATION PROFILE

If one of your network connections is assigned the Public network location profile, this command fails, and you must manually configure the Windows Defender Firewall exceptions.

- Alternatively, to enable Windows PowerShell remoting, you can run the **enable-PSremoting -force** cmdlet from an elevated Windows PowerShell window.

EXAM TIP

Windows Remote Management uses HTTP. By default, both Windows Remote Management and Windows PowerShell remoting use TCP port 5985 for incoming unencrypted communications and TCP port 5986 for incoming encrypted communications.

Using Windows PowerShell to manage remote computers

After you have enabled Windows PowerShell remoting, you can use Windows PowerShell cmdlets and scripts to manage the remote computer in virtually the same way that you manage local computers. However, you must first establish a connection with the remote computer.

After you have established a connection, you can run any cmdlets or scripts against the remote machine. When you connect to the remote computer and run a remote command against it, the command is transmitted across the network and run on the remote computer. The results are sent back to your local computer and displayed in your Windows PowerShell window.

One way to establish a remote connection and run a command is to use the **invoke-command** cmdlet. You can also use the **invoke-command** cmdlet to establish a temporary remote connection. For example, the following command retrieves the contents of the system event log from the remote computer LON-CL1:

```
Invoke-Command -ComputerName LON-CL1 -ScriptBlock {Get-EventLog -log system}
```

If you intend to run several cmdlets, or to run more complex scripts, it is useful to establish a persistent connection to the remote computer. Use the **New-PSSession** cmdlet to do this. For example:

```
$s = New-PSSession -ComputerName LON-CL1
```

You can now use the **Enter-PSSession** command to establish the persistent connection:

```
Enter-PSSession $s
```

You will now have a Windows PowerShell prompt that looks like this:

```
[LON-CL1]: PS C:\>
```

Any commands that you run in this session run on the LON-CL1 computer. The session remains active until you close with the **exit-PSSession** command.

You can also use these commands to establish remote connections with multiple computers. For example, to connect simultaneously to computers called LON-CL1 and LON-CL2, use the following command:

```
$s = New-PSSession -ComputerName LON-CL1, LON-CL2
```

Next, run the remote Windows PowerShell cmdlets against the new session:

```
Invoke-Command -Session $s -ScriptBlock { Get-EventLog -log system }
```

You can run any Windows PowerShell command remotely in this way.

Manage Windows 10 remotely by using Windows Admin Center

Windows Admin Center is a web-based management console that you can use to manage remote computers and services, including services hosted in Microsoft Azure. Windows Admin Center has two core components that enable you to manage remote devices and services:

- **Gateway** Enables you to manage servers through Windows PowerShell Remoting and WMI using WinRM.
- **Web server** Enables management through standard HTTPS communications.

Installation

To use Windows Admin Center, you must first download it from the Microsoft Download website. After download, run the installation program. Then use the following procedure to complete setup:

1. In the **Windows Admin Center Setup Wizard**, select **Next**.
2. On the **Install Windows Admin Center on Windows 10** page, select **Next**.

3. On the **Installing Windows Admin Center** page, for **Select a port for the Windows Admin Center site**, enter a suitable TCP port. The default, as displayed in Figure 4-71, is 6516. This port is used to communicate with the Windows Admin Center.

FIGURE 4-71 Installing Windows Admin Center

4. Select the **Allow Windows Admin Center to modify this machine's trusted hosts settings** check box if you want to manage computers that are not part of your AD DS forest. See more information about authentication in the next section.

5. Select **Install**. Accept the UAC prompt.

6. When you see the prompt, select **Finish**.

After installation, when you run Windows Admin Center for the first time, you are prompted for a certificate. Select the Windows Admin Certificate, as displayed in Figure 4-72.

FIGURE 4-72 Selecting the Windows Admin Center certificate

Authentication

If you connect to remote computers, either with Windows Admin Center or with Windows PowerShell remoting, you must authenticate with the remote computer. If your two computers are part of the same AD DS forest, Kerberos authentication automatically occurs. However, if you are connecting to computers in a different forest, or to non-domain-joined computers, you must configure the TrustedHosts settings.

If, when you install Windows Admin Center, you accept the defaults, then the TrustedHosts are set to be automatically configured. However, if you want to manage these settings manually, you do so by using Windows PowerShell:

1. Open an elevated **Windows PowerShell** prompt.

2. Run the following command:

   ```
   Set-Item WSMan:localhost\Client\TrustedHosts -Value 'svr1.Contoso.com'
   ```

3. When prompted, enter **Y** to confirm the change.

4. For each device you want to manage, run the preceding command, remembering to change the computer name specificied in the value parameter.

You can also use a wildcard to enable connectivity to any computer. Run the following command:

```
Set-Item WSMan:\localhost\Client\TrustedHosts -Value '*'
```

Using Windows Admin Center

After you have set up Windows Admin Center, you can start managing computers. The first step is to add computers to the available connections. Use the following procedure:

1. In the console, select **Add**.

2. On the **Add or create resources** blade, select the type of resource. Choose between Servers, Windows PCs, Server Clusters, or Azure VMs. In this case, in the Windows PCs section, select **Add**.

3. On the **Connection tags** blade, in the **Computer** name box, enter the name of the remote computer and select **Add**.

Windows Admin Center now updates to include the newly added computer. To connect to a computer, select it from the All Connections list, as displayed in Figure 4-73.

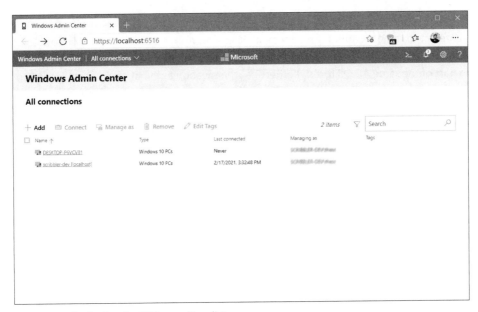

FIGURE 4-73 Reviewing the All Connections list

You can then use the navigation pane to select a specific management component, as displayed in Figure 4-74.

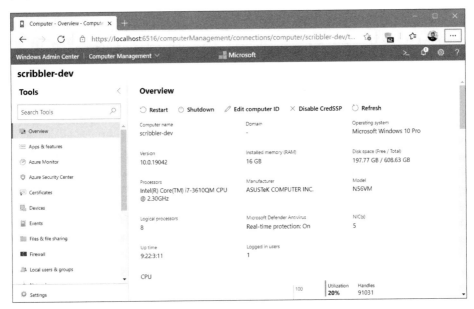

FIGURE 4-74 Connecting to a computer

You can manage many aspects of a remote Windows PC, including the following:

- Restart or shut down the computer.
- Edit the computer ID.
- Add or remove apps and features.
- Review installed certificates.
- Review the event logs.
- Navigate the file system, and manage shared resources.
- Review and configure network and firewall settings.
- Gather performance-related data.
- Configure the registry.
- Manage scheduled tasks.
- Manage services and storage.
- Manage virtual machines and switches.

Chapter summary

- Windows 10 File History is the preferred backup option that performs automatic backups of files every hour to a nonlocal storage.
- Previous Versions is a feature that allows you to recover deleted or modified versions of your files directly from File Explorer rather than via a backup or File History.
- OneDrive offers you a Recycle Bin, which allows you to recover files you've deleted from OneDrive folders and syncs with the File Explorer Recycle bin.
- OneDrive can provide a history of older versions of Office documents that are stored within OneDrive so that you can access, restore, and download previous versions of your files.
- A Windows 10 recovery drive can be used to recover your system in the event of failure.
- System Restore is useful for restoring the operating system to a previous point in time. For example, you can restore to a point prior to when your computer became unstable.
- Windows RE enables you to access the advanced startup options to troubleshoot Windows 10 startup issues.
- You can use Reset This PC to recycle a computer for use by another user or to revert the computer to its OOBE state if you experience serious problems with the computer.
- Fresh Start in Windows Security enables you to keep your personal files and some Windows settings but remove all apps, including third-party apps that are preinstalled on your device.
- Restore points are created when the Backup And Restore (Windows 7) tool creates a backup image. You can use a system image to recover Windows 10 if Windows 10 becomes unstable (for example, if your hard drive has failed and other recovery methods have failed).

- Driver Rollback allows you to revert to a previous device driver after your system begins to suffer the effects of upgrading to a new device driver that is poorly performing.

- Windows 10 Home users have Windows Updates automatically downloaded and installed on their devices. Windows 10 Pro, Education, and Enterprise customers can defer feature updates for up to 365 days, and they can defer quality updates for up to 30 days.

- Windows 10 Pro, Education, and Enterprise customers can pause quality updates for up to 35 days.

- Windows Update Delivery Optimization is a method of peer-to-peer sharing of Windows update files. This feature significantly reduces the time that a Windows 10 device is vulnerable from zero-day malware attacks. Peer caching can occur between other users on the local network or optionally across the internet.

- Administrators can use Group Policy to centrally configure and manage Windows Update behavior, location of WSUS servers, and Windows Update Delivery Optimization settings.

- If a driver update causes system stability issues, you can uninstall the update, and if necessary, you can disable the automatic application of the update.

- Event logs automatically record system activity such as logons, application errors, and services stopping and starting.

- If you enable remote management, you can pull event logs from remote computers by using event subscriptions.

- Windows 10 includes several tools to view system performance, including Task Manager, Performance Monitor, and Resource Monitor.

- In Performance Monitor, you can create benchmarking reports by creating your own user-defined collector sets and running them to generate a performance baseline.

- Windows 10 introduces the option to manage your default printer by setting the default to the last printer you used, rather than the printer at your current location.

- The built-in Search feature uses the background indexing service to index areas of your hard drive automatically, including files stored in your user profile.

- Reliability Monitor provides a graphical history of your computer's reliability and offers solutions to resolve issues.

- You can choose from a number of management tools to perform remote management.

- To configure and enable remote management settings, you must first modify the Windows Firewall configuration.

- Remote Assistance can be used to view or take remote control of a remote user's computer.

- Both Remote Desktop and Remote Assistance can be configured manually or by using GPOs.
- Windows PowerShell remoting enables you to perform remote management of any Windows 10–based computer with Windows PowerShell.
- Management console snap-ins support both local and remote connections.

Thought experiment

In these thought experiments, demonstrate your skills and knowledge of the topics covered in this chapter. You can find the answers to these thought experiments in the next section.

Scenario 1

You want to use the Backup And Restore (Windows 7) tool to create a backup of your files contained on your computer to a removable USB hard drive or SDHC memory card. You want to create a custom schedule. Answer the following questions relating to the Backup And Restore (Windows 7) tool:

1. What is the default backup schedule for the Backup And Restore (Windows 7) tool?
2. How would you modify the schedule so that you can be more specific? For example, say you want to back up the data every 30 minutes.
3. What triggers are available that could be used to begin the backup task?
4. You no longer want to use the Backup And Restore (Windows 7) tool for your Windows 10 Pro tablet. What built-in backup tool could you use instead? How could the data be safeguarded from theft?

Scenario 2

You have been asked to review the backup and restore options available within Windows 10 and OneDrive.com. Your manager is developing a backup strategy and wants to ensure that files are backed up and that users can easily access the backed-up files for at least six months. Backups will be stored offsite. Answer the following backup-related questions:

1. How would relying on the OneDrive Recycle Bin feature affect the backup strategy?
2. You want to examine how the Previous Versions feature found in File Explorer works, but you cannot see any Previous Versions listed. How do you enable Previous Versions?
3. Could the Previous Versions feature found in File Explorer offer backup and recovery of files as part of the backup strategy?

Scenario 3

Your company has recently upgraded half of its computers from Windows 7 to Windows 10 Pro. Staff members use Office and a web-based line-of-business application. The help desk manager has received several complaints from users who state a variety of problems following the upgrade, including that the following:

- Their computers are slow.
- Apps stop responding.
- Websites are slow to load.

The remaining Windows 7–based computers do not exhibit the same issues. You need to offer the help desk some advice on how to diagnose these problems and recommend how to resolve them as soon as possible.

Answer the following questions from the help desk:

1. Why might the computers be slow after the upgrade?
2. Which tool could you recommend to assist the help desk support members verify which apps are freezing?
3. You suspect that the network card could be a performance bottleneck. How could this suspicion be tested?
4. How would a network card bottleneck present itself?

Scenario 4

You work as a desktop support technician. Your Windows 10 deployment for 5,000 devices is now complete, and you are now busy supporting your users. Answer the following questions about using advanced management tools and techniques for your organization:

1. You find that you are repeatedly performing the same management task on multiple computers. At the moment, you use several customized Microsoft Management Consoles to perform the required tasks. How could you achieve this more easily?
2. A number of users are experiencing problems with their computers. You determine that the issue relates to a service that occasionally stops and is then restarted. Where can you track information about this problem?
3. What command-line tools can you use for managing services?

Scenario 5

You work in support at Adatum Corporation. Many of your users work in small branch offices. Some work from home, using work laptops. It is important for you to be able to manage these users' computers remotely. As a consultant for Adatum, answer the following questions about remote management in the Adatum organization:

1. One of your users phones the help desk, requiring assistance with an application. They need to know how to perform a grammar check with Microsoft Word 2019. They are

not very experienced, and despite your best efforts and explanation of how the process works, they are still confused. What remote management tool might you consider using in this situation?

2. Another user calls the help desk. They've lost a file and need you to locate it. They're due to leave the office for a conference this afternoon, and they tell you that's the best time for you to resolve the issue. What remote management tool would you use?

3. You try to connect to this user's computer later that afternoon, but despite knowing that the necessary Windows Firewall settings are configured, you cannot connect. Why?

4. You want to use Windows PowerShell remoting. You try to connect to a remote machine but are unsuccessful. What steps must you perform on the remote machine before Windows PowerShell remoting can work?

Thought experiment answers

This section provides the solutions for the tasks included in the thought experiment.

Scenario 1

1. The default backup schedule for the Backup And Restore (Windows 7) tool is every Sunday at 7 PM.

2. You need to edit the AutomaticBackup task in the WindowsBackup node found in Task Scheduler and configure the task to repeat every 30 minutes by editing the trigger.

3. The triggers available for the task to begin include the following: On A Schedule, At Log On, At Startup, On Idle, On An Event, At Task Creation/Modification, On Connection/Disconnect To A User Session, and On Workstation Lock/Unlock.

4. You would suggest using File History. This feature allows the backup of files and folders to a removable drive—for example, a USB drive or SDHC memory card—that may be used with the device. Optionally, the external storage may be encrypted using BitLocker To Go or EFS.

Scenario 2

1. The OneDrive Recycle Bin is not a backup facility. It will only retain files that have been deleted for a maximum of 93 days. This is less than the 6 months required by the backup strategy.

2. You would need to turn on the schedule to create restore points using either File History or the Backup And Restore (Windows 7) tool. Once the Backup And Restore (Windows 7) tool creates a backup, or when File History runs, previous versions of files will be available on the Previous Versions tab.

3. Previous Versions could provide the longevity of access to the backed-up files if the backup storage location does not become full. To ensure that the Previous Versions complied with the backup strategy, you would need File History or the Backup And Restore (Windows 7) tool to save the image to a remote storage location, such as a network-attached drive.

Scenario 3

1. Answers might vary. Several potential areas need to be investigated. The original computers should have met the minimum specification for Windows 10 to upgrade from Windows 7. The computers might be quite old and contain components that are slow in comparison to modern hardware, such as older hard drives without cache, or slow RAM memory. The BIOS or motherboard firmware might be old and need updating. The hardware device drivers might not have been updated to the latest versions for Windows 10.

2. Recommend to the help desk that it suggest using Reliability Monitor to review the stability history of the computers that are reporting app freezing. The Reliability Monitor report should identify the failing app and how often it is failing; also, the report should identify potential solutions. You should also be able to see whether other failures are occurring that might relate or contribute to the app failure.

3. Answers might vary. You could review the network card driver version and see whether there are any known issues relating to the network card and Windows 10 on the manufacturer's website. You could use Performance Monitor to review the performance for the Network Interface counter and monitor the Output Queue Length.

4. Network-related activities, such as web browsing and opening and saving resources across the network, would be slower than normal. If there is network saturation, the report should indicate that the queue length is more than 2, meaning that the network card cannot process network packets quickly enough.

Scenario 4

1. You could create Windows PowerShell scripts as required that contain the required management cmdlets. Because Windows PowerShell supports remoting, it is easy to run the script against remote computers at the same time. You must, however, ensure that the execution policy for each computer supports the running of PowerShell scripts and that Windows PowerShell remoting is enabled.

2. Use the System log in Event Viewer. You can group events based on source; in this instance, the source is Service Control Manager.

3. You can use Windows PowerShell to manage services. Also, the SC.exe and Net.exe command-line tools can be used.

Scenario 5

1. Using Remote Assistance would enable you to demonstrate how to perform the grammar check. You could take remote control of the user's computer and show them the procedure.

2. Remote Desktop is the most suitable tool. Remote Assistance requires the interaction of the user to accept your connection request and, initially, to invite you to help. Remote Desktop requires no invitations and does not require the remote user to assist you in connecting.

3. The most likely reason you can't connect is that Remote Desktop users must be granted access in addition to the Windows Firewall configuration changes being made.

4. You must start the Windows Remote Management service and reconfigure the Windows Firewall, and then Windows PowerShell remoting must be enabled. You can perform these steps by running either **winrm quickconfig** or by running **enable-PSremoting**.

Index

Numerics

O

P

Q-R

S

Plug into learning at

MicrosoftPressStore.com

The Microsoft Press Store by Pearson offers:

- Free U.S. shipping

- Buy an eBook, get three formats – Includes PDF, EPUB, and MOBI to use with your computer, tablet, and mobile devices

- Print & eBook Best Value Packs

- eBook Deal of the Week – Save up to 50% on featured title

- Newsletter – Be the first to hear about new releases, announcements, special offers, and more

- Register your book – Find companion files, errata, and product updates, plus receive a special coupon* to save on your next purchase

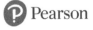